OUT OF THE GREAT TRADITION OF AFRICAN-AMERICAN THEATER—NEW VOICES, NEW IDEAS

I Ain't Yo' Uncle by Robert Alexander

Playwright Alexander puts author Harriet Beecher Stowe on trial for her role in the creation and perpetuation of black stereotypes—and the real Uncle Tom and Topsy turn out to be powerful people indeed.

Imperceptible Mutabilities in the Third Kingdom by Suzan-Lori Parks

This OBIE Award–winning drama probes the connection between African-American history and identity, beginning when the white slave traders brought blacks to the New World and created the feelings of isolation, dislocation, and alienation that remain to this day.

Before It Hits Home by Cheryl L. West

Produced at New York City's Second Stage Theater and optioned for film by Spike Lee, West's untraditional depiction of the black family—a saxophone player and his two lovers, one male, one female—challenges audiences to question their own assumptions . . . . and their own lives.

Shakin' the Mess Outta Misery by Shay Youngblood

A 1991 NAACP Theater Award nominee, this play evokes both humor and passion as stories of Southern black women recall the 1950s and 1960s in tales of struggle and survival, racism and pain, loss and extraordinary love.

COLORED CONTRADICTIONS

Harry J. Elam, Jr., is associate professor of drama at Stanford University. **Robert Alexander** is a prize-winning playwright and playwright in residence at the Lorraine Hansberry Theatre in Oakland, California.

COLORED CONTRADICTIONS

AN ANTHOLOGY OF CONTEMPORARY
AFRICAN-AMERICAN PLAYS

EDITED BY

HARRY J. ELAM, Jr.
AND ROBERT ALEXANDER

A PLUME BOOK

PLUME
Published by the Penguin Group
Penguin Books USA Inc., 375 Hudson Street,
New York, New York 10014, U.S.A.
Penguin Books Ltd, 27 Wrights Lane,
London W8 5TZ, England
Penguin Books Australia Ltd, Ringwood,
Victoria, Australia
Penguin Books Canada Ltd, 10 Alcorn Avenue,
Toronto, Ontario, Canada M4V 3B2
Penguin Books (N.Z.) Ltd, 182–190 Wairau Road,
Auckland 10, New Zealand

Penguin Books Ltd, Registered Offices:
Harmondsworth, Middlesex, England

First published by Plume, an imprint of Dutton Signet,
a division of Penguin Books USA Inc.

First Printing, November, 1996
10 9 8 7 6 5 4 3 2 1

 REGISTERED TRADEMARK—MARCA REGISTRADA

LIBRARY OF CONGRESS CATALOGING-IN-PUBLICATION DATA:
Colored contradictions : an anthology of contemporary African-American plays / edited
by Harry J. Elam, Jr. and Robert Alexander.
    p.   cm.
    ISBN 0-452-27497-4
    1. American drama—Afro-American authors. 2. American drama—20th century.
3. Afro-Americans—Drama.   I. Elam, Harry Justin. II. Alexander, Robert.
PS628.N4C65   1996
812'.54080896073—dc20   96-15948
                                                                     CIP

Printed in the United States of America
Set in New Baskerville
Designed by Leonard Telesca

PUBLISHER'S NOTE
This is a work of fiction. Names, characters, places, and incidents either are the product of
the author's imagination or are used fictitiously, and any resemblance to actual persons,
living or dead, events, or locales is entirely coincidental.

CAUTION: Professionals and amateurs are hereby warned that the plays appearing in this
volume are subject to a royalty. They are fully protected under the copyright laws of the
United States of America, of all countries covered by the International Copyright Union
(including the Dominion of Canada and the rest of the British Commonwealth), of all
countries covered by the Pan-American Copyright Convention and the Universal Copyright Convention, and of all countries with which the United States has reciprocal copyright relations. All rights, including professional, amateur, motion picture, recitation,
lecturing, public reading, radio broadcasting, television, video or sound taping, all other
forms of mechanical or electronic reproduction, such as information storage and retrieval
systems and photocopying, and the right of translation into foreign languages, are strictly
reserved. Particular emphasis is laid upon the matter of readings, permission for which
must be secured in writing.

Acknowledgments

Special thanks to Imani Abalos, who researched, gathered, and wrote the biographical sketches of all the playwrights in this volume. Ron Davies, Administrator of the Stanford Drama Department, was extremely helpful in organizing, collating, and proofreading this volume. Our sincere appreciation for the work of Rosemary Ahern, Dutton Senior Editor, and the people at Dutton Signet for bringing this manuscript to fruition. Our deepest gratitude to all thirteen playwrights for the creativity, commitment, passion, and compassion that are contained here in their works.

Contents

SECTION FOUR: The Black Family in Crisis 451

Colored Contradictions in This Postmodern Moment: An Introduction

Harry J. Elam, Jr.

We have appropriated the name for this anthology, *Colored Contradictions*, from the final moment of *The Colored Museum* by George C. Wolfe, in which the character Topsy informs the audience, "My power is in my madness and my colored contradictions." Wolfe's play celebrates the heterogeneity of contemporary African-American existence. Accordingly, this volume reflects the diversity present in recent African-American playwriting. These plays evidence new directions and spirit in African-American cultural production. Their range in subject matter, style, structure, and language underscores the recognition that "black experience" can no longer be viewed as a monolith, but must be understood for its variety, its multiple permutations and contradictions. These plays explore new ideas as well as issues of historic resonance, new dramatic forms as well as traditional realism. They press against the externally and internally imposed boundaries placed on African-American cultural expression.

We have brought these twelve plays together because of their individual strengths, but also because of their collective contribution to expanding the American and African-American dramatic canons. As Wolfe notes, there is an immediate need to revise our thinking on "what a black play is supposed to be." This collection of plays, with its divergences in form and content, is intended to provoke such a revision and to suggest how the work of contemporary African-American playwrights is redefining "black theater."

The diverse plays contained in this anthology respond to concurrent and decidedly variant social, political, and economic concerns facing black America. For African-Americans, the contemporary social and cultural condition is one of paradox, complexity, despair, and contradiction. Cornel West argues in *Race Matters* that postmodern America has witnessed "the collapse of meaning in life—the eclipse of hope and the absence of love of

1

self and others, the breakdown of family and neighborhood bonds—[that] leads to the deracination and cultural denudement of urban dwellers, especially children. We have created rootless, dangling people with little link to the supportive networks—family, friends, school—that sustain some purpose in life."[1] In contemporary America, the infrastructure and tax base of urban cities and African-American communities have been eroded, and the middle classes have largely escaped to the suburbs and have left behind decaying urban enclaves and an underclass of poor, homeless, unemployed, and impoverished people. Many African-Americans have found themselves feeling dislocated and disconnected, extremely uncertain about the present or the future. As a result they live for what Cornel West calls "random nows," "fortuitous and fleeting moments preoccupied with 'getting over'—with acquiring pleasure, property, and power by any means necessary."[2]

And yet, at the same time that African-Americans suffer in disproportionate numbers from the aforementioned ills, African-American culture is valorized worldwide. African-American entertainers and sports figures, black urban music, dance, and even dress saturate the television screens, the printed commercial advertisements, and the radio waves in this country and around the world. Increasingly apparent in the disparities and paradoxes of contemporary African-American culture and existence is that there is not one single homogenized and essentialized black experience, as widely believed and disseminated in the 1960s, but rather a matrix of black experiences. Playwright Wolfe maintains that the defining characteristic of contemporary African-American culture is its "schizophrenia." According to Wolfe, "Black American culture is a very fragmented thing. We're all trying to come up with some definition of what we are. My absolute definition of me is the schizophrenia, the contradiction."[3] He imagines "schizophrenia" not as a negative manifestation of black pathology, but as a positive assertion of the multiplicity of black identities. This "schizophrenia" represents a significant element in African-American past and present struggle and resistance.

Colored Contradictions is a unique and explicitly "schizophrenic" anthology. Never before have black gay plays, black family dramas, and black historical dramas all been collected together in one volume. Individually as well as collectively, these plays consciously foreground the interactions between race, class, gender, and sexuality. All of the works included in this volume have been produced professionally, some to considerable commercial or critical acclaim. Still, African-American playwrights have historically confronted problems of "invisibility," searching for validation in an American culture that has consistently diminished black achievement and artistic merit. Consequently, one significant function of this anthology is to bring wider recognition and increased access to the efforts of these playwrights.

Smashing Stereotypes and Embracing Icons

We have divided this anthology into four sections, each containing three plays. In the first section, "Smashing Stereotypes and Embracing Icons," the three plays explore icons, mythologies, and stereotypes from the African-American past. They examine the connection between past images and the construction of present African-American identity. The plays contained in this section consider the lasting significance of such early "relatives" in the African-American "family" as Aunt Jemima and Uncle Tom. At this postmodern juncture, when European postmodern theorists such as Jean-François Lyotard have declared that history is dead, these African-American playwrights have seized the opportunity to compose alternative histories, to control their own representations, and to expose and interrogate the misrepresentations of African-American culture and history proposed and imposed by the dominant culture. These plays probe the truth behind the stereotypes.

The first play of this section, *I Ain't Yo' Uncle*, concerns itself fundamentally with the politics of representation. Playwright Alexander puts author Harriet Beecher Stowe on trial for her role in the creation and perpetuation of black stereotypes through her now-legendary abolitionist novel *Uncle Tom's Cabin*. Since her creation of the novel in 1852 and its adaptation by George Aiken into dramatic form in 1858, the title character, Uncle Tom, has become a pejorative symbol and earned his own separate place in American history and culture. Alexander's "new jack" revision of *Uncle Tom's Cabin* challenges Stowe's stereotypical representation of Uncle Tom and the other black characters. Alexander empowers these characters to control their own representation, to re-right history by telling their own truth. As the escaped slave George exclaims at the end of the play, "Harriet, could you sit down and be quiet? This ain't about you anymore. It's about us writing our stories." Stowe is impotent to stop this new vision of her work, but must instead only watch, listen, and learn.

In this new irreverent revision, the traditional image of Tom— as self-deprecating, God-loving darky, adverse to revolutionary insurgency and escape—is continually subverted. In addition, one of the most profound changes Alexander enacts in *I Ain't Yo' Uncle* is in the character of Topsy. Rather than depicting her in period costumes or using stereotypical slave dialect, Alexander presents Topsy in 1990s hip-hop attire, spouting contemporary street vernacular. She is at once timely and timeless. Through Alexander's refiguration of Topsy, she comes to embody antiestablishment, anarchical attitudes of frustration and alienation that were as evident in slavery as they are present in black youth culture today. The contemporary representation of Topsy as well as the action of *I Ain't Yo Uncle* visibly demonstrate how the past is read through our present reality. The economics of slavery have wrapped black and white people in a system of oppression and repression in which the ramifications are still being experienced.

Carlyle Brown's *The Little Tommy Parker Celebrated Colored Minstrel Show* explores one of the most pernicious and culturally loaded images in African-American cultural memory: the blackface minstrel. Brown's project is also to explore the truth behind the stereotype. His picture of the Tommy Parker Colored Minstrel Troupe in 1895 reveals that blackface minstrelsy offered black performers a real means of survival. Even as these colored minstrel players suffered a "social death" at the hands of white oppression and exploitation, they persevered through their talents and their desire to perform.

The pivotal character, Percy, rebels against the limits placed upon him by the oppressive, white-dominated social system. Significantly, after Percy retaliates against white racism, his only chance to escape a rapidly approaching white mob is by hiding behind the demeaning anonymity of blackface makeup. Paradoxically, blackface minstrelsy, a symbol that has historically connoted the confinement and limitation of black representation, becomes the key to Percy's liberation. During the final climactic scene of *Little Tommy Parker*, all the black minstrel players apply the burnt cork makeup to their faces in an effort to save Percy. In this moment, Brown powerfully contrasts the true black faces and individual identities of these performers with the garish uniformity of the minstrel mask. This moment reveals the inherent contradictions in black participation in blackface minstrelsy. It shows the dehumanization as well as the artistry within this ritual of "blackening up." The play, through its examination of the past, interrogates the present purposes of art and reinforces the need for African-Americans to control the means of their own cultural production.

Re/Membering Aunt Jemima by Glenda Dickerson and Breena Clarke, like Brown's *Little Tommy Parker,* also appropriates aspects of the minstrel show. Dickerson and Clarke consider the iconic figure Aunt Jemima, the woman on the pancake box, "the Great Mammy of American Myth." While *Little Tommy Parker* focuses on black men, the characters in *Re/Membering Aunt Jemima* are all women. The play's subtitle, *A Menstrual Show,* explicitly parodies and revises the notion of "a minstrel show" and underscores the significance of gender in this work. *Re/Membering Aunt Jemima* reconsiders and deconstructs the negative image of Aunt Jemima, while recovering a positive space for the articulation and celebration of black womanhood.

As the play unveils the personal history of the "Great Mammy," Aunt Jemima, it purposefully connects her to the historical struggles of black women in America. Aunt Jemima in the play gives birth to thirteen daughters. These daughters represent significant black female figures from history, from the bondswoman Harriet Tubman and early activist Ann Julia Cooper, to the beautiful and tragic actor Dorothy Dandridge, to the present-day figures of Anita Hill and Desiree Washington. Together they signify the diversity of black women's identities, that black female identity is not fixed, but only understandable through its permutations and differences. And yet, the daughters' ties back to Aunt Jemima provide these women and black women as a whole with a collective identity, a collective consciousness, a shared heritage of struggle and survival. *Re/Membering Aunt Jemima* unites black women in their difference.

The playwrights' use of "Re/membering," as opposed to "remembering," is significant. It connotes processes that reconnect the social body, that bring the members all back together. Re/membering implies community-building, while it also suggests that the voices of the past must resonate on and through the fragmentation of the present. In *Re/Membering Aunt Jemima,* past experience feeds our understanding of present and future. The symbolic figure of Aunt Jemima has endured and overcome, and her place in history is Re/membered.

Black Men at Risk

The plays in this next section, "Black Men at Risk," explore issues of black male identity. Cultural critic Kobena Mercer argues that "identity becomes an issue when it is in crisis, when something assumed to be fixed, coherent, stable is displaced by the experience of doubt and uncertainty."[4] The current conditions within the American socioeconomic order have created such a crisis for

African-American men. The violence and carnage on urban streets have made homicide one of the leading causes of death for black men between the ages of 16 and 25. Voices from both inside and outside black communities have labeled black men an endangered species. These plays directly confront the current crises consuming and confining contemporary black males. They challenge traditional conceptions of black masculinity and notions of a monolithic, essentialized, and authentic black manhood. Implicitly and explicitly, *for black boys*, *Fierce Love*, and *Tod, the Boy, Tod* all revisit and redefine the concepts of "black self-determination" and "black power" from the 1960s and 1970s. In distinctly different ways, these three plays endorse the slogan promoted by the late award-winning gay filmmaker and cultural critic Marlon Riggs that "black men loving black men is a revolutionary act."

The characters in Keith Antar Mason's *for black boys who have considered homicide when the streets were too much* are identified simply by their numbers, Brother #5, Brother #19, and Brother #34. This numerical notation explicitly draws attention to the social perception that "niggas are numbers; jus' statistics for death rolls and criminal charts." Mason's project within this play is to humanize these numbers, to externalize the inner tensions experienced by young black men as they attempt to negotiate the processes of life. Through a series of monologues, the "Brothers" in the play reveal their pain and their struggle to escape being dehumanized and labeled from the moment of birth. They confront the idea that "bein' black and a man is the ultimate contradiction."

As the title suggests and as Mason acknowledges in his director's notes that precede the play, his work is purposefully a pastiche, a "signifyin(g)" revision of Ntozake Shange's *for colored girls who have considered suicide when the rainbow is enuf*. In his award-winning study on African-American literary theory, *The Signifying Monkey*, Henry Louis Gates argues that African-American literature is double-voiced, with texts talking to other texts offering critique and revision. The process of repetition and revision with a signal difference Gates terms "signifyin(g)."[5] While *for colored girls* empowers the singular and collective voices of black women and black female experiences, *for black boys* articulates the rage and desires of young black men. The play explores how the pressures placed on black men contribute to the threat of additional black homicides, which are in effect also suicide. As in *for colored girls*, an important subject in *for black boys* is love and the relationship between black men and black women. Mason repeats and revises Shange's work in order to present love relationships from the perspective of black men. The monologues of love in *for black boys* dispel myths of black masculinity and black males as lovers whose "only mind" is "between my [their] legs."

The affirmative resolution of *for black boys* again is signifyin(g) on the collective community of sisterhood that ends *for colored girls.* Mason calls for black men to love other black men by recognizing the redeeming forces of the god that is within. Each Brother comes to realize that he has "found god in me revealed unto myself." The crisis of identity is resolved through self-discovery, and black male rage is released through the power of self and collective love.

Even as *for black boys* deconstructs the myth of black male homogeneity, its representations of black masculinity are strictly heterosexual. The second play in this section, however, Pomo Afro Homos' (*Postmodern African*-American *Homosexuals*) *Fierce Love*, refigures black masculinity to include homosexuality. With humor, parody, and pathos, *Fierce Love* contests the homophobia present in the black community, the racism in the gay community, and the essentialized images of black masculinity that exclude a gay presence. *Fierce Love* explodes the concept that black and gay are dichotomous identities.

Like *for black boys, Fierce Love* asserts the diversity of black male identities. Early in the play the characters proclaim, "We are numerous and *quite* varied cruel and loving tight-assed and loose." *Fierce Love* explores the permutations, pains, and pleasures of black gay experience. It uses satire to attack the mainstream's perpetuation of derogatory and stereotypical representations of black homosexuality. Monologues within the play purposefully break heterosexual taboos and the externally imposed silence on black homosexuality by revealing, without apology, gay intimacy and desire. In *Fierce Love,* Pomo Afro Homos present homosexual eroticism not as antithetical to but as an element of a newly imagined and newly defined black masculinity.

Fierce Love acknowledges that black gay men, like the black boys of *for black boys,* are an endangered species. AIDS, homophobia, and gay bashing are very real threats to black homosexuality. In *Fierce Love,* however, Pomo Afro Homos intend for these tangible threats confronting black gay life to be met with a rededication to persevere, to survive, and to overcome. The play ends with a return to the declaration "We Are." The action of the play situates the fight for black gay rights within the historic continuum of oppressed peoples' movements. Pomo Afro Homos align their efforts to secure a space for black gay identity free from heterosexual persecution with the historical struggles to achieve black liberation.

At the outset of *Tod, the Boy, Tod* by Talvin Wilks, Tod, the title character, has lost any connection to the history of African-American battles for freedom. He is extremely conflicted over his identity. Tod, too, represents an endangered species, a young black man at risk. In this case, however, the immediate threat to Tod is himself. Unable to negotiate the various pressures working on his consciousness, Tod attempts to commit suicide. The play transpires in Tod's unconscious mind as he struggles with the meanings of being black.

Tod battles with his black middle-class guilt and with his long-standing belief that his identity has been constructed on and through what Stuart Hall terms the "recognition of self through difference."[6] Throughout his black middle-class existence, his experiences in a white prep school and in a white Ivy League college, Tod has been separated from the black masses, and encouraged by the white dominant culture to believe that he is somehow different from these other black people. Yet, rather than fully assimilating, Tod encounters conflict with the problematic isolation of the black middle class and rebels against white establishment success. He decries being different from both the white norm and the black Other. He experiences self-hatred and exhibits a self-destructive rage.

Tod struggles to reconstruct himself, to pull together his fragmented, confused, and tormented self-image. At the core of this struggle are issues vital to this postmodern moment and our definitions and understandings of blackness. Tod queries, "What is black?" He fights against essential notions of blackness. Through Tod, playwright Wilks challenges current racial ideologies that locate the "authentic" black experience soley in the urban, ghetto environment and negate black middle-class experiences. Tod's personal battle with black identity reveals "black" to be a social and politically constructed category with meanings particular to and relevant for the specific historical moments of its use.

As in the other works presented in this section, Tod eventually finds redemption through self-knowledge and love. He comes to recognize his inherent connections to the black liberation efforts of the past and discovers a new meaning of "Freedom," a new language of struggle, and a less constricting and conflicting concept of blackness. He determines to live every moment of the present to its fullest. "Live free or die!" Tod exclaims.

Tod, the Boy, Tod and the other two plays in this section reflect on the diversity that comprises and the difficulties that confront contemporary black men. All three plays explore previously underexposed aspects of black manhood. These plays contest the current crises of identity by embracing black difference and empowering alternative black male voices.

Reconstructing Black Womanhood

The voice, identity, and position of black women are the subjects of the next section, "Reconstructing Black Womanhood." Significantly, the three plays in this section give voice to black women who emanate from the margins of black women's already marginalized locations. They are poor, rural, handicapped, and incarcerated women. Their stories have largely been overlooked, silenced, or even ignored. By focusing on these previously anonymous black women, these three plays and playwrights broaden the vision of black women's experiences and show the power, insight, and transcendent meanings contained in these women's earnest negotiations of life. The title of this section is adapted from Hazel Carby's book on the emergence of black women novelists, *Reconstructing Womanhood*, in which she argues that historically, black women have "had to confront the dominant domestic ideologies and literary conventions of womanhood which excluded them from the definition 'woman.' "[7] Implicitly, the plays in this section interrogate contemporary definitions of black womanhood and "the material conditions" of black women's existence.

In *Big Butt Girls, Hard-Headed Women*, performance artist Rhodessa Jones explores an underclass of women who are intentionally silenced and ostracized by the systems of power in this country, women in prison. Jones focuses on the stories of four women: Mama Pearl, a woman in her seventies who has been in and out of correctional institutions for thirty years; Lena, a former dancer and valedictorian turned drug addict; Doris, a young teenage mother; and, most particularly, Regina Brown, a wizened prostitute. The portraits of these women are hard-hitting and raw. Jones conveys the feelings of neglect, regret, isolation, passion, and pride that shape these women's lives. Jones intensifies the social significance of these "real" and vivid portrayals by dedicating the piece to the memory of Regina Brown, who was killed in 1989 after her third release from incarceration.

Jones observes these women and their stories from her position as prison aerobics instructor. The correlation between "aerobics" and "Big Butt Girls" is not ironic nor trivial, but purposeful. Aerobics hones and shapes the body. The use and abuse of women's bodies is the center of Jones's performance piece as well. Jones reveals the pressures, constraints, degradations, and exploitations enacted on and against the bodies of these "Big Butt Girls" and "Hard-Headed Women" by their society, their lovers, their families, and even themselves. These are women caught up in a tragic cycle of poverty and limitation, crime and incarceration. Unfortunately, these are conditions that disproportionately involve African-American women. Jones intones the statistics, "85% of all women incarcerated in U. S. penal institutions are women of color . . . 50% are African-American women."

Jones's performance piece intentionally indicts and engages the audience. She challenges audience members to recognize their personal connections to these women. "Who are these women? . . . She's your mama. She's your lover. That woman who is gonna carry your child." Jones points out that the system of crime and punishment touches all our lives and that we all have a responsibility to act for social change. She calls on the audience to participate in a symbolic ceremony for Regina Brown. It is a ritual of redemption, an act that reaffirms and "re/members" Regina's spirit. Jones argues that through love, through the power of the ancestors, through the linkage of past to present and future, a body can "catch a body." The needless loss of black lives to the prison system can be overcome through collective consciousness and the formation and assertion of community.

The assertion of a community of women enthuses and suffuses Shay Youngblood's *Shakin' the Mess Outta Misery*. The play takes its name from a faith-healing ceremony and is structured around the approaching ritual of womanhood that the character Daughter will soon undergo down at the river. Daughter has been orphaned by her own mother and raised by a "sisterhood" of older black women. They are a diverse and dichotomous group. Yet their differences coalesce in the community that addresses Daughter's needs, nurtures her development, and teaches her through their examples.

Daughter functions as the conduit for the stories of these women, her "mothers." Each story, a vivid memory of black southern life in the 1950s and 1960s, has helped to forge Daughter's identity. With humor and passion, flashbacks recall the lives of these ordinary black women. Yet within the ordinary are extraordinary tales of struggle and survival, of racism and pain, of love and loss. The "her" stories are at once personal and political, a history of African-American women who have triumphed in the face of adversity and passed this legacy on to their "Daughter." The women exude wisdom, vitality, and spirit. Their ability to overcome adversity, poverty, and prejudice attests to the proclamation that "Colored people are the most amazing people on earth." Daughter is at once singular and representative of all black "daughters." In the lesson she learns from her mothers, she exemplifies the need of black women to read their present circumstances through the collective heritage of black women's struggle and survival.

Kia Corthron's *Come Down Burning* explores the harsh realities of family planning, economic welfare, and social survival in the rural mountains of the South. No men are seen within the world of this play. As in *Big Butt Girls*, the personal and political dynamics of black women's bodies are critical to the action and meanings of *Come Down Burning*. The focal character Skoolie's body is paralyzed, but she is in no way incapacitated. She moves around on a flat wooden board with wheels, negotiating her way around her home. All the appliances within the house are purposely placed lower than those in a "normal" house, tailored to her needs and specifications. She earns an income through styling and braiding hair and the performance of abortions. In *Come Down Burning*, Corthron presents abortion—a fervently contested contemporary issue of women's bodily rights—as an accepted though dangerous practice, a matter of economic necessity, an act that protects the welfare of the family and children already present. The events of the play reveal Skoolie's will to survive even as the injustices of fate "come down burning." The indomitability of her spirit prevails over any attempt to marginalize her due to her body, her class, her gender, her race, or her handicap.

At the outset of the play, Skoolie's sister Tee and Tee's three children are living with Skoolie. In addition, Tee is pregnant once again. Two of Tee's babies who did not survive lay buried in the backyard, a testament to the harshness and unforgiving nature of the family's mountain existence. Throughout their lives Skoolie, despite her handicap, has cared for and mothered her sister. On and off over the past five years, Tee and her family have lived with Skoolie. Still, the sisters are a study in contrast. While Skoolie exudes a practical wisdom rooted in her real-life experience, Tee exhibits a stubborn innocence and attempts to ignore and even transcend the material realities of their impoverished lives. Despite her dependence on Skoolie, Tee resists Skoolie's guidance. Her desire to escape Skoolie's control leads Tee to move out of Skoolie's house and to attempt tragically her own abortion rather than to await the knowledgeable hands of Skoolie.

And yet, through cooperation the sisters achieve a moment of transcendence and triumph. Tee carries the crippled Skoolie down to Tee's nine-year-old daughter Eva's school, where Skoolie confronts Eva's abusive white teacher. Both sisters overcome limitations through this act. Skoolie leaves the safety of her mountain home. Tee must summon new strength, confidence, and commitment to carry her sister over a distance of one and a half miles. Together, in this communal act, they exorcise personal demons and challenge the forces of poverty and prejudice.

In *Come Down Burning* and the other plays of this section race, class, and gender powerfully interact. These representations of ordinary, marginalized black women contain meanings that transcend the immediate even as they enrich our understanding of the particular cultural, economic, and social circumstances that affect black women's lives and shape their identities.

The Black Family in Crisis

In the final section, "The Black Family in Crisis," the interdynamics of domestic family life are the focus. Historically, African-Americans have been connected to and through extended families and socialized to think of themselves as a community. These plays struggle with definitions of family and with notions of what is community. External and internal forces threaten the security and values of the families in each of these three works.

In Wayne Corbitt's poetic *Crying Holy* and Cheryl West's award-winning *Before It Hits Home,* sons who are stricken with AIDS return home. They desire to come home and reconcile themselves with their families. In *Crying Holy,* the protagonist, Waters, a forty-year-old black gay poet, returns to his family's southern home because he "needed to go home and—rest in the bosom of my family." Throughout the play the nature and meaning of family are challenged. His nuclear family is a family of women, matriarchal and extended. At the center of the family is his mother, Mother Bell, a leader in the Holiness Church and a powerful presence in his life. Waters brings his friend Merideth, a black British anthropologist, home for support. They form part of an alternative family that once included Waters's now-deceased lover, Donald. As Merideth explains, "We queers must make our own family. Blood family tends to desert or oppress us." Her statement reinforces the need for as well as the problematic nature of "family."

While Waters makes his nuclear family aware of his HIV infection, no one in the family mentions it during his visit. Their sense of denial is strong. More significantly, his homosexuality and AIDS come into direct conflict with his mother's religious fanaticism. Mother Bell's avoidance of her son's illness is based on her belief that his contracting the disease must be false, that her religion will not allow it to be true. "They told him a lie Lord Jesus. I know IT TO BE A LIE." Waters's attempts to talk to his mother to explain the realities of his living with AIDS are rebuffed by the strong forces of her zealous denial. Waters must recognize, "I cannot go home as who I am." The last scene of the play functions as a powerful, poetic, even operatic duet as Waters and his mother both lament and give voice to their pain: they both "cry holy."

In Cheryl West's *Before It Hits Home,* the traditional conceptions of family, of mothers and fathers and sons, are questioned and conventional expectations exploded. The protagonist, Wendell, is a saxophone player, an artist like Waters in *Crying Holy.* Unlike Waters, however, he has two lovers, one male and one female. His female lover, Simone, implores him, "I want to be your family," while his male lover, Douglas, who has a wife and children, reminds him, "I'm the one with a family." Wendell himself is a father and thus already part of another "family." All these statements about and images of family are further problematized when Wendell makes a trip to the doctor's office: a waiting black female AIDS patient welcomes him to "the family," the family of those infected by this terminal virus. Clearly this is not a family that Wendell chooses. Through these and other invocations of family, West points out that the crises and concerns, the ties that bind families together, are not simply a matter of desire nor choice.

Wendell returns home with AIDS because he, like Waters, believes that "I could get stronger at home." Yet his admission of homosexuality to his mother draws an unexpected response. She enters into denial. She refuses to help her son or nurture him in his time of need. Moreover, she is unable to even stay in her own house with him. Her reactions are honest, yet they refute the traditional expectation of the selfless, loving black mother. Wendell's admission of his sickness destroys his mother's images of home and family and irrevocably damages her identity as mother in the process.

When Wendell becomes sick, it is his father, Bailey, who cares for him. Their relationship has always been an antagonistic one— so much love and so little communication. Bailey explains that "sometimes a father can't see his son for his own failures." Significantly, the father overcomes his own fears and inhibitions and reaches out to his son. Through her representations of fathers, sons, mothers, and families, West contests the sanctities, traditions, and taboos that define and delimit the black family unit. She challenges audiences, "before it hits home," to reflect on their own families, their prejudices and preconceptions that restrict and constrict true struggle, love, and communication.

Suzan-Lori Parks's Obie-Award–winning drama, *Imperceptible Mutabilities in the Third Kingdom,* concerns not just one particular family, but the African-American family as a whole and the historic experiences of African-Americans under the hegemony of a racist, white world. The play is abstract in both form and language. Parks uses symbolism, metaphor, humor, and irony to probe the relationship between African-American history and the construction of contemporary African-American identity. Parks queries "who we were when we were, who we will be when we will be and who we be now that we iz." According to Parks in *Imperceptible Mutabilities,* when the white slave traders, the "Bleached Bones Man," brought blacks to the New World, they created a "third kingdom," a liminal space between the world of Africa and America. Parks observes this "third kingdom" through history and suggests that the changes, the evolutions, or the mutabilities in African-American identity and self-knowledge are virtually imperceptible. African-Americans still suffer from the feelings of isolation, dislocation, and alienation experienced on being brought from Africa and jettisoned into the "third kingdom."

The play is divided into four sections. The first section, "Snails," focuses on the home life of three contemporary African-American women. It explores how their interactions with the dominant culture shape their self-perception and identity. At the same time, this section comments on how the dominant culture attempts to control and contain the social mobility of African-Americans. A white naturalist and pseudo-exterminator spies on these women from an anthropological distance with the assistance of a giant cockroach. The next section, "The Third Kingdom," is a threnody of Middle Passage. Its poetry recalls how the abrupt separation of Africans from their homeland literally placed them between two worlds. "Open House," the third section, enters the nightmare of a dying former slave. She recalls images of slavery and visions of slave ships. Yet, a mysterious Mrs. Smith brutally wrenches her memories, her history, from her through a series of tooth extractions. A reprise of "The Third Kingdom" follows "Open House" and reinforces the sense of dislocation from past, from history, from self, experienced by Africans in the New World.

The final section, "The Greeks," repeats and revises these

themes of cultural and personal separation. A black marine sergeant, stationed across the sea from his family, communicates with his wife and family through a series of letters. He forfeits the possibility of "quality time" with his family in his quest to achieve his "distinction" in the service. He loses his legs in the process and receives little recognition from a system that continually diminishes black achievement. Most significantly, in his absence his wife goes blind and his family multiplies in numbers and in their feelings of distance and alienation from their father, from their culture, from their history.

Parks's work repeats and reinforces issues and ideas expressed throughout this anthology. *Imperceptible Mutabilities* and other plays contained in this anthology emphasize the impact of the African-American past on the present. Parks notes the importance of righting history, of African-Americans retaining control of their own representation. Even as linguistic and structural complexity separates Parks's play from other plays in this anthology, which are more conventional in form, she is united with them in the process of renegotiating what African-American theater should be. Together these plays defy labels and expand our understanding of the inter- and intracultural connections, the collective considerations, and the individual permutations of African-American cultural expressions. Together they express and embody "our colored contradictions."

Endnotes

[1] Cornel West, *Race Matters* (Boston: Beacon Press, 1993), 5.

[2] Cornel West, *Race Matters*, 5.

[3] George Wolfe, quoted by Jack Kroll in "Theater: Zapping Black Stereotypes," *Newsweek* (17 November 1986): 85.

[4] Kobena Mercer, *Welcome to the Jungle* (London: Routledge, 1994), 259.

[5] Henry Louis Gates, *The Signifying Monkey* (New York: Oxford University Press, 1988). Gates terms his theory *signifyin(g)*, with the "g" in parentheses to differentiate it from other definitions of signifying or signifyin'. In his book, he outlines the relation of signifyin(g) to these aforementioned terms. He also traces the African and African-American roots of the traditions of intertextuality, repetition, and revision. Here I will use the term "signifyin(g)" when I am directly referring to the process as identified and theorized by Gates.

[6] Stuart Hall, "Minimal Selves," *Identity: The Real Me*, ICA Documents 6 (London: Institute of Contemporary Arts, 1987), 45.

[7] Hazel Carby, *Reconstructing Womanhood: The Emergence of the Afro-American Woman Novelist* (New York: Oxford University Press, 1987), 6.

Foreword

"Mad Flava"

Like way before I called my main man, Harry Elam, like my brain was buzzing with this idea for this book, you dig, and not just any book, this book had to be the bomb, the joint, all that and a six-pack of beer. It had to be the new jack attack on an eight track, pumping fear in yo' ear from another hemisphere. It had to have a little Shakespeare wrapped inside a niggeroe and plenty open spaces where a niggeroe can grow and grow and grow and be not afraid to contradict anything that went down before.

And that's why y'all should read this book. See, we got Pomo Afro Homos pumping that black gay pride in your ear. Yeah, and Sister Shay—Sister Shay Youngblood can be counted on to make you shed a tear or two or three, but don't take it from me—read the play, she be shakin' the mess out of misery.

You see, some of us be writing in blood and some of us be speaking in tongues. But we be out here representing. So we got Suzan-Lori Parks in the house. So you intellectually lazy niggeroes, better step—this ain't for you—'cause when Ms. Parks is through, we got some Talvin Wilks for your head, and he and Ms. Parks—they be kickin' that mad flava for yo' ear—kinda like Shakespeare wrapped inside a niggeroe, only better and much wetter when the fluid starts to flow and Wayne Corbitt is just crying holy, a muted poem sprung from his lung like a muted note blown by Miles as he smiles down on all of this kinda blue kinda new jack attack on a twenty-four-track mixing board, 'cause Kia Corthron had to come down burning kicking up mad flava, stressing the lesson for all you nappy-headed girls with big curls and yo' hands on yo' hips. So if you're timid and fronting, put the book down! This ain't for you.

Now, where else are you gonna find the complete unabridged version of Keith Antar Mason's *for black boys who have considered homicide*, 'cause those streets are kickin' up mad flava, in the same book with Aunt Jemima and Uncle Tom? See, the truth of the matter is, there has never been a book of hooks like this one, where you get to step inside the mind of Carlyle Brown, or reinvent Aunt Jemima with Glenda Dickerson and Breena Clarke.

So like I said before the downpour of words, I had been buzzing for some time with this mad idea, of putting together a book of plays by black playwrights that seemed different from all those other books of plays by black playwrights, so I dropped a dime on my partner Harry and I said, "Yo, Harry—I got this phat idea for this book of plays, and not plays that belong together, but plays that bite, contradict, sample, inform, you know, plays that be kicking mad flava, Harry—plays that be kickin' mad flava. Plays that spray bass in yo' face, twice, just in case they missed you the first time." Mad flava.

Peace, Robert Alexander

Smashing Stereotypes and Embracing Icons

I AIN'T YO' UNCLE
The New Jack Revisionist
Uncle Tom's Cabin

Robert Alexander

R OBERT ALEXANDER, playwright, is the author of nineteen produced plays. His most recent works are *Servant of the People*, a play about the rise and fall of the Black Panther Party, produced at the St. Louis Black Repertory Company in St. Louis, Missouri, in 1994; and *I Ain't Yo' Uncle: The New Jack Revisionist* Uncle Tom's Cabin, originally written for the internationally renowned San Francisco Mime Troupe. *I Ain't Yo' Uncle* toured the East Coast from Florida to Vermont in 1992. As Playwright-in-Residence at the Lorraine Hansberry Theater in San Francisco, California, Alexander has authored several world premieres for that company, including *Air Guitar*, a rock opera, and *We Almost Made It to the Super Bowl*, a tragicomedy about racism in the NFL.

Alexander's works have been produced or have received workshop productions by some of the top regional theaters in the country, including the Negro Ensemble Company; the Kennedy Center in Washington, D.C.; the GROUP: Seattle's Multicultural Theater in Seattle, Washington; the Inner City Cultural Center, the Los Angeles Theater Center, and the Mark Taper Forum in Los Angeles, California; the Hartford Stage Company in Hartford, Connecticut; Jomandi Productions in Atlanta, Georgia; the St. Louis Black Repertory Company in St. Louis, Missouri; and the San Diego Repertory Theater in San Diego, California.

The recipient of numerous writing awards, grants, and fellowships, Alexander is currently devoted to developing his microphone skills as a spoken-word artist with The Black Planet Collective, an alternative performance art band. A graduate of Oberlin College, he lives in Oakland, California. Alexander received an MFA in theater from the University of Iowa, where he was a Patricia Roberts Harris Fellow.

Cast of Characters

HARRIET BEECHER STOWE, abolitionist novelist
ELIZA HARRIS, mulatto slave
GEORGE HARRIS, runaway slave
TOPSY, slave urchin
LITTLE EVA, a dying liberal
SIMON LEGREE, a racist slave owner
UNCLE TOM, a man with an image problem
SHELBY, a Kentucky slave owner
HALEY, a slave trader
AUNT CHLOE, TOM's wife
PHINEAS, a reformed character
MARKS, a shyster
LOKER, a slave catcher
MARIE ST. CLARE, a New Orleans belle
AUGUSTINE ST. CLARE, her husband
MISS OPHELIA, St. Clare's cousin
JANE, a slave
A DOCTOR
SKEGGS, an auctioneer
MANN, a slave speculator
EMMELINE, a slave
SAMBO, a slave
CASSY, a slave, Legree's bedwench
YOUNG SHELBY

Most actors will play multiple roles.

Prologue

(*AT RISE: We hear the angry voices of the cast offstage.*)

GEORGE (*off*): Bring in the accused!

(GEORGE *enters first, followed quickly by* TOPSY *and* ELIZA *as they drag on* HARRIET BEECHER STOWE *against her will.*)

GEORGE: Bring in the accused!

HARRIET: What am I accused of?

GEORGE: Shut up and we'll read the charges. Sit down!

ELIZA: Don't hurt her.

TOPSY: Missy here is accused of creatin' stereotypes—

HARRIET: I did no such—

TOPSY (*Gets in* HARRIET*'s face*): And making me talk like a damn fool pickanniny!

GEORGE: We've been stuck with these stupid bug-eye images you made up for a hundred and fifty years!

HARRIET: I did my research . . . I visited plantations. I met dozens of girls like Topsy. I did not make you up!

TOPSY: But all I did was dance in your novel!

HARRIET: Dancing is wonderful, especially the way you dance. If I could dance like you, Topsy, I would dance all the time.

(*A spotlight shines on* UNCLE TOM, *as he enters through the audience. Like a shuffling janitor, with a handkerchief in his hand, he wipes the arms of the theatre chairs.*)

TOM: Excuse me, y'all . . . pardon me, ma'am . . . excuse me, suh . . .

24

GEORGE: See? This is the crap I'm talking about! (*To band*) Stop playing that song! Who let him in here? This is the last shuffling stereotype we need to see.

TOM: Evenin', George.

GEORGE: Get him out of here, Harriet!

TOPSY: We thought Uncle Tom was dead and long buried.

TOM: Ain't I de one everybody come to see?! Don't y'all want to see me stoop, shuffle, and bend over backwards with a smile for every white person I meet?!

TOPSY: No!

ELIZA: Nobody wants to see you. We're just trying to get on with our new lives. George is an executive now—with CLOROX!

TOM: You too, Eliza? What's y'all's beef with me?

TOPSY: You loved every master . . . you ever had.

GEORGE: You took every whipping like you got off on it!

TOM: I did?

HARRIET: There seems to be some confusion as to who's on trial here. I'm glad you've come back, Uncle Tom. I know you'll defend me. Tell them how my book helped emancipate your race.

TOM (*straightens up*): Let's get a few things straight, Ms. Stowe. First of all, I ain't yo' uncle!

TOPSY: I heard that!

TOM: Yeah, your book turned some folks against slavery, but it created a big image problem for me. "Uncle Tom," that's what they call that new Supreme Court justice, ain't it? Why did you give me that cross to carry? Why did you paint me like Jesus, instead of painting me like a man . . . a whole man?

HARRIET: I wrote what you showed me.

TOM: You wrote what you wanted to see!

ELIZA: No . . . wait! I loved Harriet's book. Used to. I cried every time I got to the part—

TOPSY: This child is tragic! It's the "black thang" we're mad about, "Lemon Drop!"

GEORGE: I find the accused—GUILTY!! . . . of writing stuff she couldn't possibly know about. A slave's experience. The black experience ... my life here in America. (*Others respond,* YEAH!)

HARRIET: We try our best and it's never enough. What is it that YOU PEOPLE want?

TOM: I wants to git paid! (*Group reacts with affirmations.*)

HARRIET: Paid, Tom?

TOM: Money!

TOPSY (*pounding her palms*): Forty acres and a mule!

HARRIET: Look, we have integration, we have equal opportunity ... we've had every kind of social program. I'm sorry, but I'm tired of being guilty and I'm tired of being the accused. I'm sick of black anger and I'm even beginning to question affirmative action! (TOPSY *must be restrained by* GEORGE.) If I get waited on before you, it's discrimination. If I bump you on the streetcar, I'm oppressing you, and if I want to study Aristotle, I'm a racist!

TOPSY: Let's off this broad, right now!

TOM: No! Tonight ... let's do our version.

TOPSY: Aw, man ... I ain't with that. (*Others protest.*)

TOM: I said we're doing this play! Wid new dialogue ... and scenes YOU left out! Scenes that show me in a new light. A true light. I want to git paid my proper respect, especially from the brothuhs and sistuhs who turn their backs. None of y'all would be here if it wasn't for me. I stayed behind so y'all could git ahead. So tonight—let me lift my voice and sing, 'til the earth and heavens ring ... ring with the harmony of my New Jack Swing.

ALL: Go, Tom, Go, Tom ...

TOPSY: Yeah, I'm housin' up some of my shit, too.

TOM: I said places, Topsy!

HARRIET: What's the point, Tom? How much could you possibly change? You can't rewrite history!

TOM: But I can change who writes it. So places, Harriet! Let's kick it! (*Exeunt.*)

Act 1

Scene 1

(*Plain chamber. Enter* ELIZA *with* HARRY.)

ELIZA: Ah, George. I'm so glad you've come. (GEORGE *regards her mournfully.*) Why don't you smile, and ask after our Harry?

GEORGE: I wish he'd never been born! I wish I'd never been born myself!

ELIZA: George! I know how you feel . . . losing your place in the factory, and that man torments you so, but try to be patient.

GEORGE: Patient! Haven't I been patient? Did I say a word when he stole credit for my invention? And then he came and took me away—for no reason. He got every cent I ever made.

ELIZA: It's not right. Why, your skin is as fair as his! But after all, he is your master.

GEORGE: My master! Right! And who made this peckerwood my master?! What right does he have to me? I'm as good a man as he is. Maybe better. He says, even though I don't say anything, he can see I got the devil in me, and he's gonna bring it out. He keeps pushing me, one of these days it's gonna come out all right! He's gonna find out I'm one whipping can't tame!

ELIZA: George! Don't do anything wicked; trust in heaven and try to do right.

GEORGE: He's been saying he was a fool to let me marry off the place—and he says he won't let me come here anymore, that I have to take another wife and settle down on his place.

ELIZA: I don't *think* so! You were married to me by the minister,

27

right in Mistress's parlor, as much as if you'd been a white man!

GEORGE: Don't you know you can't be my wife if either of our masters chooses to part us?

ELIZA: Oh, but my master is so kind.

GEORGE: But he could die, and then Harry could be sold to anybody!

ELIZA: Never!

GEORGE: Eliza, my girl, bear up now, and goodbye—I'm going.

ELIZA: Going! Going where?

GEORGE: To Ohio—to the Quakers, and then . . . to Canada; and when I'm there, I'll buy you and the boy—that's all the hope that's left us.

ELIZA: But you could be caught!

GEORGE: I won't be caught, Eliza—I'll die first. I will never be taken down the river alive.

ELIZA: Go, but be careful—I can't bear the thought of you dying.

GEORGE: My preparations are made. One last look at Harry, and then goodbye.

ELIZA: Heaven grant it not be forever. (*Exeunt.*)

(*Lights fade. End of scene.*)

Scene 2

(*A dining room. Tables and chairs. Dessert, wine, etc., on the table.* SHELBY *and* HALEY *discovered at table.*)

HALEY: I can't trade dat way. I positively can't, Mr. Shelby. Give me Tom and one of them critters I've seen running around here and dat will clear your debt fair and square.

SHELBY: My debt totals eight hundred dollars. I can get twice that for Tom. He's loyal, capable . . . honest.

HALEY: You mean honest as niggers go.

SHELBY: No! He's truly honest. He got religion at a camp meeting four years ago and I've trusted him with running everything ever since. He manages my money, my house, my horses. He comes and goes just like a free man, and I've always found him to be true and square in every way. He's got the fear of God in him.

HALEY: The fear of God in a nigger is a valuable thing.

SHELBY: And Tom's got the genuine article. Why, just last fall I let him go to Cincinnati to take care of my business matters, and he came straight back with five hundred dollars for me. Some low fellows tried to encourage Tom to make tracks for Canada. But Tom said, "My master trusted me and I couldn't." Now, if you were a man with any kind of conscience, you would let Tom cover the entire balance of my debt.

HALEY: I've got as much conscience as any decent businessman . . . none. (*Pours more wine as* ELIZA *enters.* HALEY *takes notice of her right away.*) But I tell you what—you throw in dat yeller wench right there, you'll be out of hock and I'll be out of your hair. (*Offers his hand.*) Care to shake on dat deal?

29

(ELIZA *starts clearing the dishes.* HALEY *pats her bottom.*)

SHELBY: No way I can shake on that kind of deal. My wife wouldn't part with her for all her weight in gold.

HALEY: Women always say such things. 'Cause they hain't no sort of calculation. But show 'em how many feathers and trinkets dat weight in gold will buy—

SHELBY: I tell you, Haley, this is not to be spoken of.

HALEY: Well, then—dat smart little critter I seen running 'round here. You know—the one I played catch with.

SHELBY: You mean Eliza's boy . . . Harry? Why, what can you want with the child?

HALEY: Why, I've got a friend dat's going into this yer branch of the business—wants to buy up handsome boys to raise for the market.

ELIZA (*aside*): Oh, no! Not my Harry. (*Exits.*)

HALEY: Your debt has gathered up quite a bit of interest. Might as well own up to it, I'm determined to leave here with more than just Tom. . . . So what's it gonna be . . . the wench or the critter?

SHELBY: Come by this evening 'round seven and you shall have my answer.

HALEY: See you at seven. (*Exits.*)

(SHELBY *pours himself another drink.*)

SHELBY: Maybe the answer lies at the bottom of this bottle.

(*Lights slowly fade to black. End of scene.*)

Scene 3

(*A dim light rises on* TOM *and* CHLOE *in bed inside of Uncle Tom's cabin. They are asleep. Suddenly they are awakened by an anxious tapping on the window.* CHLOE *grabs the candle and looks out the window.*)

CHLOE: It's Eliza! (CHLOE *rises from bed and opens the door.* TOM *follows.*) Git in here, gul! You gonna catch a death of a cold, running 'round on such a brutal night.

(ELIZA *enters the cabin, shaking snow off her coat.*)

TOM: What's gotten into you, gal?

ELIZA: I'm running away, Uncle Tom and Aunt Chloe. And I'm taking Harry with me!

CHLOE: Running? You? What on earth for? Massa treats you like you was Snow White—givin' you the softest job in the Big House.

ELIZA: He sold my boy! I hid in a closet and I overheard Master tell his Missus that he sold you too, Uncle Tom.

CHLOE: Sold Tom, too! Massa promised he would never sell either of us.

ELIZA: Master is so stupid he has come into this man's debt. The trader's coming to take possession in the morning. Uncle Tom, it would ease my heart if you ran away with us.

CHLOE: Don't just stand there like a stump, old man—run with 'Liza! (*He doesn't move.*) You got a pass to come and go anytime—now's the time to go!

TOM: No. If I run, too—I would bring the bloodhounds sho 'nuff.

ELIZA: But they're coming to claim ya in the morning.

31

CHLOE: Don't be a fool, Tom. Run . . . 'fore they tote you down-river where they kill a nigger with hard work and starving!

TOM: Let Eliza go—it's her right. It ain't in her nature for her to stay, and it ain't in my nature for me to run. Now, reach under dat mattress and give 'Liza a little something for her journey.

(TOM *reaches under her mattress for some money. This is a surprise to both women.*)

TOM: Massa been trusting me with tending to his business. (*Aside*) Sometimes I set aside a small commission for times like these! (ELIZA *hesitates.*) Go on—and take care of that boy of yours.

(*Sudden noise of pursuers and dogs offstage.* TOM *hurries terrified* ELIZA *to back door.*)

ELIZA: George just left for Canada. Get word to him that I ran north with Harry!

TOM: Chloe'll see dat he gits your message. Now hurry up and go. Follow de moon 'til it shines upon a river.

(ELIZA *exits,* SHELBY *and* HALEY *enter.*)

HALEY: Hey, boy! Have ya seen dat high-yeller wench and dat fair-hair boy of hers?

CHLOE: Which yeller girl you tink he talking 'bout, Tom? Lessee, dere's Dinah . . . and Jezebel . . . now would you call Jezebel yeller?

TOM: Naw, she's more honey colored . . . but her boy's got that fair hair . . .

HALEY: Now, now—her tracks in the snow lead straight to your door!

TOM: Funny thing 'bout them tracks . . . they can fool yassuh—'specially in de snow. Last winter I was tracking me a possum. Follered him clear—musta been 6 or 8 miles through dem woods—den come to find out, it was a coon!

HALEY: You're my nigger now, boy—I'll be back to deal with your hide later! Come on, Shelby. Let's git dat critter.

(HALEY *exits.* SHELBY *starts to exit, but* TOM *grabs his arm.*)

TOM: Why did ya do it, suh? Why did ya break your promise?

CHLOE: A white man's promises ain't worth the air dey was written on.

SHELBY: I swear, Tom, as soon as I get things right, I'll send my boy for ye. I'll buy you back—do you think you'll ever find it in your heart . . . to—to forgive me? Oh . . . what's the use? (*Exits.*)

TOM: Chloe, it's better I go alone and be sold than break up the whole place and have everybody sold off.

CHLOE: But why you got to be the one?

TOM: 'Cause I can b'ar it. Hold me, Chloe. Don't cry now, don't need to cry. I'll be comin back—I have faith.

CHLOE: You got a fool's faith! And a fool's faith can't help you where you're going!

TOM: Ya'll see. Long as I can do right. 'Cause I believe—if you do right, things'll come out right for you.

Scene 4

(Tavern by the riverside. Table and chairs brought on. ELIZA *enters with little* HARRY *wrapped in a bundle.)*

ELIZA: Courage, my boy. Mama won't let those slavecatchers get you. We have reached the river at last. (*Looks out window.*) Oh, no! The river is choked with blocks of ice! How shall we make it to the other side?

*(*PHINEAS *enters, looking out the window at the river.)*

PHINEAS: That thar river looks like a permiscuous ice cream shop come to an awful state of friz. (*Spits on the floor.*)

ELIZA (*aside*): The tavern scene, where we meet a scene-stealing, to-bacco-chewing, corny-ass white guy stuck in for comic relief.

PHINEAS: Chaw? (*Offers.*)

ELIZA (*gestures refusal*): Is there any ferry or boat taking people over now?

PHINEAS: Everything's stopped running.

ELIZA: Stopped running?

PHINEAS: That's what I said! But I know a feller down the road a piece that's going over with some truck this evening. If he duss to, he'll be in here to have his supper. There's a little room over there with a fireplace where you and the young'un can stay warm 'til he shows.

*(*ELIZA *curtsies & exits.)*

PHINEAS (*studying her as she leaves with* HARRY *in her arms*): That gal ain't fooling nobody. She's got too spacious a backyard for a white woman. I could make a bundle on her and her boy. I used to own a whole grist of niggers . . . 'til I met Ruth. But she said I had to give 'em up and become a Quaker if I wanted her heart and her hand. Damn, I am cursed by the woman. I never knew such pouting lips could change a man's heart.

(GEORGE *enters.*)

GEORGE: With this disguise, I've got white men tipping their hats, white ladies batting their eyes—and innkeepers open their doors. But nobody knows I'm the negro on this wanted poster. (*Displays it, posts it.*)

PHINEAS: George? What are you doing here? You're not supposed to reach this tavern until the second act.

GEORGE: Where's my wife?

PHINEAS: I ain't seen her, George. Chaw? (*Offers.*)

GEORGE: Stop lying. She crosses the river in the first act. I never did like her crossing the river before me, when I left two scenes before she did.

PHINEAS: Anyone seen the writer?!

GEORGE: I'm writing this part. You play the kind factory owner who recognizes me.

PHINEAS: That mealymouth?

GEORGE: 'Liza can cut my scenes, but she can't cut my best lines. (*Indicates poster.*)

PHINEAS (*reading, assumes new voice*): "Wanted dead or alive." George . . . this is a dangerous game you're playing. I couldn't advise it.

GEORGE: White man—if the Indians should come and capture you . . . take you away from your wife and children and keep you hoeing corn for them—I wonder if you'd abide in that condition. I imagine you'd steal the first stray horse you came upon and shoot any man who stood in your way!

PHINEAS: Really, neighbor George . . . putting the case in that— somewhat peculiar light . . . I don't know what I'd do. But this is not the right course for you—going against the laws of your country.

GEORGE: My country!? My country?! What country have I but the grave? I don't want to have anything to do with YOUR country except to be left alone by it . . . allowed to peaceably leave. And I pity the fool who tries to stop me! (*Snatches his wanted poster down.*)

PHINEAS (*looks off*): Here come the human bloodhounds. (*Raises trapdoor.*) Look . . . hide down here.

GEORGE: I'll blast my way out!

PHINEAS: Just get down in the trap while I parley with them.

GEORGE: I'm warning you, Phineas. You better not cross me.

PHINEAS: Yeah, right . . . just git! (GEORGE *hides.*) Some niggers are just not worth the trouble. (PHINEAS *slides a table over the trapdoor.*)

(HALEY *enters, followed by* MARKS *and* LOKER.)

PHINEAS: Say, strangers, care to join me for a drink?

MARKS: Why, you are excessively kind. Don't mind if I do.

HALEY: Not now. I'm tracking a nigga gal with a critter. Have you seen her?

PHINEAS: No. Describe her.

HALEY: She's high yeller—could pass for white. Speaks better English than we do.

PHINEAS: Naw!

HALEY: But the gal's no concern of mine. It's the boy I'm after.

MARKS (*to* LOKER): We'll turn the boy over to Haley and take the gal to New Orleans to speculate on.

PHINEAS (*aside*): What should I do? What would you do? That gal and her boy could bring a pretty penny. But Ruth . . .

HALEY: Well . . . have you seen her?

PHINEAS: I don't recollect seeing no one fitting that description.

LOKER: I'm looking for a runaway darkie, too.

PHINEAS: What kind of darkie?

LOKER: A mulatto chap, almost as light complexioned as you.

PHINEAS: Kind of tall?

LOKER: Yes.

PHINEAS: With brown hair? And dark eyes?

LOKER: Yeah.

PHINEAS: Pretty well dressed?

LOKER: Yeah.

PHINEAS: And a scar on his right hand?

LOKER: Yes, yes.

PHINEAS: I ain't seen him . . . but I hear he's dangerous.

HALEY: Come on, boys . . . let's search the house! (*Exeunt.*)

PHINEAS: How about some chaw? I'd like to help ya find 'em. I used to speculate on niggers myself. (GEORGE *bangs on the trapdoor/"Let me out! Let me out!" etc.*) Oh, you hush down there.

ELIZA (*re-enters*): How shall I escape these human bloodhounds!

PHINEAS (*points to trapdoor*): Ma'am . . . I think that's your husband down there.

ELIZA: What! Leave it to George to muscle in on this scene. This is a scene about a mother's love. Leave him there 'til intermission. (*Exits.*)

(HALEY, MARKS, LOKER *re-enter.*)

HALEY: Thar she is now!

MARKS: She's making for the river.

LOKER: Let's have after her. (*Exeunt.*)

(*River appears*—ELIZA *re-enters.*)

ELIZA: The river of ice! Heaven grant me the strength. Courage, my child, we shall be free or perish! (*Jumps.*)

MARKS: She's on the ice.

LOKER: I'll stop her. (*Aims rifle at* ELIZA.)

HALEY: Fool, you'll hit my property! (*Knocks rifle away.*)

MARKS: She'll be drowned!

LOKER: She's made it to the other side.

MARKS: Let's get a boat.

HALEY: Aye, to the ferry! A hundred dollars for a boat!

(*Exeunt as music rises and* ELIZA, *on opposite bank, gives clenched-fist salute.*)

Act 2

Scene 1

(*A handsome parlor*—MARIE *enters.*)

MARIE (*looking at a note*): What could possibly be detaining St. Clare? Keeping that child away so long, when he knows she's sickly. According to this note, he should've been in New Orleans yesterday. (*Noise of a horse-drawn carriage off.*) Could that possibly be them at last?

(EVA *runs in excited.*)

EVA: Mama! (*Throws her arms around* MARIE*'s neck and kisses her.*)

MARIE (*cold*): That will do! You are giving me a headache!

EVA: But I missed you, Mama. For a moment, I thought I'd never see you again. Oh, I'm so glad to be alive. (*Kisses her mother again.*)

(TOM *enters, carrying luggage, followed by* ST. CLARE *and* OPHELIA. MARIE *is taken aback by the sight of* TOM.)

ST. CLARE: Well, my dear Marie, we are home at last. The wanderers have arrived, you see. Allow me to present my cousin, Miss Ophelia, who is about to undertake our office of housekeeper.

MARIE: What's he doing here . . . coming through my front door? We've already got enough mouths to feed.

ST. CLARE: But he's a first-class coachman . . . the driver you've always needed.

MARIE: I can look at him and tell he'll get drunk. Why couldn't you bring me some diamonds or lace, instead of another nigger?

38

ST. CLARE: Aren't you going to say hello to my cousin?

OPHELIA (*offers her hand, which* MARIE *ignores*): The pleasure is all mine.

ST. CLARE: Well, what do ya think? Does this place suit you?

OPHELIA: It's rather old . . . heathenish—but I suppose with a lot of hard work and elbow grease it could be fit to live in.

ST. CLARE: What do you think, Tom?

TOM: Looks fine to me, Mas'r. These bags are gittin mighty heavy, suh.

ST. CLARE: Oh, set 'em down—set 'em down.

MARIE: Not on my good carpet.

(TOM *sets the bags down.*)

ST. CLARE: Have you no curiosity as to where I picked him up?

EVA: Uncle Tom, Papa . . . that's his name.

ST. CLARE: Right, my little sunbeam! Tom is an uncle to everyone.

TOM: Please, Mas'r . . . dis ain't no 'caision to say nothing 'bout me.

ST. CLARE: Now is no time for modesty, Tom. It was Eva who persuaded me to buy him.

MARIE: She is so odd.

ST. CLARE: Tom here is a hero. As we approached the landing, a sudden rush of passengers caused Eva to fall into the water.

MARIE: St. Clare!

ST. CLARE: And one man jumped to her rescue . . . none other than—

EVA: Uncle Tom! (*Hugs him.*)

OPHELIA (*astonished*): How shiftless!

EVA: Come with me, Uncle Tom . . . I'll show you around the house.

TOM: Can I go now, suh?

ST. CLARE: Of course you can. Eva—show him where to set those bags. One other thing, Tom . . . I want you to watch after my little Eva, day and night. She's your mistress now. Your only duty will be to attend to her. Think you can handle that? That will be all for now. (TOM *&* EVA *exeunt.*)

OPHELIA: How shiftless . . . giving a little girl a grown man.

MARIE: I thought you said he was my driver!

ST. CLARE: He is, he is. Well, what do you think of Uncle Tom, Marie?

MARIE: He is the perfect behemoth! (*Exeunt.*)

Scene 2

(A single spotlight shines on TOM *as he enters with flowers in the button-hole of his coat. He comes downstage to address the audience.)*

TOM: In this world, you make yo' luck—luck don't come looking for you. Five days on the river, spellin' out my Bible, bein' respectful, Haley give up and took the shackles off me just before the little girl went over the side. I didn't even know I could swim 'til I found myself under the water. But the Lord, he brung me up, and den her daddy, he brung me here. Now I gotta sof' bed, sof' Massa, and nuttin' to do but look after a po' little white child got the mark of the Lord on her.

    That don't impress you none. You sitting there thinking, "He ain't chained! What's wrong with him? Why don't he run? George ran!" George can pass for white. I can only pass for midnight. I'se too tall, too black, and too far South to think about running—I'm studying a different way to get back to my own. Massa St. Clare . . . he ain't got no farm to run, he ain't go no cotton to pick. . . . When I open Massa's eyes to his better nature—dat's when I'm gonna have my freedom.

*(*EVA *enters, skipping with a wreath.)*

EVA: Uncle Tom . . . there you are. Didn't you hear me calling you? *(Places the wreath around* TOM*'s neck.)* Oh, Tom . . . you look so funny. Why do you seem so sad?

TOM: I was just thinking about my own chillen. I miss them so.

*(*TOM *sits, and* EVA *sits on his lap.)*

EVA: You have children, Uncle Tom?

41

TOM: Yes. I got a son the same age as you. Willy is his name, growing like a weed last time I seen him.

(ST. CLARE *and* OPHELIA *enter, observing.* TOM *sees them, and puts* EVA *down at once.*)

TOM (*taking off wreath*): Me and Miss Eva was just having some fun pretending I was a big ox, like in the Good Book . . . dressed fo' sacrifice.

ST. CLARE (*amused*): I see.

OPHELIA: How utterly shiftless.

ST. CLARE: Cousin—there must be some other word in your vocabulary?

OPHELIA: Not for the way you live, Cousin.

EVA: Papa, Papa, Uncle Tom has children. Do you think we could buy them and then we could all be together?

ST. CLARE: Well, Eva, what a fine idea.

TOM: We could all be together, but some of us still wouldn't be free.

ST. CLARE: Well, Tom, as a free man I doubt you'd dress and eat as well as you do here.

TOM: I'd rather have poor food, poor clothes, poor everything, and have them be mine, than have the best if they belong to somebody else.

ST. CLARE: That's a new light on the matter. And where has my little Eva been?

EVA: I've been in Tom's room, hearing him sing.

ST. CLARE (*laughs*): Hearing Tom sing, hey?

EVA: Oh, yes! He sings such beautiful things, about the new Jerusalem, and bright angels, and the land of Canaan. But, Papa . . .

ST. CLARE: I dare say all darkies are blessed with the gift of music. Some spirituals are better than opera.

EVA: Yes. And he's gonna teach them to me and I'll read to him from my bible. (*Grabs* TOM*'s hand.*) Come, Uncle Tom . . . I'm ready for another lesson. (TOM *and* EVA *exeunt.*)

OPHELIA: How can you let her carry on with Tom in such a way?

ST. CLARE: Why not? You would see no harm in a child caressing a large dog—even if the dog were black . . . but let a child touch a nigger with thoughts, feelings, and a soul and you shudder. You Northern hypocrites all tickle me. You would not have them abused, yet you keep your distance from them as you would a toad in a lily pond.

OPHELIA: There is some truth in what you say. I think you are very wrong to keep them as slaves—and yet, I couldn't bear to have one touch me.

ST. CLARE (*yells*): Topsy! Cousin, you'll be happy to know I made a little purchase for your department. (*Yells.*) Here, Topsy! (*Whistles, as if calling a dog.*) Here, girl! (*Whistles again.*)

(TOPSY *enters and folds her arms like a 20th-century rapper.*)

TOPSY: Yo', G! What it is!

OPHELIA (*moves behind* ST. CLARE): Good gracious, St. Clare.

ST. CLARE: Don't worry—she won't bite. Come on, Topsy . . . give us a song and show us some of your dancing.

TOPSY: Easy enough, G! Kick the ballistics!

(*Music rises in the background as* ST. CLARE *becomes a human beat box.*)

TOPSY (*raps*): I can pick as much cotton as any man/And bag it all up with one hand/I can milk all yo cows 'fore the sun comes up/And fit all my belongings into a little tin cup/No job is too big, no job is too small/I'm Topsy Turvy, I can do it all. Word.

(TOPSY *does breakdown dance.*)

ST. CLARE (*laughing*): That's enough, Topsy.

OPHELIA: Well, of all the things! If I ever saw the like!

TOPSY: I was just gittin' warmed up—G!

OPHELIA: Why does she call you G?

TOPSY: 'Cause he's the Governor 'round here, and I'm the governed.

ST. CLARE: I couldn't resist buying her. I thought she was a rather funny specimen on the Jim Crow line. (*Smothering a laugh.*) Topsy . . . Miss Ophelia is your new mistress. I'm leaving you in her charge. See now that you behave yourself.

TOPSY: Word, G! You sticking me with Snowflake?

ST. CLARE: Snowflake!

OPHELIA: Now, St. Clare . . . I don't see the point in you bringing another one of these plagues into your house. You've got negroes crawling through the woodwork like cockroaches. I can't set my foot down without treading on one. I can't understand for the life of me why you would want to bring home another one . . . especially this one!

ST. CLARE: For you to educate! You're always preaching about educating. So here's a fresh . . . raw specimen. Go on!

OPHELIA (*advances to* TOPSY): How old are you, Topsy?

TOPSY: Dunno, missis.

OPHELIA: Don't you know how old you are? Didn't anybody ever tell you?

TOPSY: Nope.

OPHELIA: Who was your mother?

TOPSY (*grinning*): Never had none.

OPHELIA: Never had any mother? What do you mean? Where were you born?

TOPSY (*sarcastic*): Never was born.

OPHELIA: You mustn't answer me in that way. I'm not playing with you.

TOPSY: I ain't playing with you, either!

OPHELIA: Who was your mother and father?!

TOPSY: I told ya . . . never had no father . . . no mother . . . no nothin'. I was raised by a speculator, with lots of others. Old Aunt Sue used to take care of us.

ST. CLARE: She speaks the truth, Cousin. Speculators buy them up cheap when they are little, and get them raised for the market.

OPHELIA: Have you ever heard of heaven, Topsy? (TOPSY *grins, bewildered.*) Do you know who made you?

TOPSY: Nobody, I knows of . . . I 'spect I just growed!

ST. CLARE (*laughs*): You'll find virgin soil there . . . nothing to pull up. You can plant your own ideas and just watch 'em grow! (*Exits laughing.*)

OPHELIA: Follow me, you benighted innocent.

TOPSY: Yes'm.

(*As* OPHELIA *turns her back to* TOPSY, TOPSY *seizes the end of the ribbon* OPHELIA *wears around her waist, and twitches it off.* OPHELIA *takes the ribbon from her.*)

OPHELIA: What's this? You naughty wicked girl, you've been steal-ing this!

TOPSY: I guess Massa tied me up in this ribbon when he gave me to ya.

OPHELIA: Don't tell me a lie—you stole this ribbon.

TOPSY: Maybe I did.

OPHELIA: You must be punished! (*Boxes her ears.*) Now what do you think of that?

TOPSY (*laughs*): That don't hurt me none . . . dat won't even hurt a skeeter! (*Runs off laughing.* OPHELIA *follows indignantly.*)

Scene 3

(*Lights come up on* TOM's *small room as he is discovered polishing his boots. He is wearing fancy new clothes.*)

MARIE: What are you doing, Tom?

TOM: Just puttin' a shine on my shoes, ma'am. You can tell a lot 'bout a man from de shine on his shoes. Do you want me to put some spit and polish on your shoes when I'm done?

MARIE: No, thank you, Tom. I just came up here to see if you were comfortable.

TOM: Oh? De ober day, I kinda got de impression you didn't like me, Miss Marie.

MARIE: I know, but I saw how you were looking at me.

TOM (*scared*): No ma'am, you'se wrong!

(MARIE *moves closer to* TOM, *running her fingers through his hair.*)

MARIE: I sure love the feel of your hair, Tom. It's so soft—just like cotton. (MARIE *sits down on* TOM's *bed, raising her legs suggestively.* HARRIET *enters, watching.*)

TOM: Suppose Massa St. Clare comes barging in here.

MARIE: I don't care. The one he loves is Eva. Please, Tom.

(HARRIET *enters* TOM's *space, angrily.*)

HARRIET: Jungle fever, Tom?!

TOM: I ain't do nuffin!

HARRIET: I didn't want my novel adapted. The theatre is Satan's playhouse! I never had a scene like this in my book.

46

MARIE: I know. You never even imagined it.

HARRIET: How do you know?! Get out!

MARIE: Don't I have a right to tell my story?

HARRIET: No! Now get out!

MARIE: But everybody else is making changes.

TOM: Wasn't no need for you to go bringing this up. You're making me look bad in front of all these sisters.

MARIE: What am I in this damn play for anyway? (*Exits.*)

HARRIET: How could you let her in here, Tom? What were you going to do if I hadn't stopped it? (TOM *gives her a look that says it all.*)

TOM: Wake up and smell the magnolias, Harriet.

HARRIET: No—you wake up! We need this scene in a book that argues for your emancipation?! But my novel only helped start the Civil War—what do I know? (*Starts off.*)

TOM (*exiting*): Harriet, people need to know these things happened.

HARRIET (*off*): Why?

TOM: 'Cause the truth will set you free!

Scene 4

(*A plain chamber.* TOPSY *is discovered sweeping the floor. She is singing her rap to herself as she sweeps.* JANE *enters with laundry to fold. As she folds the laundry, she stands annoying* TOPSY *. . . taunting her.*)

JANE (*sing-song, like a child*): Topsy is ugly. (TOPSY *keeps sweeping.*) Don't nobody wantchu! Topsy is ugly.

TOPSY: I'm gonna show you ugly if you don't shut up!

JANE: Topsy is dirty! I've got new earrings—you've got nothing.

TOPSY: You better fold dem clothes somewhere else.

JANE: Topsy is a nigger.

TOPSY: No more nigger dan you be.

JANE: I've got good hair . . . you've got bad hair. (TOPSY *starts sweeping furiously.*) I've gotta boyfriend . . . you can't get one. Nobody wants to shovel no coal.

TOPSY: Goddam it, bitch! (TOPSY *strikes* JANE *with the broom.*)

JANE (*crying*): Stop it, Topsy . . . I was jus' playin' . . .

TOPSY (*pulling* JANE*'s hair and scratching her like a cat*): You play too much . . . bitch! (*Snatches* JANE*'s earrings off of her ears.*) Nice earrings, Janie! (*She throws the earrings to the ground and pounces on* JANE, *beating her with nonstop punches, trying to pull her hair out of her head.*) You dink you white or something!

JANE: Eva! Eva! Please help me, Eva!

TOPSY: Miss Eva can't help ya none . . . your butt is mine now. I don't bit mo' care who you call! (*She continues to beat* JANE.)

JANE (*crying overlap*): Miss Eva! Miss Eva, help me!

48

(EVA *enters running.*)

EVA: Oh, Topsy! Topsy! You have been very wrong again.

JANE (*pointing to her earrings, crying*): She broke my earrings!

TOPSY: You lucky dat's all I broke.

EVA: Oh, Topsy. What makes you do so? Why did you spoil Jane's
earrings?

TOPSY: I dunno . . . I 'spects it's cause I'se so wicked.

JANE: She got the devil in her, Miss Eva . . . no other way to explain
it. Everything was fine until she showed up. I'm telling my
cousins on you. (*Exits crying.*)

TOPSY: Yo' cousins can't whup me! I despises all dem cream-colored
niggers.

EVA: What makes you so bad, Topsy? Don't you love anybody?

TOPSY: I'se black . . . no one loves me.

EVA: Oh, Topsy. I love you.

TOPSY: Y'do? (EVA *nods.*) Then gimme dat dress you're wearing.

EVA: You can have this dress, but you must promise to be good.

TOPSY: Oh, I shall be real good, Miss Eva. Never had nobody give
me something so pretty.

EVA: I'll go take it off now, and it's yours. (EVA *exits.*)

TOPSY: Better had gave me dat ugly-ass dress. (TOPSY *smiles devil-
ishly at the audience.*)

(HEAVY 'G' *[stage manager or band member] enters, dressed in modern
clothes and carrying a boom box.*)

(TOPSY*'s rap*)

I'M TOPSY TURVY I'M WICKED AND I'M BLACK.
ALL YOU YELLOW-ASS NIGGERS BETTER WATCH YOUR
BACK.
I'M WICKED AND I'M SO SO MEAN.
I'M THE BADDEST BLACK NIGGER YOU EVER SEEN.

LET ME TELL YOU ALL A LITTLE TALE.
'BOUT SOME STEPS, A FAT BITCH, AND A PAIL.
SEE ONE DAY OLD AUNT SUE
BROUGHT HER MONKEY ASS DOWN TO MY ROOM.

TOPSY TURVY WITH A WICKED GRIN PUT A BUCKET ON
    THE STEPS.
GUESS WHAT, THE BITCH FELL IN!
BUT I DIDN'T GIVE A SHIT, I JUST LAUGHED
WATCHING AUNT SUE JUST ROLLING WITH HER FAT ASS.
I DON'T GIVE A DAMN IF SHE DIED TODAY,
OLD PEOPLE ALWAYS GOT SOMETHING STUPID TO SAY.
A NIGGER'S LIFE DON'T MEAN SHIT YOU SEE.
SHE'S A BLACKIE JUST LIKE ME
EVERY PLANTATION I'VE BEEN SOLD TO I'VE BEEN THE
    ONE THAT'S
PUTTING MY FOOT THROUGH ASS-STEPPING OFF IN YOUR
    FACE.

I AIN'T SPEAKING FOR THE HOUSE NIGGER
I'M TALKING FOR THE BLACK RACE
THE ONE'S OUT SWEATIN' IN THE FIELD AND FOR WHAT
SO A KNOW-NOTHIN' PECKERWOOD CAN SIT ON HIS
    BUTT
I DON'T CARE IF ALL THE WHITEYS DIED TODAY
WHITE PEOPLE ALWAYS GOT SOMETHIN' STUPID TO SAY

MEANWHILE I'M IN SPACE
JUST WALKING AROUND—A STUPID GRIN ON MY FACE
JAMMING TO MY BEAT BOX
CUTTING THE FOOL
'ROUND HERE THAT'S MY GOLDEN RULE

BUT REMEMBER, I'M TOPSY, I'M WICKED AND I'M BLACK
I STAND HERE WITH MY EVIL ASS READY TO ATTACK
I KEEP YELLING AND 'BELLING LIKE I DO IT
'CAUSE THAT'S THE ONLY WAY I KNOW TO GET
    THROUGH IT.

(*Exit* HEAVY 'G'. TOM *enters.*)

TOPSY: Watchu want, ol' coot? We ain't *even* gotta scene together.

TOM: We do now. Look, we're both new to dis house, but I'm old to
    dis airth. So, let me lace yo' shoes fo' you. Tread lightly 'round
    white folks.

TOPSY: And they'll stomp all over you! I ain't treadin lightly 'round
    nobody! 'Specially that old dried up Miss Feely.

TOM: Tell ya how to handle Miss Feely. Look—white folks feel good when they dink dey teaching us sumpthin. Let her think she's teaching you sumpthin! You'll have her eatin' outcho' hand like a heafer at feeding time. Now come on—I found a nice piece of wood. I'll whittle you a top.

TOPSY: Don't be making me no boy thang!

TOM: Excuse me, Miss Topsy—how about a doll baby, then?

TOPSY: Okay.

TOM: What kind of hair you want on it?

TOPSY: Nappy—just like mine.

(*Exeunt.*)

Scene 5

(*Chamber. Enter* GEORGE, ELIZA. GEORGE *kisses* ELIZA *on her neck.*)

ELIZA: Oh, George. (GEORGE *abruptly stops kissing her.*) What troubles you?

GEORGE: I can't even kiss you without thinking about those devils. If something had happened to you—

ELIZA: We're in Ohio now. We're halfway to freedom. (*Noise off.*)

GEORGE (*paranoid, pulls out his pistol*): What's that?! Who's there?! (GEORGE *aims his pistol in the direction of the door.*)

ELIZA: It's nothing.

GEORGE: Damn them! I hate each and every one of them—making me run like a scared rabbit.

ELIZA: But the Quakers have been so kind.

GEORGE: I hate them all! I hate every ounce of white blood in me!

ELIZA: George!

(PHINEAS *enters without knocking, dressed like a Quaker.* GEORGE *points his gun at him.*)

GEORGE: Halt, I say! (*He relaxes when he sees it is* PHINEAS.)

PHINEAS: Verily, friend, how is it with thee?

GEORGE: I should shoot you for leaving me stuck in that crawl-space. (*Puts gun away.*)

PHINEAS: Don't be mad at me . . . it was your wife's idea.

ELIZA: Phineas, what has caused this metamorphosis?

PHINEAS: I was driven by a strong argument. Them lips would per-

52

suade a man to assassinate his grandmother! But forget my love life for now! There's a posse of slave catchers sitting down in the tavern having a taste. They are after you, George. So, what's to be done?

GEORGE: I know what I shall do! (*Takes out his pistol.*)

ELIZA: Please . . . I pray there will be no shooting around Harry.

PHINEAS: Let's get outta here.

GEORGE: I will stand and fight them alone if I must. Phineas, give me your wagon and direct me. I will drive alone to the next stand.

PHINEAS: Tho'ut need a driver, George. I know a thing or two about the road that thee don't.

GEORGE: I don't want to involve you in my war.

PHINEAS: Involve me, brother, involve me!

ELIZA: But Phineas . . . you're a Quaker now!

PHINEAS: Oh, Ruth . . . hell, I won't even tell her! Let's vamoose!

(*Exeunt as the lights fade to black.*)

Scene 6

(*A rocky pass in the hills. Large set, rock and platform.* PHINEAS *enters with* HARRY *in his arms.* GEORGE *supporting* ELIZA.)

PHINEAS: Come on up into these rocks! Run! Come up here; this is one of our old hunting dens. Come up. Hurry. (*They ascend the rock.*) Whoever comes here has to walk single file between those two rocks in fair range of your pistols . . . d'ye see?

GEORGE: I do all the fighting. Agreed?

PHINEAS: Thou art welcome to do the fighting. But may I have the fun of looking on? Look. Our hunters are debating down here, looking up, like hens getting ready to fly up onto the roost.

GEORGE (*about to shoot*): I'll fire a warning shot, straight between their eyes.

PHINEAS (*knocks* GEORGE*'s hand down*): Thou hast promised only to shoot in self-defense.

GEORGE: Why should I let them fire first?

ELIZA: Shhh. Duck down.

PHINEAS: They're moving up.

(HALEY, LOKER, *and* MARKS *enter.*)

MARKS: Well, Loker, your coons are fairly treed.

LOKER: Yeah. I saw them going up this path. See? Here's their tracks.

GEORGE (*rising on the rock*): Gentlemen, who are you down there and what do you want?

MARKS: We want a party of runaway niggers. One George and Eliza Harris, and their son.

54

HALEY: That little monkey belongs to me!

LOKER: I'm an officer and I've got a warrant for their capture. D'ye hear? Hey boy . . . ain't you George Harris, that belonged to Mr. Harris of Shelby County, Kentucky?

GEORGE: I'm George Harris, but I belong to no man. My wife and child I claim as mine. We have arms and we mean to defend ourselves. The first one to come in range is a dead man!

MARKS: Oh, come . . . surely you jest, young man. That ain't sensible talk for a nigger.

LOKER: We've got the law on our side . . . so you better give up peaceably.

GEORGE: To hell with you and your law, white man!

HALEY: Nigger, I'm losing my patience with you. (HALEY and MARKS *draw their guns and fire at* GEORGE. *He dodges their bullets and fires back.* ELIZA *screams.*)

GEORGE: It's nothing, Eliza . . . they can't hit me.

PHINEAS (*draws* GEORGE *down*): Stop your cocky speechifying and shoot them rascals.

LOKER: Hold your fire . . . let's take 'em back alive.

MARKS: The buck's worth just as much to me dead or alive, and he's less trouble—dead. (*Fires again, but* GEORGE *hits him.*)

GEORGE: I've got one of them wounded.

PHINEAS: I guess I must join thee, brother. (PHINEAS *fires off a round.* ELIZA *screams.*)

HALEY: I must've hit one. I hear them squealing.

LOKER: I never was afraid of niggers, and I ain't going to be now. Back me up, Haley.

(*Music as* LOKER *dashes up the rock.* ELIZA *throws a rock.* LOKER *appears to be struck. He staggers for a moment, then springs to the top.* GEORGE *seizes him. A struggle.*)

GEORGE: Mister Slave Catcher . . . thee is not wanted here. (GEORGE *throws* LOKER *off the rock,* HALEY *retreats, helping a wounded* MARKS.)

HALEY: Those critters mean to kill us! (*They run.*)

GEORGE (*Embracing* PHINEAS): We did it, my friend! We did it!

Act 3

Scene 1

ST. CLARE: There are the bills, Tom . . . and the money to liqui-
date them.

TOM: Yes, massa.

ST. CLARE: Well, Tom . . . what are you waiting for? Isn't it all right
there?

TOM: Suh . . . you'se a man set apart from the rest.

ST. CLARE: . . . That's not in the script, is it? This is the scene where
you say you love me, and tell me to stop drinking!

TOM: Other massas buys and sells slaves. You just buys us—never
sold one.

ST. CLARE: I never could, Tom.

TOM: Give us light work, kind words, good living.

ST. CLARE: I hope I do.

TOM: Nobody ever seen you pick up a whip, or send anyone to the
whipping jail.

ST. CLARE: This system of ours is the devil's invention, to turn masters *and* bondmen into beasts! No, there's misery enough in
slavery all by itself without adding cruelty, Tom.

TOM: Misery enough, suh: that's right! (ST. CLARE *now wishes the
conversation to end, but* TOM *goes on.*) Suh, seeing as you understands how that is (*Retreats a psychological step*)—I knows a few
things about blacksmithing.

ST. CLARE: Well, you never stop surprising me.

TOM: I've always dreamed of one day having my freedom and own-ing my own blacksmith shop. I could open it up right behind your place, then after I builds up my savings, I could go back to Kaintuck and buy my wife and all of my young'uns . . .

ST. CLARE: Tom—do you know how many white men fail in business?

TOM: But I ain't white.

ST. CLARE: I forbid you to worry yourself with such foolish dreams. Now go along with those bills.

TOM: Why you keep us, suh? Why you need us darkies?

ST. CLARE: You need me, Tom—*and* I love you people. You make this house feel so alive, with your singing and your humor. And when I see your faces shining with gratitude—why, I'm grateful myself, that I've the means to make so many happy.

(OPHELIA *enters.*)

OPHELIA: Come along, you shiftless mortal!

ST. CLARE: Aw, hell . . . what new witchcraft has Topsy been brewing?

OPHELIA: Cousin . . . I cannot be plagued by this girl any longer. She stole all of my bonnet trimmings.

TOPSY: I didn't steal nuffin! My dolly needed a jacket!

OPHELIA: Here, Tom . . . you take her. Where's Eva?

ST. CLARE: In her favorite bower by the lake.

OPHELIA: Why, the dew is falling. She mustn't sit out there with her terrible cough.

ST. CLARE: Oh, nonsense. That cough is nothing. She has caught a little cold, perhaps.

OPHELIA: That's the way Cousin Ellen was taken. (*Exits.*)

ST. CLARE: Oh, hogwash! (*Laughs.*) Well, Tom I'd say you've really got your hands full now. Don't forget the bills. (*Exits laughing.*)

TOM: Right, suh. (*Sighs.*)

TOPSY (*cries*): Missy locked me in the closet. Missy can't b'ar me, 'cause I'm black. Nobody can love niggers, and niggers can't do nothing. And I don't car if nobody ever loves me!

TOM: I love you, Topsy.

TOPSY: Dat don't count—you'se blacker than me!

TOM: We've got to love ourselves.

TOPSY: But we'se ugly. Everybody says so. I'd be better off if I could be skinned and made over white.

TOM: Topsy, have you ever heard of Africa?

TOPSY: Africa? What's dat?

TOM: That's where we come from, Topsy. It's on de ober side of the big water. It's full of tall trees dat bar fruit, wid lakes, and mountains, and all de people's is black. Dey even got black kings and queens dat live in fancy palaces, bigger than de big house. We are Africans, slaving in a foreign land. Your black skin would be pretty in Africa.

TOPSY: You makin' it up.

TOM: No—a young slave named Eliza—she done run away now—she used to read to me all about de place we come from.

TOPSY: Dey got books about us?

TOM: Plenty of 'em.

TOPSY: I'se born. I'se born in Africa. (*To doll.*) We'se Africans! See my dolly? I'ma gonna dress her up real nice and pretty like de kings and queens in Africa. I gonna make dat Janie so jealous! (*Runs out.*)

TOM: Topsy! (*Exits.*)

Scene 2

(EVA *and* TOM *are discovered sitting by the lake, reading from the Bible.*)

TOM: Read dat passage again, please, Miss Eva?

EVA (*reading*): "And I saw a sea of glass, mingled with fire." (*Stopping and suddenly pointing to the lake.*) Tom, there it is!

TOM: What, Miss Eva?

EVA: There's a sea of glass mingled with fire! Look in those clouds, they look like great gates of pearl; and you can see beyond them—far, far off—it's all gold! Uncle Tom, sing about the "spirits bright."

TOM (*sings*): I see a band of spirits bright
        That taste the glories there;
        They are all robed in spotless white.
        And conquering palms they bear.

EVA (*points to heaven*): I'm going there, to the spirits bright, Tom. I'm going before long.

TOM: One day we will all go thar and be free. But I hope my people will be free before we gits thar.

EVA: Do you wish you lived in Africa, Uncle Tom?

TOM: If Africa is the only place I can be free, den I wish I lived dere.

ST. CLARE (*enters*): Ah! There's my little Eva . . . blooming like a rose. Are you feeling better, my dear?

EVA: Papa, I've had some things I wanted to say to you a great while. I must say them now, before I get weaker. There are many things here that make me sad . . .

59

ST. CLARE: What could that possibly be?

EVA: I feel sad for our poor people. Oh, Papa . . . I wish they were all free. There must be a way you can free them. When I am dead . . . please free them for my sake.

ST. CLARE: When you are dead? Please stop such foolish talk. You know you're getting stronger every day.

EVA: Don't deceive yourself. I'm not any better. I'm going, Papa. And these poor people love their children as much as you love me. Tom loves his children and wants to be with them. Oh, please do something for them. Make them free!

(EVA *sinks to the ground.*)

ST. CLARE: What have you been filling this girl's head with, Tom?

TOM: Nothing, suh—but the truth.

ST. CLARE: Carry her to her chamber. (TOM *lifts* EVA.) This evening air is too chill for her.

TOM: Now I hear you white folks choking back your tears, getting out your handkerchiefs—and I hear you bloods going, "Drop the bitch." This child done all she could to get me my freedom. But y'all can't take credit for what she did.

(TOM *sets* EVA *down carefully, comes downstage as* ST. CLARE, OPHELIA, MARIE *gather around deathbed.* TOPSY *enters and watches from wings.*)

Scene 3

MARIE: Augustine . . . Cousin Feely . . . tell me she's better.

ST. CLARE: Hush! She is dying.

MARIE (*kneeling*): Dying?! My baby, my only child!

EVA (*raising her head*): Papa . . .

ST. CLARE: Yes, darling Eva . . . what do you see?

EVA: Angels!

ST. CLARE (*looks away*): I can't bear this!

TOM: Look at her, Massa.

EVA: I see joy . . . I see love . . . I see peace . . . I see freedom, Papa . . . promise me, Papa—Tom will have his freedom as soon as I am gone.

ST. CLARE: You know I could never refuse you anything.

EVA: Mama . . . Mama . . . (*Dies.*)

MARIE: Oh, no! (*Sobs.*)

(*Lights fade on tableau.*)

INTERMISSION

Act 4

Prologue

(*Loud shouting offstage.* TOPSY *drags on* HARRIET, *followed by* GEORGE, *who is writing feverishly in a notebook.* ELIZA *and a very tired* TOM *not far behind.*)

TOPSY: How you liking it so far, Harriet?

HARRIET: Maybe I didn't see everything—maybe there were things I left out—but I notice you all had scenes you didn't bother to change.

TOPSY: Yeah, but dat rap I did was SLAMMING! I wrote dat shit myself.

ELIZA: Fingertips, girlfriend—fingertips.

HARRIET (*finds* TOM): Tom—you were right to have a scene with Topsy. I'm ashamed I didn't think of that. And the way you . . . stand up to people. But why didn't you tell Topsy about Jesus? Aren't you a Christian, Tom? What happened to your faith in heaven?

TOM: All we know is this world—yet all we talk about is heaven. I still have plenty faith. But I try to put my faith in people.

GEORGE: Look, Harriet—I wasn't even in the second half of the original play. Now I've got a few changes I want to make.

HARRIET: Heaven help us—does everybody have to be a writer now?

LEGREE (*enters*): That's what you get, you damn Yankee agitator.

ALL: Simon Legree!

LEGREE: You spoiled a good thing! Slavery was the best thing that ever happened to these niggers. Don't you agree? You've had your freedom for some time now, and what have you done with it? You measure your success by the number of new black TV shows you get each season.

TOM: Legree—shut the FUCK up and get offstage 'til yo' entrance.

LEGREE (*laughs*): I will see you later . . . Uncle Tom. (*Exits.*)

TOPSY: Yeah, well, Harriet, you sure got him right.

TOM: Okay, Topsy. Now, places everybody. (*Exeunt.*)

Scene 1

(*A plain chamber in a settlement in Canada;* GEORGE *writing.*)

ELIZA (*enters*): Why did you walk off your job today?

GEORGE: Teaching bores me. I was not born to teach.

ELIZA: But your students are former slaves like you and me. Remember our promise when we moved into this settlement— we must each reach one to teach one?

GEORGE: All I ever teach from is the Bible. And Christianity is the white man's religion.

ELIZA: We're in Canada—we can be a family, together and free— and all I hear is white man this, black man that!

GEORGE: My students say I'm a white man. They say, "Your massa was your daddy."

ELIZA: They're just children, George.

GEORGE: You want to know what their fathers say?

ELIZA: George!

GEORGE: "Don't trust a half-breed."

ELIZA: You know who you are. You've got to trust yourself and hold on to that. If you don't want to teach, work in the freemen's mill. You have a brilliant mind: you could start a new factory. This community needs you!

GEORGE: I thought I would feel different on free soil. But the devils here are no different. "This community" is an isolated speck on a white sea. We would be crushed should that sea turn violent. My people—the masses of black people—live south of

64

here, under conditions that can no longer be tolerated. But they're blinded by their ignorance. They do not see the strength of our numbers. They cannot see that freedom is theirs to be taken. I can't be free until my people are free.

ELIZA: "I." "Me." "My people." "My freedom." What about us? You need God, George. You need to let him into your life!

GEORGE: Fuck God!

ELIZA: Blasphemy, George?

GEORGE: I am tired of your God! And I am tired of your turn-the-other-cheek Christians, dressed up in their Sunday finest, sitting in their pews, praying for freedom, instead of taking their freedom.

ELIZA: I want the same thing for our people that you want. But for us to be a strong people, we must build on a strong foundation. And that rock is the family. Where do you think you're going?

GEORGE: I'm going to see some people.

ELIZA (*sees he has a gun*): I need you, George—I need you alive! You're no good to me dead. (*He won't stay.*) Picking up a gun won't make you any blacker, George.

(GEORGE *exits.* ELIZA *exits opposite.*)

Scene 2

(*Gothic chamber. Slow music.* ST. CLARE *discovered, seated on sofa.* TOM *at left.*)

ST. CLARE: Oh, Tom, my boy, the world is as empty as an eggshell.

TOM: I don't know what to tell ya, suh.

ST. CLARE: What happened to the Tom I used to know? I used to envy your simple faith.

TOM: I'm puttin' my faith in you, suh.

ST. CLARE: My lawyer has drawn up some papers. I plan to make you a free man. I know Eva will smile on me for doing this.

TOM (*nonchalant*): Thank you, suh.

ST. CLARE: Is that all you've got to say?

TOM (*after a beat he offers his hand;* ST. CLARE *shakes it*): You doin' the right thang.

ST. CLARE: Well, go upstairs and get my fountain pen, and I will sign your papers. Is there something else, Tom?

TOM: Well, suh—seeing how Topsy's been kicking up so much sand, I was hoping you'd give her to me to raise.

ST. CLARE: Oh, Tom, if you insist, you can have her, but I would advise against it. You'll soon learn you can't carry the whole world on your shoulders.

OPHELIA (*enters, dragging on* TOPSY): What are you doing there, you limb of Satan? You've been stealing something ... I'll be bound.

TOPSY: Keep your grubby paws off of me, Miss Feely. 'Tain't none of your business.

ST. CLARE: Hey! What is all this commotion?

OPHELIA: She's been stealing!

TOPSY (*sobbing*): I 'hain't neither.

OPHELIA: What have you got in your bosom?

TOPSY: I've got my hand d'ar . . .

OPHELIA: But what have you got in your hand?

TOPSY: Nuttin.

OPHELIA (*grabs* TOPSY's *hand and opens it*): I don't believe it. She has stolen Little Eva's earrings.

TOPSY: I reckon I did. You gave everybody earrings but me. Ain't I a girlie?! I got as much right to look pretty as your dead little Goldilocks.

ST. CLARE: Give me those earrings!

TOPSY: I ain't givin' you nuttin!

ST. CLARE: Are you defying me, you little monkey?

TOM: Topsy, dis is one of dem times you should tread lightly.

(TOPSY *runs and stands behind* UNCLE TOM.)

TOPSY: Don't let dat ghost put his paws on me!

OPHELIA: Stop calling us names!

TOPSY: Stop calling me monkey! I guess you're still wondering how Goldilocks got sick all of a sudden. (*Takes out a lock of* EVA's *hair.*) I guess it never crossed your mind a little monkey like me had anything to do wid it.

ST. CLARE: What's this?

TOPSY: It's a lock of your dead daughter's hair.

TOM (*turns around and takes the lock*): Who learned you about dis?

TOPSY (*snatches it back*): Aunt Sue did! You can't have it!

ST. CLARE: You little savage! (*Snatches it from* TOPSY.)

TOPSY (*runs away*): Goldilocks wasn't the only one around here dat I gave a haircut. Pretty soon all you ghosts will start dropping like flies. (*Exits.*)

ST. CLARE: Tom, you wanted her . . . now take her and get out!

(TOM *follows her out.*)

ST. CLARE: Don't worry, Cousin—she can't really work spells. I must escape this unhappy house for a while. Excuse me, Cousin—I'll just walk down to Bourbon Street and hear the news. (*Exits—leaving unsigned paper.*)

OPHELIA: I never realized how much Topsy hates us. (*Exits.*)

Scene 3

(TOM *enters with his packed suitcase.* MARIE *enters, picks up* TOM *'s freedom paper.*)

MARIE: What's this, Tom?!

TOM: My Freedom Paper. Massa St. Clare gonna set me free for Little Eva. God bless her soul! Did he sign it yet?

MARIE: No. All this time I fooled myself you liked it here, Tom.

TOM: I do, Missy . . . but I can't turn down no chance for freedom.

MARIE: I give you all the freedom you'll ever need.

TOM: Missy, let's you and me just forget about each ober.

(OPHELIA *enters hastily.*)

OPHELIA: Marie . . . Uncle Tom! Come with me right away!

MARIE: Gracious me, what's the matter now?

OPHELIA: It's Cousin St. Clare . . . he's been shot!

MARIE: Shot?

TOM: How bad is he?

OPHELIA: Come now. Let's hurry!

MARIE: Oh my God . . . first Eva . . . now Augustine. I do believe this house is cursed!

(*Enter* ST. CLARE *wounded, supported by* TOM *and* A DOCTOR, OPHELIA *following. They lay* ST. CLARE *on the sofa.* TOPSY *enters and watches from the wings.*)

ST. CLARE (*raising himself feebly*): Tom—my poor fellow!

69

TOM: Yes, Massa.

ST. CLARE: I have received my death wound.

TOM: Oh, no, no, Massa!

ST. CLARE: I feel that I am dying . . . Tom—pray!

TOM (*sinking to his knees*): I do pray, Massa . . . that you'll sign for my freedom. (TOM *snatches the paper from* MARIE *and shoves the pen and paper into* ST. CLARE*'s hand.*)

ST. CLARE (*weakly*): Oh, Tom, I am too weak . . .

TOM: Try not to speak, suh . . . just sign.

ST. CLARE (*weakly*): But . . . I've . . . I—(*Dies.*)

TOM (*hysterical*): Sign it! Sign it!

DOCTOR: I'm afraid he's gone.

MARIE: Oh, no . . . not my Augustine. (*Cries, then realizes what she's inherited.*)

TOM: You sign—Miss Marie.

MARIE (*Waves the paper away. Clutches* ST. CLARE.): Augustine! (DOCTOR *helps her off.*)

TOM (*shoves the paper in* OPHELIA*'s face*): You sign, Miss Feely. You know Massa wanted me to have my freedom.

OPHELIA: I can't help you, Tom. I have no authority. (*Exits.*)

(*Lights fade on tableau of* TOM, TOPSY, ST. CLARE.)

Act 5

Scene 1

(*An auction mart.* UNCLE TOM *and* EMMELINE *at back, as various spectators step forward to inspect the merchandise.* MARKS *and* MANN *come forward.*)

SKEGGS: Hello, Alf. Good to see you here.

MANN: I heard St. Clare's darkies were on the market. You'd never catch me buying one of dem spoiled niggers. St. Clare raised them to think they was as good as white.

SKEGGS: Well, whoever gits 'em 'll soon whip their airs out of 'em.

MANN: There's some that whipping don't affect. (*Takes out a wanted poster of* GEORGE.) George Harris, runaway slave. Wanted for murder in five states. He killed his former master and set all de darkies free. Then he went on to the next plantation and did the same thing. He's riding with a gang of some 20 darkies. Call themselves Black Thunder.

SKEGGS: Why, hanging ain't good enough for some niggers.

MANN: Last word, they were seen headin' this way.

SKEGGS: Coming this way?

(*Enter* LEGREE.)

LEGREE: And who's this pretty little bitch? How old are you? Old enough, I guess. I know someone at home's gonna have her eyes opened when she sets 'em on you.

EMMELINE: Ah! You're hurtin' me!

71

LEGREE: What you lookin' at, boy? Well—a nigger with his boots black—bah! (*Spits on them and steps on them.*)

TOM: You're scuffing my shoes, suh.

LEGREE: Show me your teeth. (*Seizes* TOM *by the jaw and opens his mouth.*) Good, good. Where was ya raised, boy?

TOM: In Kintuck—boss.

LEGREE: What have ya done?

TOM: I had care of Massa's farm.

LEGREE: A likely story.

(MARKS *enters.*)

MANN: Marks! You're here at last!

(EMMELINE *whimpers.*)

SKEGGS: Stop that, you minx. No whimpering here. Gentlemen, to-day Skeggs Traders is pleased to announce the sale of the prize of the St. Clare stable. De best-trained nigger in all of Louisiana, Uncle Tom, but first we have on consignment this pretty little plum called Emmeline. This prime unspoiled quadroon girl is only fifteen years of age. Okay now, the bidding begins at five hundred. Do I hear six? (MARKS *raises his hand.*) Okay, I got six hundred, do I hear seven? Sugar and spice, don't she look nice! Come on—don't sit on your hands. (LEGREE *raises his hand.*) Okay, I've got seven . . . do I hear eight hundred? Who's gonna teach her the facts of life? (MANN *raises his hand.*) Eight hundred . . . do I hear nine for this pretty little plum? (LEGREE *raises his hand.*) I got nine hundred . . . nine hundred. Going once . . . going twice . . . sold to Mr. Legree!

EMMELINE (*crying*): Oh, no . . .

SKEGGS: Stifle yourself wench! (*Smacks* EMMELINE, *as* LEGREE *forks over the money.* GEORGE *enters disguised, drawing wary glances from the others.*) Now, I want to close today's sale by offering you this most valuable article known as Uncle Tom . . . the most useful nigger ever raised . . . coveted for his brawn and his brains. Gentlemen in want of an overseer, now is the time to bid. Let's open the bid at seven hundred. Do I hear eight? (MARKS*'s hand shoots up.*) I got eight . . . do I hear—(MANN*'s hands go into the air.*) Nine hundred already. Do I—(LEGREE*'s hand goes up.*) I got a thousand. Do I hear eleven hundred. (MANN *raises his* *hand.*) I got eleven . . . do I hear twelve? (LEGREE's *hand goes up.*) I got twelve . . . do I have thirteen? (GEORGE *raises his hand, and* LEGREE *looks at him hatefully.*) I got thirteen from the Spaniard. Is thirteen the lucky number . . . going once . . . twice . . .

LEGREE: Fourteeeeen!

SKEGGS: Good! I got fourteen. Do I hear fifteen? (MANN *raises his hand.*) Do I hear—

LEGREE: Sixteen hundred! (*Pulls out his pistol.*) And dare anybody to bid against me!

SKEGGS: Sixteen hundred . . . going once . . . going twice. Sold to Mr. Legree. (GEORGE *exits, making obvious eye contact with* TOM, *who seems confused because he thinks he recognizes the stranger, but can't be sure.*)

LEGREE: Here's your damn money. This is highway robbery and you know it. The nigger is only worth half of what I'm paying for him. (*He grabs* TOM *and* EMMELINE.) Now, come along. You two varmints now belong to me.

(LEGREE *exits, with* TOM *and* EMMELINE *roped behind him.*)

SKEGGS (*giving a few bucks to* MANN *and* MARKS): Good job, fellows. Legree don't suspect a thing. (*All laugh.*)

(*Young* GEORGE SHELBY *enters. They stare at the stranger, sizing him up as a sucker.*)

SHELBY: Pray, strangers . . . could you give me some information?

MARKS: I'm a lawyer. I will *give* you nothing.

SHELBY (*slow to get it*). Oh . . . of course. (*Gives him money.*) Could you tell me where Mr. Augustine St. Clare dwells? (*The three look at each other.*) Father sent me to buy back a Negro from him—old Uncle Tom—and convey him to our Kentucky home at once!

MARKS: St. Clare "dwells" in the grave. (YOUNG SHELBY *is taken aback.*) Uncle Tom's been sold to a Mr. Legree—further down the Bayou. But his plantation's such an out-of-the-way, desolate place—it can only be reached by steamboat. I'm afraid you'll never find it, unless—of course—

SHELBY: Will you direct me there? (*Flashes money.*) I promise the reward shall be ample.

MARKS: Enough said, stranger. Come—we've got some time to kill before the boat leaves. Allow me to show you the French Quarter. There is a house in New Orleans . . .

SHELBY: What's it called? (*Exeunt.*)

MANN: What a card! Marks played that sap like a banjo!

SKEGGS (*as they exit*): He's gonna drain him dry!

Scene 2

(*The garden of* MISS OPHELIA'*s house in Vermont.* TOPSY *is discovered playing with her doll baby.* OPHELIA *enters with a book.*)

OPHELIA: There you are, Topsy—I see you've found the garden.

TOPSY: Yes'm.

OPHELIA: Yes, this is my favorite place. (*Looks out.*) My, what a pretty sunset.

TOPSY: Yes'm.

OPHELIA: Well, Topsy . . . do you think you'll like it here in Vermont?

TOPSY: Yes'm.

OPHELIA: You know this is a free state. There's no slavery here.

TOPSY: No niggers, either.

OPHELIA: Now, Topsy. You mustn't use that word here. Is that clear?

TOPSY: Yes'm.

OPHELIA: Here in Vermont, your people are called Nee-groes. Now, Topsy, I know I must have seemed very cruel to you at first . . . I-I was wrong for hitting you and locking you in the closet. I'm sorry, Topsy.

TOPSY: Dis de first time anybody ever said dey was sorry to me.

OPHELIA: Things are going to be a lot different here. I inherited you from my cousin's estate, but I don't want to own you—I want to adopt you. From now on, I want you to call me . . . Mother.

TOPSY: You's gonna be my mama?

OPHELIA: Is something wrong with that?

TOPSY: You's white. Why would you want to be my mama?

OPHELIA: Because I love you, Topsy. (*Places her hand on* TOPSY.) Now, Topsy . . . a day will come when I will give you your freedom papers, but you've got to prepare for that day. You remember passing through New York. All your poor black brethren idle in the streets near the depot, some begging, some asking for work. To live here in the North, you will need to learn to read, to sew, to do arithmetic.

TOPSY: What?

OPHELIA: Numbers, Topsy. You must learn how to add and subtract numbers. Now, are you ready for your reading lesson?

TOPSY: You got any books on Africa? Uncle Tom said there were plenty books on Africa.

OPHELIA: There is nothing you want to read about in Africa. Remember . . . call me Mother, and I shall call you Daughter.

TOPSY: Yes . . . Mother.

OPHELIA (*sits and opens the book*): Let's begin by reading from *McGuffy's Reader*. (*Reading*.) "Mary had a little lamb, whose fleece was white as snow."

(TOPSY *sits next to* OPHELIA, *who reads to her, as the lights fade to black.*)

Scene 3

(*Rude chamber on* LEGREE *plantation; lights up on* TOM *sleeping in old clothes.*)

(CHLOE *enters.*)

CHLOE: Poor Tom. Y'all done forgot me—old Aunt Chloe, the one left behind to raise all Massa's children, plus my own. Nobody else rewriting me: I gotta save myself from the pancake box. Last night, I had a dream. Dreamed I died and went to heaven and St. Peter told me to go 'round to the back door. So I go 'round to the back. Niggas everywhere. I go and knock. An old man slides a peephole open. "Watchu want?" I told him I want to have a meeting with God. He said, "But God don't want to meet you!" And he slammed the peephole shut. Then I turned and I saw my Tom, standing on an auction block. (*Approaches* TOM.) Tom, my husband, I done told you what you needed to do.

TOM (*half-wakes*): Chloe . . . ? Where . . . ?

CHLOE: You downriver now, old man! Now what you got to say about faith?

(*Exits.*)

TOM: Chloe—Chloe! (*She is gone—he is fully awake.*) Why me, Lawd? Why I got to be born a nigger in this white man's world?

(GEORGE *enters, disguised.*)

GEORGE: Tom!

TOM: Who there?

GEORGE: It is I, George. George Harris. Eliza's husband.

77

TOM: George? . . . You was at the auction today. (GEORGE *smiles*.) This ain't in the script, either.

GEORGE: I've come to lead you to freedom. Tomorrow night, I will strike like a panther at the Fulton Plantation. Then my posse shall pay your Mr. Legree a visit. Be ready. (*Hands him a gun—* TOM *has never held one before*.) You hold your freedom in your hand, Tom. (TOM *weighs the gun*.) We shall fall on our oppressors with fire and sword! We're gonna see these swamps run red with slaveowners' blood.

TOM: Did something happen to Eliza?

GEORGE: She and Harry are safe in Canada.

TOM: What she think about this? (GEORGE *dismisses the question*.) What gonna happen to your son?

GEORGE: I'm doing this for my son! I can't claim my father—but my son can be proud of me.

TOM: Gimme some bullets. (GEORGE *does*.) Gimme some mo'.

GEORGE: I need the rest.

TOM: How many bullets the Army got? How many guns? How many men they got looking for yo' hide? (GEORGE *scoffs*.) Say you cuts every slaveowner's throat 'round here. Say you burns down every plantation. What white folks gonna do to the rest of the slaves? How many gonna pay the price for what you done?

GEORGE: Old man, either use that gun or it could be turned against you.

(TOM *lays the gun down*.)

TOM: God help you, George.

GEORGE: This (*the gun*) is the only God I know. (*Exit*.)

TOM (*picks the gun up*): What I'm gonna do with this? White people got to learn to be civilized—how they gonna learn unless we teach 'em? Real change comes from people's hearts, not from guns. But don't we got a right to defend ourselves? (*Hides it carefully*.)

(*End of scene*.)

Scene 4

(*Blues chords rise in the darkness. The lights slowly rise, and* TOM *is discovered center stage with a hoe in his hand, miming plowing the fields. He sings a "work song" from the era.* TOM *continues singing, and comes down to a rude chamber as* LEGREE *enters pulling* EMMELINE *by her ear.* SAMBO *follows, carrying a whip.* LEGREE *hears singing above and below* TOM*'s moaning.*)

TOM (*singing*): "Keep so busy workin' for the master" (*three times*), "Ain't got time to die."

LEGREE: Shut up, you black cuss! Do you think I want to hear your infernal howling? (*Turns to* EMMELINE, *pulling her by the ear.*) You didn't ever wear earrings?

EMMELINE (*trembling*): No, Massa . . .

LEGREE (*pats* EMMELINE *on her buttocks*): If you be a good gal and do right by your master . . . you can have as many pairs of earrings as your heart desires. You needn't be so frightened. I don't intend to work you very hard. You'll have the finest times with me and you'll live like a lady . . . if you know how . . . to be a good gal.

EMMELINE: No! Please, let me work de fields. I don't wanna be no lady.

LEGREE: Oh?! You're going to be contrary. I'll soon take all that out of ye. (*Points to* SAMBO.) See what you'll get if you try to run away? Now come here, wench, and pleasure me.

EMMELINE (*bites* LEGREE*'s hand as he pulls her to him*): Kill me first!

LEGREE: Oh! You want to be killed, do you? Come here, Tom. I didn't buy you just for common work. I mean to make a driver

79

out of you. Now take this ungrateful wench and flog her.
You've seen enough to know how.

(SAMBO *hands* TOM *the whip.* TOM *looks at it—hesitating.*)

TOM: I ain't flogged no one—never. No possible way you'll ever
make me. (*Drops the whip.*)

LEGREE (*picks up the whip*): You stupid cuss. This will learn ya.
(*Strikes* TOM *with the whip.*) Now tell me you can't do it!

TOM: Massa, I's willing to work from can't see to can't see, but I will
die first 'fore I raise my hand again' anyone.

LEGREE: Boy . . . you belong to me . . . body and soul!

TOM: No . . . my soul ain't yours . . . my soul belongs to no man.

LEGREE: It don't? We'll see. Here, Sambo! (*Hands* SAMBO *the whip.*)
Give this dog such a breaking-in as he won't git over it this
month or next.

EMMELINE (*clings to* TOM): Please! Have mercy!

LEGREE: Mercy? You won't find any in this shop. Now flog him
within an inch of his miserable life.

(SAMBO *raises his whip, but* TOM *appeals to him.*)

TOM: Sambo . . . my brother. The white master always pits one
darkie against the other. If anyone should whip me—let him
do it. Do not burden yourself with his evil deeds.

(SAMBO *thinks for a moment, then laughs as he strikes* TOM. LEGREE
grabs EMMELINE *and throws her to the ground, raising her skirt to
have his way with her.*)

LEGREE: Come here, bitch!

(*Music rises, underlining each crack of the whip, as* EMMELINE *shrieks in
pain.*)

(*Lights slowly fade to black.*)

Act 6

Scene 1

(TOM, *whipped, wakes in a shed.* CASSY *enters and kneels by his side, holding a cup to his lips.*)

CASSY: Drink all ye want. I knew how it would be. It isn't the first time I've been out in the night carrying water to one such as you.

TOM (*returning cup*): Thank you, Missis.

CASSY: Don't call me Missis. I'm a miserable slave like yourself . . . a lower one dan you could ever be. It's no use being stubborn, even when you've got right on your side. You're in the devil's hands now. He is the strongest and you must give up!

TOM: Don't know nuffin' 'bout givin' up.

CASSY: You don't know anything about it. I do. We're on a lone plantation, ten miles from any other. In the swamps; not a white person here who could testify if you were burned alive just like that po' brave soul who's been trying to free all us slaves. The Army caught him, but they didn't kill him. They just handed him over, no questions asked, to that posse of fine southern gentlemen. They strung that po' boy up, for all the slaves to see, makin' him an example to all us darkies not to raise no gun against no white man.

TOM: I know de man. He was here last night. Poor George!

CASSY: Don't do ya no good to know anything, sometimes. Dis man we call Massa, there's no earthly thing he's not bad enough to do. Did I want to live with him? Wasn't I a woman delicately bred? And he!—Father in heaven! What was he and is he?!

81

And yet I've lived with him these five years, and cursed every moment of my life, night and day.

TOM: You oughta run. You and Emmeline.

CASSY: Run? I wouldn't git far before someone would tell on me.

TOM: You must have faith, de others will keep their mouths shut.

CASSY: Those miserable low dogs? Every one of them would turn against you the first chance they got.

TOM: And what made 'em like dat? No, see, if I give in, even a little, I'll git used to it, and bit by bit, I'll grow just like 'em. No, I've lost . . . my wife . . . my chillens . . . everything in this world, but I refuse to lose myself and the truth I believe in.

CASSY: Well, there are not many like you. I'll be back tomorrow to bring you some more water.

TOM: No, tomorrow I'm going to work and you're gonna run—

CASSY: Run?

TOM: Reach under dem rags. (CASSY *finds gun.*) Now you take that. This time you and Emmeline are gonna be all right.

(CASSY *hides gun under her things and exits.*)

Scene 2

(A rough chamber. LEGREE *enters. Sits.)*

LEGREE: Plague on dat Sambo, to whip Tom like that right in the press of the season. (CASSY *steals on and stands behind him.*) That feller won't be fit to work for at least another week. How could I have let dis happen . . .

CASSY: Yes . . . it's just like you.

LEGREE: Hah! You she-devil. You've come back, have you?

CASSY: Yes. I've come back; to have my own way, too.

LEGREE: You lie, you jade! I'll be up to my word. Either behave yourself or stay down in the slaves' quarters, and fare and work with the rest of them.

CASSY: I'd rather live in the dirtiest hole in the quarters than under your hoof!

LEGREE: But you are under my hoof! So you listen to reason. (*Grabs her wrist.*)

CASSY: You listen to reason! (*Pulls away from him.*) Keep yo' damn hands off of Emmeline! Why did you spoil that girl?

LEGREE: Jealous, is ya? Aw, Cassy . . . I'll make it up to you.

CASSY: Simon Legree, you better take care! You know you're afraid of me, and you've got good reason to be; for I've got the devil in me, and dere is no way you can beat it out of my soul.

LEGREE: Aw, Cassy, why can't you be friends with me again? What has brought about this change in you? You've turned cold . . .

83

hard-tempered. Can't you behave yourself decently? (*Puts his hands on* CASSY.)

CASSY (*pulls away*): You talk about behaving decently. But you haven't the sense to keep from spoiling one of your best hands.

LEGREE: He had to be broken in.

CASSY: You shall never break him!

LEGREE: Oh, I shall break him, and I shall break you as well, 'cause you ain't nuthin' but a nigger . . . next thing to a monkey. And the blacker the skin, the tougher the hide and the more I got to whip 'em and that Uncle Tom is the blackest nigger on the face of the earth, and I intend to have his soul.

CASSY: How did you ever git dis way?

LEGREE: Was born dis way . . . grew up dis way, and I intend to die dis way. I am a white man, created in the image of God. God forbid if Satan should ever come to earth, for all you wretched darkies will rise from Satan's furnace like crows, swooping down on white people. But no nigger shall ever rule a white man . . . Now you go and fetch me Emmeline—'cause your thin yeller skin won't hold up well to flogging.

CASSY: You go and do your own damn fetching!! 'Cause you took the last thing you ever gonna take from me. (*Exits.*)

LEGREE: Something has gotten into all dese cussed darkies ever since I brought Uncle Tom to my farm! (*Exits.*)

Scene 3

(MISS OPHELIA's *garden in Vermont.* OPHELIA *and* TOPSY *are discovered, reading.*)

OPHELIA: That was wonderful, Topsy. Now I have something else for you to read.

TOPSY: But, Miss Feely, I'se so tired.

OPHELIA: Now, Topsy . . . I told you what to call me.

TOPSY (*sighs*): Yes, Mother.

OPHELIA (*hands* TOPSY *a piece of paper*): Now come on and read this. It won't take you long.

TOPSY (*struggles*): To—all interested parties. Topselia St. Clare is—here—by de-clared a free per-son as of June . . . 29th, in the year . . . 1849, in the township of Andover, Vermont. (*Looks up.*) You mean . . . I'se free, Miss Feely, I'se free?

OPHELIA: Yes, Daughter . . . you are free.

TOPSY: I can go anywhere I want—do anything I want?

OPHELIA: Yes, but carry your freedom papers with you at all times. Well . . . aren't you going to say anything, Topsy?

TOPSY: Oh . . . yeah . . . goodbye.

OPHELIA: Goodbye? Whatever happened to "Thank you?"

TOPSY: Right. Thank you, and goodbye.

OPHELIA: Where are you going? It's almost suppertime.

TOPSY: New York. (*Folds up her paper.*)

OPHELIA: Are you running away?

TOPSY: I ain't running. I'm free.

OPHELIA: Just because you have your freedom papers, it doesn't mean you can leave, Topsy.

TOPSY (*waves the paper*): It says right here dat I'se free. Or is dis another lie?

OPHELIA: But Topsy . . . I'm your mother—I love you.

TOPSY: Git yo' hands off of me! No ghost could ever love me! And no ghost could ever be my mama!

OPHELIA: Are all white people ghosts to you, Topsy? Am I a ghost?

TOPSY: Yeah . . . you're the ghostliest of dem all. Sometimes I can look right through you. I touch yo' skin and my hand goes right through yo. I don't see nuffin—I don't feel nuffin . . . no feelings ever come back from you.

OPHELIA: I have feelings, Topsy, and you are hurting them right now.

TOPSY: Well, dat's just too goddamn bad—ain't it?

OPHELIA: But Topsy—where will you go? What will you do? How will you eat? How will you live?

TOPSY: Don't worry about it, Miss Feely. I'se free! (*Runs out.*)

OPHELIA: Wait, Topsy—all we need is more time!

(OPHELIA *exits calling after* TOPSY. *Lights fade to black. End of scene.*)

Scene 4

(LEGREE*'s plantation.*)

LEGREE: Curse the woman! She's got a temper worse than the devil! I shall do her an injury one of these days, if she isn't careful. Am I haunted, or were the hands whispering against me? And Sambo—was the dog looking at me crosswise just now? (*Enter* SAMBO, *sullen.*) What's the matter with you, you black scoundrel?

SAMBO: You sent me to find Miss Cassy? (LEGREE *waits.*) She wasn't dere.

LEGREE: She's got to be around the house somewhere.

SAMBO: No, Mas'r. I been all over de house and I cain't find nothing of her nor Emmeline.

LEGREE: Bolted, by God! Call out the dogs! Saddle my horse! (SAMBO *starts.*) Stop! Are you sure they're really gone?

SAMBO: Yassuh, I's sure, Mas'r.

LEGREE: All right, Sambo, you jest go and walk that Tom up here. (SAMBO *exits.*) I believe this nigger means to measure himself against me. He's stirred something up and I'm going to know what. I'll have it out of his infernal black hide! I *hate* him—I *hate* him! And isn't he *mine*? Can't I do what I like with him? Who's going to stop me? (SAMBO *drags on* TOM.) You get out. (SAMBO *hesitates*—LEGREE *threatens, he goes.*) Well, Tom, do you know I've made up my mind to *kill* you?

TOM: It's very likely, Mas'r.

87

LEGREE: I—have—done—just—that—thing, Tom, unless you tell me where my two bedwenches run off to. (TOM *is silent.*) D'ye hear? Speak!!

TOM: Got nothing to tell, Mas'r.

LEGREE: Are you trying to tell me you don't know? Speak! Do you know anything?

TOM: I know something, Mas'r, but I can't tell nothin'.

LEGREE: Listen up. Since the day you got here you've stood against me; now, I'll conquer ye or kill ye! One or t'other. I'll count every drop of blood there is in you, one by one, 'til you give up!

TOM: You can drain my body dry, but I can't give up to you. Do the worse you can, my troubles will be over soon. But unless'n you change, yours will never end.

LEGREE: Shut up! (*Strikes* TOM *down with the butt of his whip.*) How do you like that?

TOM: Is dat your worst? (*Spits out blood.*)

LEGREE: No! (*Kicks him again—*TOM *feebly raises his hand.*)

TOM: There ain't no more you can do.

(CASSY *enters, gun drawn, with* EMMELINE *behind her.*)

CASSY: Truer words were never spoke, Simon Legree.

LEGREE (*laughs*): Nigger, you wouldn't dare.

CASSY: I'm tired of hearing that word. (*She blows him away.*)

(*Onstage characters freeze.* SAMBO *enters and stares at body.* GEORGE *enters.*)

GEORGE: Cut, cut, cut. Who's writing this? Harriet! Get in here! Who said the women get to shoot him?

(HARRIET *enters.*)

HARRIET: This is not the ending I wrote! Cassy . . .

CASSY: You wrote every word of the rage that's in me! You just didn't give me a gun.

HARRIET (*remembering who did*): Tom . . . ?

(YOUNG SHELBY *enters.*)

SHELBY: Is this the plantation of Mr. Simon Legree?

(*Others step back—*CASSY *indicates* LEGREE.)

SHELBY: Oh! Er—(*Steps over the body.*) Excuse me. I understand that he purchased a negro named Tom? (CASSY *points to* TOM, YOUNG SHELBY *kneels by him.*) Oh, Uncle Tom, do wake—and speak once more! It's your own little Master George.

TOM: Massa George?

SHELBY: I have come to buy you, and take you home.

TOM: You's late.

GEORGE: You're always late!

HARRIET: Yes—and me above all. I am very, very late to understand. I was blind to so many of your feelings. I misinterpreted, I misrepresented and distorted you! (*Nobody disagrees.*) My book should just be forgotten. It should be burned. I'm guilty!

CASSY: Case dismissed. (HARRIET *is surprised,* GEORGE *bristles.* CASSY *shrugs.*) She tried.

HARRIET: But not hard enough!

GEORGE (*polite but firm*): Harriet, could you sit down and be quiet? This ain't about you anymore. It's about us writing our stories. Tom, we all changed our endings. Why didn't you change yours?

TOM: If I live, nobody'll remember. (*Coughs.*) My dying stays in everybody's face.

LEGREE (*rises from dead*): Nigger, please! (*As cocky as ever.*) Thank you, Harriet . . . for immortalizing me. (*Bows and exits.*)

GEORGE: Wait, I'm losing track here. Whose script are we in now?

(*Suddenly a boom box blares.* TOPSY *enters from audience with box, dressed in modern hip-hop clothes. She sets the box on the stage and directly addresses the audience.*)

TOPSY: Dat's right. Topsy-Turvy in effect. This ain't no motherfucking play. I'm the governor of this bullshit story! Harriet didn't make me up. Well, well, well . . . look at all these crackers and peanut butter. We'se ready for a picnic. (*These two lines vary according to the racial mix of the audience.*) What you lookin' at?! You see something you like?! You wanna leave?! I oughta fuck you up! I see the way you look at me when I get on the bus . . . you sit there, scared . . . tensed . . . clutchin' yo' purse . . . hoping I don't sit next to you. Well, fuck you! I shot a bitch 'cause she looked at me wrong. I burned down

Uncle Tom's condo with the nigger still in it. I love to hear glass break. I love to watch shit burn. I love to hear mother-fuckers scream. Word!! (TOPSY *freezes.*)

TOM: Any volunteers to take Topsy? Ya'll think she come from nowhere? Do ya 'spects she just growed?

(*Blackout. End of play.*)

THE LITTLE TOMMY PARKER CELEBRATED COLORED MINSTREL SHOW

Carlyle Brown

CARLYLE BROWN is a playwright and founding artistic director of The Laughing Mirror Theater, an experimental ensemble company devoted to the research and development of Black American theatrical forms. His play *Buffalo Hair* was one of six plays included in the 1992 Mid-West PlayLabs Conference sponsored by the Playwrights' Center in Minneapolis, and was produced by the Penumbra Theater Company in St. Paul, Minnesota, in 1993. *The African Company Presents Richard III* was produced at the Arena Stage in Washington, D.C., in 1992–93, and toured nationally during the 1994–96 season. *The Little Tommy Parker Celebrated Colored Minstrel Show* was produced Off-Broadway by the Negro Ensemble Company at the Master Theater in New York City in 1991 and was nominated for six Audelco Awards. In addition, both *Little Tommy Parker* and *The African Company* are winners of the Penumbra Theatre Company's National Black Playwriting Award.

Brown has received several commissions, including *The Blue Nail* for the Arena Stage. He is the recipient of National Endowment for the Arts, McKnight, New York Foundation for the Arts, and Creative Artist Public Service fellowships. Brown has performed an original one-man show, *Sea Never Dry*, at the Arizona Theater Company in Tucson, Arizona. He has also worked as associate director for the opera *He Who Says Yes (Der Jasager)* by Bertolt Brecht and Kurt Weill, presented at the Banff Centre for the Fine Arts in Alberta, Canada.

Currently under commission with the Houston Grand Opera in Houston, Brown is writing a new book for *St. Louis Woman*.

Characters

HENRY
DOC
TAMBO
SOLOMAN
ARCHIE
PERCY
BAKER

Upstage is an open-sided replica of a railroad car. A private Pullman car of the late 19th century. It is raised by a shining, metallic maze of wheels, gears, and cogs. The interior of the car has two conventional train seats facing each other with a fold-up table between them, two sofa chairs, a stool, and a wood-burning stove.

It is early in the evening, in the winter of 1895. The rear windows of the car are facing east, looking across the icy Mississippi River toward the faint shores of Illinois.

DOC is sitting by the window reading a book. TAMBO is strumming his banjo in one of the sofa chairs. HENRY is shining his shoes on the footstool, popping his rag in accompaniment to TAMBO's melody.

Property List

Suitcase
Coat hooks on wall
Steamer trunk
Small wooden bench
3 sets blankets, sheets, and pillows on triple bunk beds
Carpetbag under bunk beds
Coat hooks on far right upstage wall
Wall-hung oil lamp
Shelf over window
2 dry goods canisters on shelf
Leather armchair
Wood stove
Firewood box
Coffeepot on stove
Shelf behind stove
1 fry pan
2 small cooking pots
6 coffee cups
6 water glasses
Hurricane lamp in window
Carpetbag on platform
Chair on platform
Wisk broom on hook on wall
Steamer trunk below platform
Chair
Ladder to platform
Shelf on wall
2 tambourines
Coat hooks on wall

Broom in corner
Bench against wall
Table
Small wooden bench
Carpetbag
Notices on wall
3 banjos, one with case
Shoeshine brush and rag (HENRY)
Book (DOC)
Washbasin
Firewood
Newspaper (*The Clipper*)
Scissors
Comb
2 tablespoons (ARCHIE)
Trick top hat (HENRY)
Trick water glass (HENRY)
Bottle of moonshine whiskey
Box of cigars (HENRY)
Cigar boxes with blackface makeup (ALL CHARACTERS)

Costume Plot

Act One

HENRY
White shirt, light vest, dark trousers, and tie

TAMBO
White shirt, dark vest, dark trousers, and tie

DOC
White shirt, pattern vest, dark trousers, and tie

SOLOMAN
Overcoat, scarf, derby hat, dark jacket, white shirt, dark vest, dark trousers, and tie

ARCHIE
Overcoat, white shirt, suspenders, and dark trousers

PERCY
Overcoat, scarf, dark jacket and tie, white shirt, derby hat

Act Two

ALL CHARACTERS
During the course of the second act, the characters change into either a uniform dress of tailcoats, ties, vests, trousers, and top hats, or a variety of gaudy, clownish clothes typical of the minstrel costumes of the time.

Act One

HENRY: That song put me to mind when I was a kid shining shoes outside the 11th Street Opera House in Philadelphia. I wasn't no older than that boy Archie. There was some big-time minstrel group playin' in the Opera House and the place was slowly gettin' packed. I was makin' as much as a nickel a shine. There was this old colored man standing just a little ways from where I had my shine box set up. And he was just a shoutin', "Place ya bets. Place ya bets. Boy can play the coronet while jiggin'. With every note and every beat as clear as if each had been done alone. Not a slur or stumble will you hear, but only the sweet-soundin' noise of the most educated music. Place ya bets, place ya bets." Well, he was a funny-lookin' old colored man and he was standin' right next to the playbill of the Opera House where they had a picture of the minstrel group blacked up and another one of them in they regular face. Everybody had to pass me and him to get into the theatre. He was attractin' a whole lot of attention, funny-lookin' the way he was, standin' next to that playbill and shoutin'. "Place ya bets, place ya bets." Pretty soon he had him a crowd and I was shinin' a lot a shoes.

Before ya know it, some of these high-class gentlemen is makin' jokes 'bout this old colored man. "You can't play and dance." You can't do this and you can't do that. But they was holdin' up their money to bet. When time come for that old colored man to cover them bets, he walk over to me and he say, "Boy, what's yo name?" I say, "Henry." He say, "I'm glad to know you, Henry. My name is Moe. Moe Joe Jefferson. Moses Joseph Jefferson. It's a good Christian-American name," he say. He say, "I know you hear me braggin', but I can play this horn and do a jig for truth. And I can win me that money, 'cause they don't believe in me, but I do."

He say, "All I need from you is ya shine money to cover them bets." I said, "My shine money, you can't take away my shine money." He say, "I'll double ya shine money, boy. Besides, you wasn't shinin' no shoes at all, 'til I come along with this here crowd." He say, "Don't holler 'bout what's fair, just be fair." It was a strange way a lookin' at things, but I know'd somehow he was right and I give him my shine money. He played a tune somethin' like the one you strummin', Tambo. And his jig sound just like a man playin' the trap drum. Here's my hand to God, it sound just like a wailin' trap drum. He wasn't just playin' and dancin' at the same time. He was havin' a duet with hisself. A duet between his mouth and his feet. One time he took that horn out his mouth and he say, "Shine ya shoes, Henry, shine ya shoes. Make ya self some shine money." Well folks watching that old colored man puts they feet on my shine box and I shine and I pop my rag to the beat and now me and Moe Jefferson is a trio. Folks forgot all about the minstrel show, they was havin' a ball with me and Moe Joe. That old colored man dance his natural behind off. He cut the most amazing steps you ever saw. Played and did flips and never missed a note. And his music. His music was different. He put his stressin' in a lot a funny places, so it had a raggedy, loose kinda sound, like a stumblin', strong, drunk man refusin' to fall. Like that music they call rag, that they play in the houses and the parlors. Man, the people was all off the sidewalk and out all into the street. Inside, the Opera House was almost empty. The theatre manager come with the police and make us get from round there. But hell, it didn't do em no good, 'cause the crowd come with us. We was out in the streets, so Negroes was allowed to see our show. In fact, it was the most mixed house I ever seen. All wanted to see Moe Joe Jefferson do his thing. We fell into this saloon down 11th Street and once that owner saw that crowd, he didn't mind no colored in his place that night. There was this other old colored man in there, hunched up at the piano. One of his legs was way shorter than the other and he didn't have but three fingers on his left hand. He caught on quick to what was goin' on, and boy, we was now a regular goddamn band.

Moe Jefferson danced on top a the tables, on the bar. Seem like he was dangling off the ceiling and around the walls, too.

I popped my little dere rag, 'til I couldn't pop no more. My arms was like lead. I musta fell asleep in all that ruckus. I woke up in a corner with Moe Joe's coat coverin' me. The place was empty 'cept for the porter. Everybody was gone. The crowd, Moe Joe Jefferson and my shine money.

DOC: Sound like them old-time parades, with the big bass drums and brass instruments. High-steppin' guys with them frills on their shoulders and shiny brimmed hats. And the drum major prancin' and dancin', cuttin' turns and hittin' them hard military corners. When you get a bunch a guys that can high-step and play, boy it's somethin' else.

HENRY: That tune was somethin' else. That tune and Moe Joe was the same. How he moved, when he paused, the way he changed up. It was all in the music. The way the music was, that's the way Moe Joe did it. (HENRY *scats a tune.*) Percy's always hummin' a tune that goes somethin' like that, only slower. How do it go, Tambo? (HENRY *clumsily hums the tune and* TAMBO *hums along for a few bars to set it straight.*) Yeah, that's it. What is that?

TAMBO: That's Percy's song.

HENRY: Percy wrote that?

TAMBO: Yeah.

HENRY: What does he call it?

TAMBO: He doesn't call it anything. It don't have a name.

HENRY: Well, what are the words? How does it go?

TAMBO: I don't really know all the words.

HENRY: Well, sing it for me and just hum what ya don't know.

TAMBO: It wouldn't make any sense without all the words.

HENRY: Well, just play it for me then, Tambo.

TAMBO: I kinda don't want to do that, Henry.

HENRY: Why not?

TAMBO: I don't want to. It's Percy's song.

HENRY: It's Percy's song? What's that got to do with it?

TAMBO: For one, Percy don't really like hearin' it.

HENRY: What do you mean he don't like hearin' it? He's hummin' that tune all the time.

TAMBO: He don't realize he's doin' it.

HENRY: How can you hum somethin' and not realize it?

TAMBO: Irregardless, he don't. Look, Henry, I don't want to sing Percy's song. It's Percy's song and I don't want to sing it. Can you understand that?

HENRY: What is the matter with you, Tambo? Damn, is this some kind a secret society song or somethin'? What do you think I'm gonna do, steal Percy's song?

TAMBO: Now, did I say that? Did I say I thought you was gonna steal Percy's song? I just don't want to sing the guy's song. The answer is no. Anyway, if you wanted to steal his song, you wouldn't be the first.

HENRY: Now, what is that supposed to mean?

DOC: Henry. Tambo. Y'all stop all that nonsense. Tambo, what is it 'bout this song that upsets you like this?

TAMBO: I don't want to talk on it. It's not my place or none a my business. It's just a song. Just that kind of a song. You know how it is when ya try to put somethin' out of your mind and without thinkin' about it, you be hummin' some tune or singin' some song, where there's somethin' in it or somethin' about it, that's full of what you tryin' to forget.

HENRY: Yeah, well, I kinda see what you mean, still I'd like to hear the words to that song. It's catchy. Hell, Percy don't have to know if it bothers him that much.

TAMBO: But I'll know, Henry. No, I'm not gonna do it.

HENRY: Whatever you say, Tambo, but I'll tell ya somethin'. We all haves our ups and downs in this business. Everybody falls, makes mistakes, messes up. So aside from catchin' hell every day, what could it be that puts you in such an uproar over singin' Percy's song?

TAMBO: Alright, I'll tell ya what it was, but I don't want to sing Percy's song. And for godsakes, don't let Percy hear nothin' 'bout it. He'd have himself a natural fit.

HENRY: We ain't go say nothin'. That's a promise. Ain't that right, Doc?

DOC: A' course we ain't gonna say nothin'. Go on, Tambo, tell us about it.

TAMBO: He wrote that song for a young girl outa Memphis, name a Rachel Green. I guess she was about nineteen. She was as black and shiny as your shoes, Henry. Like a black stone just out the sea. Like a raven, she was, black and pretty. The smoothest skin you ever saw. She had this way 'bout her, a cockin' her head and rollin' her big, black eyes up at ya, like she wasn't quite gettin' what you was sayin'. Them eyes could knock a man down. She was shapely too. Yeah, that girl had a fine body on her. If you could keep your eyes from lookin' into hers, you would see what a fine figure she had. Percy was doin' pretty good then. He was a feature singer and I was an endman with the Hall and Thompson's slave troupe, outa Albany. We was in Memphis. Percy sang this song he wrote, "De Darkies Dancin' Do." They loved it. It cracked everybody up. Everybody. Audience called him back three times. Three times. I guess you know what that does for your act after the show. When he looked into that gal's big black eyes, that was all there was to it. He was in love. . . . She wanted him to make his mark in her program. Percy said, "Mark? Girl, I can sign my name, read and write both words and music. Sing and dance, play the piano and kiss you so's your hair'll uncurl and stick straight up in the air like a pickaninny." Well, boy, that girl laughed. Then she got shy. Started talkin' 'bout how Percy was too fast for her. She was talkin' alright, but Percy had pulled a string in her too. He left the troupe and stayed in Memphis. I didn't see Percy again, until '83 or '84, one. We teamed up and played the ends together. There was a lot a work for a colored man in minstrelsy in those days.

DOC: It sure was. And '82 was the best, but those days are gone now.

TAMBO: We was makin' fifteen, twenty, twenty-five, sometimes thirty-five dollars a week. Apiece!

HENRY: Thirty-five dollars? Oh, sound like ya'll was in the big time.

TAMBO: Seem like every penny Percy made, he either sent it to her or bought her somethin' with it. He was showin' this country girl a whole nother life she could only dream of. Only he didn't know he was primin' that well for somebody else to drink. We finished 6 weeks at Koster and Bial's. We had some time on our hands. Percy bought this solid gold wedding ring. Took me along for best man, and we started takin' trains to Memphis. That's when he started writing this song. On that train. All day and night on that clickety, clackity, rickety, rackity excuse for a train. With all the bumpin' and jerkin' he never took that paper out his lap or that pencil out his hand, 'til we got to Memphis. Boy was he happy. He had done it. It was finished. . . . She was waitin' on him at the station. Waitin' on him to lay it on him. There was another guy, she said. They was in love. They was already married. He was a schoolteacher. He was even there, standin' right down the other end of the platform. . . . Tall, skinny, yella nigga.

DOC: A schoolteacher? Well, what happened then?

TAMBO: Percy, a course, took it pretty bad. It was 'bout six months later, we walk into this theatre in New Haven to see a minstrel show. There was this skit in the second part. The two white guys in the skit was blacked-up. One was dressed like a woman. Supposed to be a colored woman. The man was singin' the woman this song. . . . It was Percy's song. It was bad enough that they was singin' the man's song, but the way they did it, was what made it so bad. A joke song, 'bout a couple a simple coons in love.

DOC: How they get the song in the first place?

TAMBO: I don't know, Doc. Seems like I got this picture in my mind a the last time I seen that song was crumpled up in Percy's fist. Or mabey it was blowin' away in the wind, skippin' down that platform and her chasin' after it. I guess she was kneeling down to pick it up, trying to straighten it out. I don't really remember.

HENRY: Mabey she sold it or lost it or somethin'.

TAMBO: I don't know, Henry.

DOC: That's a doggone shame.

HENRY: It sure is. Hey Tambo, I didn't know.

TAMBO: It's alright, Henry. Forget it. Just don't say nothin' 'bout it to him.

DOC: You know Tambo, I hates to say it, but Percy sure has gone down through the years. With all that drinkin' and carryin' on. Maybe it's that Rachel Green girl, like you say, or somethin'. But that boy used to show a whole lot a talent.

HENRY: It ain't talent you need out here, Doc. It's a advertising agent, an advance man, a line a bull, and lots a dough-ray-me.

TAMBO: I say amen to that.

DOC: It be worst than that. You need all a them. Shoot, none of us gone get rich and very few gone be famous, no matter how good you is. But Percy, he played the stage. He done Shakespeare. Othello and Aaron the Moor. In some a dem good houses too. In Philadelphia and New York. Why, he's the only negro, aside from Sam Lucas, to play Uncle Tom.

HENRY: Percy played Tom?

DOC: Sure did. Ain't that right, Tambo?

TAMBO: Yep. The guy who usually played Tom, a white man a 'course, took sick. Percy knew all the lines, you see. Of course the management didn't like the idea one bit, but the house was sold out. The show had to go on.

DOC: He was good too.

TAMBO: How, you seen it, Doc?

DOC: Sure I seen it. If I was around I wasn't gone miss somethin' like that. A Negro playin' Uncle Tom. Why that's history. Sure I did. I remember, it was in Chicago. Percy was with that guy. . . . You know, I keep forgettin' that guy's name. What's his name? The guy what owned the place.

TAMBO: Jacobs.

DOC: That's right. That's him. You know, I ain't never looked at it that way before.

TAMBO: Looked at what?

DOC: The way Percy put it, so to speak, in that play. Every time I seen *Uncle Tom's Cabin* there was always a white man playin' Uncle Tom. Of course, I know he's supposed to be a colored man, but they always make him more fool than man. Shoot, we all makes our livin' playin' the fool. And sometimes that livin' ain't half bad, if it don't do nothin' but fill ya stomach. But all that nonsense does nothin' but hides what's real about the story. Slavery and the way it was and all. But that night I saw Percy do it, it was altogether different.

HENRY: What was different 'bout it, Doc?

DOC: Well, the way he played him. He was pure. Devout as a deacon. He had no need to hurt. The only hurt he ever felt was for other people. To him, his bond was with the Lord, and whether he was slave or free that was a constant. I just never looked at it that way before.

TAMBO: You seen Percy do Uncle Tom in Chicago?

DOC: Yes I did, and I know what you wonderin', Tambo. I didn't know ya'll then, but you wonderin' if I recognize you back dere in the chorus playin' a overgrown pickaninny girl.

HENRY: Oh no, Tambo, don't tell me. A pickaninny girl? What color was your dress?

TAMBO: It was eight dollars a week and cakes. That's what color it was.

DOC: Don't take it to heart, Tambo. You was pretty cute.

HENRY: Cute? O'wee, I bet you was bonafide cute. A regular big, hairy-leg, knocked-knee princess you musta been. God I wish I'd been there.

TAMBO: Ya'll get on from out here.

HENRY: I'll be doggone, a pickaninny girl.

DOC: What's that noise? Somebody's out there.

HENRY: Who is it?

TAMBO: Is it Percy?

DOC: It's Soloman and the boy, comin' back with the firewood.

HENRY: If Soloman's comin' back in here, there goes the peace and quiet. (*Enter* SOLOMAN *and* ARCHIE.)

SOLOMAN: Baker get back with that engine yet?

TAMBO: No. You seen Percy out there?

SOLOMAN: No. Not since we left the hall.

ARCHIE: That's all you be doin', Doc, readin' all the time.

DOC: That's how you learn, Archie.

SOLOMAN: Stoke that fire, boy.

ARCHIE: Yes sir . . . wish I knew how to read.

SOLOMAN: He shoulda been back by now.

HENRY: Baker ain't lookin' for no engine. He's in that hotel, wrestlin' with one a them big-behind saloon gals.

SOLOMAN: You see, Henry, you think it's funny. But it ain't funny. It ain't funny one damn bit. Maybe you never seen it, but I have. I seen it, I tell ya.

ARCHIE: Seen what, Soloman?

SOLOMAN: Stoke the fire, boy.

DOC: Come on, Soloman. There's no need to holler at the boy. Ain't nothin' gonna happen.

SOLOMAN: Go on, Doc. You know better than that. You know better. Tell 'em, Tambo. Tell 'em what I'm talkin' 'bout.

TAMBO: Most all of us been run outa towns before, ain't no big deal 'bout that.

SOLOMAN: It's how we gets run out that worries me. Man, we got to start figurin' 'bout gettin' hell out a here, after this thing is over with.

HENRY: Soloman, you heard the man say he was goin' to hire a engine. So why come in here causin' a lot a worriation?

SOLOMAN: Worriation? Worriation! Henry, you don't know what ya talkin' 'bout. I know railroads. I been workin' the rails mosta my life. Drivin' spikes, brakeman, Pullman porter. There's no trains leavin' out a here tonight. Nothin' movin' out there tonight. The rails is all iced up and the snow is swept up and piled high on the tracks. In weather like this you need a brakeman for every car. We got to figure on a brakeman, a fireman, and an engineer.

HENRY: Soloman, the man knows as much about it as you do. What are you worryin' about?

SOLOMAN: What am I worryin' 'bout? What am I worryin' 'bout! Henry, you got a memory short as the hair on your head. I suppose you wasn't over there cowerin' in the corner when we come rollin' in here today and them people was shootin' at this railroad car. I guess you blind and can't see these bullet holes in this here parlor car, everywheres.

HENRY: You wasn't exactly standin' up and wavin' at 'em yaself.

DOC: All these towns out here are wild. Country's wild. The people are wild. They was only shootin' at the sign.

SOLOMAN: Well, they sure missed a whole lot. It's cold as the devil in here now, with these bullet holes everywheres.

DOC: Soloman, it don't do no good to dwell on it. Like ya say, we ain't movin' outa here tonight. We got to go down to that very same hall and do a show anyway. You can't get away from that. And we'll do us up a good show. Them people'll be laughin' so much and laughin' so hard, it'll be all they can do just to keep their bellies from waddlin'.

ARCHIE: Keep their bellies from waddlin'.

DOC: I'll tell ya what we'll do. When we come in with the cakewalk, we'll play Dixie.

HENRY: Oh, they'll love that. When your ass is in a quandary, just sing Dixie to the dummies.

TAMBO: You ought to put that in the show, Henry.

SOLOMAN: You ought to smoke cigars made a dynamite.

ARCHIE: Cigars made a dynamite.

SOLOMAN: Archie, will you stoke that fire.

DOC: Soloman, leave the boy alone.

HENRY: If he stokes that fire anymore, we'll be cakewalkin' to Dixie in here.

SOLOMAN: It's cold out there and it's damp in here. That's the way the goddamn railroad is. Iron and steel, nothin' warm 'bout it. That's the way these people are in this town, ain't nothin' warm about 'em. I'm goin' to find a engine myself so's we can get while the gettin's good. I know the railway better than Baker do anyway.

HENRY: Yeah, Soloman, that's a good idea. Why don't you go look yourself.

TAMBO: See if you see Percy out there somewheres. Tell 'em to come on in out that cold. Ain't that long before showtime.

SOLOMAN: Okay, Tambo.

DOC: And don't you be out there too long yourself. Show starts eight o'clock ya know, and we gots some things to work out.

SOLOMAN: I'll be back. I ain't miss a performance yet, have I?

ARCHIE: You want me to go with you, Soloman?

SOLOMAN: No, stay here. (SOLOMAN *exits.*)

DOC: Henry, why do you try to aggravate Soloman all the time?

HENRY: Man, I ain't botherin' Soloman. He's just so damn negative all the time. That guy been workin' on the railroad too long.

TAMBO: Say, Doc, how 'bout a haircut?

DOC: Sure, Tambo, have a seat. How you want it?

TAMBO: Just a little trim will do.

DOC: Alright, we'll get you all slicked down. Leave it to me.

ARCHIE: Mr. Jones, would you read me the paper?

HENRY: Not now, Archie.

ARCHIE: How 'bout you, Doc?

DOC: I'm cuttin' Tambo's hair right now, Archie.

TAMBO: I'll read you your paper, Archie. Where is it?

ARCHIE: Thank you, Mr. Tambo. Here it is.

TAMBO: *The Clipper.* Where did you get this?

ARCHIE: Mr. Baker give it to me.

TAMBO: Baker give it to you? You didn't have to pay for it, did you?

ARCHIE: No sir, he give it to me.

HENRY: Read the paper so we all can hear it, Tambo.

TAMBO: Yeah, alright. What you want me to read, Archie?

ARCHIE: I don't care. Anywheres. What's that? What does that say?

TAMBO: That's the "Deaths in the Profession" column.

ARCHIE: That. Read me that.

TAMBO: "Deaths in the Profession?"

ARCHIE: Yes sir.

TAMBO: Okay, if that's what you want. Let's see, "Deaths in the Profession." . . . You don't mind if I skip around and just read the
good ones, do you?

ARCHIE: No sir.

TAMBO: Alright. "Deaths in the Profession." "D. B. Moody, known
to old-time circus people as Dibolo, fire eater and clown, died
a few weeks ago in his home in Chicago, Illinois from catarrh
of the stomach." Catarrh of the stomach?

ARCHIE: What's that he had on his stomach, Mr. Tambo?

TAMBO: Catarrh. Catarrh of the stomach. What is that, Doc?

DOC: Damned if I know.

HENRY: Do my ears deceive me or did I hear Doctor Syntax say that
he didn't know somethin'?

DOC: Come on, Henry. I never said I knew everything. Just most
things, that's all.

HENRY: Just most things.

DOC: He didn't die of catarrh of his stomach, he died from eatin' fire.
You supposed to die if you eat fire. Just like you, Henry. When

you die, it won't be because somebody beat your behind to death, but 'cause a your big mouth teasin' people all the time.

HENRY: Alright, alright, I'll stop.

DOC: I'm glad to hear it.

HENRY: I always listen to country wisdom, even if it's more country than wise.

DOC: Go on, Tambo, and read the boy his paper.

TAMBO: "Dolly Varden, who twenty years ago was well known as an acrobat and clown, was found dead . . . in a room at his home in this city. The deceased . . . forty years of age and at one time . . . with the late Barney Carroll, performed a bareback riding act with circuses. Mr. Varden was a dwarf and used to ride on Mr. Carroll's head around the ring. He afterward performed with Melville and Sebastian. His death was due to . . . as-fix-action." As-fix-action?

DOC: As-phyxi-a-tion. He was suffocated. He couldn't breathe.

TAMBO: ". . . Due to as-phyxi-a-tion and as the gas jet was turned on it is thought to be a case of . . . suicide."

DOC: Now that's sad.

ARCHIE: Well, why couldn't he breathe?

TAMBO: If you breathe gas, Archie, you'll die.

ARCHIE: But he coulda turned the gas off.

HENRY: He don't know what suicide means.

TAMBO: Suicide, Archie. He killed himself.

ARCHIE: What do you mean, he killed himself?

TAMBO: He killed himself. He . . . he didn't turn off the gas, 'cause he wanted to die.

ARCHIE: It say in dere, for real . . . that he wanted to die?

TAMBO: Yeah. That's what it means.

ARCHIE: He crazy. He a man and his name is Dolly, too. How come he wanna make hisself die, Mr. Tambo, how come?

TAMBO: I don't know, Archie. It doesn't tell you that.

ARCHIE: He's crazy. Wanna make hisself die.

DOC: Either a you guys remember or ever heard of Japanese Tommy?

HENRY: Japanese Tommy? Japanese Tommy. Wasn't he a dwarf?

DOC: Yeah, a little slant-eyed colored guy.

TAMBO: A colored dwarf?

DOC: Wasn't but so or so high. Three feet or so at the most. He could dance, sing, and play the violin beautiful. He was with George Christy in the 50's. He was the only colored I ever heard of, outside a Juba Lane and Blind Tom, if ya count concert music, to play minstrelsy before the war. Not for his talent, but 'cause he was a little, slant-eyed colored dwarf. Variety is a hard life, Archie. You ain't got no business gettin' mixed up in it if you ain't prepared for some trouble. Folks'll clap and cheer for you like hell, if ya different and strange to 'em. If you're colored or a dwarf or both. But that don't go off stage. No, sir. Some mens just can't take it, is all.

ARCHIE: Japanese Tommy didn't make hisself die, did he?

DOC: No, I don't think so, but to tell ya the truth, Archie, I don't know whatever happen to Japanese Tommy.

TAMBO: Hey, y'all, listen to this one.

HENRY: Tambo, I've 'bout had enough of them deaths in the profession.

DOC: Thank you, Henry.

TAMBO: Just let me read this last one. Please. Come on ... "A. J. Castile, stage carpenter of the Standard Theatre, St. Louis, Missouri, died Feb. 6th in that city from the effects of a pistol shot wound in his foot ..."

HENRY: A pistol shot wound in his foot?

TAMBO: ". . . He was shot on Dec. 18th while standing in the lobby of the theatre by McCune Holiday, advertising agent of the house, who fired at Richard Burke, the treasurer. The bullet missed its mark—," meaning Burke "—and struck Mr. Castile . . . in the foot. . . ."

DOC: Holy smokes.

HENRY: That advertising agent was trying to shoot the right guy, he just missed, that's all.

TAMBO: ". . . The immediate cause of death was blood poisoning and pneumonia."

ARCHIE: What did he die from?

TAMBO: A bullet.

ARCHIE: Oh, well, at least he didn't make hisself die.

HENRY: Say, Tambo, if you got to read that paper, why don't you read the minstrelsy and variety column and let's hear what it say 'bout what's doin' in Missouri.

TAMBO: Alright. Minstrelsy and variety . . . minstrelsy and variety . . . Kansas, Ohio, New York, Missouri . . . here it is. "St. Louis—the cold weather had a depressing effect on business last week and cut down the receipts at all the houses . . ."

DOC: All the houses. That's bad.

TAMBO: "At the Olympic Theatre, *The Politician* would have drawn considerable money if the weather had been pleasant. Wonderland Muses—Topsey, the talking horse; Thompson, the tattooed man and nail king. Scofield, the juggler; Whale Oil Gus and the two-legged pig are in the Curio Hall . . ."

ARCHIE: Topsey, the talking horse?

DOC: We can be glad we're not playin' St. Louis.

HENRY: I'd like to see that pig, though.

ARCHIE: Me too. That's got to be somethin', a two-leg pig.

TAMBO: ". . . Kansas City—the coldest weather of the winter knocked business last week. Coats Opera House, last week, was dark."

HENRY: What's the date on that paper, Tambo?

TAMBO: The 16th. February 16th.

HENRY: Today's the 28th, ain't it? It's been like this for almost going on two weeks.

DOC: What's it look like out there now, Henry?

HENRY: Can't see nothin' out there but snow and ice. Will ya look at that ice. I never seen so much ice floatin' on a river. Puts me to mind of that scene in *Uncle Tom's Cabin* where Eliza is crossin' the river. Runnin' 'cross the ice. Looks like one a them parlor pictures of heaven. Come here, Doc. Take a look at all that ice on that river . . . you ever seen anything like that before?

DOC: Yeah, but not on the Mississippi. This is the coldest winter we've had in a long time.

TAMBO: Well, Soloman don't have to worry 'bout no hostile crowd in the house this night. We be lucky if we gets any house at all in this weather.

DOC: Who knows? Folks still might turn out. If it's been like this for two weeks, people be feelin' plenty cooped up. They probably ready to get out for some entertainment.

HENRY: I could see it if we had an advertising agent or an advance man, but we a little troupe with a phoney draw, playin' little out the way towns like this one. Who ever heard of Hannibal, Missouri?

DOC: That's why they might turn out. Nothin' comes here and they ain't nothin' to do.

HENRY: Well I hear what you sayin', Doc, but still things can get funny with Baker and his catfish-lookin' self.

TAMBO: What you sayin' Henry? You think Baker might skip out on us?

HENRY: No, I don't think Baker's gonna do that. He spend a lotta money buyin' this parlor car. He might skip out on us, but he won't skip out on it. He ain't a white man for nothin'. He ain't no fool.

ARCHIE: What make y'all think Mr. Baker would run off on us?

HENRY: 'Cause he's a crook.

ARCHIE: Mr. Baker ain't no crook. Why would he hire him if he was a crook?

HENRY: Why would who hire who?

ARCHIE: Mr. Baker. Why would he hire Mr. Baker?

HENRY: Why would who hire Baker?

ARCHIE: Tommy Parker.

HENRY: Tommy Parker? How the hell is Tommy Parker gonna hire Baker?

ARCHIE: 'Cause it's his show. *The Little Tommy Parker Celebrated Colored Minstrel Show.*

HENRY: Man, Tommy Parker's dead.

ARCHIE: Tommy Parker's dead? When he die?

HENRY: He dies every time we do this show.

ARCHIE: Oh, I get it now. You just made me your straight man.

DOC: He's not joking with you, Archie. I think you been flim-flammed. Tell me, you probably workin' for nothin', 'til he sees how you work out. Am I right?

ARCHIE: Well, he say until Tommy Parker get back.

DOC: Well, Tommy Parker ain't coming back. This ain't Tommy Parker's company. It's got Tommy's name alright, but Baker pays the bills, when he pays 'em. Tommy Parker ain't in it neither. Like Henry said, Tommy Parker's dead. Been dead a long time.

HENRY: And Baker wasn't no friend a his neither. He's never even met him. Why, Baker ain't never even seen a show that Tommy Parker was in.

ARCHIE: What happens when people find he ain't showin' up?

DOC: That's when Baker tells his little story.

ARCHIE: Story?

DOC: Yeah, why Little Tommy Parker can't be with us this evening.

TAMBO: He's told a story in every little one-shack town we been in since we left Philadelphia. All through Ohio, Tennessee, Kentucky, Kansas, and now Missouri.

DOC: He walks on the stage all sad and draggy, like. He gets before the house and he say, "Ladies and gentlemen, I am deeply grieved and burdened to tell you that Little Tommy Parker cannot be with us this evening." Then he say when he died. It's always that mornin' or that afternoon. Mornings for matinees and afternoons for the evening show. Of course we can only do one show in a town, but Tommy Parker's been known to die twice in one day.

HENRY: He don't never die a no diseases. Folks don't take too kindly to a bunch a Negroes in they hall just exposed to small-pox or somethin'.

TAMBO: He died once savin' a little white boy from a fire.

HENRY: He's been killed by a few no account Negroes. He fell off a train once and broke his neck.

DOC: He's drowned in a tub, been run over by a horse, fell out a window, cut his throat shavin'. . . . Let see, a woman give him poison once and he's been hit by stray bullets all over the country. . . . That's it, Tambo, you all slicked down now.

TAMBO: Thank you, Doc.

ARCHIE: How did he really die?

DOC: Probably from a lifetime a nothin' but eel and ale on his stomach. Poorness. I done forgot now.

ARCHIE: But, he was famous.

TAMBO: Yeah, but he was colored, too.

ARCHIE: I can't believe it. Tommy Parker's dead.

HENRY: How, you know somethin' 'bout Tommy Parker, boy.

ARCHIE: Yes sir, I seen him.

DOC: You seen Tommy Parker? Where at?

ARCHIE: In Maguire's Opera House in San Francisco, when I was real little.

HENRY: San Francisco? San Francisco is a long way from Kansas City. You come all the way from there with that crooked medicine man we found you with?

ARCHIE: No sir. I was with a couple a others before him.

HENRY: A couple a others? Look to me boy like you got to start lookin' at the world the way it is. I thought Soloman was supposed to take this boy under his wing.

TAMBO: Now, Henry, don't you start to being so hard on the boy.

DOC: Leave 'em alone Tambo, things is already hard. Let 'em learn him.

HENRY: Archie, what was you doin' with that medicine man we found you with, back in Kansas City?

ARCHIE: Dancin'.

HENRY: I knows you was dancin'. What I'm askin' you is what was you dancin' for?

ARCHIE: So people come 'round to see. Then the medicine man, show what he got to sell. Roots and snake oil and thing.

HENRY: Right, Archie, right. You was dancin' so he could sell his roots. You understand what I'm sayin' to you boy? You was dancin' so's he could make money. He didn't love you. He wasn't tryin' ta give you no break, else he wouldn't run off on you.

ARCHIE: I suppose you right, Mr. Jones.

HENRY: You doggone right, I'm right. And it's the same thing with Baker. Lyin' to you, talkin' 'bout when Little Tommy Parker get back. Boy, I bet you better mind what's goin' on round here. It all ain't no cakewalk.

DOC: Hush up now, Henry. You made ya point. Boy done made a few mistakes. Hell, ain't nobody payin' for it but him.

HENRY: Doc, what you talkin' 'bout? What is the matter with you? We ain't seen this kid before the day before yesterday. Now he's supposed to take Sammy Nash's place. He's supposed to be the sixth colored minstrel—tonight.

TAMBO: The best thing to happen to us, is for Sammy Nash to run off. He didn't belong in no show business noway. Share-cropper could take that nigga's place.

DOC: Tambo, please don't use that word.

TAMBO: Sorry, Doc.

HENRY: Yeah, but can the kid dance? Can he sing? What can he do? Boy, can you dance?

ARCHIE: Yes sir, I can.

HENRY: What you was doin' before them medicine shows?

ARCHIE: I watch shows in the Opera House.

HENRY: "I watch shows in the Opera House." What kinda shows?

ARCHIE: You see . . . people use to say I was a stage-door-Johnny baby. My mama was a chorus girl . . . but I never seen her. The scrubwoman, Molly, looked after me. She always cleanin' the Opera House, so I get to see a lot a shows. I mean I usta. Lots a dancin' too. I even seen Tommy Parker there. Mr. Jones, really, I can dance. (SOLOMAN *enters.*)

SOLOMAN: I found him. I found the engineer.

TAMBO: Did you see Percy?

SOLOMAN: Haven't seen him.

TAMBO: I'm gonna go look for him.

SOLOMAN: See if ya can find Baker, too.

DOC: Don't go out there, Tambo. Percy'll be back and then we'll have to go lookin' for you.

SOLOMAN: But we got to find Baker. That engineer say he won't hook up to us 'til he gets his money first. Say he won't do no business with no colored man. Bet I know more 'bout them engines than he do. . . . Y'all done let the fire go out.

ARCHIE: I'll do it, Soloman.

SOLOMAN: Well, do it then.

DOC: Will you leave the kid alone.

HENRY: Soloman, will you stop? Will you stop? You not the only one in here. We all know what's goin' on as well as you do.

SOLOMAN: Well, you're not actin' like it.

HENRY: Not actin' like it? What? Man, you talk 'bout bullets in the goddamn walls, hell, there's one through my derby and I had it on my head. You don't know no more 'bout it, than anybody else.

SOLOMAN: Listen, I'm tellin' ya'll somethin'. Ya'll think I'm just scary, but I'm tellin' ya, somethin' is wrong out there. Folks is travlin' 'round in crowds, wanderin' about. Somethin' ain't right, I tell ya.

DOC: Soloman, stop being so spooky, now. Tells us what you think is goin' on out there.

HENRY: Mabey you can dress up in your old Pullman porter coat and disappear in the crowd.

SOLOMAN: You being devilish, Henry, and ya think you funny, but you know, I got me an old Pullman porter coat. That coat is lynch protection. That's why I keeps it. Lynch mob pass right by a negro wearin' a Pullman porter coat. Jimmy Rogers minded what I told him, he got him one a these coats. It was that what saved them boys down in Texas with Handy, back in '90.

DOC: I remember somethin' 'bout that. What was it? They wouldn't let them boys in the hospital or somethin', wasn't it?

SOLOMAN: No, it was worse than that. One or two a them boys caught the pox. The sheriff and the county folks and all them people, they wouldn't let 'em out. Had them boys corralled there in that railroad car, with no food, no water, no place to relieve themselves, nothin'. Well, you see, one night Jimmy Rogers he put on his Pullman porter coat and he get out the trap door. He crawl to the outside of the circle where they all was. He stands up and quite natural, they catch him. They ask him what he's doin' round there and Jimmy say, he just come over to see what's goin' on. So they tell him to mind his business and get from round there. Well it just so happen that the Clyde Kelly Minstrels was playin' in the next county. You know, with Morris and the Woods brothers and them. They come over the next night and do a parade and stage a show out in the street. Meanwhile, some of them sneaks them boys out in woman's clothes and some kinda way, they make it out there. And I know we got to get out a here, I know that.

DOC: Soloman, listen, we was just talkin' 'bout the thing before you come. Now we all know Baker ain't goin' nowhere without his high-class, low-life parlor car. He'll be back before showtime. I guarantee it. Where's the paper? Give him the paper. Look in there. Look in the minstrelsy and variety section. Business is bad all over. Mosta the theatres is closed up. We go out there to that hall and might find it empty. You worried 'bout a mob, but you ought to start figurin' on how we gonna get paid.

SOLOMAN: Alright, it might be empty. But what if it's full?

DOC: What if it is? Look, Soloman, we are performers. We make the show. We make 'em laugh. Not Baker. Not the engineer or anybody else. Can't nobody sit in a seat in that hall that's got ears and eyes and not laugh and relax and have themselves a good ole time, when we steps out in front of them footlights. When we swing, we'll make 'em weary. We're performers, man. Every bullet hole in here'll be a nickel and every nickel a laugh. We make it happen. The stompin', the knee slappin', all of it. We make 'em feel. And when we be hittin' it, we can make it grow and get bigger and bigger and bigger, 'til it's about to bust. And then we make it bust. Bust it wide open. You know how it is when you on. You can hear it even after the curtain goes down. Tricklin' out the doors. For a long way off there's a merry feelin' that we put out there. We're performers, Soloman. The way out a here ain't the rails, it's on the stage. We do like we supposed to do and we can leave this here little town, how and when we get ready. Come on now, Soloman, let's all put on shine and get ready to do our stuff.

SOLOMAN: I must look pretty foolish to y'all, don't I? Move, Archie, I'll stoke that fire. . . . I must look pretty foolish. I feel pretty foolish. You know George Roland said to me one time, he said, "Soloman, you best performer I seen come out a Virginia in a long time." That comin' from him made me feel pretty good. Applause used to make me feel good. Lately, it don't sound no different to me than the roll of them iron wheels over them iron rails. I'm tired of it. I've had enough. It's a dream world and a kid's game. We're performers alright. On stage and off. Two hours a night you somebody. Mabey yourself, who knows? Two hours, and the rest of the time we're performers playin' who the hell knows what. That's our best performance. I quit the railroad. Had me a good job as a Pullman porter—supreme performers. I quit to play minstrelsy to get off the rails, and I been ridin' trains ever since. I'll tell you one thing. I'm gettin' me to Chicago when this run is through. I got a sister there, got her a roomin' house. Her husband say he can get me a job in the train depot as a redcap. I may see trains all the time, but I won't be ridin' on none, and when minstrel shows come in on the rail, I'm stayin' home sick.

HENRY: You lucky, if you got a halfway decent job in Chicago. You ought to stop complainin'. If it wasn't for that and this business, how else you gonna live? Bustin' sod? Pickin' cotton? Sharecroppin'? You'd be doin' the same thing you'd a done in slavery and still get yourself in a mess a trouble. They'll still be folk out there lookin' to put ya in a fix. All any of us ever do is try to please white folks, and that ain't no easy thing to do. What you gonna do, go back to Africa?

SOLOMAN: Well, Henry, that wouldn't exactly be a bad idea.

HENRY: You'd last about as long in Africa as that. (*Snaps his fingers.*) All them wild niggers runnin' round. Big mosquitoes, lions, bears . . .

DOC: There ain't no bears in Africa, Henry.

HENRY: Well, gorillas then. Same difference.

SOLOMAN: I'm not goin' to Africa, Henry, I'm goin' to Chicago. But if'n I was goin' to Africa, I don't suppose that wild niggers runnin' round be no worst than wild white folks.

HENRY: And I say amen to that. But I go along with Doc, we're performers. Nothin' special, just pleasin' white folk, only we gets paid better for it.

TAMBO: Wait a minute, now. Hold on. There's more to it than that, and Henry, you'd be the last to say it isn't so. We haves us a good time, mostly. We travels all over. We go to the colored sections and we be the heros and the stars. Rainbows among the chanty shacks. We gets that good cornbread and things. The best liquor.

HENRY: Even if it is corn liquor.

TAMBO: Even if it is corn. Kids followin' us everywhere, old folks takin' us in and pretty girls, high yella or otherwise, is fair game to us. All the good musicians and players come round and they is always a party for us. Ain't no better life for a colored man in America, as far as I'm concerned.

DOC: Maybe it was that way once, but times done gone hard, now. Blackface gettin' ready to go out a style. Right there in the paper, it got advertisements for "massive minstrel shows." Thirty-five white minstrels, thirty-five coloreds, fifteen Japanese, fifteen Bedouin Arab Moors.

ARCHIE: What's a bedin' abby moor?

HENRY: A moor is what they call Negroes, before they call us niggers.

DOC: Well it ain't exactly that way, but besides comedians and singers, dancers and musicians, them shows got jugglers, acrobat, tumblers, whirlin' Dervishes and every kind a freak. If a man could get work in that mob, he wouldn't be makin' no money and nobody's gonna be able to see what he can do in all that crowd. They say that Bufflo Bill is gone do a big show out in some park in New York. Gonna be the biggest show ever. Our little one-rail type a show is almost finished.

SOLOMAN: Well, it's workin' with those white minstrels that bothers me. I don't likes it, especially when it comes to the dancin'. It doesn't matter what you call it. The Lancashire Clog, the Hornpipe, the Virginia Essence, it don't make no difference. The way they do it, it all looks and sounds like the same thing to me. It don't have no swing and it has nothin' whatsoever to do with the music. They ignore the music altogether. They takes the best dances and bastardizes them. Bastardizes them and turn around and become famous and make a whole lot a money 'cause they claim they the originators a this dance and that dance. What they call a speciality, ain't nothin' but colored folks' social dancin'.

DOC: I first started doin' minstrelsy on that steamboat, the Banjo, right here up and down the Mississippi River. In my father's time, he worked on the same paddleboat, only down in the engine room shovelin' coal. He told me a white man named David Keys used to slip down there and pass a jug around and chew the fat. Talked real artistic. Wanted to see some steps by the light of the furnace fire, with their loomin' shadows in the background. Come to find later, this David Keys is a big hit with a new speciality dance. Man, that dance wasn't nothin' but the Buzzard Loope, he seen on that riverboat.

SOLOMAN: That's what they do. They copy. Copy and make all the money.

DOC: Well, all of 'em ain't like that.

SOLOMAN: Sure they is. Every one of 'em. I wouldn't show none of 'em nothin'. Not a step, not a note, nothin'.

HENRY: I would. Tell 'em anything they want to know. Corn whiskey is lemonade, the moon is a cupcake, eatin' whole red peppers'll make ya good wit the ladies. They the most gullible people on the face of the earth. Believe everything but the truth. Shute, even Archie know 'bout that. Why you think them Indians can sell so much a that snake oil? Charlie Griffith used to sell, or I should say, try to sell snake oil. Man, he wasn't makin' a penny. But he's kinda red, ya know. Got high cheekbones and good hair. He let his hair grow. Got him a bunch a bird feathers. Wrapped a little tiny towel 'round his little waist. And what he have in it, garlic, vinegar, raspberry soda, and a pinch a saltpeter. He couldn't sell that junk as a Negro, but as an Indian, he was a snake oil professor. Shute, Charlie made him enough money to get him a little place just outside a Charleston.

SOLOMAN: Well, I don't know 'bout all that, but the only one of 'em any good at all is that Ray Bantam. He's about the best when it come to the Virginia Essence.

TAMBO: What did you say?

SOLOMAN: Ray Bantam.

TAMBO: Ray Bantam? You done got too old, Soloman. Your mind has give out on you. The best cakewalker and Virginia Essence dancer in the country, in the world today is Buster "Tambo" Williams, whom you have the distinct and historic pleasure of addressing.

DOC: Oh, oh. Oh, oh!

HENRY: Speak, brother Tambo. Speak.

SOLOMAN: Well, you good Tambo, but I don't know. You at least got to give the man credit.

TAMBO: I don't got to give the man nothin'. Listen, in 1882, me and Doreen Wilson won the cakewalk in Madison Square Garden with glasses a water on our heads. Doreen had a crystal stem glass, the base set in her hair. I had a water glass set on top a my top hat, just so. We high stepped everybody out a there and didn't spill a drop. Ray Bantam! Man, you crazy. You are lookin' at the absolute and total grand master of the pedestal feat.

HENRY: The nigger's not lyin' either. He's good.

DOC: Henry, please. Don't use that word.

HENRY: Alright, Doc, I'm sorry, but he is.

SOLOMAN: I admit Tambo's a good dancer, especially cakewalk, but I don't believe he can do a cakewalk with a glass 'a water on his head and not spill a drop.

TAMBO: Soloman, I can . . .

HENRY: Wait a minute, Tambo, don't say nothin' . . . Soloman, how much don't you believe that Tambo can dance with a glass a water on his head and not spill none?

SOLOMAN: What you mean, how much?

HENRY: I mean that if he can do it, then when you get your eight dollars, if you get your eight dollars for the week, they belongs to me.

SOLOMAN: Eight dollars, huh? He's gonna do it in here?

HENRY: In here, Tambo?

TAMBO: I'll do it on a cockroach's toenail if you want.

SOLOMAN: It's a bet.

HENRY: Well, alright. I have somewheres here in my bag of musical tricks, somewheres a splendid top hat, fit for a pedestal genius. . . . Here you be, grand master Tambo. And to show you how much confidence I have in the elegance of your steps, I shall fill this here waterglass with the last of my elixir of corn.

DOC: For God's sake, don't spill that on the floor, Tambo. It'll put a hole in it.

SOLOMAN: Hold on a second now, wait. Now listen, there can't be no tiptoein' or shufflin' round. You got to bonafide cakewalk to win . . . and you got to do at least 16 bars.

TAMBO: Soloman, bonafide is the only kind a cakewalk I do.

DOC: Get out your fiddles, gentlemen. Archie, you claim to play spoons, well, now's the time to lay into 'em.

HENRY: What'll it be, Master Tambo?

TAMBO: How 'bout a little "Shine."

DOC: One—two—three—four, one—two—three—Hey! (TAMBO *performs a splendid and original cakewalk before his companions without spilling the whiskey. He finishes to applause.*)

ARCHIE: That was real good, Mr. Tambo.

HENRY: What did I tell you, Soloman? What did I tell you?

SOLOMAN: Oh, go on, Henry. That was alright, Tambo. But it's the most money I ever paid to see a Negro dance.

ARCHIE: That was good. I liked that.

DOC: It was Henry y'all should a been lookin' at. Look like his heart was gonna stop, if Tambo had a spilled that moonshine.

HENRY: But he didn't, did he?

SOLOMAN: Man, that stuff is so thick it would a stuck to the sides a the glass.

ARCHIE: That was somethin' else, Tambo.

TAMBO: Thank you, Archie. You should a seen me do it with Doreen.

ARCHIE: Can I try?

TAMBO: Try what?

ARCHIE: The cakewalk.

TAMBO: Not in here, Archie. You'll knock everything down.

ARCHIE: Let me try, Mr. Tambo. I can do it.

TAMBO: Well, I guess so. Why not. Go ahead.

ARCHIE: I mean with the hat and the glass a moonshine.

TAMBO: Oh, you can't do that, Archie.

ARCHIE: Yes I can. Let me try.

DOC: Let him have a shot at it, Tambo.

SOLOMAN: Sure, let the kid try. You think you can do it, Archie?

ARCHIE: Yeah, I think so.

HENRY: He ain't tryin' nothin'. Not with my whiskey on his head, he ain't. You can wear the hat, but get yourself a glass a water, boy.

SOLOMAN: Two weeks on the kid. Sixteen dollars. Double or nothin'. What you say, mouth?

HENRY: You on. Boy, you're gonna need at least that much to pay for the damages. Go on, Tambo, give 'em the hat.

TAMBO: Alright, Archie, let me balance the glass for you. . . . Okay, there you go.

SOLOMAN: Alright, now, I'm countin' on you, Archie. Let's show these nega-roos how to hush they mouth.

DOC: What you want us to play, Archie?

ARCHIE: Same thing as Tambo, "Shine." (ARCHIE *performs a cake-walk every bit as spectacular as* TAMBO*'s.*)

TAMBO: Well, I'll be doggone.

HENRY: You'll be doggone? What you think 'bout me? Man, I thought I was through losin' my shine money.

SOLOMAN: Pay up, Henry! Archie, you done show'd these Negroes what kind a dancin' you can do. I'm gonna take you out and we goin' spend Henry's money together.

HENRY: They talkin' already 'bout spendin' my money.

DOC: Where you learn to cakewalk, Archie?

ARCHIE: I seen Tommy Parker do it. Lots a times. At Maguire's Opera House. Look like he was flyin'. He was flyin'. He was somethin' else. Somethin' else.

HENRY: Why this boy Archie is a regular man a the world. This calls for a drink, that's what this calls for. Archie, pass around them water glasses there. Gentlemen, shall we partake of a little shine? (*Pouring.*) Doc, Tambo, Soloman.

ARCHIE: What about mine, Mr. Jones.

HENRY: Sorry, Archie, but this is to you, not for you. Gentlemen, I propose a toast to Archie, that little boy, with them great big dancin' feet.

ALL: To Archie. (*Before they can complete their toast,* PERCY *crashes through the door and falls to the floor. Shocked at his appearance, they all freeze.*)

END OF ACT

Act Two

DOC: Lord a mussy, Percy, what happened to you?

TAMBO: Percy, where you been, boy? You look a mess.

PERCY: I been out there, walkin'.

HENRY: Out there walkin'?

SOLOMAN: You trackin' water all over the floor, Percy.

DOC: Never mind trackin' water on the floor, can't you see the man's freezin' to death. Go on over by the stove there, Percy, and warm yourself up. Get out a them wet clothes. I'll get ya a blanket.

TAMBO: Here, let me take ya coat. Archie, take these wet things and hang 'em up by the door there.

DOC: Wrap this around you, Percy. There you go. That's better, isn't it?

HENRY: Here, Percy, suck down on some a this awhile. This'll warm ya up.

TAMBO: Well, Percy, tell us what happened. Where you been?

PERCY: Like I said, I was out there walkin'. I was with this girl, from down in the town.

HENRY: Oh, I shoulda known. Boy done started already. Yeah, and where you find this girl at, Percy.

PERCY: She was hangin' round out here, lookin' to meet herself a minstrel man.

HENRY: Oh yeah, I sees it now. And you was out there to make sure she found herself one. Look like she had you rollin' in the snow.

PERCY: I guess I musta fell down once or twice in the snow.

124

TAMBO: Percy, ain't no use in you tryin' to fool me. I knows you, Percy. Tell us what really happened. How you get all messed up like that. Where you been?

PERCY: I been hidin' . . . I been hidin' in an old packin' crate, down by the riverside.

SOLOMAN: What was you doin' hidin' in a packin' crate for? Who was you hidin' from?

PERCY: Some a them town folk was after me.

SOLOMAN: Oh, my God. Oh, my God.

PERCY: Ain't nobody there now. I gave 'em the slip. It happened hours ago. I been in that cold, old packin' crate for so long, I don't know how long. First I was too scared to move . . . and then I want to make sure nobody seen me come here.

SOLOMAN: I knew it. I knew it, I told you so. Didn't I tell you so? It was in the air ever since we got here. They was waitin' for one of us to get out a line, from the first. They wants to see a show alright. They wants to see some niggers dance. See 'em dance in the air, from a rope. What we gonna do now? I told you, mabey nothin' movin' out a here tonight. How am I gonna get to Chicago now? What are we gonna do?

DOC: Soloman, don't panic. We got to be calm. Come on now. Hold yourself together. Come on, Soloman. Hold on, let's hear Percy out. Mabey it ain't all that bad.

HENRY: It's bad, ain't it Percy?

TAMBO: For God's sake, Percy, tell us what happened.

PERCY: I was walkin' down the street with this girl. We had come out the ice cream parlor and we was just walkin' down the street. Walkin' down the street, when we walk by this bunch a white folk. Mens mostly, but there was some women there too. They didn't like the way we look. We was uppity niggers. We dressed like we thought we was somebody. First, they made us get down from off the sidewalk and start callin' this lady the usual lot a dirty names. They followed behind us and throw snowballs at us. One knock my hat off. I stopped and I bent down and I was pickin' it up off the ground; and then I was thinkin' to myself, shit, even all them poor white trash, together, couldn't afford this hat. My hat. And I stood up and I turned around and I cussed 'em. I bet they never heard such cussin' from a colored man. I called 'em every lowdown, dirty name I could think of. I called 'em names upon names. I called 'em.

TAMBO: You wild, crazy nigger.

SOLOMAN: You played right into their hands. You know that? Right into their hands. Don't you know by now, that's what they do?

DOC: Soloman, take it easy.

SOLOMAN: Take it easy, hell. He's gone off like a damn fool and got us all in a mess.

TAMBO: Percy, what in God's name was on your mind?

PERCY: What was on my mind? What was on my mind, why there was nothin' on my mind, Tambo. For the first time in my life, there was nothin' on my mind. I was free as an animal in the woods. If there was anything on my mind, it was survival. So I ran. I ran away and left that poor girl standin' there. I had my back to her and I was runnin', but I could see her lookin' at me, just the same, with that strange, confused look I seen somewhere before. . . . That mob was dead behind me and every now and then, I could feel some of they hands grab for me and slip off. . . . The theatre was just up the street. I barely managed to turn into the door, much less close it behind me and drop the latch. . . . But they broke it down and pretty soon they had me cornered in the aisle. I had no choice then. I had to pull out my little rascal and fire on 'em.

SOLOMAN: You fired your pistol?

PERCY: Bang! Pop! You should a seen 'em, it was as if they had been wronged.

SOLOMAN: Oh, God help us.

PERCY: "The nigger's got a gun! The nigger's got a gun!"

TAMBO: Did you shoot anybody?

PERCY: What difference does it make if I shot anybody? They'd come to get me just the same.

TAMBO: Did you shoot anybody?

PERCY: No. I wasn't tryin' to hurt nobody. I just wanted some runnin' room. I just wanted to live.

TAMBO: Goddamn it, Percy, where do you think you are? Who do you think you are? You ain't nobody to these people. You nothin' to these people. They don't care if you suppose to be some kinda a big star in show business. You just another nigger to them. What makes you so proud?

PERCY: Listen, I didn't mean to get you all in no trouble. Only one really in any trouble in here is me. I been out there thinkin' 'bout it. I thought about it, believe me. First I thought I'd hightail it out here. I'd run for it. My best bet would be the river. If the ice was thick enough all the way across, I could make it all the way to the other side. How far across would you say that was, Doc?

DOC: I don't know, Percy, but you can't get across that river that way.

PERCY: Then I figured I got me but one chance. You see, I lost them folks over by the riverfront. I seen 'em from where I was hidin' in that old packin' crate. They didn't look for me very long. It's cold out there. No tracks in the slush. The cold done sent them home. They're warm inside their houses by now, eatin' their supper and thinkin', I'm a long way gone by now. Or else freezin' down by the river.

SOLOMAN: They seen your face. They must've seen your face.

PERCY: They did. I know, they did. Some of 'em gonna be sure to reconize me. But I don't think they would reconize me if I was in the black and playin' the ends.

TAMBO: What you talkin' 'bout?

HENRY: You talkin' about doin' the show?

PERCY: Oh, we've got to do the show. You don't do the show and ya'll be in the same fix I'm in. You got to do a show if they kill me afterwards. The billboard call for six colored minstrels. What's gonna happen when they see five colored minstrels. We gonna be in the same fix all over again. They gone be mad as it is, when they find out Little Tommy Parker ain't gonna show. Oh, we got to do a show. . . . Boys, listen to me, that's my only chance, to hide myself behind this blackface in the show. You got to do this for me, and if they reconize me, well I guess I'll just have to let it go.

ARCHIE: What's gonna happen, Soloman?

SOLOMAN: It's gonna be alright, Archie, just stay by me.

HENRY: Ain't there nothin' else we can do?

PERCY: If there is, Henry, I don't know what it is. I don't see I got no other choice.

DOC: Well, you talkin' 'bout doin' one hell of a show, to make that audience tonight be anything less than a mob.

PERCY: You all will have to give the performance of my life.

TAMBO: Well, if you're gonna black up, whose gonna take your part? Who's gonna be the middle?

PERCY: Henry. Henry could do just as good a job as me. Better!

HENRY: Say what? Better?

PERCY: Hell, Henry, you a better interlocator than I am, anyway.

HENRY: Oh, go on Percy.

PERCY: No man, I mean it. I'm not just sayin' this. I'm only doin' this bit 'cause that's the way Baker wants it. Sure I pushed him on it. I didn't want to wear black. Like Tambo say, for me it was the middle or nothin'. He went for it, don't you see. God knows, he's never seen you up front. You're good, Henry. You're more composed than me. You look better in your clothes. The only reason you not doin' it instead a me is 'cause this is the white man's idea a minstrel show. Come on, Henry, what do you say?

HENRY: You done got me by the nose this time, Percy. I likes to play the middle, I shore do. I don't know about who's better, you or me. That don't really matter. But I do likes it an I don't like puttin' on this black stuff noway.

DOC: I don't know how you'll figure you goin' to get away with all that. We just now figure out how to squeeze this boy into the act and now you'll want to go changin' parts.

PERCY: Ain't nothin' to it, Doc, ain't nothin' to it. You talk about doin' a minstrel show. Puttin' on blackface. I done worn that face. I done worn that face out. I got things in my carpetbag, I can't remember the last time I had 'em on. Ya'll know I ain't been Bones in years. I got these long toe shoes, stick way out. And these real big pants with extra material in the back, so's I can put a pillow or somethin' in dere and make it look like I got a great big behind.

TAMBO: I can't believe this is you talkin', Percy.

PERCY: Man, I even got a pair a false lips. Big libba-lickin' lips. . . . Do ya hear me, boys. I'm the one got to go outside. I'm the one got to do the show. I'm askin' you now, boys, do this for me. Will you help me, Henry?

HENRY: It was never a question of whether or not we was goin' to help ya, Percy. We gonna help, we ain't got no more choice than you.

PERCY: Tambo?

TAMBO: You don't even have to ask me that, Percy.

PERCY: Soloman, what about you?

SOLOMAN: Sure, I'm with ya, but I sure wish you hadn't a done it.

DOC: Done what? He ain't done nothin' but been born black. Go on if you want to. Put on your Pullman porter coat and walk down to the depot.

SOLOMAN: I ain't got no Pullman porter coat. I ain't never got it back from Jimmy Rogers. That coat is gone. Well, if we gonna do it, let's get started puttin' on shine.

HENRY: Archie, you know how ta put on cork?

ARCHIE: No, Mr. Jones, I never did it before.

HENRY: Well, come on sit over here on this stool, then. We gonna make you black.

ARCHIE: Make me black? I am black.

HENRY: You ain't black enough.

SOLOMAN: Give 'em a good mouth, Henry.

ARCHIE: What's wrong with my mouth?

HENRY: It ain't big enough.

ARCHIE: What he mean, Soloman?

SOLOMAN: You know, the mouth. The lips. That white stuff Henry got over there. Every minstrel's mouth is just a little bit different. You can't copy another person's mouth, cause it's ya character, who you gonna be onstage. Now when Henry through blackin' ya up and makin' ya mouth, you take a look in the mirror and remember what ya see. So when you on stage, you try to be the guy with that mouth.

HENRY: What are you, Soloman, a mouth and lip philosopher? This man is crazy.

DOC: He's right about one thing there, Archie. When you all done, you go look in the mirror and take a good look at yourself and all of us and then you get your laughin' over with before we go out on that stage.

PERCY: Yeah, ain't that the truth. It tickles you to death when you first see that greasy black face on somebody ya know.

HENRY: First time I seen it, I was like this kid, in my first big minstrel show. Forty guys onstage and a chorus a twenty girls. I look down the line as we about to do the openin' number and I sees this colored guy with his face all blacked up. Boy, I liked to die. Fell on the floor, rollin' round, holdin' my belly. That was one short run for me.

TAMBO: Speakin' a openin' numbers, we best mind what Doc be sayin' and work out our stage business. Now, what about Archie? What's he gone do?

HENRY: Archie can play them spoons. Let him follow along with you and Percy, rattlin' them bones, then do his routine. You see, Percy, before you come in, we was havin' a drink to Archie's dancin', I mean, that was what our little toast was for, Archie's dancin'. Him and Tambo was havin' a cakewalk contest in here and Archie put somethin' on Tambo's behind. . . . Keep ya face still, Archie. . . . Cost me sixteen dollars. You see, it went somethin' like this—sight unseen, me and Soloman makes this bet, on if the kid can do the cakewalk with a glass a water on his head, like Tambo do. Well, I'll be damn if he don't do it. . . . Archie, stop twistin' up ya face like that. . . . I tell ya, the whole thing is a routine if I ever saw one. I mean it's a setup.

DOC: You mean, we let the kid do the same thing with Tambo, onstage?

HENRY: Yeah, why not? Boy, if I have to tell you to keep your face still, one more time.

ARCHIE: Yes sir. I'll be still.

SOLOMAN: I get it now. Tambo gets to braggin' about his speciality dancin' and we make a bet and I lose. Now the kid wants to try. We doubles the bet and he does it. What you think about that, Tambo?

TAMBO: Well, the contest don't have to turn out that same way all the time.

DOC: But it ain't that funny, less the kid wins.

TAMBO: Yeah, I suppose you right, Doc. Okay, I guess that's alright with me. How we gonna set it up?

PERCY: Well, why don't you ad-lib it. Soloman could give you a cue, Tambo. He could say somethin' like, "Say, Mr. Tambo, they tells me you is a great dancer." Tambo, you good at that kinda stuff. Soloman, you make the bet with Henry and you'll pass it back and forth and feed it to Archie.

TAMBO: That'll work.

SOLOMAN: You think you can do all that, Archie?

ARCHIE: Sure I can do it.

SOLOMAN: Don't get too big for ya britches, now. Don't start showin' off.

HENRY: Showin' off? Soloman, we in the business a showin' off.

SOLOMAN: Oh Henry, hush. This is your big chance, Archie. You gonna have to stand tall and speak up. Say, listen. Let me tell you one thing, too. When you get out there, look in people's face if you have to, but don't look in they eyes. I been meanin' to tell you that. You got a tendency to look people dead in they eye. That's okay round us, but out there, you look white folk in they eye and they wanta know, "Nigger, what you lookin' at?"

HENRY: What are you now, Soloman, the stage manager? The dog-gone mouth philosopher, stage manager.

SOLOMAN: I'm not gone stand for too much more a your slights, Henry. I ain't botherin' you. Every time I say somethin', you got somethin' to say about that. I'm not gone stand for much more, you hear me?

HENRY: Take it easy, Soloman. I'm sorry. I was only teasin' with you.

SOLOMAN: Well, stop teasin' me, then. I done told you, I'm tired of it. Everybody don't like to be made fun of and laughed at all the time. Why I got to be your fool, huh? What I got to be a straight man for you for. I'm supposed to be stupid, so you can look smart? Don't do that to me no more, goddamn. I ain't your nigger. I'm tired. I'm tired of it, I done told you. Do you hear me? Do you hear me?

DOC: Soloman, easy. Easy.

SOLOMAN: Son of a bitch.

HENRY: Soloman, look at me. Look at me. Soloman, I know what's wrong with you. I know what's botherin' you. We all got the same things on our minds. We all nervous. But Soloman, look here. (*Indicating* ARCHIE, *nearly in black face.*) Look at that face. Look at it. Archie's back there. He's back there, behind that face. He's in there, Soloman. Touch him. Go on, touch him. Can you feel him in there? Feel his heart beat? He's in there, breathin', Soloman. Back there, behind that face. Who is that in there? (*Pointing at* SOLOMAN.)

SOLOMAN: Me.

HENRY: That's right, Soloman, that's right. And who is that?

SOLOMAN: That's me. Soloman Rastus Edwards the Third.

HENRY: That's right, Soloman, that's right. I'm sorry, Soloman. I didn't mean nothin'. I swear I didn't.

SOLOMAN: I'm sorry too, Henry. Forget it, I'm alright now. I'm alright.

ARCHIE: Don't worry 'bout me, Soloman. I know how to dance. I can do it. Don't be scared. We gonna knock 'em dead.

SOLOMAN: You a good boy, Archie. You a good boy. You a god-damn fool, but you a good boy.

TAMBO: You got black smeared all over ya lips, Percy. Let me help you out.

PERCY: Thank you, Tambo. (*Sitting down facing each other,* TAMBO *and* PERCY *put on their blackface makeup, each using the other as a mirror.*)

TAMBO: Last time we did this, musta been ten years ago.

PERCY: In New Haven.

TAMBO: Yeah, that's right. It was when we met. Remember that? You was standin' over by the stage door of the Park Theatre. Pattin' your feet and noddin' ya head to the music from in-side. I said to you, "Hey fella, what you doin'?" You said, "I'm listenin' to the music, fixin' to get myself a job." I said, "Where you gonna get a job at, standin' by that stage door?" You say, "I'm gonna get a job inside this theatre. Tomorrow night I'm gonna play Mr. Bones." I asked you how you gonna do that? You turn around and say, "When the manager sees me and what I can do, he's gonna fire that guy who's in there now." Then you start to rattle them bones the way you used to do. Hog bones, wasn't they? I started laughin' at you . . . and what was that you said to me?

PERCY: I said, "I see you carryin' 'round that banjo. Mabey you need a job too. You want me to get ya one playin', Mr.

Tambo?" Yeah, that was quite a night, Tambo, out in the street in the spotlight of a gas lamp.

TAMBO: I believes in the night. I believe that the night tells us everything. It's mostly in the night when we're safe. When no one can see us, like they do in the light a day. There's a feelin' that comes with the night. Seems like it only comes at night. Night's like when you was a kid, layin' on your pallet on the floor, dreamin' 'bout places. Listenin' to the whistle blow, far off on a train goin' somewheres you ain't goin'. But I could dance. Lord, I could dance and I know'd it. I can hear my daddy's fiddle now. I can see him standing up there leanin' on the porch post, playin' on his fiddle. Gettin' us to dance and jump and wear ourselves out. I wanted to be in minstrelsy badder than a little bit. I was so young and dumb and countrified, I believed for the longest time that somewhere out there, there was really colored folk, like in a minstrel show. Can you imagine that? Boy your mind is quick and big when you young. . . . That night, that's when we start to put together that "Say, Man" routine, remember that?

PERCY: Yeah, Tambo, I remember.

TAMBO: That was some doggone stump speech. What it was?

PERCY: It was the Wizard.

TAMBO: Yeah, that was it, the Wizard. How it go, again? You started it up, didn't you? Do it, Percy. Gimmie the line.

PERCY: Say man, ain't you the fella what . . .

TAMBO: Yeah, I remember you, now. It was in . . .

PERCY: That's right. The very place. It was at that place . . .

TAMBO: You know, that place ain't there no more . . .

PERCY: No foolin'? Well, why they close it?

TAMBO: It was 'cause a her.

PERCY: You mean . . .

TAMBO: The very one. They say that she . . .

PERCY: No foolin'?

TAMBO: Here's my hand . . .

PERCY: I can't believe it. It can't be true.

TAMBO: I saw her myself.

PERCY: Where at?

TAMBO: She was over there on . . .

PERCY: No, she wasn't over there.

TAMBO: Oh, I'm tellin' ya the truth, it shocked me too. She was over there with . . .

PERCY: Oh no . . .

TAMBO: And . . .

PERCY: Oh, that's a terrible bunch.

TAMBO: Yes and besides that, she had . . .

PERCY: Well, I declare. I never heard such. Was it . . .

TAMBO: Yes, indeed it was. A great big little . . .

PERCY: Oh that's nice. Perfect size. Did she happen to say who . . .

TAMBO: As a matter a fact, she did. She told me . . .

PERCY: Oh no. No way, no way.

TAMBO: Yes, she did. She said that a . . .

PERCY: It can't be true.

TAMBO: She swore on a stack a bibles. Said it was . . .

PERCY: Excuse me, cousin, but what time is it gettin'?

TAMBO: It's just the other side a half past . . .

PERCY: That late already. I better get goin'. Well . . .

TAMBO: I certainly will. And you . . .

PERCY: They'll be glad to hear it.

TAMBO: Mabey, before you go, you would . . .

PERCY: Why, certainly, I'd love to. Just let me clear my throat. . . . Ladies and Gentlemen. I stands here before you, plainly speakin' to say that what the Wizard was is what the Wizard does and what the Wizard does is the wonderment of what the Wizard was for when he opened his opus lips and paraded his oracular tongue about the capes and estuaries of his gums the owl would dare not hoot and the sparrow went to hush his beak to listen to the Wizard speak and low in his throat was a garglin', like an old hound dog 'bout to bay and as we sweetly listen dis is what the Wizard say . . . "I'll give the blind sight and make the lefties right, all the toothless'll bite and what's loose'll be tight, they'll be a Hot Time In The Old House Tonight."

TAMBO: And then we did that number, "A Hot Time In The Old Town."

PERCY: You snatched up your banjo and started playin'. Started hittin' them catguts, boy. And then you started dancin'.

TAMBO: You mean, we started dancin', swirlin' and spinnin' round and high-step prancin'. I hit that last note and you stretched out your arms and slowly let 'em fall as ya say.

PERCY: Gentlemen, be seated.

TAMBO: I drop down on that alley floor, while you stay standin', singin' that old-time minstrelsy song. Lord, it was all in the music and the night and the feelin'.

PERCY: Tonight the feelin' is kind a sad.

TAMBO: Yeah, I know it . . . But the next day, we both got that job. After that night, we were a natural. Mr. Bones and Mr. Tambo, the union of the Ends.

PERCY: It was a good act, Tambo. But as good as it was, we were never as good as that night in the alley when we was doin' it for ourselves.

TAMBO: Yeah, I know . . . I know it. Percy, I got to clear up somethin' between us. There's a wedge between you and me and I had more than my share a drivin' it. I don't know what's gonna happen tonight. I want to clear the air between you and me, so maybe we can drive out that wedge.

PERCY: Let's drive it out, Tambo.

TAMBO: "Bones and Tambo." We didn't just get us a job, we got us a bill as a speciality. Performin' in the spotlight of a made-up gas lamp. I remember how we got into many a stage door, cause a you. You was fast-talkin' and charmin'. We was a hit, Percy. I do believe we like to nearly made it. But it seemed to me like every night after that first night in the alley, I was playin' more and more in the shadows. I been jealous a you Percy. I been envious. I can't tell you why. I wasn't raised that way. I just felt like I was gettin' crumbs in your shadow. Don't get me wrong, they was good crumbs and lots a times they was sorely needed. But I was standin' in your shadow, when I should a stood up and cast a shadow a my own. When you gave up bein' Mr. Bones and puttin' on black, it didn't just cut the act, it cut me out. I even played a little pickaninny girl in the chorus, while you was the star, playin' Uncle Tom. You was good in that part, Percy. Better than the white boy. But it puzzles me how you played it. How you played a guy who loved from his heart no matter, whatever his troubles was, despite his own hardships. I know, like now, you come in here all of a sudden and decide you gonna put on black. You ain't never stop to consider that we might get tired a wearin' this stuff ourselves. I knows we had us some hard times, but you selfish and over-proud.

PERCY: I didn't know you felt that way, Tambo. I didn't know you was keepin' count, otherwise, I'd a kept a tally myself. I remember that night too. I likes the nighttime myself. That's why I was out in it. In it for the feelin'. You wasn't no more broke and hungry than me. What I had in me was mine. Just like you, I had nowheres to go with it but out back in a alley. If I can't find no way to express what I have in me, how am I gonna give it to you? Don't you got your own? Wasn't we tryin' to share it? You talk 'bout rememberin' nights. I remember a night back in Memphis. You didn't help me that night. Why didn't you do somethin'? You could've stopped it. You was just standin' there with your hands in your pockets. You could've done somethin'. Why didn't you help me then?

TAMBO: Why didn't I help you? I did help you. What else was I suppose to do? You went plumb wild and crazy, like you did today. When she told you what she had to tell you and she looked off down that platform towards that young boy. Without a sign, you took off mad as March. By the time we got down there, you had done squeezed the life out a that boy. And Rachel, she was. . . . She was beside herself. And didn't I take to the air with you. I was on the run too, you know. And not for nothin' I did. I was there with you when we was sleepin' in swamps and marshes. In barns and hollows along the roads. Meanwhile back in Memphis, that boy was just another colored boy dead. No big deal in Memphis or Hannibal here or anywheres for that matter. You didn't have to do it. You didn't have to kill that boy.

PERCY: I didn't want for it to go that way. He took from me what was mine.

TAMBO: She wasn't yours.

PERCY: What you mean, she wasn't mine?

TAMBO: She wasn't anybody's girl.

PERCY: She was my girl.

TAMBO: You just had your mind fixed on her, is all. It was what you wanted.

PERCY: She was mine.

TAMBO: No.

PERCY: How in the hell would you know?

TAMBO: I know, Percy. I know.

PERCY: Oh, I see. I see it all now. As clear as new moonshine drippin' from a midnight still. You knew way back when. From the time I got her that ring, before I wrote the song, you knew. Why didn't you say somethin' to me? Do you love it so much when I'm down, Tambo? Is it you down there sittin' in that front row seat, danglin' ya feet in that spotlight? Is it you, Tambo?

TAMBO: I don't know what to say to you, Percy. Even if you would a listened to me, I just didn't know how to tell ya. . . . It was just one night out on the town for me. You was lookin' for somethin' else. Somethin' you thought was special. I didn't believe in all that, but you did. You believed it so hard, you throwed it all, all ya dreamin' onto that girl, 'til you made yourself love her so much. Even if you would've listened to me, I didn't know how to tell you. But you got to believe one thing, here this night, Percy. I didn't know nothin' 'bout the song. I didn't have nothin' to do with whoever took your song.

PERCY: Oh, you didn't take my song. Oh, I appreciate that, anyhow. I kinda wish you hadn't taken what you just now took. . . . Sure is funny, ain't it. I was all fired up to give away that song and turn around and get mad when they just takes it from me. A word to the wise might have been sufficient. I don't mind so much bein' poor and by now I begin to grow accustomed to the scorn, but the one thing that I truly thought was mine, was the time, Tambo. The time was mine and you just took it away.

ARCHIE: Excuse me, but can I say somethin'?

SOLOMAN: Hush now, Archie.

DOC: Let the boy talk if he want to.

ARCHIE: Molly, the scrub woman. The one I told ya'll about. The one took care a me when I was little. Molly usta say, that it was wrong to fault the past for the way you livin' now, 'cause the past don't never change.

HENRY: That boy is smart. He got plenty sense. That boy is alright.

SOLOMAN: Sure he is, that's my boy. Ain't you, Archie?

ARCHIE (*Looking out window*): Yeah, Soloman. Hey it look like a lot a lights out there.

HENRY: That's the lights from some town across the river.

DOC: That can't be right, Henry. There ain't a town across the river here.

ARCHIE: I don't think so neither, 'cause these lights is movin'.

SOLOMAN (*Looking out window*): Oh, hell boys. Them lights is lanterns and torches. They done figured it out. They comin' to get us.

TAMBO: Hide in the trap, Percy.

PERCY: They gonna find me in there. They done figured it out.

DOC: Get in the trap, Percy. Go on.

TAMBO: Percy, get down in the trap.

HENRY: Get in the trap, Percy. We'll cover for ya.

PERCY: No, I'm not goin' down in there. They gonna come in here and tear this place apart lookin' for me and I don't want them draggin' me out from down in there. I don't even want 'em comin' in here.

SOLOMAN: But Percy, listen. When you get down through the trap and crawl under the car and get yaself behind the wheel, then when they come in lookin' for you, you can go on and slip off.

HENRY: That ain't gonna make it, Soloman. All them folks ain't gonna jam themselves in this parlor car. None of 'em comin' in here. They goin' to make us all go outside, you know that.

TAMBO: I know. I know what we can do, we'll all go outside. I mean, we all look the same in this blackface. They'll be confused. We'll all probably just come out with nothin' but a good ole' whippin'. I mean, he didn't hurt nobody. Nothin' really happen to anybody.

DOC: They'd just make us take off that blackface. And what about Henry? He ain't blacked up. What about him?

HENRY: If they got it all figured out and they reconize his face, I'll make out. Percy and me don't really look that much alike, anyway.

SOLOMAN: I say we hides him in the trap. There got to be a way we can hide him.

DOC: Ya'll lookin' for a needle in the haystack. Ain't no way outa this but to go outside. Lease wise Percy won't be out there by hisself . . .

PERCY: Uh, uh. Yes, I will. I'm goin' solo. It's show time ya'll. This the kind they don't never let us miss, if they can help it. We ain't the only ones out here hidin' behind this face. Them, out there, they hidin' too. For the price of admission, for a nickle some poor son of a bitch who ain't got no more hope and future than me can laugh at this ugly, miserable, stupid face and feel like he is somebody. That's why there's a show. That's why it's a blackface show. . . . Hey, Henry, how 'bout givin' me one a them cigars a yours. We'll give a little style to this routine. A bit a that moonshine wouldn't be bad for the nerves none. I wish I had me an exit line, boys . . . wait . . . I got one. Yeah, boys, it's like the time I usta barker for an old tent show. I usta say, "Hurry, hurry, step right up, ladies and gentlemen. The possibilities are endless, but the end is all the same." Good-bye boys. God bless you and good luck. (*The door slams as* PERCY *exits.*)

ARCHIE: Why he do it, Soloman? How come he went out there?

SOLOMAN: Nothin' else he can do, Archie. (*Voices of an unruly theatre audience rise.* BAKER *enters and comes down to the forestage to stomping jeers and applause.*)

BAKER: Ladies and Gentlemen! Ladies and Gentlemen! Please, Ladies and Gentlemen, please! . . . Ladies and Gentlemen, I am deeply grieved and burdened to tell you this evening that Little Tommy Parker cannot be with us tonight. He died yesterday, quietly in his home, after a long and distinguished career on the stage. In honor of his passing, we hope you will enjoy The Little Tommy Parker Celebrated Colored Minstrel Show!

END

RE/MEMBERING
AUNT JEMIMA:
A Menstrual Show

Breena Clarke.
Glenda Dickerson

GLENDA DICKERSON, director, writer, folklorist, educator, and actor, has directed such actors as Debbie Allen, Lynn Whitfield, Charles Brown, Phillip Michael Thomas, and Robert Townsend. She has worked on Broadway, Off-Broadway, regionally, and internationally. Dickerson has conceived and/or adapted numerous vehicles for the stage from various dramatic and nondramatic sources, including *Jesus Christ, Lawd Today, Owen's Song: The Unfinished Song, Rashomon, Torture of Mothers, Jump at the Sun, El Hajj Malik*, and *Every Step I Take*. Dickerson also conceived and directed *Eel Catching in Setauket: A Living Portrait of a Community*, an oral history, creative performance project that documents the lives of the African-American Christian Avenue community in Setauket, Long Island.

She has performed two original, one-woman shows, *Saffron Persephone Brown: The Flower-Storm of a Brown Woman* and *Spreading Lies*, as well as acting in *The Trojan Women, a Tale of Devastation for Two Voices*.

Glenda Dickerson is a professor and chairperson of the Department of Drama at Spelman College. She lives in Atlanta, Georgia.

BREENA CLARKE, founding artistic director of The Narratives Performing Company, is a writer, actress, and journalist whose career as an arts professional has been quite varied. She made her Broadway acting debut in *Reggae* in 1980, and has appeared with several Off-Broadway theater companies. Clarke's directorial and acting work has appeared at the First and Second National Festivals of Women's Theater in 1983 and 1984, and on many college and university campuses. She has worked as an Equity stage manager and has taught acting and speech at The Duke Ellington School of the Arts in Washington, D. C. Ms. Clarke is assistant to the Deputy Managing Editor of *Time* magazine and Associate Editor of *Black Masks* magazine. Her writings have appeared in *Heresies: A Feminist Publication on Art and Politics, Conditions, Quarto*, and *Women and Performance*. She is currently completing a novel about black life and experience in Washington, D. C. *Re/Membering Aunt Jemima, a Menstrual Show* received its world premiere at the Lorraine Hansberry Theater in San Francisco, California, in 1992. Breena Clarke lives in New York City.

All roles are played by Menstruals 1, 2, 3, 4, and 5. The role of La Madama Interlock-It-Togetherer remains constant. All the other roles are divided up variously among the other four Menstruals.

Playmagicianwrights' Notes

Only the black woman can say "when and where I enter, in the quiet, undisputed dignity of my womanhood, without violence and without suing or special patronage, then and there the whole Negro race enters with me."

—Anna Julia Cooper

Contemporary Black women are all but invisible in a popular culture and society which fears and loathes us unless we can be fitted comfortably into a recognizable stereotype: the Mammy, the Sapphire, the Jezebel, the Tragic Mulatta. The playmagicianwrights chose to use the minstrel format and its most potent device—innovative word-play (malapropisms, puns, conundrums, and double entendres) in an attempt to write Black female identity into existence on the world stage. Thus, this postmodern Menstrual Show is created to provide a "place" or context for the latter-day African-American woman performer.

—Breena Clarke
Glenda Dickerson

Act One

(The stage is bare. The space is somehow reminiscent of a circus or carnival sideshow. The lighting is harsh, such as would be found in an old-time minstrel show.)

LA MADAMA INTERLOCK-IT-TOGETHERERER: Stereotypes, be seated!
Contrary women and sympathetic gents.
I extend a welcome on behalf of the greatest show on earth:
THE AUNT JEMIMA TRAVELING MENSTRUAL SHOW!!!!!!!
We have come out tonight to bring you an evening of oddities, peculiarities, eccentricities, and comicalities of the distaff side of the Sable Genus of Humanity. We will fondly reminisce about the lovable bright side of Negro life down on Col. Uncle Sam Higbee's sunny plantation, home of Aunt Jemima, the Grand Mammy of American myth. With bones on the right and tambourines on the left, we begin.

(COMPANY sings)
WE ARE HERE TO PERFORM AN ACT OF MAGIC, WE ARE
HERE TO PERFORM AN ACT OF MAGIC.
WE'RE GOING TO WEAR THE MASK
OF THE JOLLY MAMMY
PITCH OURSELVES
OFF THE PANCAKE BOX.
WE'RE GOING TO FIND OURSELVES,
LOVE OURSELVES,
IN THE BIG, FAT MAMMY OF LIES.
OH, MAMMY, DON'T YOU KNOW
WE'LL RESCUE YOU WITH MAGIC

DON'T YOU KNOW WE'LL SALVAGE YOUR BAD NAME
WHO DO WE HATE?
LET'S PULL OURSELVES TOGETHER
WHY DO WE HATE?
LET'S GIVE IT ONE MORE TRY
WE'RE GOING TO PULL OURSELVES TOGETHER
AND NOT HATE OURSELVES
PULL OURSELVES TOGETHER
SO WE'LL FEEL ALRIGHT
WE ARE HERE TO PERFORM AN ACT OF MAGIC
AN ACT OF MAGIC TO PERFORM.

(*A skirmish breaks out between two* MENSTRUALS.)

MENSTRUAL: You is just a creature of white imagination.

MENSTRUAL: You ole house nigger! I'll defile and mutilate your body until you look just like Bo Akutia!

LA MADAMA INTERLOCK-IT-TOGETHERERER: Mistresses! I will not put up with this ingenious vituperation by proxy. Go back to your scats. We will now present a true copy of the ups and downs in the life of Aunt Jemima, the most famous colored woman in the world.

MENSTRUAL: Aunt Jemima was born in a box.

MENSTRUAL: She was discovered covered with feces . . .

MENSTRUAL: And branded with the letters KKK.

MENSTRUAL: She never did get over that sad beginning.

LA MADAMA INTERLOCK-IT-TOGETHERER: Her parents are unknown and she just sprung up on Col. Uncle Sam Higbee's plantation.

YOUNG JEMIMA: I was naked as a jaybird until I was 12.

MENSTRUAL: A humble old fellow named Uncle Ben worked in the fields on Col. Higbee's plantation. He was from Sara Leeon and knew everything there was to know about growing rice.

MENSTRUAL: Hadn't been for Ben, Col. Higbee would've been groanin' stead of growing rice.

MENSTRUAL: Uncle Tom was the butterler in the Big House. He knew how to read and conducted secret services for the other slaves in the arbor by the stream.

MENSTRUAL: Who keeps snakes and all bad things from hurting you?

MENSTRUALS: God does.

MENSTRUAL: Who gave you a master and a mistress?

MENSTRUALS: God gave them to me.

MENSTRUAL: If the master be unreasonable, may the servant disobey?

MENSTRUALS: No.

MENSTRUAL: (*Sung.*) No no no no! (*Spoken.*) The Bible says, "Servant, be subject to your masters with all fear."

(*Singing*)
I AM A POOR PILGRIM OF SORROW
I'M LEFT IN THIS WIDE WORLD TO ROAM
NO HOPE HAVE I FOR TOMORROW
I STARTED TO MAKE HEAVEN MY HOME.

MENSTRUAL: Oh let us pray, for an end to suffering, for no more beatings, and for shoes to fit on our feet.

MENSTRUALS: (*singing*):
NO HOPE HAVE I FOR TOMORROW
I STARTED TO MAKE HEAVEN MY HOME.

MENSTRUAL: From a very young child, Jemima would see things dart by out of the corner of her eye. Sometimes she felt something watching her over her shoulder.

MENSTRUAL: Uncle Tom told her it was nothing but the devil. But a maroon woman name of Nanny knew it was the Three Blood Mysteries.

YOUNG JEMIMA: Who dat?

NANNY: Who dat?

YOUNG JEMIMA: Who dat?

NANNY: Who dat?

YOUNG JEMIMA: Who dat say who dat when I say who dat?

NANNY: Dat yo' womanhood coming down on you.

LA MADAMA INTERLOCK-IT-TOGETHERERER (*singing*): I am menarche!

MENSTRUALS: Nanny, Nanny, Bomanny. Banana, fanna, fo-fanny.
Fee fi momanny, Nanny!
Sees her comes and sees her goes.
Sees her ass the bullet throws.

LA MADAMA INTERLOCK-IT-TOGETHERERER: Nanny was renumerated to be able to catch bullets with her ass-perity. She was

HNIC in the kitchen. Jemima was her Novitiate Scotiate. When Nanny put on her necklace of English soldiers' teeth and decided to fly back to Africa,

MENSTRUAL (*singing*): Geechee, Geechee Geechee Ya Ya Ya Ya Oohh!

LA MADAMA INTERLOCK-IT-TOGETHERERER: Jemima became head cook. Jemima soon developed a repetitious as a fast, efficient cook with a repertoirishus of delicious dishes, but her skilletacious with pancakes brought her the most refrown. Other Mammy cooks tried in vain to get her famous recipe. When them rascals come up against Jemima's irascible nature, they give up in disrepair.

YOUNG JEMIMA: Griddle cakes pipin' hot! Come and get 'em.

MENSTRUAL: Col. Higbee was forever sniffin' 'round the kitchen cause he couldn't get enough of them delicious pancakes. Miss Ann suspicioned that his hunger went beyond a simple hankering for pancakes.

MENSTRUALS (*singing*):
SOMEONE'S IN THE KITCHEN WITH DINAH
SOMEONE'S IN THE KITCHEN, I KNOW.
SOMEONE'S IN THE KITCHEN WITH DINAH
STRUMMIN' ON THE OLD BANJO.
FE FI FIDDLE DI OH, FE FI FIDDLE DI OH
FE FI FIDDLE DI OH,
STRUMMIN' ON THE OLD BANJO.

(MENSTRUAL *chases* AUNT JEMIMA *with Col. Higbee puppet*.)

YOUNG JEMIMA: Lawd, Col. Higbee, I don't know nothin' about birthin' no babies.

LA MADAMA INTERLOCK-IT-TOGETHERERER: The birth of that baby was any-minunint. So Col. Higbee sent for the midwife.

MENSTRUAL (*conjuring—singing*): Amazing Grace, how sweet the sound.

LA MADAMA INTERLOCK-IT-TOGETHERERER (*singing*):
The first of Aunt Jemima's thirteen daughters was named Dorothy.

MENSTRUAL (*singing*):
MY OLD MAN WAS A WHITE OLD MAN
MY OLD MAMMY'S BLACK,
WONDER WHAT I'M GONNA DO

BEING NEITHER WHITE NOR BLACK
I GOT THE BLUES.

LA MADAMA INTERLOCK-IT-TOGETHERERER (*sing simultaneously*):
THAT BABY POPPED FROM UNDER HER MAMA'S SKIRT
SINGING THE BLUES.

LA MADAMA AND MENSTRUAL (*singing*):
I GOT THE TRAGIC MULATTA BLUES.

MENSTRUAL: Col. Uncle Sam Higbee kept eating a steady diet of his favorite pancakes.

YOUNG JEMIMA: Pancakes with a personality!

LA MADAMA INTERLOCK-IT-TOGETHERERER: And he whipped up three more daughters in Aunt Jemima's mixing bowl: Marie, a child born with a rattlesnake in her hand. Pecola, a little red baby who bawled melodramatically all the time. And Dysmorfia, who was half black and half white, but the black skin didn't show as long as she kept her clothes on.

MENSTRUAL: Col. Higbee was sitting on the porch one day, sipping on Southern Comfort and watching his four beautiful but mixed-up daughters.

LA MADAMA INTERLOCK-IT-TOGETHERERER: Marie's skirts made a superstitious swishing sound as she danced to music in her head.

MENSTRUAL: The other three was sitting in the sunlight trying to tame their mama's naps, fussing at her all the time.

AUNT JEMIMA: What you gals doin' here? Ain't you got nothing better to do than fool with my naps?

PECOLA: Want to sit with somebody uglier than me.

AUNT JEMIMA: What's de mattah wid you? Fore we come across de water, everybody look lak me. I ain't ugly. You just thinks I is.

PECOLA: Yes, ma'am, you is. Your lips is too big. Dey looks lak bees been stingin' you.

DYSMORFIA: My lips is too big, too, but you can't tell cause I holds em in like this.

AUNT JEMIMA: Don't be ridiculous. Why you got all dat cornstarch on your face?

DYSMORFIA: In case de black creep out from underneath my clothes.

DOROTHY: Mammy, how come you ain't 'shamed of the way you look? How come you always so happy?

AUNT JEMIMA: Ain't got nothing to be ashamed 'bout. I got pretty black skin, I got a beautiful, long neck, I got a fine, rounded shape. I got plenty to smile about.

MENSTRUAL: Does it seem to you lake dem gals favors Miss Ann's towheaded chillun?

LA MADAMA INTERLOCK-IT-TOGETHERERER: Yep, das why she made Col. Uncle Sam sell 'em off de place.

(*Laughter.*)
Bid 'em in, bid 'em in.
We got fine ones, tall ones, black ones too,
brown ones, yellow ones just for you.
Bid 'em in! Bid 'em in!
We got young ones old ones, babies too,
fine mulatta gals tried and true.
Bid 'em in, bid 'em in.

MENSTRUAL: Dorothy was sold to Paramount Pictures, where she became a tragic star. She committed suicide at a young age and asked to be buried as they found her—scarf, gloves, and underwear intact. Marie was sold as a "fancy gal" to High John de Conquer in New Orleans. Dysmorfia and Pecola was sold as a matched pair, but Pecola soon escaped and passed for white up North.

THE DAUGHTERS: Mam, Mam, Mammy, goodbye.
Mam, Mam, Mammy, don't cry.
Goodbye Ma!

LA MADAMA INTERLOCK-IT-TOGETHERERER: As Jemima watched her girls carted off, she wrapped her half-combed naps in a old greasy rag. She looked Col. Higbee in the eye and grinned a grin so brilliantine that it could flatten out naps dead straight.

MENSTRUALS: From this day forth Jemima became known as "Auntie."

(*Menstruals sing "16 Tons"*)

LA MADAMA INTERLOCK-IT-TOGETHERERER: Long about this time, a big slave name of Two Ton arrived on the plantation. Two Ton got his name 'cause he could pick two ton of cotton any day of the week.

(MENSTRUALS *enter with two bales of cotton.*)

(AUNT JEMIMA sings *"Some Enchanted Evening"*)

(MENSTRUALS *sing "16 tons"*)

MENSTRUAL: Two Ton was constantly trying to outdo himself in the weight of cotton he could pick. (*Sung.*) Col. Higbee discombobulated the balls on the weighing machine so that the bolls Two Ton picked needed an ever-increasing weight of balls to balance 'em. Pretty soon the man bust his balls pickin' them bolls. Oh, he bust his balls picking them bolls.

LA MADAMA INTERLOCK-IT-TOGETHERERER: Two Ton died with his hammer in his hand. But he left Aunt Jemima with three little hammers to remember him by:

MENSTRUAL (*sings simultaneously*): He bust his balls picking them bolls.

LA MADAMA INTERLOCK-IT-TOGETHERERER: Anna Julia, a woman who risked all to learn to read; Rebecca, a strangely beautiful child called by the thunder to preach to free Black slaves; and Bondswoman, a girl with freedom on her mind. Nothin' but freedom on her mind, she had nothin' but freedom on her mind. Bondswoman!

MENSTRUAL: I will follow the North Star and the moss on the trees.

(MENSTRUAL *sings "Feet Don't Fail Her Now"*)

(*As* BONDSWOMAN *flees for freedom she encounters* MEDICINE WOMEN, HAIRDRESSERS, *and other adventurers.* MENSTRUAL 2 *sings "Feet Don't Fail Her Now."*)

LA MADAMA INTERLOCK-IT-TOGETHERERER: And now, Contrary Women, FOR SALE, CONGO SQUARE SNAKE OIL! CONGO SQUARE SNAKE OIL! CONGO SQUARE SNAKE OIL! An ointment of power and purity. You can take it for relief from those monthly discomforts; take it to cool off from those private summers; take it to soothe the mysterious misery of the rainy-season clitoridectomy. Congo Square Snake Oil! COON GRIN CONKOLENE! COON GRIN CONKOLENE! It will flatten out naps dead straight. It will flatten out naps dead straight! Mistresses and creatrix, all diminutives must fade 'cause Madam C. J. Moonwalker knew best the tricks of the tress stress trade.

(MENSTRUALS *sing "Feets Don't Fail Her Now" and "Flatten out Naps Dead Straight" in duet style.*)

MENSTRUAL: Chilluns! Get yo' Aunt Jemima Rag Doll Family!

LA MADAMA INTERLOCK-IT-TOGETHERER: What're you doing sprinkling salt and pepper on those babies?

MENSTRUAL: I'm seasonin' 'em up. So's they'll be fit for the hog meat gang. These is goin' to be A-number-one pickaninnies.

LA MADAMA INTERLOCK-IT-TOGETHERER: But you don't season them up by putting salt on them.

MENSTRUAL: Huh!

LA MADAMA INTERLOCK-IT-TOGETHERER: You're supposed to fatten them up with choice victuals and give them only light tasks until their bodies are strong and fit for hard labor.

MENSTRUAL: Oh.

LA MADAMA INTERLOCK-IT-TOGETHERER: A smart master like Col. Higbee knows you get your money's worth out a slave if you season them up right from the start.

MENSTRUAL: Cardamon bay thyme o-reg-an-o allspice?

LA MADAMA INTERLOCK-IT-TOGETHERER: O-REG-a-no Rosemary bay garlic and thyme.

MENSTRUAL: Back down on the plantation, Aunt Jemima went out every night, and looked down the road her daughter had traveled. One night from out de moonlight step a smooth brown man of mystery.

(MENSTRUAL *sets down a bottle of Karo Syrup near* AUNT JEMIMA.)

MENSTRUAL: This smooth, brown man of mystery was dripping wet 'cause he just swim from Dominica. He whispered to Aunt Jemima how he could make a thick, smooth, sweet syrup he'd concocted in the islands that would glide slowly and flavorfully down a stack of she pancake. "Karo, Karo syrup." This famous, secret syrup "Karo" with its husky, sweet flavor made a fitting accompaniment to Aunt Jemima's delicious American breakfast.

MENSTRUAL: Ooo-wee! How she loved she Karo!

(*Singing*)
KARO, KARO SYRUP
HOW SHE LOVED HER KARO
KARO, KARO SYRUP
HOW SHE LOVED HER KARO.

LA MADAMA INTERLOCK-IT-TOGETHERER: All in due time, Bonds-woman came back over her Great Underground Railroad. She discovered that she had three new husky, sweet sisters: Sap-phire, "I will not be tamed by any man"; Susie-Faye, "I will be-come president of the Planned Parenthood Confederate-ation of America"; and the newborn baby, Freedom Fighter. (*MEN-STRUAL does rap beat box sound.*) "When I grow up I'm gonna be involved in so many slave revolts and shootouts I'm gonna be on the FBI most wanted list."

MENSTRUAL: Where in the name of wonder, did all these mokes come from? (*Karo Music theme played.*)

LA MADAMA INTERLOCK-IT-TOGETHERER: Bondswoman gathered up her new sisters and a whole lot other mokes. And led them all out to the Promised Land.

MENSTRUAL: Well head 'em up and move 'em out.

MENSTRUALS: (*singing*):
O FREEDOM
O FREEDOM
O FREEDOM OVER ME
BEFORE I'LL BE A SLAVE
I'LL BE BURIED IN MY GRAVE
AND GO HOME TO MY LORD AND BE FREE
AND GO HOME TO MY LORD AND BE FREE.

(*All bid goodbye to* AUNT JEMIMA— *"Oh Freedom" repeats.*)

MENSTRUAL: Aunt Jemima continued as Higbee plantation cook.

LA MADAMA INTERLOCK-IT-TOGETHERER: Whenever there were guests, Aunt Jemima was called upon to make huge stacks of her fluffy, light pancakes.

MENSTRUAL: Coax as long as dey might, guests at Col. Higbee's plantation never could get out of her the secret flavor of dem wonderful pancakes.

AUNT JEMIMA: That's my secret, you just eat 'em.

LA MADAMA INTERLOCK-IT-TOGETHERER: When the great War Between the States broke out, Aunt Jemima, Uncle Tom, and Uncle Ben was the only darkies who stayed on the place. Uncle Ben and Aunt Jemima kept each other warm at night and they steamed up two little twin converted rice cakes: Aminata, a headstrong girl full of determination, and Anita, a tall, beautiful, serious scholar.

MENSTRUAL: Emancipation came like a bolt out of the blue. Uncle Ben decided to walk back to Africa and took Aminata with him. Uncle Tom hitchhiked up to the Yarvard Law School to begin meretricious matriculation. Anita went with him to learn at his feet. Bye, Ma!

AUNT JEMIMA: Bye, baby!

MENSTRUALS (*singing*):
KUMBAYA, MY LORD, KUMBAYA
OH, LORD, KUMBAYA.

LA MADAMA INTERLOCK-IT-TOGETHERER: So it was just Aunt Jemima left on the plantation with Col. Uncle Sam. Col. Uncle was so poor he didn't know what to do. Then one day R. T. Davis of the Davis Milling company went ashore at Higbee Landing and tasted Aunt Jemima's scrumptious pancakes. He flipped out.

MENSTRUAL: Ooh wee! Gosh oh! Gosh dern! Hot dern!

LA MADAMA INTERLOCK-IT-TOGETHERER: He persuaded Col. to let Aunt Jemima share her recipe with others. Col. said he would consider it for a price. And so Aunt Jemima left her home to begin her travels up and down America. Aunt Jemima was interdicted to the world at the World's Columbian Exposition in 1893 . . .

MENSTRUALS:
PANCAKE DAYS IN HERE AGAIN,
MM, MMM, MMM, MMM,
MM, MMM, MMM, MMM
PANCAKE DAYS IN HERE AGAIN,
MM, MMM, MMM, MMM,
MM, MMM, MMM.

AUNT JEMIMA: I'se in town, honey. I'se around.

MENSTRUAL: R. T. Davis set her up in a booth in The Great Agricultural Hall to advertise his new packaged pancake mix based on Aunt Jemima's own recipe.

MENSTRUAL: Everybody was there at the World's Fair. All the well-known speakers and great doers of the African peoples was there. Paul Laurence Dunbar:

MENSTRUAL: Jump back, honey, jump back.

MENSTRUAL: W. E. B. Du Bois:

MENSTRUAL: The problem of the 20th century, is the problem of the color line.

MENSTRUAL: Frederick Douglass:

MENSTRUAL: It was the blood-stained gate, the entrance to the hell of slavery, through which I was about to pass.

MENSTRUAL: And Ida B. Wells:

MENSTRUAL: A Winchester rifle should have a place of honor in every home.

MENSTRUAL: But the center of all this was Aunt Jemima. Eerybody at the Fair wanted to taste them golden brown cakes. She was a sensation!

AUNT JEMIMA: Lawsy, we ain't never goin' to be able to make enough pancakes for all dem white folks.

LA MADAMA INTERLOCK-IT-TOGETHERER: Aunt Jemima flipped more than one million pancakes and gave each one an identity by telling antidotes of how all America had come to love her pancakes.

AUNT JEMIMA: Ole Miss Ann was mighty hard on us niggers. She would take a needle and stick it through my lower lip and pin it to the bodice of my dress and I'd have to go roun' all day with my head drew down that a way and slobberin. It felt like I was goin' crazy. (*All laugh uproariously.*)

MENSTRUAL: Aunt Jemima, your cheerful demeanor has much to do with the popularity of your pancakes. They have become America's favorite breakfast. Aunt Jemima, the committee on awards bestows upon your pancake flour the highest medal and the diploma of excellence.

LA MADAMA INTERLOCK-IT-TOGETHERER: But honors did not turn her head.

AUNT JEMIMA: Dis honor should go to Col. Higbee. His kind words spoken to me years and years ago, expressing his appreciation for my loyalty and cheerful service, mean more to me than my present fame. But when R. T. Davis offered me the opportunity to make so many families happy with the ease and satisfaction of serving my mouth-watering pancakes—it was irresistible. My pancakes delighted Col. Higbee and his guests. Here they are delighting thousands. Thank you.

LA MADAMA INTERLOCK-IT-TOGETHERER: While Aunt Jemima was flipping pancakes, she could hear true women in the tent next door—lifting as they climbed.

MENSTRUAL: We now issue the call to all the women's bodies throughout the country. The time is short, but everything is ripe. Remember, earnest women can do anything.

MENSTRUALS (*singing*):
LIFT EV'RY VOICE AND SING
'TIL EARTH AND HEAVEN RING.

AUNT JEMIMA: Her is a veri-table paramour of genuine ass-ets. (*As* COL. HIGBEE.) She put her ass-ets on ma table and Ah'm gwine to kick her veri-ass-ity. (*As* AUNT JEMIMA.) Colonel!

MENSTRUAL: The painful, patient, and silent toil of mothers to gain a fee, simple title to the bodies of their daughters, the despairing fight, as of an entrapped tigress, to keep hallowed their own persons, would furnish material for epics.

MENSTRUAL: Only the black woman can say, "When and where I enter, in the quiet, undisputed dignity of my womanhood, without violence and without suing or special patronage, then and there the whole Negro race enters with me."

AUNT JEMIMA: Her is the legiti-mate of the spurious equivocator. (*Imitating the voice of* COL. HIGBEE.) . . . but I don't care who huh husband is, she better not be quivocatin' in my face. (*As* AUNT JEMIMA.) Colonel!

MENSTRUAL: Remember, earnest woman can do anything.

MENSTRUAL: Ladies, shall we step next door and sample Aunt Jemima's temptalatin comestibles?

MENSTRUAL (*as* ANNA JULIA): Compositivelytrary not! I would rather leave public life.

MENSTRUAL: When Aunt Jemima laid eyes on the speechifyer, seemed like to her it was the little girl who risqued all to learn to read.

AUNT JEMIMA: Anna, Anna, child is that you? Anna Julia Two Ton!

ANNA JULIA: O, Mammy, all through the darkest period of the colored women's oppression in this country, a period full of heroic struggle, a struggle against fearful and overwhelming odds that often ended in a horrible death, I have prayed to once again see your greasy face.

LA MADAMA INTERLOCK-IT-TOGETHERER: And so, Aunt Jemima is reunited with her daughter, Anna Julia, who became a founding member of the National Association of Colored Women and a proponent of the tenets of the cult of true womanhood.

AUNT JEMIMA AND TRUE WOMEN (*singing*): (First verse of "Lift Every Voice and Sing")
No more auction block for me
No more auction block
No more auction block for me; no more auction block for me
Facing the rising sun of a new day begun
Let us march on, til victory is won
No more auction block for me
No more auction block for me
No more auction block for me; no more aucton block for me!

LA MADAMA INTERLOCK-IT-TOGETHERER: After the World's Fair, Aunt Jemima served as the official trademark for The Davis Milling Company's pancake flour for three decades. She became a traveling spokesperson spreading the word of her clean, sweet, pure pancake flour.

AUNT JEMIMA: My pancake flour is made in a sanitary napkin mill by millers of long experience. At the Aunt Jemima mills the ingredients are exactly mixed as ah once mixed them by hand. Other manufacturers have sought the secret of my famous pancakes. They've never achieved it. Lawsy, they never will.

MENSTRUAL: Aunt Jemima's personal appearances soon made her smiling face a familiar sight to all Americans. She appeared in advertisements and commercials all over the world.

AUNT JEMIMA: Wake up, wake up to Aunt Jemima's old south recipe. Pancakes so light! So tender! They melt in your mouth.

MENSTRUAL: Aunt Jemima even published a book of her famous recipes called *Aunt Jemima's New Temptalatin' Menus and Recipes*.

LA MADAMA INTERLOCK-IT-TOGETHERER: Weary from her world travels, Aunt Jemima loved to take the Orange Blossom Special home to her little shack at Col. Higbee's. After soaking the tiredness out of her feet with epsom salts, she would put them up and listen to the "Amos 'n' Andy" show. That was Aunt Jemima's favorite show 'cause her daughter, Sapphire, had a starring role. One Sunday night, while she was chuckling over Sapphire's muleheaded ways, Aunt Jemima got a shock. She heard on the radio that R. T. Davis had hired out her services to the Quaker Oats man.

MENSTRUAL: Aunt Jemima decided she better pay the Quaker Oats man a visit to take his measurements. She fortified herself with a pint of Jack Daniel's and rolled her Thunderbird through the rolling hills of Rolling Rock till she come to the Quaker Oats man's house. She found him to be susceptible to Friendly Persuasion and he egregiously a-greed to introduce her famous buckwheat pancakes to the world.

AUNT JEMIMA (*singing*): A surprise from the good old days. Buckwheats with the taste men hanker for. Mornings when the windowpanes are frosty, a hankering comes to men—a longing for the tang and robust savor of real, old-time buckwheats. Perhaps your husband says nothing whatever about it. Perhaps he himself does not know just how tempting, how delicious, good old-fashioned buckwheats really are. But deep down in all men there is a sparkle of youth waiting to be awakened at the breakfast table and millions of women right now are wakening it—giving their husbands light, fluffy cakes with the true, old-fashioned buckwheat kick. Man, you don't know what you've been missin'.

LA MADAMA INTERLOCK-IT-TOGETHERER: When the politically incorrect, internationally acclaimed Aunt Jemima diversified, she made so much money that she bought herself a full-length mink coat and hired herself a chauffeur to drive her around in her Cadillac convertible.

MENSTRUAL: However, those who knew her best, those who knew her even from the time when she first came up from her little cabin home, found her still the same simple, earnest, smiling Mammy cook.

AUNT JEMIMA (*tipsy from champagne*): I'se in town, honey. I'se around!

LA MADAMA INTERLOCK-IT-TOGETHERER: The new celebrity-fide Aunt Jemima was called to represent her race in many different forums, ranging from county hog-calling contests to the Miss America pageant.

(*A crowned Miss America enters.*)

MENSTRUAL: I'm not going to be a bitch with a problem or a ho' with an attitude. Just because I have a crown on my head, doesn't mean my perception is different from anyone else. I'm going to live the life I sing about in my song.

LA MADAMA INTERLOCK-IT-TOGETHERER, MENSTRUAL (*singing*): I'M GOING TO SING IT IN MY SONG.

AUNT JEMIMA (*entering drunk and disorderly*): Dysmorfia, is that you gal, up there showing everything you should hide. Ah never thought a child of mine would act so common. You better come over here and sit down before ah miss your america for you. Why ya'll don't just bring in the auction block and sell 'em all together?

LA MADAMA INTERLOCK-IT-TOGETHERER: Aunt Jemima, why don't you come backstage. We have some black coffee for you.

(*Officials try to calm* AUNT JEMIMA.)

AUNT JEMIMA: You better get your hands off of me! Somebody get me a Coca-Cola!

(*singing*)
I'SE IN TOWN, HONEY.
I'SE AROUND
SMOKING HOT, DELICIOUS AND BROWN
MY OLD FASHIONED PANCAKES HAVE BROUGHT ME RE-KNOWN
YOUR GROCER HAS A FRESH SUPPLY,
NOW THAT FALL IS HERE.
MY GRIDDLE CAKES PIPING HOT
WILL BRING YOUR FAMILY CHEER.
I'SE IN TOWN, HONEY
I'SE AROUND!

LA MADAMA INTERLOCK-IT-TOGETHERER: Oh yeah, I'se in town, I'se around; isn't she wonderful? Thank you, thank you! Get off the goddamn stage! (*Menstruals take off* AUNT JEMIMA.)

Contrary Women and Sympathetic Gents. We beg your indulgence in observing the following rules of hall. We implore you to scratch, belch, nurse your children, hoot, holler, and sing along with the players. Ladies, if during our brief intermission you feel the need to urinate, don't be daunted by the long lines in the public accommodations of this hall. Feel free to use one of the many chamberpots placed discreetly throughout the house. Gentlemen, feel free to urinate wherever you wish as you are accustomed to doing. But whatever your pleasure, don't tarry too long because we'll be back with more of the Aunt Jemima Traveling Menstrual Show!

(*End Act One*)

Act Two

MENSTRUAL (*singing*): I got catbones, I got please have mercy candles, I got Florida water, I got enemy go away dust, I got High John de Conquer root.

I am Menopause. I will change your life in a hot flash.
I am Menopause. I will change your life in a hot flash, hot flash.

AUNT JEMIMA *and* MENSTRUALS (*singing*):
IT SEEMS TOO GOOD TO BE TRUE
THAT RAGTIME FEVER'S DYING OUT
SEEMS TOO GOOD TO BE TRUE
SEEMS TOO GOOD TO BE TRUE

IT SEEMS TOO GOOD TO BE TRUE
THAT RAGTIME FEVER'S DYING OUT
SEEMS TOO GOOD TO BE TRUE (*Including All* MENSTRUALS)
SEEMS TOO GOOD TO BE TRUE
AND WE SYNCOPATED, HYPNOTIC SENTIMENTALISTS
WILL SOON RETURN TO OUR BARBARIC HAUNTS

SEEMS TOO GOOD TO BE TRUE
SEEMS TOO GOOD TO BE TRUE
IT SEEMS TOO GOOD TO BE TRUE; THAT RAGTIME FEVER
    IS DYING OUT
SEEMS TOO GOOD TO BE TRUE; IT SEEMS TOO GOOD TO
    BE TRUE!

LA MADAMA INTERLOCK-IT-TOGETHERER: Aunt Jemima, America's Grand Mammy of lies, remained true to fact and tradi-

160

tion. Tinseltown beckoned. Beating out scores of imitators, Aunt Jemima won the coveted role of the faithful colored retainer in an epic motion picture of the old south.

MENSTRUAL: And the winner for Best Actress in a Supporting Role is: Aunt Jemima.

AUNT JEMIMA: Thank you, friends, Coloreds . . .

MENSTRUAL (*whispers*): colleagues.

AUNT JEMIMA: . . . colleagues and members of the Academy. Ah hope that my winning this award will be an insurrection . . .

MENSTRUAL (*whispers*): inspiration.

AUNT JEMIMA: . . . inspiration to the youth of my race, that it will encourage them to aim high and work hard, and take the bitter with the sweet. Ah did my best and God did the rest.

LA MADAMA INTERLOCK-IT-TOGETHERER: Back down on the plantation, Aunt Jemima was polishing her Oscar and eatin' on a watermelon when she swallowed a seed. Her stomach growed and growed and growed and growed until a tiny little baby burst out of her mouth.

MENSTRUAL: That tiny little baby was the spittin' image of her mama. That's how Aunt Jemima got her thirteenth daughter.

MENSTRUALS (*singings*):
HALLELUJAH, HALLELUJAH . . .

MENSTRUAL: I was an Aunt Jemima Cake Mix Miracle conception, cause Menopause had long since changed her life and plus Aunt Jemima didn't have no man! Nobody was nommo surprised than Aunt Jemima, but she just accepted the miraculous me, and named tiny little baby me Tiny Little Desiree.

MENSTRUAL: One day while Aunt Jemima was changing Tiny Desiree's diapers, her new Princess telephone rang. It was *Time* magazine calling.

LA MADAMA INTERLOCK-IT-TOGETHERER: Aunt Jemima! Aunt Jemima! Your daughter Aminata has fled Africa and thrown herself on the mercy of the World Court. She says she ain't having no clitoridectomy.

AUNT JEMIMA: Clitoridectomy? What dat?

LA MADAMA INTERLOCK-IT-TOGETHERERER: Dat's when dey cuts off your whosit.

AUNT JEMIMA: Who sit? What sat?

LA MADAMA INTERLOCK-IT-TOGETHERERER: Whosit is the whatsit what sits where Au Set sat.

AUNT JEMIMA: Where das at?

LA MADAMA INTERLOCK-IT-TOGETHERERER: Fool, it down dere 'tween your thingamabob and your thingamajig.

AUNT JEMIMA: Naw ! You inFlBulatin'!

LA MADAMA INTERLOCK-IT-TOGETHERERER: If youse a female you don't suppose da mention it.

AUNT JEMIMA: Now dat yo mention it, I do 'blieve I'se heard of dat.

LA MADAMA INTERLOCK-IT-TOGETHERERER: Uncle Ben say she got to have a clitoridectomy before she gets married.

AUNT JEMIMA: O-o-oh! Hush you mouf. Has she got the nervousness?

LA MADAMA INTERLOCK-IT-TOGETHERERER: No!

AUNT JEMIMA: Has she got the *catalepsy*?

LA MADAMA INTERLOCK-IT-TOGETHERERER: No!

AUNT JEMIMA: She been hysterical?

LA MADAMA INTERLOCK-IT-TOGETHERERER: No!

AUNT JEMIMA: Oh, Lord, don't tell me my chile's been masturbatin'! (*Falls out in a dead faint.*)

(*Carnival sounds are heard.*)

LA MADAMA INTERLOCK-IT-TOGETHERERER: It was Fat Tuesday in the Cathedral of St. John de Divine. De Hoodoo Queen of New Orleans come to hold a big celebration for de folks at midnight. Her skirts swished when she walked and all de folks stepped back and whisper,

MENSTRUALS: "Das de mos powerful woman dere is."

LA MADAMA INTERLOCK-IT-TOGETHERERER: And now ladies and gentlemen, the moment we has all been waitin' for. The Hoodoo Queen of New Orleans will sing her latest platinum hit. She will be backed up as always by the world-famous Three Blood Mysteries!

(HOODOO QUEEN *enters to beat of drums.*)

HOODOO QUEEN AND THREE BLOOD MYSTERIES (*singing*):
HAVE YOU HEARD OF MOTHER EARTH?
SHE WANDERED IN THE GREAT GULF
TO GIVE US LAW
AND SEARCH FOR HER CHILD.
HER LAP IS WHERE WE SIT—IS WHERE WE'RE AT.
HER BED, FROM WHERE WE GET OUR LAWS
IS THE PLACE OF BIRTH
OF SLEEP
AND DREAMING,
OF LOVE
OF LOVE
AND DEATH.
ALWAYS,
EVERYWHERE.
WIDE-LEGGED EARTH,
EVER-SURE FOUNDATION, FOUNDATION OF US ALL.
HER LAP IS WHERE WE SIT.
LAP OF THE EARTH
HER LAP IS WHERE WE'RE AT.
LAP OF THE EARTH
LABIA/LIP/MOUTH OF THE WOMB.
MOUTH OF THE RIVER
MOUTH OF THE VESSEL
MOUTH OF THE WOMB.
WIDE-LEGGED EARTH—YEAH
HAVE YOU HEARD OF MOTHER EARTH?
SHE WANDERED IN THE GREAT GULF
TO GIVE US LAW
AND SEARCH FOR HER CHILD.
HER LAP IS WHERE WE SIT—IT'S WHERE WE SIT.
EVER-SURE FOUNDATION, FOUNDATION OF US ALL.
EVER-SURE FOUNDATION
HAVE YOU HEARD OF MOTHER EARTH?
EVER-SURE FOUNDATION!

MENSTRUALS: Horrible events have taken place here!
Horrible events have taken place here!
Horrible events have taken place here!

MENSTRUAL: That night—strange and mysteriolacious goings-on got
      loose. The sanctity of the body of the Hoodoo Queen of New Or-
      leans was *violated* by a roving band of peter-poppin' preppy pistols.

MENSTRUAL: When time come for the trial, eleven white male jurors and one Aunt Jemima was called for jury duty.

HOODOO QUEEN: Do you like oral sex, he said to me.
I said no.
Have you ever had sex with a white man.
I said no.
I couldn't breathe.
I said no.
I said no.

MENSTRUAL: When the eleven white male jurors told Aunt Jemima that the Hoodoo Queen asked for it—that she got what she deserved—Aunt Jemima had some doubts. But in the end, she agreed with them.

MENSTRUAL: The jury brought in a not guilty verdict. When the Hoodoo Queen stood up and walked out the courtroom with her head still held up high in the air, the swishing sound her skirt made sound just like a rattlesnake to Aunt Jemima.

AUNT JEMIMA: Hoodoo Queen, was you born and raised on the Higbee plantation?

HOODOO QUEEN: Mammy, don't you know me? Ise your own daughter Marie.

AUNT JEMIMA: Oh, lord, my own chile! I betrayed my own chile. Guilty as sin, guilty as sin. (*Singing.*) . . . Them preppies pistols is guilty as sin.

HOODOO QUEEN: That's alright, Mammy. I'll fix 'em.

MENSTRUALS AS THE THREE BLOOD MYSTERIES:
Oh, she said NO!
Oh, she said NO!
Great God Almighty!
She said NO!

AUNT JEMIMA: She was not on trial. She was not on trial.

MENSTRUALS: No, Mammy, no, she was not on trial.
No, Mammy, no, she was not on trial.

AUNT JEMIMA:
I should have hung the jury.
Guilty as sin.

MENSTRUALS: She said NO!
She said NO!

AUNT JEMIMA: Guilty as sin.
Guilty as sin.

MENSTRUALS AND AUNT JEMIMA: Great God Almighty,
That's the bottom line.

HOODOO QUEEN: I'll fix 'em.

LA MADAMA INTERLOCK-IT-TOGETHERER: The NAACP decided to
   boycott Aunt Jemima pancake mix because of her disgraceful
   behavior at the Hoodoo Queen's trial. Aunt Jemima wrote a
   red-hot letter to the NAACP.

AUNT JEMIMA:

Dear Madame President:
      Only those in our own race have used the name of Aunt
   Jemima to mean someone that is not desirable. Aunt Jemima
   built a monument to herself with pancakes and the advertisements admit she was a Negro. She is as American as ham and
   eggs. Please know it would be impossible for you to be more
   proud of being a Negro than I. Sincerely, Aunt Jemima.

MENSTRUAL: In later years, Aunt Jemima had to undergo several
   debilitating operations, including a mastectomy and a hysterectomy. She had the diabetes so bad, she had to get her
   feet amputated even though she didn't want to.

AUNT JEMIMA (*singing*): I BELIEVE THE FATE OF MY FEET
SHOULD BE LEFT UP TO GOD.
DON'T LET THEM TAKE THEM
DON'T LET THEM TAKE THEM
DON'T LET THEM HANDLE ME WITH THEIR HOT HANDS.

MENSTRUAL (*singing*): A staggering thought! To amputate the feet
   of someone who doesn't want it to happen.

AUNT JEMIMA (*singing*): I BELIEVE THE FATE OF MY FEET
SHOULD BE LEFT UP TO GOD.
DON'T LET THEM TAKE THEM
DON'T LET THEM TAKE THEM
DON'T LET THEM HANDLE ME WITH THEIR HOT HANDS.

MENSTRUAL (*singing*): AFTER HER AMPUTATION, AUNT JEMIMA
   COULDN'T TRAVEL NO MORE,
SO THE QUAKER OATS MAN RETIRED HER TO THE PANCAKE
   BOX TO LIVE.
HE CUT OFF HER FEET AND RETIRED HER TO THE PANCAKE
   BOX TO LIVE.

AFTER HER AMPUTATION, AUNT JEMIMA COULDN'T
 TRAVEL NO MORE, SO THE
QUAKER OATS MAN RETIRED HER TO THE PANCAKE BOX
 TO LIVE OUT HER DAYS.

MENSTRUAL: When Aunt Jemima went to the pancake box to live, it
 caused a furious fibrillation in her family.

MENSTRUALS (*singing*): AUNT JEMIMA ON THE PANCAKE BOX?
AUNT JEMIMA ON THE PANCAKE BOX?
AINCHA MAMA ON THE PANCAKE BOX?
AIN'T CHURE MAMA ON THE PANCAKE BOX?

MENSTRUAL: Rebecca was a mover and shaker, and begged her
 mother to fly away with her off the pancake box.

REBECCA: Come, Mammy, let's fly away togetherer.

AUNT JEMIMA: Ah got the arthur, baby, and when the arthur gets in
 your joints, you can't even twist 'em.

REBECCA: Mammy, my spirit eye tells me, thee are destined to die
 very soon if thee remains where thou art. Come take my hand,
 and thee can walk through the walls of the pancake box.

AUNT JEMIMA: Rebecca, ain't that that apostrophe that keeps gittin'
 you in so much trouble?

REBECCA: Thee and me can converse with the angels.

AUNT JEMIMA: That sounds like you letting the devil in the church.
 No, baby, Ah'll jes stay where Ah is.

MENSTRUAL: Tiny Desiree and Sapphire were at each other's throats
 and Bondswoman was the peacemaker.

TINY DESIREE: Mama, you gettin' too old to sit up on that box.

AUNT JEMIMA: Really, I don't mind. Not if it keeps my white folks
 happy.

SAPPHIRE: The white woman is the white man's dog, and the black
 woman is his mule. We do the heavy work and get beat
 whether we do it well or not. You never find me sittin' up on
 no goddamn box flipping pancakes for some white man!

BONDSWOMAN: Sapphire, you and Tiny Desiree both shut up!
 Ain't none of us free to do what we want as long as our mama
 is a slave. Now you two need to be trying to see how you can
 work together to liberate our mama. Tiny Desiree, you the
 youngest. You got too much mouth for such a little girl.

TINY DESIREE: At least I ain't like Sapphire. I can't stand that evil, treacherous, bitchy, stubborn thing. I ain't nothing like Sapphire. I is the Anita-thisis of Sapphire.

SAPPHIRE: I ain't none of them things folks call me. I just ain't afraid to express my bitterness, anger, and rage about our lot.

BONDSWOMAN: Mammy, you got to work to end your own oppression.

AUNT JEMIMA: Why should I complain about makin' $7,000 a week playing a mammy? If I didn't I'd be making $7 a week actually being one.

PECOLA: Mammy, we have a gift for you, a television.

MENSTRUAL: The last refuge for the lonely woman.

PECOLA: Mama, if you pass me on the street, you mustn't see me. Or own me. Or claim me.

AUNT JEMIMA: Oh, how dreadful, daughter deah!

PECOLA: Mama, I got to go out into the world and find myself.

AUNT JEMIMA: Pecola, honey, you grease them legs good befo' you goes anywhere.

PECOLA: Yes ma'am. (PECOLA *exits. Music: "Trouble of the World."*)

MENSTRUAL: After her crazy daughters left, Aunt Jemima began singing while she set her new television to the channel where she could see the confirmation hearings for Uncle Tom.

AUNT JEMIMA (*singing*):
THERE IS A BALM
IN GILEAD
TO MAKE THE WOUNDED WHOLE
THERE IS A BALM
IN GILEAD
TO CLEANSE THE SIN-SICK SOUL.

MENSTRUALS: Here come de judge
Here come de judge
Everybody knows that here come de judge
Court's in session
Court's in session
Order in de court
Cause here come de judge.

MENSTRUAL: Judge, judge, smile so we can see you.

JUDGE: Your mama can find me in the dark.

MENSTRUAL: Aunt Jemima was shocked to see her other daughter Anita sitting up there.

ANITA: Let's face it. I am a marked woman. I don't have a patron and I don't have a pass. The senators fear that affirmative action now means that Americans will have to hear edumacated colored folks talk about pubic hair, long dongs, big breasts, and bestiality in Senate chambers.

MENSTRUAL: The judge had no trouble slipping into America's most beloved minstrel role.

JUDGE (*singing*):
I BEEN 'BUKED AND I BEEN SCORNED
I BEEN 'BUKED AND I BEEN SCORNED
I BEEN 'BUKED AND I BEEN SCORNED
I BEEN TALKED ABOUT SURE AS YOU BORN.

MENSTRUAL: She got trashed and he got confirmed! Simple as that. Umph!!

AUNT JEMIMA: Ah need . . .

LA MADAMA INTERLOCK-IT-TOGETHERER: Need what?

AUNT JEMIMA: Ah need . . .

LA MADAMA INTERLOCK-IT-TOGETHERER: Need what?

AUNT JEMIMA: Ah need to . . .

LA MADAMA INTERLOCK-IT-TOGETHERER: Need ta what?

AUNT JEMIMA: Ah—nee—ta tell.

LA MADAMA INTERLOCK-IT-TOGETHERER: Need ta tell what?

AUNT JEMIMA: A—ni—ta tell on Uncle Tom.

LA MADAMA INTERLOCK-IT-TOGETHERER: Lowest life on the highest court!!!!!

MENSTRUAL: As time went on, Aunt Jemima became more and more of an embarrassment to all the limited partners in her corporation. The Quaker Oats Man tried to teach Aunt Jemima how to dress for success, but she refused to keep up with the changing times.

AUNT JEMIMA: I ain't havin' no skin peel. I ain't takin' off my head rag. And I ain't havin' my naps pressed. I'm a real woman, not a composite like Betty Crocker.

MENSTRUAL: Col. Uncle said, "We should just manumit Aunt Jemima, and run her out of town." The Quaker Oats man said, "You got a point there. Let her fend for herself. Let's do it."

MENSTRUAL: After her long, faithful years of service, the food inspectors came to evict Aunt Jemima from the pancake box.

MENSTRUAL: She was sixty-six years old and weighed three hundred pounds. She had arthritis, high blood pressure, and diabetes.

MENSTRUAL: The cops said she shouted that she would kill anybody who tried to evict her.

AUNT JEMIMA (*singing*):
IT'S A GODDAMN SHAME
WHAT THEY DO TO ME
WHAT WILL IT TAKE
TO SET ME FREE?
GODDAMN, GODDAMN!
DON'T READ MY PAP SMEAR
FOR A YEAR
THEY FINALLY TELL ME
I'M FILLED WITH FEAR
CANCER'S EATING UP MY WOMB
MOTHER EARTH, YOU'LL BE MY TOMB
WHAT THEY DO TO ME, GODDAMN
HYSTERECTOMY, GODDAMN
WHAT THEY DO TO ME, GODDAMN
CLITORIDECTOMY, GODDAMN
WHAT THEY DO TO ME, GODDAMN
MASTECTOMY, GODDAMN
CANCER WRECKTED ME, GODDAMN
CANCER WRECKTED ME, GODDAMN
GODDAMN! GODDAMN! GODDAMN!
GODDAMN! GODDAMN! GODDAMN!
IT'S A GODDAMN SHAME
WHAT THEY DO TO ME
WHAT WILL IT TAKE
TO SET ME FREE?

AUNT JEMIMA: Ah'm a free Black woman. Here is my free papers dat ah carries in my shoe.

MENSTRUAL: They said she charged at them with a ten-inch knife. Her right hand was blown away by the first shot. She looked surprised.

MENSTRUAL: The second shot blew a hole in her chest. She fell back into the kitchen and bled profusely.

AUNT JEMIMA: America who caused the daughters of Africa to commit whoredoms and fornications, upon thee be their curse. Though we are looked upon as things, we sprang from a scientific people. Ah bore 13 children, AIN'T AH A WOMAN!!

MENSTRUALS: Aunt Jemima had 13 daughters!
Marie, a child born with a rattlesnake in her hand.
Dorothy, her tragic mulatta chile.
Pecola, a little melodramatic red baby.
Dysmorphia, who was half black and half white.
Anna Julia, a woman who risked all to learn to read.
Susie-Faye, Aunt Jemima's earnest child.
Rebecca, called by the thunder to preach the gospel.
Bondswoman, a girl with freedom on her mind.
Sapphire, a girl who could not be tamed by any man.
The twins, Anita and Aminata,
Freedom Fighter,
and the cake-mix-miracle baby, Tiny Desiree.

MENSTRUAL: They say she is dead, but we know she hurled herself, naked, a black bombshell into the center of the battle.

MENSTRUALS (*singing*):
AUNT JEMIMA ON THE PANCAKE BOX?
AUNT JEMIMA ON THE PANCAKE BOX?
AINCHAMAMAON THE PANCAKE BOX?
AIN'T CHURE MAMA ON THE PANCAKE BOX?

AUNT JEMIMA (*leaping off the pancake box*): I can walk like a ox, run like a fox, swim like a eel, yell like a Indian, fight like a devil, spout like a earthquake, make love like a mad bull, and swallow a nigger whole without choking. I can catch bullets with my assperity. Sometimes I send them back with interest and sometimes I transform them into balls of cotton.

MENSTRUAL: Turning her back on us, she went to live in the moon forever.

TINY DESIREE: The woman on the pancake box today is not Aunt Jemima. Everybody thinks it is because it looks just like her. But it is me, her microwave miracle daughter, Tiny Desiree. I have no compunction about skin peels and pearl earrings.

MENSTRUAL: At the great World's Fair in '93, people could see Aunt Jemima in person. Sadly today we can not. But what she did lives on—that and her smile.

MENSTRUAL: She is with us always and asserts herself in our daily lives and offers us a strategy.

LA MADAMA INTERLOCK-IT-TOGETHERERER: Thank you for coming out tonight. Be sure to tell your friends that the greatest show on earth will be coming to their town soon. Soon, soon they, too, can hear the Aunt Jemima Traveling Menstrual Show announce:

(*Reprise opening song.*)

AUNT JEMIMA: I'se in town, honey. I'se around.

(*Curtain.*)

SECTION TWO

Black Men at Risk

for black boys who have considered homicide when the streets were too much

Keith Antar Mason

KEITH ANTAR MASON, performance poet and artistic director of The Hittite Empire, a black male theater collective based in Santa Monica, California, has been performing his own award-winning works in a variety of media since 1979. Mason's literary achievements include spoken-word recordings. He is the founder of blackmadrid, a Black poetry-jazz-rap-griot recording collective that has created new works for New American Radio, BarKubCo Music, and New Alliance Records. He is the founding director of the Los Angeles Black Repertory Company in Los Angeles, California. Mason has performed at Los Angeles–area venues such as Highways Performance Space in Santa Monica, Beyond Baroque, LACE, the Laguna Beach Art Museum, and the Santa Monica Museum of Art. He has also performed around the country at such locations as the High John's Warehouse in Harlem, New York; the Alternate ROOTS Festival in Atlanta, Georgia; and the Cleveland Performance Festival in Cleveland, Ohio.

Commissioned by Lincoln Center Theater as part of its annual Serious Fun Festival, *49 Blues Songs for a Jealous Vampire* was performed by The Hittite Empire in New York City in 1992. In 1991 Mason curated "Black December," a monthlong festival that celebrated Black culture and the legacy of the African diaspora in Los Angeles. *for black boys who have considered homicide* was produced originally in Los Angeles and toured nationally in 1993. In March 1995 Mason and The Hittite Empire performed *Underseige Stories*, written and conceived by Mason and the Hittite Empire, in Pittsburgh, Pennsylvania.

Active in numerous arts organizations, Mason is on the steering committee of the National Performance Network and is involved with the Saturday Morning Literary Workshop, the Cool Black Collective, and the California Multicultural Men's Movement. Keith Antar Mason lives in the Los Angeles area.

Dedication

in loving tribute to henry dumas

Director's note

my love for the living arts developed in me early i saw the ballet and wanted to be a dancer my father immediately got me a baseball glove from that rejection denial overprotective nurturing gesture, i escaped into the fantasy world of books . . . years later while in college i saw ntozake shange's **for colored girls who have considered suicide when the rainbow was enuf** i was numbed overwhelmed spoken to directly another experience added to the horizon of my own potential . . . what i am saying is that for years i had to gather the life forces around to create my vision to share with you . . . and that i could not have even begun this quest if it had not been for other black artists that preceded me . . . so i say this in praise of them and their magic and i ask you now to grant me permission to share my vision with you.

thank you for supporting black artists throughout the world we live for moments like this.

> i prayed to god
> he heard my cry . . .
> selah-selan
> amen.
> —keith antar mason

Characters

Brother #19
Brother #8
Brother #17
Brother #3
Brother #34
Brother #5

Costumes: The brothers are dressed in black jeans, black T-shirts with red numbers (each individual brother's number on his own shirt, this is their identification), and they are barefoot.

Set Description: The stage is a closed-off alleyway. There is a three-step fire escape landing USR. There is a noose hanging DSC.

(*Lights dim.*)
(*All brothers ent. one at a time, take their position.*)

BROTHER #19
(*it's a game to him*):
who is my god
who is my mother
who is my father
do you care for me
do you love me (*pause*)
do you love me (*hold pose*)

BROTHER #8
(*noble*):
who is my god
who is my mother
who is my father
do you care for me
do you love me (*pause*)
do you love me (*hold pose*)

BROTHER #17
(*disbelief*):
who is my god
who is my mother
who is my father
do you care for me
do you love me (*pause*)
do you love me (*hold pose*)

BROTHER #3
(*disrespect*):
who is my god
who is my mother
who is my father
do you care for me
do you love me (*pause*)
do you love me (*hold pose*)

BROTHER #34
(*passion*):
who is my god
who is my mother
who is my father
do you care for me
do you love me (*pause*)
do you love me (*hold pose*)

BROTHER #5
(*it's the news to him*):
who is my god
who is my mother
who is my father
do you care for me
do you love me (*pause*)
do you love me (*hold pose*)

(*Music up, Stevie Wonder's "Secret Life
of Plants." All Brothers break into frenzy
movements screaming in pain.*)

BROTHER #5:
sweat and strain muscle and bone

(*All brothers, except #5, run to back wall
and continue frenzy movements.*)

boxes and fences
fancy trips and covered by night
the blues and pain
and yellin'
rollin' down a pectoral
taut
it's tight
movement
it's hilarious
a black boy's moan
cattin' fallin' dancin'
no words no no tears
just movements
just pain
don't touch him
don't nobody touch him
leave him alone
this is a cemetery a graveyard

of countless souls screamin'
jazz
and looney tunes
cartoons and monsters crawlin'
no joke
we are bones
children of the hellfire
don't touch him
we are animals
gone to madness
say a psalms
the last hurrah
laced and leathered bound
but the madness kills
the tender flesh scorched
the blessings and promised me
you did it
who ever you are
bring me out
bring me home
to myself
bring us to ourselves
this corner this maze
his rhythms
his chants
kindlin' and foldin' workings
pray a psalms of him
reveal his life
he doesn't witness his own soul
is circumcision
his strengths
pray a psalms
he's lost words
brazen flash
smoke and dance
prayers and unseen
thought
the makings of a god sweat strain muscle and bone
let him be revealed
let him be bared
take a number
any number niggers are jus' numbers
any age jus' a number take a number

(Each brother turns on his line and faces audience.)

BROTHER #34:
in basic training

BROTHER #3:
on the corner

BROTHER #17:
at howard university

BROTHER #19:
in a tomb

BROTHER #8:
in hot water, mississippi

BROTHER #5:
takin' numbers any number niggers are
jus' numbers any age

ALL BROTHERS:
and this is for black boys who have
considered homicide
when the streets were too much

*(Lights up.
All brothers clap, then break up as if in
a football huddle, start to play games.
Then break into two lines facing off at
each other but at a distance.)*

play ball man
come on
pick me
mighty mouse
built a house
how many bricks did
he leave out

(#19 points at #3, they all laugh.)

yeah
devil and the pitchfork
i'll be the namer

red rover
yeah man

red rover
red rover
send big head
on over (*they all laugh*)

ALL BROTHERS:
batman
he took her
to the movies
batman
the movies were

groovy
batman
he took her to his house
batman
and threw her on the couch (*they all freeze*)

(*#8 pushes #3 CS; all brothers sit in different spots on stage but still in their
face-off lines.*)

BROTHER #3
(*bragging*):
man it wasn't like
that for me
i had been playin'
ball
all that early mornin'
and i was sweatin' hot
we had played kick
ball
on the lot in front of
Molls grocery store
and
half breed michael
had thrown a brick
on butch's foot
'cause
butch
had
tagged the back of
his head
with

one of them round
rubber balls
you play with
in gym class

but it was hot
that mornin'
my white tee shirt
was gray with sweat
and my body
was changin'
and playin' ball
wasn't the only
thing i felt
like playin' all day

so when cody
and his gal
sharlene
came by from the grocery
store
my mind stopped
playin' ball
i started walkin'
home

boy it was hot all of a sudden
and kool-aid wuzn't gonna do
nothin'
but sharlene
spoke
seems like
ole' cody
decided that he might
catch some action
with the fellas
and everybody knew
i wasn't no fool
have to fight
to the death
with mad man cody
over his gal sharlene
so when i caught up

with her
i was gonna go home
and watch
some t. v.
and take a bath
a cold one

but the next thing i know
i was carryin' her bags
for her
and her smile
did something to me
umh umh
bout goin' over her house
for some kool-aid

by the time i was on her front porch
and i swear to god
that wuz' as far as i
was goin'
i was nobody's fool
cuz' cody
was known to be
treacherous and crazy
he put eyes out
and busted heads
with baseball bats

but she pulled me
and her waist
jus' jus' touched
my waist
and she noticed my tremblin'
and i was scared
all the way back to the
kitchen
and wuzn't nobody home

boy i wanna play house
today she said
real low and winkin'
you know how to play
house don't you

*

well, i did
i knew how to play house
and it wuzn't goin' to be said
that i never had played
house before
shhuudd i had my rep (*slaps a high five with* #8)
to protect

yeah, i know how to play
as i kinda looked out
the back window
hopin' that her aunt
wuz' gardenin'
and to see if
cody wuz' still
playin' ball

then i felt her on me
on that couch
and all i can
remember is that kool-
aid never tasted sweeter
never (*slaps high five with* #8)

BROTHER #8:
you got took out by
a friend's gal

BROTHER #3:
umh umh

BROTHER #19:
by an older gal

BROTHER #3:
umh umh
and all i could do
wuz' jus' play ball (*they all laugh*)

BROTHER #5:
it ain't always fun
it ain't always the kick
or the late night party
it should

be
sometimes you get
really took out

ALL BROTHERS:
fo' real
that's fo' real

BROTHER #34

> (*Lights dim. Spot on #34.*
> *Stands, cross to DSC.*):

he stood
naked in front of his mirror
always smilin'
jus' baptized on fish friday
and the cool of the evenin' leavin'
purple blazed in his mind
his radio caressed him
his music made love to him always
always smilin'
splashed his cologne his scent

before and after
he was the life of their dances
too much even naked in his mirror
and by the time it was dark
he would have selected which
dance was goin' to be his

and by the time it was dark
he would have selected which
dance was going to be his
what world would he conquer
ernest would step
like fog leans up against
the lakes in forest park
softly he would touch
jus' enuf for them to know
that music ran with him
and
they wanted to be seen
no one else would do

*

he was deliberate
watched all the others before he would
move
remembered those from other times, who
acknowledge his presence
serene
as if no music was playin' he would move
regardless
jus' enuf to let them know
he could dance

he mainly danced with his shadow
she was there
but he knew after the music
wuz' no longer there
he would go home
alone
a memory of a good time
and he didn't want
to be anything else but
that—a dance, unforgettable dance

he wuz' hot
as red pepper in greens on sunday
and those that wanted
him on the sheets
had to be more than themselves
he never ever made love—ever since—she had
        left him
he danced

and he would allow for them
to dance to his
real music
the waiting was over
and she would
have herself what she wanted—a ball
after all it wuz' always planned
and he wuz' always smilin'
but she could not believe in him
he knew that before the dance
but all he wanted was a dance

*

she could demand no better performance
and he wuz' all gentle man
twice a gentle man
but there wuz' no room for excuses
or reason
he knew before they danced and lied
and promised each other anything
that she could not believe in him

ernest would cling then to his pillow
wished that he smoked
or looked like somebody that she dreamed
about
then naked in front of his mirror he'd
smile
she'd think that she had pleased him
done him the greatest favor of all
but he knew she didn't believe in him

and he would baptize himself again
and pour himself out
a river
while she would gather herself
and watch for a while him bathin'
but he said nothing
and she would leave
havin' danced with him
no kiss goodbye
and maybe he felt like
it would have been better
for him to come home alone
again
dried himself
and cried himself to sleep
and all he wanted wuz' to dance
and his radio played
no music
and he tried to remember her
she had taught him
take care of yourself
in the rain
and in this pain
that you feel

remember big boys
don't cry
especially niggas
with thick lips
and cute black asses

she taught him to dance
and to forget nights that he went home
alone
she had come and she had promised
and she had loved him
beyond compare
and he now the conqueror
surrendered himself
his dance to her
his movin' life to her
and she seized it
and taught him to dance naked
especially nasty dances
that no one would ever find out about
on the sheets now between his wet black
legs
that covered his waist
that touched his navel

but he wanted to dance some more with
her and he knew she did not believe in him
because she was not there
but he had been seen
in a world that he had conquered
and he clung to his pillow
and cried himself
to sleep
alone because she
did not believe in him
and she was no longer there
jus' a wet memory
between his sheets

BROTHER #19
(*stands, crosses to CS*):
man you let some colored girl
stop you from dancin'

good dancin'
soul savin' dancin'
my dance is too
electrifyin'

> (*Music up. "Just Another Part of Me,"*
> *Michael Jackson. All brothers stand and*
> *dance.*)

to stop dancin'

> (*Music fades. #19 takes CS; all brothers*
> *take their seats.*)

man it's a solo
trip
into my own happiness
can you see
me
on some dance floor
all red not subdued
and when i'm hot
i'm sizzlin' hot
and the music is spinnin'
head
and eyes are rollin'
and i'm jus' startin'
to move
the way
the water rolls
the way brazil
curves into the
atlantic
the way l.a.
slides
into the pacific
i'm rollin'
like a new wave
a rushin'
crimson prince
royal blood
and i am too hot
to trot baby girl
so don't try to
stop the tide

the tidal wave
and heads
turnin'
and the music
flowin'
like pharoah
turnin'
and the music
flowin'
like pharoah
turnin' out
some ancient
rhythms
between my thighs
and my feet
the joy of
sunday revival
turn my dance
out
no way out no way
my dance is too well thought out
to be turned out

(*#19 poses, showing his dance.*)

ALL BROTHERS:
(*they copy #19's pose.*):
my dance is too well thought out
to be turned out
my dance is too well thought out
to be turned out
my dance is too well thought out
to be turned out

BROTHER #5
(*he shows his dance*):
my dance is too 4 corners
to be turned out

(*Music up. "Just Another . . ."*)

ALL BROTHERS
(*they copy #5's dance.*):
4 corners

4 corners
4 corners

BROTHER #34
(*he shows his dance*):
my dance is too psychedelic soul
to be turned out

ALL BROTHERS
(*they copy #34's dance*):
psychedelic soul
psychedelic soul
psychedelic soul

BROTHER #8
(*he shows his dance*):
my dance is too cool jerk revolutionary
to be turned out

ALL BROTHERS
(*they copy his dance*):
cool jerk revolutionary
cool jerk revolutionary
cool jerk revolutionary

BROTHER #3
(*he shows his dance*):
my dance is jus' too sexy
to be turned out

ALL BROTHERS
(*they copy his dance*):
sexy
sexy
sexy

BROTHER #17
(*he shows his dance*):
my dance is jus' too dangerous
to be turned out

ALL BROTHERS
(*they copy his dance*):
dangerous
dangerous
dangerous

BROTHER #8
(*he saves #19*):
soul savin'

ALL BROTHERS
(*they all copy*):
soul savin'
soul savin'
soul savin'

BROTHER #19
(*he shows his dance*):
white boy

ALL BROTHERS
(*they all copy*):
white boy
white boy
white boy

BROTHER #5
(*he shows his dance*):
dog

ALL BROTHERS
(*they all copy*):
dog
dog
dog

(*Music fades out.*)

BROTHER #3
(*angry, furious; he takes CS*):
i must be mistaken
some monster
i know
i can tell by the way you look
at me
you tighten up
and never smile
like aggression can only
be symbolized
by me
like the male gender
and colored black means

death carrier
potent poison
lethal
like the only mind i
have is between
my legs
and all it does is piss
the sewage out
the raw unadulterated
mean-ness
and i know
some how i know
i want to live
a long time but
i am gonna die
some obscene
joke
cuz' you clutch
yourself around me
hold back
all the good things
even precious smiles
from me
some how i know
i wuz' born to die
to die too soon
and i don't understand

and that's the confusion you see
that's the fear
you feel
i am no more than
the stacked up
cemented
aggression
black tornado
come back from
oz no hell
born to die
and i mus' be
a zombie
walkin' the streets
the livin' dead

*
and my brain
my dick
the curse
          of the male gender
colored black
colored black
with nappy hair

and you only feel
afraid
but i know
how fear kills
i know
i live it
standin'
on the corner
holdin' the wall
like a firin' squad
and some how i know
i wuz' born to die
a zombie
live or dead
the male gender
cursed
colored black
and too damn
aggressive
jus' by being born

BROTHER #5

(*He clears his throat, all brothers form a
line CS, one behind the other according
to height, with the tallest USC, shortest
DSC, freeze. #5 walks to the front.*):

I have fallen to the ground
i have no face

ALL BROTHERS

(*all brothers dart out of line, dart back
in and freeze on #5's lines*):

take a number any number

BROTHER #5:
this bold and dangerous act

ALL BROTHERS
(*all brothers dart out of line, dart back
in and freeze on #5's lines*):
niggas are numbers
jus' statistics for death rates
and criminal charts

BROTHER #5:
we lose meanin' once
any one learns the word

ALL BROTHERS
(*all brothers dart out of line, dart
back in and freeze on #5's
lines*):
nigga

BROTHER #5:
and it's hard
to live being that
and nothing more
it's a drag

ALL BROTHERS
(*all brothers dart out of line, dart back
in and freeze on #5's lines*):
being a nigga

BROTHER #5:
and other verbose and
superfluous metaphors

ALL BROTHERS
(*all brothers dart out of line, dart back
in and freeze on #5's lines*):
all niggas are numbers
important only
to coroner's reports
and the mortician's business
take any number

BROTHER #5:
countless thousands
has been candidates

dying to be number one
and it's hard to prove

ALL BROTHERS
            (*all brothers snap fingers then dart out of
            line, dart back in and freeze on #5's lines*):
dead
niggas don't count

BROTHER #5:
it's hard to prove
numbers don't have
any values outside of
themselves
jus' like

ALL BROTHERS
            (*all brothers snap fingers then dart out
            of line, dart back in and freeze on #5's
            lines*):
niggas
            (*They break, go sit in their places.*)

BROTHER #5
takin' odds
ain't takin' chances
and the countdown
is critical
takin' tolls
ain't supplyin' me
with the right that a man
a god-like child
with a future
can understand
takin' numbers
ain't supposed to mean
takin' my life
and validatin'
my demise
ain't i worth
nothin'
takin' numbers
that don't add up
subtract or divide
can only make

multiplyin' a fruitless
endeavor
that is justified
contemptible
not with standin'
routine

ALL BROTHERS:
niggas take a number
a ho' card any number
any integer

BROTHER #5:
but seekin' no sympathy
please
jus' remove
the bitterness
remove the anger
jus' keep it away
from me
this pain of bein'
dehumanized
and programmed
no damned
can no longer be tolerated

ALL BROTHERS
        (*they drop on all fours, then crawl DSC*):
niggas are numbers any number
take a number

BROTHER #19:
an address
represents a nigga's house

BROTHER #8:
a phone number
allows you the privilege
of dialin' him up at
two o'clock and callin'
him

ALL BROTHERS
        (*they form a horizontal line across the
        stage*)
nigga

BROTHER #5:
jus' keep it away from me
keep that pain
never endin' never healin'
terminal curse
affliction away from

ALL BROTHERS
(*raise to a sitting position with backs to
audience*):
nigga nigga nigga

BROTHER #5:
keep it away from me
i hear it everywhere
i been travelin' so long
and gone so far
turned over as many new
leaves that bud in the spring
and i can't count them any more

ALL BROTHERS
(*snap*):
dead niggas don't count
count

BROTHER #5
(*he screams and drops to his knees
as if having a spasm or
seizure*):
damn take the nigga
off me
take it and don't hurt
nobody else with it
let nigga die
let the nigga die
and promise me

BROTHER #8
(*jumps up and exits USL*):
one

BROTHER #3
(*jumps up and exits USR*):
two

BROTHER #19
(*jumps up and exits USL*):
three

BROTHER #34
(*jumps up and exits USR*):
four

BROTHER #17
(*jumps up and exits USL*):
five

BROTHER #5
(*tenderly; rises to knees*):
promise me
that takin' numbers
don't mean takin'
names
cuz'
ain't no nigga died
and left you boss
on purpose
(*Smiles, gives audience the finger, exits.*)

BROTHER #3

(*lights dim, spot on #3.*)
(*#3 ent. USL crosses to steps, sits.*):
a new moon caught in his throat,
an easy kinda bad this motherfucker ridin'
the bus
listenin' to RUN-DMC "It's like that, an that's
    the
way it is."
there's this smile between the layers of skin—
    that burns cold
        when your eyes meet his—you fear his
        hard dick—his
rebop tennis shoes
camoflages
the sudden impact of his destiny—he's tall as
usual—thin—dangerous
ridin' this bus—smokin' this moonlit cigarette—
    runnin' his dark
hands—over

frizzy braids—bein' more afrikin than he knows—
the wind—the cold—the
hard times
everyday etchin' his groove on the back seat of
    this
bus
thinkin' about the feel of pussy and how it
    feels—he
ain't got no words
no sacrifices
jus' crossin' streets—into another world

> (*Lights dim where he leaves, up on trash
> can. He crosses DSL to trash can.*)

and can't nobody go
not even his best friend
not even coked-up death
not even
crack
not even
free-basin'
can't keep up with him
cool
and the smile finally surfaces
reaches his teeth—flashes his gold tooth—
    cuz' he knows
he knows the nigga
truth.

> (*Lights fade to black.*)

ALL BROTHERS
> (*Lights are dim.
> All brothers are chanting from BS. #34
> stalks like a zombie randomly chanting
> across the stage. #3 dances or does
> karate moves across the stage.*)

and slush funds
and hideaways
and late brides
and dizzy spells
all signs all omens
the marked cup of death's drink
and favorite sons
and loosen waist bands

all powerful signs
and prayers and voodoo ritual
and brooms and gourds
and bone dust of ancestors
all worshippin'
drawnin' near and nearer
the fire's heart
and one twin flame
blue as night
and the ash white of day
all signs all omens
the drum and the chants
the swirlin' dance of naked feet
shift light dirt around
collect no caked
upon the feet and the graves
of ancestors
the federal cuts
the black bourgeois
salt stuffed mouths
and sewn lips
all signs all omens
the naked screams of
pain cut bodies
stick pinned
and lynched
drippin' blood
from a lover's eye
all signs all omens
all boys bein' born
and the swarm of flies
the draft bill
the surge of manhood
the circumcision
all the powerful signs
the chant whistles
the fix
the needle
the glory
all signs all omens
the sex stains
the first taste
the smoke

all the signs all the omens
the jam
the quick thrust
in rusted chains
of beads of sweat

>   (#34 *wipes sweat, gives someone in the*
>   *audience a candle.*)

listen
the drum
the kintago's call
the old one's finger nails
all signs all omens
the braidin' of hair
the piercin' of left ears
the votes

>   (#34 *screams, "American let me in."*)

the bus rides
all signs
all the signs of the times
the naked children
dead and strangled
the omen
the master of the vineyard
the comin'
the returnin'
the ancestral search
the burnin' flame
the brand of fear
the death
the death wish chant and nightmare scream of
     this life

>   (*Music stops.*
>   *#8 sneaks onstage under a black cloth,*
>   *takes squatting position on top step USR.*)

all signs all omens
all signs all omens
of the times
of this times

>   (#34 *conjuring in front of steps in a*
>   *frenzy*):

time
time

time
all omens
all signs

BROTHER #8
(*Lights full up.*
He pops up out of sheet.)
jus' dust and hot heat
lingerin' heat
and glistenin' black skin
and hot cauldron water washed
the dirt from him
his musty groin
and the sighin' relief
and squeezin' pain after the fight
was all the moon made him see

the moanin' moon pale white
an open cut over his left eye
and too many scars
seen and gleemingly unseen

and the rush of humid heat
poured out a sponge rag
made from a pair of old pants
too tight now for any other job

mozambique drenched of life
stenched of life
blood clotted life
wuz' a street fighter first
then a nigga
that thought he escaped from hell
and went to live in hot water mississippi
not far from bayou louisiana

and when white men bet
he would fight
not for the few dreams that
he bashed heads for
but for life
the life that
toe-jam and sweat wuz' made of

black skinned
and thick jointed

he escaped
loneliness to
hot water mississippi
not far from bayou louisiana
turned blood red
in the ring of life
the circus of life
where his fists did tricks
and his teeth tore flesh
like any animal that
stalks a prey
mozambique
wuz' a black man's terror
and believed the bigger
the battle
the more of himself
that would escape from

hell
and as long as he had a dick
he could turn a trick
for life
clung to him
like them tight pants used to
pungent twisted life
curled in every sighin' sigh
whether makin' love or killin'
see death come by two means
both wuz' for money
and hell had a price to be paid
he had won his bargain
and he didn't blame the devil
or anybody for that matter
all he knew wuz'
that red piss ants stung his feet
when he slept naked
and the heat jus' hung
hung heavy like his nuts heavy
and full of life
and when the fight wuz' over and the bleedin'

stopped
there wuz' more money to be made
either by a woman's need
or the throw of the bones
and his magic
could always throw
them bones
cuz' he won jesus's robe from
satan and wuz' wearin'
the blood stained garment
every day and every night
rain or shine
but he wore it hot
filled with musty heat
and he loved the smell
of exotic places and people

he wore jesus' death shroud
but life hot life
flowed in him
under the pale moanin' moon
singin' 'bout death
mozambique

> (*All brothers chant*
> *"Mozambique" 3x's offstage.*)

wuz' a revolution
with big coarse hands that touched
everything the same way
you knew life was on his side
it wuz' scared not to be
he made punks and women
made daggers and dreams come
far and few were his own dreams

cuz'
mozambique had escaped
from hell
and won
jesus's black death robe
and he jus' wears it
under a moanin' moon pale white
escaped from hell

to hot water mississippi
not too far from bayou louisiana

mozambique turned over
            (*All brothers chant "Mozambique" 3x's
            offstage.*)
one night tired
tired of livin' himself
tired of hearin' them jeers
and cries the lusts
death came over him
this nigga
this nigga
turned man
and when the gatherin' crowds
saw him it was too late

cuz' 'stead of the
conqueror root drink
makin' him crazy
made him
mozambique
            (*All brothers chant "Mozambique" 3x's
            offstage.*)
keeper of the word
of ogun
            (*All brothers chant "ogun" 3x's offstage.*)
warrior of damballa
            (*All brothers chant "damballa" 3x's off-
            stage.*)
all life forged them a god
creativity
and the moanin' moon
pale and white
laughed
            (*All brothers laugh.*)
laughed a cry of terror
cuz' mozambique hands
            (*All brothers chant "Mozambique" 3x's
            offstage.*)
that always touched the same way
grabbed a white man
a gambler

throwin' bones
who thought the money wuz'
what he wuz' playin' for
not his life
but mozambique
>   (*All brothers chant "Mozambique" 3x's*
>   *offstage.*)

kissed that black death robe he wuz
wearin'
and the blood
flushed the air
jus' dust and heat
black skinned
and scarred muscles
and the fire next time

the burnin' heat came
from the sheriff's gun barrel
blue smoke and dust
and heat lingerin' round
and this time mozambique
had escaped

escaped satan
left hot water mississippi
not too far from bayou louisiana
so beware children
so beware
any nigga
that change
his name to
mozambique
>   (*He exits laughing.*
>   *Lights dim.*)

>   BROTHER #5
>   (*Lights dim.*
>   *He tiptoes in CSL, frightened by the*
>   *laughter, crosses to CS, stands*):

see late at night
when i was little
real little
and scary

scared of the dark mainly
and of the movie
where everybody
went into this hole
but never came out again
i would
rock myself to sleep
and worry 'bout peein'
on myself
if i couldn't make it to
the bathroom on time
but the only thing that
saved me wuz' a voice
on one of
my auntie's
records
i wuzn't
suppose to touch
and her voice
would soothe me
calm me down
her name wuz'
NINA SIMONE
and she say hush little
baby don't you cry
late at night
and sometimes
i'd be watchin'
instead
of sleepin' on that couch
watchin'
my auntie
kissin' her boyfriend
and knowin'
that Nina wuz
singin' to me
see Nina
could put a spell
on me and keep me safe
and i saw her
in the shadow
with her hair
combed

back
and she wuz'
a princess
a black princess tough and proud
a high priestess of soul
i would close my eyes
and see her
chasin' the werewolves
from around my house
especially from underneath the back porch
and basement
and when i woke up the next
mornin'
NINA SIMONE would be back
in her album jacket
and i would hold her
secretly on them
warm afternoons
when it wuz' too hot to go
outside and play
and everybody
always wanted to watch
dark shadows
at three
but i would hold
NINA SIMONE close
cuz' i knew
she would put
a spell on Barnabus Collins
and Angelique the witch
but one afternoon
         (*Music: Storm sounds.*)
it was rainy
and my cousin
had cut his finger
almost off
and everybody
went to the hospital
to see 'bout him
and left me at home
to watch dark shadows
alone
         (*Lights go black.*)

and the lightenin'
>   (*Lights: Strobe.*)
sparkled
and the lights
>   (*Lights up and down, up and down,
>   then remain dim.*)
flickered
and that old t.v.
jus' faded on out
and i jus' ran on into
my room
cuz' everybody
wuz' gonna blame me
i knew i wuz' gonna
get
blamed
for it
and it wuz' dark
all over the
house
and wuzn't no body home
but me
but i wuz' too big
to be cryin'
but i sho'll did want to
>   (*He runs around, stops in front of steps,
>   sits on floor.*)
and it seemed like all them monsters
wuz' jus'
a plottin'
ole dracula wuz' in the closet
>   (*He jumps, looks SL.*)
and the werewolf
wuz' under the bed
>   (*He jumps, looks underneath
>   himself.*)
and jack the ripper
wuz' pickin' the lock
>   (*He jumps, looks SL.*)
on my bedroom door
when all of a sudden
from out of my
bedroom window

i could hear
Nina singin'
my song
hush little baby don't
you cry
       (He sings "Summertime.")
and i didn't
i went and listened
not mindin'
the rain drops
splashin' me
every once in a while
seemed like
Nina had got around
the lady downstairs
in our apartment buildin'
had the same
album my auntie
did
and when she
flipped it over to the
other side
NINA SIMONE
the high priestess
of SOUL
saved me again
cuz' she put a
a sleep spell
on and
i fell asleep
to the sound of her voice
holding her in my arms
at the same time
i knew
then
NINA SIMONE
was alright
with the kid
alright with the kid
that was about 1967 st. louis

      (He rushes off USR.
      Lights go to black.)

BROTHER #17
(*Lights spot on #17.*
He ent. USR, crosses DSR in front of steps,
stares blankly then sits on bench.):

she is counting pennies
endlessly again
her back against the yellow
kitchen wall
beans are cooking
her right hand . . . sliding
them into the slot
klink klink   klink klink
half her face is lax
and her tongue
is swollen
rolling over
she screams monkey shouts
and you must pour out
the pennies again
she starts to count
you smell the excrement
she cries
and you don't want
to remember
how her hands
guided you to make
letters
she taught you to
count by giving
you kisses
you close your eyes
her left one bulges
never relaxing
she counts the pennies
klink klink   klink klink
her left arm is
hard and withered now
she cries
as you clean her up
her right hand clenches
the beans boil over
and the steam sizzles

she holds you tightly
and you must break away
dizzy
give her the pennies
she chokes on spittle
the beans need stirring
your back stiffens
she's bleeding again
from the nose
you rush
cold water startled
the flesh spasms
you smell yellow cold
phlegm
and go back now
to cutting onions
you remember
her house dresses
the pretty flowers
she sat around
the house
now you wait
she is counting
pennies
her right hand
shaking
klink klink   klink klink
she helped you
paint finger paintings
hung them on the wall
by the pantry
her face has no
mystery
you have her eyes
now . . .
klink klink   klink klink
        (*He drops the pennies. Lights go to*
        black.)

    BROTHER #3
        (*Music: Siren sounds.*
        Lights barely visible on #3. #3 stumbles
        onstage, falls USR two feet from steps.)

nobody
came
nobody
saw

the necessity to
come

jus' white hands
and oxygen

it wuz' jus'
another routine
autopsy

no i.d.
wuz' needed

nobody
came

what sense did
it make

and i wuz'
determined
to hold on

but it wuz' all the
way cross town
on the south side

and they turned
off the siren
half way there
and i couldn't scream

i wanted to live
i wanted to live

even jus' bein' a nigga
wuz' more

than jus'
dyin'

but nobody came
get that knife
out of me
turn the lights back on

and those
gloves
smeared
blood
heavy blood
stained
get that knife
outa me

and go faster
faster
turn the siren back on

nobody
came

nobody
saw

it wuz' jus'
another routine
autopsy

(*He slumps on floor.
Music: Sirens up.*)

INTERMISSION

(Lights dim.
Music: "It Don't Hurt Now" by Teddy
Pendergrass.
All brothers ent. talking loudly, as if at
a house party. Music fades out.)

BROTHER #19:
hey man did you deal with a strong one before
man so strong you didn't know what wuz' up
she out did john wayne
and laid you more than you did her
the strong and silent type
gave it up before she realized and suffered
the changes and didn't tell you
didn't let you know
only called to say that she should-could-would
    luv' you
but never did when she got there because
bein' silent wuz' golden and she wuz' jus' be-
    ing a lady
a killer—holdin' everything in
and seemingly lovin' you and bein' there
'cause no matter what you were doin' even if
you were doin' someone else
'cause her strength her martyrdom
wuz' to be guaranteed
bought lock stock and barrel
out macho-ed
ricardo montalban
cuz' somehow
her happiness lays in pointin' out
how guilty you should be at eleven o'clock
and you on the job and some redneck listenin'
in and dockin' you for personal calls
silent but fired up
mouth twisted
    (He puts hands on hips and twists up
    his mouth.)

BROTHER #8
(*Jumps up as if he were his woman, gets in #19's face and curses him out. Sits back in place.*):

dog nigga
chicken shit
motherfuckin'
bastard

BROTHER #17
(*Jumps up as if he were his woman, gets in #19's face and curses him out. Sits back in place.*):

dog nigga
chicken shit
motherfuckin'
bastard

BROTHER #34
(*Jumps up as if he were his woman, gets in #19's face and curses him out. Sits back in place.*):

dog nigga
chicken shit
motherfuckin'
bastard

BROTHER #3
(*Jumps up as if he were his woman, gets in #19's face and curses him out. Sits back in place.*):

dog nigga
chicken shit
motherfuckin'
bastard

BROTHER #5
(*Jumps up as if he were his woman, gets in #19's face and curses him out. Sits back in place.*):

dog nigga
chicken shit
motherfuckin'
bastard

BROTHER #19:
baby what happened to your strong and silent
        image.
stonewall
the strong and silent wonder woman of the
        third millennium
cracked
and somehow i got knee deep
in the definitive female trouble
every month it seems
and i ain't scared to tell
you 'bout yourself
queen kong
but name callin' don't
get it.

naw you silent did it
i don't be a conjurer like you
i need real language not sad looks
i don't read tea leaves
and know that love is apparent
jus' cuz'
you strong and silent
so cuz' you did me some favors
don't mean i'm ob-bli-gated to your fantasies

i don't understand your sendin' me
things in the mail c.o.d.
and nothin' books have
blank pages
meant to be filled
with your love notes
not mine

cuz' when i love
you know it
and when i don't
have a pot to piss in
you know it
and when i'm worthless
it's your vision of me
not mine

*

and if i made a fool
of you
all good guys don't win
and ever since
i lucked up on myself
and that wuz' a miracle
i have been clear
and straight forward with my passions
dislikes and dances
and you know that
so be strong
and be silent
but get the hell outa my face
with your pain
cuz' now that you 'put out' with me
and i'm layin' in the lowest forms
of life
i still want to dance
i still want to sing my song
i still want to be the luckiest
myself I can be
so take that strong odor perfume
and take that silent death wish
to some other shrink
cuz' dr. jeckle and mr. hyde
moved

    ALL BROTHERS
      (*heckling*):
desperate

    BROTHER #34
      (*rises, takes CS*):
so what if i'm desperate
we have all been desperate
at one time or another . . .
for a smile or a trick
or treat surprise called
love
but it must have been jus' that
a temporary condition on your part
and you saw a bargain in another window
and went shoppin'
or maybe it wuz' my music that

reminded you of him
that someone else
and you couldn't look at me no more
and i should have seen you had
changed your mask
but i didn't notice
it was halloween
and i wanted that trick or treat
surprise called love
and the jack o'lantern smile
candle flames and all
and i could deal with that
desperately loving you
before and after all saints day
becuz' the blessin' had not gone
away
or maybe i wuz' jus' the last door
you knocked on
before you were due back home
back home with him
before thanksgiving could be shared
by us before the christmas holidays
happened inside of me
i wanted your trick or treat
surprise called love
cuz' you knocked at my door
colorfully dressed but with
no disguise you needed my love
so this halloween
i'm not gonna celebrate
becuz' i don't want any
ghosts comin' back to haunt me
ever again
                    (*He backs USL to wall.*)

BROTHER #8
                    (*sneeze, cough, wheeze; all brothers un-
                    wanted exit USR and USL.*):
i'm used to bein' alone now
the pain of emptiness
lets me know that i am
the loser i wuz' afraid
of bein' . . . i'm used to bein'

a nothin' of a man
a shell: if i held you
then it wuz' a lie . . .
and now i fear that no one else will come
along and save me
and i need to be saved . . .
i'm used to bein' alone
the graveyard of myself
this head cold
and sufferin' that burns
lightly slightly
glancin' touchin' my mind
every now and then
i'm used to bein' alone now
really i am . . . bein' without
and jealous of your new lover
the one you dream about now
the one you touch
the one that loves you back
and i'm used to bein' alone now
livin' in the presence
this graveyard of myself
wonderin' if i'll love again
becuz' i loved you . . . oh yeah
i loved you more than i love god
or any other . . . i'm used to bein'
alone now . . . this graveyard of myself
and the burnin' inside hell
the hell that's inside this now
this presence . . . i loved you
i'm used to bein' alone

ALL BROTHERS
            (*chant in unison*):
they say
they say
they say

            (*All brothers ent. USL and USR. Look
            at #8, take their places.*)

        BROTHER #5
            (*#5 continues toward audience DSC*):
i couldn't love you
that i wuz incapable of that human function

and it did not hurt
no not 'til you believed them
and it hurt me
not to be kissed by you an held by you
and i wanted you to hold me
and i know black boys are not supposed to
        want to be
loved
but i didn't know that not until
you told me that-that-is
what they-they say
they say i dogged before i lived
and bein' black and a man
is an ultimate contradiction
that i am no longer ashamed of
no matter what they say
and i don't want to be free of love
ever no matter what they say
and my love my real love
touched me and saved me from the coldness
that all the world knows
that i carried longer than any other
as long as we talkin'
'bout hope
they say i have none
but i've screamed my hopes at you
and you heard me
you saw me for all that i wuz' worth
before they ice picked me
and left me bleedin' long
before i discovered the injury
and you had no bandages
you a mouthful of razors
and i didn't know that i wuz'
supposed to be so strong so
unfeelin' that knife wounds
would heal without my lovin'
no matter what they say
i loved
i loved you fo' real fo' yourself and
then-then that's when i learned
that niggas were stupid first
and never could they be touched

so indiscriminately
and it's been a while
and a whole lot of talk
since the last time the water
had been turned to blood
and i don't know why they say
what they say
but i want you to hold me now
i want you to love me
i want you

to be the only thing in my life
that can heal me
see me and feel
the wounds and doubts
no more
don't ever think
that i
can come without you ever again
i am not able to be
can't get it together without you
and my love knows me better than myself
no matter what they say
so fuck the given circumstances
and the bold night action
'cause the rain is gonna fall all over
st. louis
and i'm gonna need a place to be
warm and i ain't figured out
how to be someplace all alone
with no one else
unless it wuz' a tomb
and my love
my love
resurrected me
down on sarah and finney
no matter what they say
i love you
and that's bein' myself
so selfishly that you can't
even be in on the hellified joke
and i love you
and i love you

BROTHER #34:
and i love

BROTHER #8:
and i love

BROTHER #17:
and i love

BROTHER #3:
and i love

BROTHER #19:
and i love

BROTHER #5:
and they didn't say that
i loved you and bring back
my kindness
my joy that i gave to you
i know you need it too
but bring it back
share it with me it is ours to share
not to be

BROTHER #3
interfered with

BROTHER #19
tampered with

BROTHER #8
fucked with

BROTHER #5
brought down

BROTHER #17
hoodoo'd

BROTHER #34
trampled kicked or ice picked

ALL BROTHERS
(*chanting*):
they say
they say
they say

BROTHER #5:
a lot of shit
and it only hurt when you looked at me
and saw nothin' there to love anymore
and when a mirror returns no reflection
no image
no warmth i learned
to cry
while sittin' on the side of the bathtub
listenin' to your resolution
i loved (*he sighs*) man
man i loved you
more than i ever loved
myself
no matter what they say
        (*Lights dim. Spot on #17*).

BROTHER #17
        (*kneels in prayer*):
i am the rain
in the forest
the footprints
left by the hunters
playin' life and death
games
i come to make love to you
under a stormy sky
no stars

i make the tree bark slick
like sweat-covered skin
i am close
seconds away
a misty breath
from cold night's mouth
i am pressed down shadow in the grass
our bed from dust moistened earth

i am rain
fallin' gently
over
you
let me in

the head waters rushin'
makin' white water
splashin' between your rivers
crisscrossin' your flesh
the earth

i make ponds
ripplin' beyond your limits
seconds away rushin' water
fallin'
each beat
separate
drops
findin' lakes
and streams

i am rain
silent
in the dark
rain
holdin' still
the foot prints
of the hunter
playin' life and death
games

i come to make love to you

>   *(Lights fade to black. Music fades in:*
>   *"It Don't Hurt Now.")*

BROTHER #19
>   *(Music fades out. Laughs rolling around*
>   *on floor, takes CS):*
well then what did i expect somehow i didn't
     expect this
naw it's funny it's hysterical
but it's nothin' that i expected
see i disappeared
damn somebody mojoed me
cop'd my soul and pooofff
i had vanished
could you please give me back
though . . . shit i need my raps

my black phone book addressed to my self
it's a secret . . .
i didn't know you worked for the
c.i.a. and wanted to play i spy with me
i want my dark stare
and my musty sweat and my gym
shoes not to mention my groin
what you gonna do with that
the only time it works is when i want it
to and you accused me of workin' overtime
so bring back my industrial revolution
see industrial espionage
was not needed i wuz' god given to myself
the patent and copyright belongs to the
owner and the product cannot be
removed consciously or subconsciously
and any way bein' invisible was a by-
product of me overcomin' our sufferin'
a long time ago
and cat woman always got caught
with the goods and
why you want me to be a buried
treasure where i can't be myself
i like the way i fuck
the way i make love on sunday afternoon
put my razor blades back in the
razor only i can dress that sharp
put the shine back smile and leave
my tooth paste alone
stop playin' with my music and dancin'
me with some off the wall nigga
that you think reminds you of me
dark boys are made one of a kind
that ain't news it's jus' the truth
see i been gone too long
and my homecomin' wuz' a celebration
that i invited you to attend
not a house cleanin' party
were you supposed to rack up
police   police   come quick

ALL BROTHERS
      (*nervously, looking around:*)
Hey man! Be cool!

BROTHER #19:
somebody done practiced
black magic   witchcraft
sorcery and made me disappear
and i want my hairs my cool
my kick my hairline trigger
my rap what you gonna do with
my mmm's and ahhh's
if i'm not there that's masturbation
and you can do that alone
without me
and your needin' me that much don't
justify
stealin'
and your charms and guile
jus' makes you a cat burglar
bring me back
and handle me with care
jus' don't drop me off somewhere
when you get tired of hidin' me
you hid me for too long anyway
i'm jus' now over hearin'
the echoes of the good effects
i had on myself
hey officer
mister lawman
            (*Other brothers exit in a hurry.*)
ain't it aginst the law
to steal personal property
like love and kindness
and expect expect
the person that you stole it
from to get along without them
i can't believe it
i'm shocked that my aroma
and muscles and joints and sprains
could be sold
advertised in essence magazine
and bought at your pawnshop
that's fencin'
bring me back
and that is the only
expectation

i want all my secrecy
brought back
cuz' i jus' learned
i jus' learned the value of it
my damn self

BROTHER #17:
(*Other brothers ent., making
sure the coast is clear.*)
(*Brother #17 is drinking
from a bottle.*)
and what wuz'
who wuz' that
that thing in the night
that clung to me feverishly
as if i wuz' the baddest
the protector
the man
and all the time
i wuz' the holder
the beloved
the damn sacrifice
i placed myself there
on your altar
and you killed it
i mean you killed my love
tried to at least
and this is not a love
poem
about a bad time
where anyone can get
off on or conclude it
with some snide
remark that's jus'
the breaks
no this is not a love
poem bein'
clever is not my thing
i abandoned god
i abandoned life
and wuz' willin'
to be there
on your word alone

and you in some
religious rite
murdered
something so
intrinsic
that i am not
gonna be
nice no so here comes
the nigga the dog
the no good
m.f. (motherfucker)
naw this ain't
no love poem
you hurt me
you hurt this black
m.f. (motherfucker)
and i ain't been
man enuf
to tell you
and you bein' a
pretty thing
ain't got
nothin' to do with
it
nothin'
what manner of
night creature are
you

       (He draws a knife, lunges forward. All
       brothers rush to him, subdue him, take
       the knife and bottle.)

ALL BROTHERS:
be cool man

BROTHER #17:
fine . . .
i'll be cool
i'll be ice
i'll be jus' fine
but i jus' wanna let
her know
i ain't been man enuf
to tell you

that i wuzn't gonna leave
no matter what the odds
were or what they are now
cuz' my blood
tied knots and
i stopped then
and i cried all the pain
away
and i still
pray for you
and i jus' wanna know
when you comin'
back
to me
see i'm man enuf
to still love
but it's gonna do
what it wants

   BROTHER #3
     (*all brothers move away from him*):
yeah, yeah, yeah
i know what you said
you love me
but i don't think
you meant it
see a mouth
can say anything
and yours
an unsated lust
addicted to sayin'
you love me
and makin' it all right
after you done
been
good-bad
mad as hell
and don't want to see
me no more
cuz' you said
you love me
so much
daddy

i can't live without you
take me to the movies
drive me downtown
let's go out for dinner
call me tonight
and have some other nigga answer yo' phone
and you love me right
i'll be good
don't cha know
i'm such a good man
the one you wanted
a kind man
a gentle man
and when we get to lovin'
i got to keep my eyes open
cuz' it's like a bus station
homeless lovers
the love addicts
the insane lovers
keep comin' in on us
peepin' toms
all of them
your friends
and
you love me right
more than
patti labelle
loves to sing
more than
dr. martin luther king
loved to dream
a love you say
is so pure
an unsated lust
and i should be
good to you always
but bein' good to you
is gettin' harder
and harder
by the second
and watchin'
the clock
at this bus station

ain't love
it's jus' cold here
so don't say
you love me
take all
your talk
and ship it
federal express
and when you finally
get around
to lovin' me
make me close
my eyes
this time
tonight please

ALL BROTHERS
                    (*all brothers stand, turn backs to audi
                    ence, put on shades, turn back, pick up
                    newspapers, then take places standing*):
nightmare
we all look the
same
you look like
the dope man
persona murder
not until you feel
the knife
in your thigh
biting your pussy
don't say no to me
i suspect the circumcision
of your pearl tongue
will quiet you huh

BROTHER #8:
OPEN YOUR EYES
WHAT DO YOU THINK THIS IS?

BROTHER #34:
OPEN YOUR EYES
WHAT DO YOU THINK THIS IS?

BROTHER #17:
OPEN YOUR EYES
WHAT DO YOU THINK THIS IS?

BROTHER #19:
OPEN YOUR EYES
WHAT DO YOU THINK THIS IS?

BROTHER #3:
OPEN YOUR EYES
WHAT DO YOU THINK THIS IS?

BROTHER #5:
OPEN YOUR EYES
WHAT DO YOU THINK THIS IS?

ALL BROTHERS:
and power is a open hand
slap against the mouth
forcin' flesh to touch
in the way rumors get started
and teeth grip
against your stomach comes
the scratches of rope
that itches even while you sweat

BROTHER #8:
and time . . . shit time becomes
elastic

BROTHER #34:
and time . . . shit time becomes
elastic

BROTHER #17:
and time . . . shit time becomes
elastic

BROTHER #19:
and time . . . shit time becomes
elastic

BROTHER #3:
and time . . . shit time becomes
elastic

BROTHER #5:
and time . . . shit time becomes
elastic

ALL BROTHERS:
sappin' with memories

of gossamer lightnin'
burn the sky
with the smell of cologne
and sulphur on his skin
you know him forever now
inside you
he scrapes his name
in tender flesh
he kisses the acid drippins
away . . . you stretch the chains
of love . . . mediaeval axemen
come to you now
and the axe chops off the glans
you close your eyes
in this second of victory
and a gauntlet smashes bone

BROTHERS #8 & #34:
bitch, i said look at me

ALL BROTHERS:
hawked spit stings
and he smiles
this champion

BROTHER #8:
who am i?
your eyes flare
night-the boogey-man
motherfucker
and the knife
plunges into the chest
like cuttin' a piece
of bar-b-que
he laughs

BROTHER #34:
who am I?
your eyes flare
night-the boogey-man
motherfucker
and the knife
plunges into the chest
like cuttin' a piece
of bar-b-que
he laughs

BROTHER #17:
who am i?
your eyes flare
night-the boogey-man
motherfucker
and the knife
plunges into the chest
like cuttin' a piece
of bar-b-que
he laughs

BROTHER #19:
who am i?
your eyes flare
night-the boogey-man
motherfucker
and the knife
plunges into the chest
like cuttin' a piece
of bar-b-que
he laughs

BROTHER #3:
who am i?
your eyes flare
night-the boogey-man
motherfucker
and the knife
plunges into the chest
like cuttin' a piece
of bar-b-que
he laughs

BROTHER #5:
who am i?
your eyes flare
night-the boogey-man
motherfucker
and the knife
plunges into the chest
like cuttin' a piece
of bar-b-que
he laughs

*(All brothers continue laughing as they cross
to trash can, drop newspapers in and exit.)*

BROTHER #8
(he picks up cube USL, crosses to CS,
puts it down and sits on it):
once upon a time

once upon a time
i wuz' dedicated to the world
then i went to
st. louis u
three buildings of
insatiable lust
caverns of unholy
thinkin'
once
i wuz' dedicated to the world
a monument
dedicated to third world
struggles
then i went to
201 north grand boulevard

no woman
i don't want you
you can't be serious
i'm me
and i told you what i
wuz' gonna do

i come from a world
where a word is word
and the only thing that i wanted wuz'
for your success also
no woman i don't want your
organization
take it
no you can't
bully rag me
it's my way
yu knew when
i came
i wuz' the messiah

once i wuz' dedicated
to the people

then i went
and volunteered
myself
to advance the cause
cuz' black people
deserve the best
even
when they are
the boss

no woman
you are president
yes you can amen
that way
yes it's gonna
happen

once i wuz' dedicated
to my people's struggle
it's gonna happen
cuz'
creatin' new life
is a solid occupation
that black people
invented
don't bring me down
i'm not some white
god barren
non carin'
i care
but don't make no punk
outa me
once upon a time

i wuz' dedicated to the world
but bein' good
is such a task
made harder
by the second
i told you
i promised you
the best

now let me be
once upon a time
i wuz' dedicated
to black people and our
culture
then i went to
st. louis u
three buildings of
insatiable lusts
made into a punk
and
bein'
good made
harder
every second

BROTHER #17
(*Ent. #3, stand with #8 watching #17,
he's trippin'*):
you be made a man
the same way jesus wuz' made a saviour
in my hood bocors cut the foreskin
and bloody priests remember the hard ons
and the bad days counted in ten seasons and
    new moons
and the women wait with two swords and flat
    ten breasts
on the naked streets for hoodoo gods
and Akan dogs barkin' at drive-by shootings
lightnin' rods strike and this be the law
of Moses crossin' the red sea into the wilderness
the children of Ifa dance
the crack man comin'
as conquistador and the sun is hot in
the flesh of this holy boy
spendin' his last day in hell
before he resurrects:
the cool jerks are ready for revolution
they are prayin' for a sign
amen
(*#3 and #8 sit on steps, passing a bottle
of whisky to #17.*)

BROTHER #34
*(Ent. #34 cross to DSL, makes reference
to #3, #8 & #17.)*

the threesome
good brothers
the blood
in each
the same
each the river
worker side by side
if one wuz' pete
the other wuz' repeat
the other
redundant
but brothers
they toasted life
together
in jeans and tee shirts
at the place
and they saw
her
she worked
there
usually
durin'
the day shift
but one of the girls
wuz' sick
and she needed
the extra
money

pete
caught her
but her eyes
saw all three
she needed the money
she needed the love
perhaps

pete loved her
(#8 turns his back to #3 & #17.)
took it serious

and worked
for the time they would
start
livin' together
brothers
all three
but then she started
cancellin' dates
callin'
and apologizin'
for not bein' there
and
repeat got
too busy
to go drinkin'

at the place
he took
up some strange
hobby
            (*#17 turns his back to #3 & #8.*)
that didn't include
the brothers
he had to be alone
to think things out
said
he needed his independence
            (*They all freeze.*)
wanted to be free
of social categories
but pete
jus' drank
and redundant
drank more often
himself
couldn't
keep a conversation goin'
always
lookin' away
from them
whenever they
did get together
brothers

all three
the same blood
the same river
then pete
noticed
that she didn't
work at the place
                    (*Exit #8 USR.*)
he had stopped
goin' they all had stopped
goin'
                    (*Exit #3 USR.*)
there
it hurt
too much
and drinkin'
and watchin'
the ice melt
was a strange
habit
all three
watched
the ice melt
not bein' able to look
at each other
jus' the ice
the cold ice
meltin'
between
the together
brothers
watchin' the cold
ice meltin'

brothers
jus' cold ice
meltin'
                    (*#34 exits USL.*)

          BROTHER #17
              (*still sitting on steps*):
there is something winter time about my people

their blood poured before the blue corn wuz'
    planted
and came through stone before light
wuz' even a strange consideration—the impulse
    of philosophers
grinded
into history as the loop garous
made for change through struggle
like a black boy beggin'
for a quarter the dirt on his feet
makin' him blacker than the rabbit hole
that led him to wonderland
where the glans of his penis
wuz' snipped
to find the cure for cancer
and the KKK sought ways
to start the end of the world
because winter is a time for sacrifice
and to dream of summer
when mother and father and child
will sleep in the same bed of comfort
yet death
is more than a tarot card
the end of winter is clear
no spring will jump forth
it would have turned to dust
exposed to sunlight
after bein' a child of the night
howlin' in the lunacy of wantin'
death to be freedom
a promise
that can never be given only took
and made to walk the streets
on the way to the queen's garden party
but winter has the gavel now
and it put on an executioner's mask
there is something owed to history
by my people
chosen
to be winter and history wants our faces
i have seen the winter on our faces
and that is what history wants from us
to go through stone as flesh and blood

a rolled stone that never surmounts the
        mountain top
only to grind us back down while
the superior ones want their place in myths
the mountain of our bones
go unnoticed and the cold wind of this winter
takes our youth
unrooted
icy bones jutted into space
there is no spring comin'
no matter how many bonfires we light
history wants our faces
not composit drawings
cold and gray comin' close to our/likeness
history wants our faces: time places events
time places events
how many were lynched
who sailed the middle passage who
fought in the rock house wars
the documents of blood
in south carolina
in south afrika
time places events
and names
history wants names
"Hush hush
somebody's callin' my name."

    BROTHER #19:
finally
i found the job
that promised me
some happiness
real work
and my education
has paid off
sittin' behind
my own desk
a systems design engineer
soft ware
air conditioned
and a salary
that would mean i would jus'

be comfortable
for the rest of my life
i was proud of myself
five years of hell
and then i graduated
guaranteed a job
and home safe
had been an intern
and they knew my expertise
and it
didn't cost nothing
nothing really
straight laced
shirt and tie
but i could deal with that
that's what i wanted
jus' to be comfortable
the rest of my life
and i was willin'
to work for that
i didn't have to wear
brown shoes with a
gray suit
i knew better
i could be black
and still make it
i could still dance
and program
and fly
and be black and make it
jus' be comfortable
the rest of my life
that's all i wanted
and if it meant workin'
late then i would
and i did
and closing up shop
after the sun
had gone down
meant that i could
relax
sleep late
tomorrow mornin'

it was saturday
anyway
and i knew
a white boy
who told
me he would
die and come back
a black boy
so he could live
jus' one saturday night
i laughed
drank my coffee
and went to my own
desk
and i was gonna be
comfortable the rest
of my life
and i could deal with
that and the parking lot
was empty at first
no one was there
only the beauty
of my shadow
fallen against the ground
and i was black
and gonna be comfortable
the rest of my life
but then
sirens and lights
and a hundred blows
against my head
and
my blood
was showed to me
and mouths
screamin'
ugly words

BROTHERS #3, 5, 8, 34, & 17:
rapist
nigga boy
i'm gonna kill ya
put him in the car

and the sirens
and the lights
the reds and golds
the blues

BROTHER #19:
and i wuz' gonna be comfortable
the rest of my life

BROTHERS #3, 5, 8, 34, & 17:
do you know her
what were you doin' there
come on
all you wanted
was to rape her

BROTHER #19:
i was stripped
made to stand there
and
picture
framed

and the ink
covered my swollen knuckles
could you please give
me my clothes
what am i bein' held for
i wuz jus' workin'
late
so i could relax
saturday

BROTHERS #3, 5, 8, 34, & 17:
line up is he the one
is he the one
that's him isn't it
don't he look like
the one
he can't hurt you now
we have him
the nigga
bastard rapist
we ought to kill him
now

BROTHER #19:
i wuz' black
and i woke up
late saturday
mornin'
in a cell
identified
read my rights
written off
i wuz' black
and i wuz'
gonna be comfortable
all my life
a hard worker
identified
black
and i could deal with
that
straight laced
gonna be black
and comfortable
all the rest of my life

BROTHERS #3, 5, 8, 34, & 17:
identified
black
identified
black
identified
black
and wanted
for rape

BROTHER #5:
wanted
but with no reward
to no avail

I overheard those whispers
lies
dark phrases

i wuz' alone
in a holdin' cell

gettin' ready
to be released

and across from me

i heard
a dark boy moan

wanted
but with no reward
to no avail

and i felt like holdin' him
or my voice ringin'
but
i felt
like tremblin'
a tremblin'
wave of joy

not with my empty arms
or broken heart

i felt like
the first scream
of the last
slave freed

not chained
not naked
not raw
not bandaged
and brine water poured
to purge the flesh

i felt like
holdin'
not holdin' down
no more pain
served with
the best intentions
i felt revealed

ALL BROTHERS:
i felt revealed
unto myself

BROTHER #5:
i felt revealed
unto myself
and i left
me

i left me
and took flight

ALL BROTHERS:
i felt revealed
unto myself

BROTHER #5:
and i left me
the me that
swallowed
too much
hate
too much pain
too much
coarse
and vulgar-nights
filled
with death
and hatred

i left me
wanted
but with no avail
and found
god
dark phrases
dark phrases
dark boys
black boys
dark boys
black boys
and i found god
dark phrases

revealed
unto myself
dark phrases
revealed
unto myself
dark spirits
revealed
unto myself

and i found god
i found god in me
and i found me

and i found god
revealed
unto myself
and i found god in me
and i found me
dark phrases
a dark skinned god
i found me

and i found me

BROTHER #5:
and this is for black boys
who considered homicide
but decided to be themselves

FIERCE LOVE
Stories from Black Gay Life

Pomo Afro Homos

(Postmodern African-American Homosexuals)

Brian Freeman
Djola Branner
and Eric Gupton

Pomo afro homos (Postmodern African-American Homosexuals) consists of Brian Freeman, writer, director, and performance artist, who worked as stage manager for the Negro Ensemble Company in New York City in the 1970s before he became a member of the San Francisco Mime Troupe for eight years; Djola Branner, poet, dancer, and Afro-Haitian dance teacher; and Eric Gupton, actor, singer, cabaret artist. Pomo Afro Homos originated from Black Gay Men United and was inspired by Marlon Riggs's documentary film *Tongues Untied*. Pomo Afro Homos was the first gay group to be funded by the National Endowment for the Arts Expansion Arts Program.

Pomo Afro Homos has toured throughout the United States and Europe. The group gave its debut performance, *Fierce Love: Stories from Black Gay Life*, at Josie's Cabaret and Juice Joint in San Francisco in 1991. Other performances include *Dark Fruit*, first performed in 1991 at the New York Shakespeare Festival's Public Theater as part of *Moving Beyond the Madness: A Festival of New Voices*. Pomo Afro Homos also performed *Dark Fruit* in 1992 at Josie's Cabaret and Juice Joint, and in 1993 at Alice Tully Hall in New York City as part of the Lincoln Center Theater's annual Serious Fun Festival. In 1994 Pomo Afro Homos presented *More Fabulous Fun Stories* at Highways Performance Space in Santa Monica, California.

Brian Freeman and Eric Gupton live in San Francisco, California. Djola Branner lives in Minneapolis, Minnesota.

Order of scenes:

We Are (D. Branner)

Men on Mens (B. Freeman)

I Don't Want to Hear It! (B. Freeman)

The Visitation (*Text*: B. Freeman/*Choreography*: D. Branner)

Sad Young Man (B. Freeman)

Red Bandanas (D. Branner)

Good Hands (E. Gupton)

The Just Us Club (B. Freeman)

Black Like Me (D. Branner)

Silently Into the Night (D. Branner)

Toward a Black Queer Rhythm Nation (B. Freeman)

We Are (Reprise).

We Are

DJOLA: We are
oceans of darkness
glimmers of light

BRIAN: We are
numerous and varied
flamboyant and dull
pious, perverse

ERIC: We are
the who's who
and the who's not

DJOLA: We are
centuries of silence
milliseconds of sound

BRIAN: We are
numerous and *quite* varied
cruel and loving
tight-assed and loose

ERIC: We are
unlike and quite similar to
all the age old myths

DJOLA: We are young
Well . . . relatively young
gifted, black, and gay
and these are some of our stories
our passions and fears
our victories and tears

        drink them like water
        savor them like wine
        spread them like fire

(ERIC *sings an a cappella improvisation.*)

DJOLA: We are
        an endangered species
        But our stories must be told
        our lives
        forever real
        must be cherished
        and our love
        forever rising
        must be
        has got to be
        no doubt about it
        as strong as our ancestors'
        and twice as fierce.

Men on Mens

(*Two director's chairs are set stage center. The Weather Girls' "It's Raining Men" plays in the background.*)

ANNOUNCER (*offstage*): Cable access 62 presents "Men on Mens."

(BLAIN *and* ANTOINE, *two flaming black queens, enter and sit in a parody of talk show hosts Siskel and Ebert. They stare out as if addressing a television camera. Music fades out.*)

BLAIN: I'm Blain Edwards.

ANTOINE: I'm Antoine Merriweather.

TOGETHER: Welcome to *Men on Mens.*

ANTOINE: The show that used to look at movies from a men's point of view.

BLAIN: But now we've dropped all that pretense and we just look at mens!

ANTOINE: Our first mens this week is 49er tight end Roger Craig.

BLAIN: Touch me in the morning, then just close the door!

ANTOINE: We can't confirm rumors that Roger plays in more parks than Candlestick, but that hard pumping butt alone gets—

TOGETHER: Two snaps up!

(*A brother enters wearing an "Act Black" T-shirt and beret, glasses. He is a cross between a member of* ACT-UP *and the ultimate black revolutionary. He wears the logo of a black fist overlapping a pink triangle on his T-shirt.*)

REVO: SILENCE EQUALS DEATH!!! FIGHT AIDS! FIGHT BACK! FIGHT BLACK!

BLAIN: 'Scuse me. Hello? Catch the breeze, Louise, this isn't seventies night here.

REVO: Brothers! My brothers! Seize the time!

ANTOINE: Is he talking about Morris Day?

BLAIN: I don't think so.

ANTOINE: Who are you?

REVO: I'm from ACT-BLACK, a revolutionary organization of postmodern African-American Homosexual Men.

BLAIN: Pomoafrohomos?

ANTOINE: I got the tea, thank you, Aunt Bee.

REVO: Brothers. Join the struggle. We demand an end to these demeaning depictions of Black Gay Men as snap-happy sissies perched above the masses—

ANTOINE: Don't pull my pearls, Peola.

REVO: An end to mainstream media misappropriation of Negro Faggotry.

BLAIN: Look, Eldridge, we *did* politics in college.

BLAIN AND ANTOINE: Hated it!

REVO: Is that it? Do you truly believe that our concerns run no deeper than joviality, fashion, and sex?

ANTOINE: Yes, I am deeply concerned.

BLAIN: Deep as it gets.

REVO: Well, we are here to serve notice that any supposedly straight actors who continue to exploit the mannerisms, vocabulary, signifying strokes and secret traditions of Black Gay Men for purposes that do not serve *our needs* will be outed!

BLAIN & ANTOINE: What!!!

REVO: Outed! Courtesy of a toll-free hotline we have set up in every Black Gay Club coast to coast. (*He snaps.*)

BLAIN: You wouldn't!

REVO: Ask Whitney (Houston)!

BLAIN: What if we did a show like "Men on Safe Mens"?

ANTOINE: Yeah. Give us a minute to think about this.

REVO: Think fast, brothers. The revolution is at your front door, and knocking. Hard. Will you join the struggle? What time, I said what time, I said what *time* is it? (*He snaps.*)

(*Blackout.*)

I Don't Want to Hear It!

(A working-class brother in a Raiders jacket and cap enters and confronts the audience.)

BRO: Gay? What is that, huh? Do I look like somebody's Gay to you? Yeah, I like to catch a little taste of the other side now and then. That don't make me nobody's punk. Why people got to go put their business all out in the street? What am I supposed to do, go up on my roof tell everybody ga . . . ga . . . ga . . . ? Forget that! I have a job. I have a family. I don't want to hear it. I come home from work the other day, the kids got Oprah on. I look and I see these white boys and some Uncle Tom colored ones up there talking that gay . . . I turned that mess off, yes I did. I said, "Timica. Lakeisha. Go on upstairs. Do your homework. I don't want to hear it. You watch too damn much TV anyway. That was just some mess." See, me and my old lady have an understanding. I go out couple of nights a week, take care of my business, jump in the shower when I get home. She don't say nothing. Then when she wants to go out—to Safeway or the beauty salon, over her mama's house—hey, she don't hear nothing out of me. That's fair. Why these men got to dress up like second-rate women? Is that your gay? I'm out last week trying to take care of my business and this "thing"— look like a Natalie Cole train wreck—wants to sidle up to me. Asks me do I "go gay"? I said, "I don't go gay. I don't know gay." I said, "Gay? I don't want to hear it. I don't want to motherfucking hear it!"

(Blackout.)

The Visitation

(Operatic music plays as RONALD, *an opera queen in sweater and scarf, enters acting quite impatient.)*

RONALD: Donald?

DONALD *(always from offstage)*: Yes, Ronald?

RONALD: Have you seen my contact lenses?

DONALD: The green ones or the blue ones?

RONALD: Never mind. Dearest, I know that our relationship can never equal the one you have with Leontyne Price, but if you don't hurry we'll be late.

DONALD: I'm coming, but my styling gel hasn't set yet.

RONALD: Look, my little snowflake . . .

DONALD: Yes, my Godiva chocolate drop . . .

RONALD: Hurry!

DONALD: Can we stop at Popeye's on the way? I am famished.

RONALD: Popeye's? Fried chicken? Darling, we don't eat fried chicken. I refuse to have this discussion again. You can get a nice pâté at intermission.

DONALD: Go get a cab! *(He passes him an umbrella.)*

(The sound of rain fades in. RONALD *struggles without success to hail a cab.)*

RONALD: They never stop for me. *(He opens an umbrella.)*

(A loud thundercrack. An African spirit magically appears. The rain changes to drums as the spirit, using Afro-Haitian dance, takes con-

264

trol of RONALD*'s spirit, allowing* RONALD *a moment's break from his bourgeois obsessions to indulge in a tribal dance. When* RONALD *is wrecked the spirit departs. Drums fade out and rain sounds return.*)

RONALD: Donald, let's stay home and rent a video.

(*Blackout.*)

Sad Young Man

(Aretha Franklin's "Hey Now, Hey" plays. Brian enters with a stool and a tote bag of props. Music fades.)

BRIAN: Cultural baggage. My cultural baggage. *(Sets bag aside.)*

They say the blacker the berry the sweeter the juice, and I was born in the berry, that's Roxbury, the black section of Boston. My dad, an Adam Clayton Powell, Jr., wantabee, had a small business hanging wallpaper in the new suburban homes of the Jewish folks who fled our neighborhood as too many black folks moved in. My mom, a Diahann Carroll wantabee, Mom could pass—that's a black thing, you wouldn't understand—and worked as a fashion model for Bonwit Teller. We owned our own home, even if it was a slum. We went to an integrated church, until we realized we could find better music on Sunday mornings.

At age six I shook the hand of Reverend Dr. Martin Luther King, Jr., on the steps of the Boardman Elementary School—in Roxbury! I thought I was shaking hands with Jesus, and refused to wash mine for a week, a sin for which my parents nearly slapped the black off of me. We were the very model of a modern negro family.

(Pulls out family portrait.)

One day a photographer came through our ghetto with a Polaroid Land camera and a pony and for a dollar you could get your picture taken like you were riding "My Friend Flicka." When Mom came out to pay the photographer, he noticed her runway-trained stride and asked her to pose for a project he was working on about model Negro families—that is, pose without

266

the pony. Mom put on her Jackie Kennedy outfit, she posed. Dad came home, put on his Sunday suit, he posed. I put on my blue then green then blue iridescent suit, I posed. He got a set of pictures, we got a set of pictures, never saw the man again. But six months later, my mom, having gone to night school and become a schoolteacher, was shopping in a school supplies store for positive images to pin up in her classroom for Negro History Week—now, this is before we were black and before we had a month. In between the red hearts for Valentine's Day and the bunnies with baskets for Easter she found a set of cardboard cutouts labeled *The New Negro Family*, featuring herself (displays the cutouts), my dad, and somebody *else's* child. For my parents, it was an *Ebony* magazine dream come true! But for me, what a nightmare. It seems some art director in some corporation somewhere had decided I wasn't black enough to be in my own family. Humiliated, I retreated into my books and Johnny Mathis records, vowing that one day I'd be more than a New Negro, I'd be a New, New Negro. I'd be different.

(*Johnny Mathis record, "All the Sad Young Men," plays.*)

Oh, Johnny, I'm so sad. (*He pulls a box of Oreos from his bag and tries to swallow one as if it were poison, then throws it away and pulls out a picture of Johnny Mathis and a Curious George doll.*) Johnny, George, let's run away together, huh? Just us guys. We'll go somewhere we can be new, new, Negroes together. Okay, Johnny? Okay, George? (*Looking at George.*) Oh, well, you can come, Johnny, but George-Negroes can sure be monkeys sometimes, George, but monkeys can't be Negroes! (*He puts George away.*) But you and me, Johnny, we'll go somewhere, okay? Do you have good hair, Johnny, or is that a process? Should I get a process? Johnny, how come I never see you with girls on TV? I have a secret, Johnny. I love you, Johnny, I love you.

(*Song ends. He is now a teen.*)

My resourcefulness lands me at an exclusive Latin preparatory school for boys, but my bus ride brings me home to a poor black neighborhood on fire. As I jam my head with a language that white people haven't spoken in two thousand years, my brother, a Huey Newton wantabee in six-inch platforms and double-breasted "pleather"—pleather? That's plastic leather, we couldn't afford real leather—kicks open my door and announces, "Nigger, either you are part of the solution or part of the problem!" Confused by the contradictions, I do drugs, lots of them, and hang out with hippies, one of whom, black, seduces me! But one tripped-out blow job does not a "homo" make, and I decide to become part of the solution and I invite an Angela Davis wantabee from a girls' Latin preparatory school to a Roberta Flack concert. (*Roberta Flack's "Sweet Bitter Love" plays in the background.*) With her ten and my twelve inches of "fro" we are two black dandelions, in a field of a thousand. We can sort of see Roberta through people's necks, but we don't care. We're in love.

As I slip my hand through her dashiki, my nose through her co-conut-scented hair, and my tongue past her cinnamon-flavored lips, I think, "This is a dream." Someone else's.

(*Music ends. He is now a college student.*)

A professional actor performs at my Ivy League college and he's really great and during the post-show discussion I ask all the right questions and we are really communicating and after the post-show discussion we talk and talk and he says, "Why don't we go back to my hotel and we can talk about *your* career?" My career? Wow! So we walk back to his hotel room and on the way we're talking and we get to his hotel room and he says, "Why don't you sit next to me on the bed?" And I'm like, "Wow, these New York actors are really into breaking down barriers, and we're talking, talking, and he says, "You don't mind if I take my pants off?" and I'm like, "Is this 'the method' or what?" So I take my pants off and we're talking, talking and we're no longer talking and, well, uh . . . he comes in my mouth! I race out the hotel room, back to my dormitory, and vomit in the middle of the quadrangle. A security guard comes over and asks, "Yo, blood, what's up? Something go down wrong?" *Phew!*

Ashamed. Confused. I decide to give heterosexuality one last chance and I invite a sister from the BSU, that's the Black Student Union, that's another black thing—are you beginning to understand?—I invite her to see *Lady Sings the Blues.* But she lets me know that word is out amongst the brothers in the BSU that I am "that way" and she just couldn't be seen with me. "That way"? Was it my clogs? My hot pants? My glitter tops? I am out and outraged now. I abandon the BSU for the GSU, the Gay Students Union. I run for office, and I put an

end to rumors that I'm big fag on campus by becoming offi-
cially elected *the* big fag on campus.

(*College graduation music plays underneath.*)

At my inauguration, I realize the brothers in the BSU are through
with me, the sisters in the BSU don't know what to do with
me. The white kids in the GSU think they have a real black
thing on their hands who they truly do *not* undertstand—but
they will—they all will. 'Cause I remember the words that Rev.
Dr. Martin Luther King, Jr., spoke that day, so long ago, on
the steps of the Boardman Elementary School in Roxbury.
"Sometimes, I get weary. Sometimes, when I get criticism from
other Negroes, oh, I get weary. But I have faith. Yes, I have
faith."

(*Blackout.*)

Red Bandanas

(*A* RAPPER *enters wearing dark shades, a cap turned backwards, and a red bandana around his neck.*)

RAPPER: Yo, yo, yo. What's up? What's up? . . . (*adlib.*) . . . Yo, M.C., are you ready? Kick it!

(*Music—101 b.p.m. minus-one—starts. Two more* RAPPERS *in dark shades, caps, and bandanas enter.*)

(*chorus*)
Red(Red)
Bandanas(Bandanas)
Red Bandanas mean fuck me
(mean fuck me, mean fuck me)

when worn
in the right hip pocket
in the right crowd
like Castro
or Christopher Streets
but mine is worn
around the neck

it means
that I'm remembering granddad
who wiped the sweat
from his brow
onto it
or used it to catch
the contents
of a cough

270

or laundered it
and wore it around his neck.

Give it up, say

(*chorus*)
Red(Red)
Bandanas(Bandanas)
Red Bandanas mean fuck me
(mean fuck me, mean fuck me)
say, Red(Red)
Bandanas(Bandanas)

Give it up. (*8-count dance.*)

Red Bandanas mean fuck me
when worn
in the right hip pocket
in the right crowd
like Castro
or Christopher Streets
but mine is worn
around the neck

it means
that I'm remembering Moms
who placed it in
the palm of my hand
and dried the tears
she'd cried with it
'cause her daddy'd died
with nothing but his

(*chorus*)
Red(Red)
Bandanas(Bandanas)
Red Bandanas mean fuck me
(mean fuck me, mean fuck me)
(*Repeat.*)
Go 'head, go 'head, go 'head, go 'head, go 'head
(Go 'head, go 'head, go 'head, go 'head, go 'head)

Give it up. (*32-count dance.*)

Red Bandanas mean fuck me
when worn

in the right hip pocket
in the right crowd
like Castro
or Christopher Streets
but mine is worn
around the neck
(around the neck, around the neck)
(I said, mine is worn
(around the neck)
mine is worn
(around the neck)

(*Two* RAPPERS *exit as first* RAPPER *ad libs. Blackout. Music fades.*)

Good Hands

(ERIC *enters with a chair.*)

I hadn't been inside this club for half an hour when I decided to
go to the back room. Now every once in a while when you're
about to get busy it's as simple as getting the job done—and
on this particular night I wanted to get the job done *right*.

So I made my way down the hall (*sitting in the chair*), and sat
on this bench. A fifty-year-old balding white guy stuck his head
in the room, looked at me real nervous-like, and made his way
out the room. A few minutes behind *him* was a sixty-year-old
bald white man. He came in, sat next to me, and grabbed his
crotch. He looked at me, I looked at him, and he made his
way out the room. Now, I don't know if this was a freak show
in three acts or what, but directly behind him was *the* blond
Adonis—six foot one, piercing blue eyes, and tan for days.
Walking real slow and checking me out real hard, he came up
to me and said, "Suck my dick." Well, I looked at him and said,
"Uh-uh. I don't think so."

This was obviously a sign for me to take my black ass home
(*standing up*) because wasn't nothing happening in the back
room. When all of a sudden this body, this spirit, this man
walked in the room, and as the brother made his way to the
bench, I said, "Good God! We 'bout to get busy!"

(*He sits down in the chair again.*)

So I stretched my legs out, slowly unbuckled my pants, and pulled
up my briefs real tight so he could get a better look at my
hard-on. He responded by touching his crotch. Then I drew
circles outlining my balls right up to the tip of my dick. He

273

responded by squeezing his legs together. Now, this man was absolutely magnificent. Sturdy in stature, big beautiful brown eyes, and skin the color of fertile soil. He unbuckled his pants and skinned the head back down on that big, black, beautiful dick. I wasn't far behind when I took out my cock and matched his rhythm, going up and down, and up and down. Now, I didn't want to make the first move. You see, sometimes when you make the first move you're considered pussy. Well, the truth is I'd have been pussy for him any old day. I just didn't want him to know it.

And like a dream he walked toward me. I unbuttoned his shirt and these nipples jumped out like Hershey's Kisses—I thought I was going to die. And then he reached down and grabbed those dicks and worked those good hands. Up and down, and up and down. And I felt so good as our chests rose and fell at the same time, and when he looked in my eyes I saw his heart yield. And I knew it was just a matter of time before we would both explode.

We stood there for a minute, caught our breath, and he said: "You know the white boys get real nervous when they see the two of us in the same room. Some of the brothers do too. But I like you. I like the way you feel, the way you touch, the way you take your time. Now some of the brothers want to pass the fluids. I can't do that, but there are so many things I can do. I tell you what *I* like to do. I like to pull that jimmy out. Run my hands under that man's balls until his dick sticks straight up. I run that jimmy over that dick, take my teeth out, and work that dick. Maybe I'll get a chance to do it with you sometime."

(*Blackout.*)

The Just Us Club

(Three effeminate black gay men enter. They are not the prettiest. They lip-synch to Diana Ross's "Ain't No Mountain High Enough" and act out a Supremes routine. Music ends.)

PEACHES: I'm Peaches.

POPCORN: I'm Popcorn.

PEPPER: I'm Pepper.

ALL: And we're the Just Us Club. Just Us!

PEACHES: This is a very exclusive organization.

POPCORN: Oh yes! Very.

PEPPER: Don't get your hopes up.

PEACHES: 'Cause kids, we are tight.

POPCORN: Tighter than the Eastern Stars.

PEPPER: Tighter than Oprah's weave.

PEACHES: Airtight! Babies, you couldn't work your way in here with a razor. So don't try it. Don't even consider it, unless you meet the requirements.

PEPPER: Grand Matron Mother May I Peaches?

PEACHES: Yes, Most Revered Sister Daughter Pepper?

POPCORN: We do like our titles.

PEPPER: Why don't you spell out the requirements for the children?

PEACHES: I will, when I'm ready.

PEPPER: And what would help our highly esteemed Grand Matron Mother May I credit-to-her-community Peaches get ready?

PEACHES: If you would shut up, back off, and back me up.

PEPPER & POPCORN: Alright.

PEACHES: You know how Michael—yes, that Michael, is there really any other?—you know how Michael and his fine brothers sang A, B, C—

PEPPER & POPCORN: *"A, B, C, so easy as 1, 2, 3, as simple as Do, Re, Me, (etc.)."* (PEACHES *becomes Michael and takes off with the song, moonwalks, spins, etc.*)

PEACHES: Whew! Like I was saying, our requirements are as simple as P.B.U.

POPCORN & PEPPER: P.B.U.?

PEACHES: Poor, Black, & Ugly!

POPCORN: Is that a read?

PEPPER: Is that *shade?*

PEACHES: Naw, daughters. It's just the truth. It's—

ALL: Just Us!

PEACHES: See, Mother and her lovely daughters here had grown weary of the roles we were relegated to in "gay" society.

POPCORN: At the clubs, I was everyone's best girlfriend, nobody's dream date, and got real tired of "making do" with that two in the morning trade. I was the Millie Jackson of the Tenderloin. The clean-up woman.

PEPPER: See, I didn't have that problem 'cause when the "siddity set" had a party—that's all them Bryant Gumbel–lookin' boys—I was *on* the A-list.

PEACHES: You mean "A-list" as in armed and extremely dangerous.

POPCORN: To be "a"-voided at all costs.

PEPPER: Naw, I was in the "clique." Long as I didn't stick my head out the kitchen, and kept rattling them pots!

PEACHES: You mean as long as you ironed your headrag. And I was through doing my Jennifer Holliday impersonation. "No, no, no way" I was getting into that dress again. The glamour was gone. With our loud selves and nelly ways we was on the outside of a society on the outside. And what did we get out of it?

POPCORN: Not much, so we said "fuck it," and hooked up our own thing.

PEPPER: That's right!

ALL: Just Us!

PEACHES: No longer do we peruse the classifieds, hoping to spot BGM seeks average-looking nelly thang. Major attitude & cheap cologne fine by me.

POPCORN: No longer do we linger by the phone on weekends, knowing that "real men" would probably call Lassie for a date before they call us.

PEPPER: Naw, girl, we get together, play a few hands of Bid Whist.

POPCORN: Fix a cute snack.

PEACHES: And wear as much cheap cologne as we please.

PEPPER: How's my hair?

POPCORN: Your curl activator needs recharging.

PEPPER: Bitch. (*They cat fight.*)

PEACHES: Daughters! Remember, we don't dish here!

POPCORN: I'm sorry, Pepper.

PEPPER: I love you, Popcorn. (*They hug.*)

PEACHES: So boys, the next time some hot number dumps you, and you want to get the real read from mother, don't call me. Don't even leave a message, 'cause me and my sisters will be busy—like Re Re says, "doin' it for ourselves."

ALL: JUST US!

PEACHES: First item on the agenda.

PEPPER: I motion we reclaim vogueing for the nellie sissies.

POPCORN: Madonna never did get it right.

PEACHES: All in favor?

ALL: Ay!

(*"Everybody, Everybody" plays as they vogue. Blackout.*)

Black Like Me

A MAN *enters in Americanized African garments and speaks with a royal attitude.*)

Don't call me a Black Gay Man. Don't call me a Gay Black Man. I'm an Afrocentric Homosexual Male. Get it right. And I like my men like I like my coffee. Dark. Strong. And Flavorful. Sumatra, Kenyan, Ethiopian. Don't cut it. Don't blend it. Don't put no "Swiss Miss" nor "Mocha Mix" on the table. Brother to brother, black on black, all the want-to-be's step way back. Many claim to be but few are black enough for this black man.

(*Blackout.*)

Silently Into the Night

DJOLA (*As he enters he sings "You Are My Friend" like Patti LaBelle*): He was my boon-coon buddy, my main man, my best girlfriend. I mean we ate, drank, sang, danced, prayed, cried, and screamed together. We had to quit hanging so tight 'cause everyone thought we were lovers and neither of us could get any play. But I loved me some Aman.

I worked only two blocks from the hospital, so I spent my lunch hours with Aman during those last three weeks. And I remember this particular morning I woke up and decided I wouldn't wait until lunch to see him. I would go in before I went to the office. He was in ICU by then. The respirator was going. He was in a coma. Had been for a couple of days. Even in the stillness, there was such pain in the room. And I just stood there, watching his chest rise and fall, and pretty soon I was breathing in the same time, our last dance you might say, 'cause everything else in the room was suspended. I felt him rise out of his skin and drape one of those lanky arms around me. Funny, I thought, here he was consoling me. We were communicating somehow, and I looked at his body, heaving, and said, "Well, girl, this is another fine mess you've gotten yourself into." He laughed, withdrew his arm, and slunk back into his skin.

I looked up from the computer just before lunch and thought about Aman. Felt him. When I stopped by the hospital after work, the nurse told me he had passed away around noon.

My friend Bolla a.k.a. Miss Process, the Margaret Meade of psychic healing, picked up Aman's mother at the airport. She knew she was trouble the minute she stepped off the plane with that gray hair piled high as the control tower and those patent leather pumps, and bag to match. Aman hadn't seen his mama in eleven years but she quickly set about the task of laying him to rest. She let Bolla pick the outfit to lay him out in. She chose that nice bright Guatemalan shirt, the one I gave him, some turquoise drawstring pants, and a sharp African crown for his head.

Now if the hippies who burnt sage and dangled crystals all over the man while he was in the hospital thought Mama was spooky—they swore that the oldest brother, who Aman hadn't seen in *thirteen* years, was a monster. A fundamentalist Lutheran preacher, who felt it was his duty, especially since mother had summoned him, to preside over the funeral. Six foot one and every inch a Christian as Aman was queer. If you knew Aman you know that was some serious faith. The brother made arrangements to have the funeral at a mortuary in Bayview Hunter's Point.

It was a *long* drove out to Bayview. Me and Lance, my hippie, my lover, drove behind the family limo. The first mile was quiet. Then we came to a stoplight at 16th & Mission and this huge Negro in a white suit and red shirt, hair greasy enough to stir-fry broccoli in, steps from the curb. I don't know this man from Adam but he opens the door and jumps into the back seat. Explains that he has been invited to speak at the funeral by Aman's brother, who is riding in the limo up ahead. I look at Lance, he looks at me, and as the stoplight changes from red to green the Negro prays silently to himself. The car reeks of Aqua Velva.

(ERIC *and* BRIAN *enter singing "Precious Lord."*)

DJOLA: (*over song*) Once in the mortuary, I wonder if I can get through the service. Get through the mother, who has asked me to take pictures with her Kodak Instamatic, and especially through the brother, who is on a mission of his own. (*Becoming the brother.*) "There were so many questions in my heart as I began this journey to San Francisco. Why had Aman and I grown estranged? Why had over a decade passed since we laid eyes upon each other? Why had we—like Cain and Abel—been unable to confer our love as flesh, as family upon one another? Yes, so many questions in my heart. And in my search for answers the Lord in his wisdom led me to my hometown church's sister congregation over in Oakland. In that temple of worship, a man was referred to me by his most generous pastor, a man who might provide some hard-sought answers. In his mercy, that gentleman is with us today and has consented to speak." Now, ninety percent of the congregation is lesbian and gay. People are sighing. Seriously sighing as Mazola head, the man in the white suit, strides to the altar. (*Becoming the man.*) "I didn't know Aman, so I can't comment on his life, but my life, too, was filled with desire. Every minute of every waking day was a living hell because all I thought about was having my way with men. And before God I can't lie, I *had* my way with *many* men. I could not get through the day without visiting the Pendulum, or the Blue & Gold—that's closed now, or the dirty bookstores, the Eagle Creek—that reopened, the Steamworks, or the toilets at the library, or the northside of Lake Merritt. But I *have* found Jesus, and there is comfort in his hand." The brother shouts, "Repent!" Mama shouts, "Amen!" And I can't take it anymore! I am gone, down the aisle, out the front door, and into the street.

(ERIC *and* BRIAN *exit.*)

I want a cigarette, it's been three months but I would really like a cigarette. Lance follows me into the street. Why does he look so fucking calm? But before I can say anything fifteen, twenty, thirty people pour into the street, some crying, others pulling their hair, others screaming. We are a collective mess. I decide after *two* margaritas that a cigarette definitely will not resolve the hurt. Or the anger. I call my sister in L.A. and threaten to haunt the bitch for the rest of her natural life if she ever pulls a stunt like that. We organize another memorial service—minus the blood relatives. I sing, Miss Process lights candles, and we bid a fond farewell to Aman's spirit at the ocean. And I wonder, why do so many of our brothers bundle up their pain and go off silently into the night?

(*He sings as he exits. Blackout.*)

Toward a Black Queer Rhythm Nation

(*Heavy metal music [Whitesnake's "Bad Boys"] plays as a young black gay enters dressed in the style of the "Queer Nation" kids: leather jacket, white T-shirt, babushka on his head, chains around the neck. He dances like a nerdy rocker and sings along, strumming an air guitar.*)

KID: "I'm the black sheep in my family!" (*He cuts off music.*) Whitesnake. Cool, huh? They're racist. They're sexist. If you could actually hear the lyrics, they're probably homophobic, but they are so cool! Do you think if you're black and you're gay and you listen to heavy metal, that's a truly transgressive act? Huh? I'm trying to be a rebel, but I'm having trouble finding a cause. I used to hang out with the Queer Nation dudes. They swear they are truly transgressive, but they bother me, they really bother me. Last meeting we were having a discourse on the efficacy of staging a protest at Toys "Я" Us. This is going on for hours and I'm thinking like if some six-year-old future homophobe wants to buy a Mr. Potato Head, let him. We keep going round and round and I finally stand up and say, "Yo, dykes. Dudes. I am feeling oppressed by all this clonedom here. I don't want to put stickers on my leather jacket, that reminds me of my parents' Volvo!" Then Joey, this white dude I went to art school with—thinks he is real hip—he says, "Oppressed? Your parents make more dough than the Huxtables. When they learned you were gay they threw a coming out party. You've never felt oppression in your life." I say, "Yo, dude. Don't talk to me. (*He flips the finger.*) Deconstruct this!" Then Aurora, this face ring lesbian, you know (*he indicates various points of piercing*)—Aurora jumps in: "As a woman, w-o-m-y-n, who continually struggles with the white male hegemony of

282

this organization, I am in solidarity with the oppression being felt by my black gay brother . . ." And I'm like, "Spare me your seventies self-righteousness! I can get that at home!" So I split. I head for the Stud. Guess what? It's old clone night. Everyone is over twenty-five. Nothing but "muscle bunnies" (*he flexes*) all pumping away to that dun-dun music. DUN DUN DA DA DA DUN DUN. (*He dances in a seventies disco style.*) Please! Talk about oppressive! But I'm too pissed to care, so I order a drink and start drowning my sorrows in Calistoga when I hear this sound:

(DJOLA & ERIC *sing the melody from "We Are" on mike.*)

KID: I think, "Whoa! Is there benzine in Calistoga?" So I order a beer, but two sips, I hear it again:

(DJOLA & ERIC *sing another phrase of the melody.*)

KID: This is seriously challenging what little cool I have left. I look around the club to see if anyone else has heard it, but everyone is still pumping away DUN DUN DUN DA DA DUN DUN. Everyone except the one other black person there. (DJOLA *enters dressed like an urban dance hall diva.*) We'd seen each other before but never spoke.

DJOLA: You had a lot of attitude. I thought you were tired.

KID: You had a lot of attitude. (*To audience.*) But we look at each other and—

(KID *and* DJOLA *both sing the melody.*)

KID: Like close encounters of the third kind! And he says—

DJOLA: This club is tired.

KID: So we split for the Box, this funk and soul club, and on the way I tell him what happened at the meeting and he says—

DJOLA: Those white boys are tired.

KID: And I think well, that's a rather simplistic analysis of a complex sociological construction. But then, I'd never thought of it that way before. I thought, you know, we're all gay here, so we're all . . . you know. Well, we get to the Box.

DJOLA: It had *snowed* in there. Can't they leave us anything? Tired.

KID: The crowd was kinda monochromatic. But the DJ was playing rap, hip-hop, industrial. . . .

DJOLA: That white girl is seriously tired.

KID: But I'm having a mood swing for the better and we start to dance, but before we can break a sweat, it happens again.

(ERIC *sings the melody on mike.*)

KID: The two of us look around and see this brother coming toward us like Nanook of the north fighting his way through a blizzard. He pops out of the crowd and says—

ERIC: Ow, ow, ow, my ass! I'm here to dance. Let's kick it!

(*Music: C & C Music Factory's "Let's Rock and Roll." They all dance. They talk as they dance and music plays.*)

KID: Kick it? We blasted off! It was just the three of us dancing with each other, but it felt like the Starship Enterprise had particle-beamed us into another reality.

DJOLA: I looked up at the DJ booth and saw Sylvester push that white girl out the way. He said, "Honey, that's cute, but let's get real!"

ERIC: Willi Smith and Patrick Kelly were up on that stage, modeling the fiercest drag I'd ever seen.

KID: And James Baldwin was behind the bar, pouring free drinks for himself and everybody else. He pops me open a Calistoga. I tell him about the meeting, then about my real fear, that maybe what Joey said is true, that maybe I am just a spoiled suburban brat with nothing more than an armchair understanding of oppression. James says (*becoming James Baldwin*), "My dear young boy. *You* are a Black Queer growing up in America. I think you've hit the jackpot! Work it, my dear. Work it!"

(*They all dance. Lights fade, silhouetting all dancing their own dance together.*)

We Are (Reprise)

(ERIC *and* BRIAN *sing as* DJOLA *recites.*)

DJOLA: These are *some* of our stories
        our passions and fears
        our victories and tears
        drink them like water
        savor them like wine
        spread them like fire

        We are
        an endangered species
        But our stories must be told
        our lives
        forever real
        must be cherished
        and our love
        forever rising
        must be
        has got to be
        no doubt about it
        as strong as our ancestors
        and twice as fierce.

(*Fade to blackness.*)

TOD, THE BOY, TOD

Talvin Wilks

TOD, THE BOY, TOD

TALVIN WILKS, playwright and director, began his writing and directing career with the premiere of *INCUBUS: An American Dream Play* at the 1985 Edinburgh Fringe Festival in Scotland. His play *Tod, the Boy, Tod* received its world premiere production at Crossroads Theater Company in New Brunswick, New Jersey, in 1990. The Group, Seattle's Multicultural Theatre produced the West Coast premiere of *Tod, the Boy, Tod* in Seattle, Washington, in 1993. *Tod, the Boy, Tod* also received a grant from NBC's New Voices of the Nineties program.

Wilks is a founding member of The Spin Lab, a six-member theater collaborative based in New York City that premiered *The Trial of Uncle S/M* as part of the Performing Garage's Visiting Artists Series. Wilks's plays include *Occasional Grace*, produced by En Garde Arts in New York City, *The Life in Between*, and *Bread of Heaven*, staged as part of the 1994 Genesis Festival of African American Voices.

Wilks's directorial projects include *The Love Space Demands* by Ntozake Shange, *The Mystery of Love* by Sekou Sundiata, *Unquestioned Integrity: The Hill/Thomas Hearings* by Mame Hunt, *Lost in Translation* by Craig Harris, and *The Hamlet Project*. He was the first workshop director for Crossroads Theater Company's African American College Initiative Program, and has served as the Literary Manager and Playwright-in-Residence at The Group, Seattle's Multicultural Theater. Talvin Wilks lives in Seattle.

The horror carries the endorsement of centuries and the entire life span of a nation. It is a way of life which reaches back to the beginning of recorded time. And all the bestiality, whenever it occurs and however long it has been happening, is narrowed, focused and refined to shine into a black child's eyes when first he views his world. All that has ever happened to black men and women he sees in the victims closest to him, his parents.

A life is an eternity and throughout all that eternity a black child has breathed the foul air of cruelty. He has grown up to find that his spirit was crushed before he knew there was need of it. His ambitions, even in their formings showed him to have set his hand against his own. This is the desolation of black life in America.

—*Black Rage,* Grier & Cobbs

If we can bring back on ourselves, the absolute pain our people must have felt when they came onto this shore, we are more ourselves again, and can begin to put history back in our menus, and forget the propaganda of devils that they are not devils.

—*The System of Dante's Hell,* LeRoi Jones

Characters

Tod, the Boy, Tod *African American, Age 27*
Mary Martha, the Virgin Mother *African American, Age 48*
Reverend Joe, His Holy Father *African American, Age 50*
John, the Psychiatrist, the Bearer of Truth *Jewish American, Age 50*
The Committee of Social Reform *Caucasian (American)*
      Committee Executive, *Age 67*
      Committee Senior, *Age 48*
      Committee Junior, *Age 27*

Set

The set is an altar in the form of a dream-like exaggeration of JOHN THE PSYCHIATRIST*'s office. Central to the set is a 4 x 6–ft. long ebony table that rests on a low sloping rake perpendicular to the stage. The rake is hard polished wood with an oriental rug that runs the length of the table. There is a black leather swivel chair at each side of the table. The four corners represent the hierarchy: down stage center sits* TOD, THE BOY, TOD; *stage right sits* MARY MARTHA, THE VIRGIN MOTHER; *stage left sits* REVEREND JOE, HIS MOST HOLY FATHER; *upstage center sits* JOHN THE PSYCHIATRIST, THE BEARER OF TRUTH.

At the back of the rake begins an isolated wooden bookshelf that is the width of the rake and ten feet high. There is a ladder on wheels that rolls on brackets across the bookshelf. The top of the bookshelf serves as a conference table for the COMMITTEE OF SOCIAL REFORM. *At each of the three positions there is a black telephone and a working microphone. The set should have the feel of an isolated unit suspended in darkness. The entire back wall is draped with a white cyc which serves as a canvas for mood lighting. The canvas changes colors as the play progresses.*

Act 1

Prologue: The Story of Tod

(TOD, THE BOY. TOD *appears in isolation. "The Story of Tod" is his incantation. There is a flash of lightning followed by an electrical sound of thunder as the story begins.*)

TOD: Once upon a time, not so long ago, there was Tod. Now these were the days when Tod was very strong and confident. These were the days when he was very secure in the concept of himself, when he was still innocent, a strong warrior, a child, the pride of his people he left behind.

Now during this time, Tod, our hero, garnered many awards and achievements. He was among the best and the brightest in spite of his slight "handicap" which no one seemed to notice, or if they did, they kept it to themselves. Oh, how Tod thrived in this new found land . . .

(*A blackface minstrel appears in the style of Al Jolson.*)

Until one day, Tod was approached by evil, and evil was black, as evil always is. Evil told him that he had become a token of the system, that he shouldn't believe what they say because he wasn't really accepted. Well, this Tod did not believe and he rebuked this first temptation.

(*The minstrel exits and then reappears in the guise of a sixties militant.*)

But evil approached again with a stronger hand and told him that he had conformed to the system, and had been changed, his voice was different, his thoughts were different. This, Tod, also did not believe.

(*The minstrel exits and then reappears as a nineties rapper.*)

291

But evil approached again and told him that because of this change, he could be held accountable for the misdeeds of the system. That he was guilty for their crimes. But why was evil haunting him, reminding him with this temptation to look back upon his shame. So to evil, Tod said, "begone," and closed his mind and his heart, and evil seemed to stay away.

Until that glorious day, not so long ago, the voice of the system bestowed upon Tod a new identity, and they gave him a certificate that said, "Yes, Tod, you are special, Tod, you are not like them, Tod, you are one of us."

This Tod believed, because wasn't this what they were saying all along. His long, lost friends who weren't bussed to the Montessori school, his parents whom he never understood anyway. Wasn't he now finally accepted by the system? Wasn't this what he was sent out to achieve? And wasn't this like the voice of God, speaking to him? And so he listened, and his heart was filled with joy until he noticed that his skin was starting to fade, and his blood was thinning out, and there were no more awards, and he was no longer special because he was one of them. And suddenly he felt alone, and suddenly he felt black, blacker than he had ever felt before. There were faces he did not know, words he did not understand. My mother, I do not know her. My father, I do not know him. No one speaks to me, me, in my language. And this is where the story begins, not once upon a time, but now. Woe is me, woe is Tod, from the moment he believed he was different, his soul was lost, perhaps forever . . .

Scene One—The Storm of Social Ills

(*The Storm of Social Ills contains the sounds of* TOD*'s mind that lead him to the ritual sacrifice. A radio signal is faintly heard. There is a flash of lightning followed by thunder. The sound of high static is heard. Voices are muffled in the static until they slowly become distinguishable. They are the voices of* THE COMMITTEE OF SOCIAL REFORM *delivering a newscast. The messages fade in and out with the static. The storm continues . . .*)

VOICE COMMITTEE EXECUTIVE: In a related story today the case of Tawana Brawley . . .

VOICE COMMITTEE SENIOR: In Forsythe County a parade for freedom has disclosed . . .

VOICE COMMITTEE JUNIOR: Social order broke down today in the nation's second largest city . . .

VOICE COMMITTEE EXECUTIVE: . . . racism once again has reared its ugly head . . .

VOICE COMMITTEE SENIOR: . . . in a process labeled purification . . .

VOICE COMMITTEE JUNIOR: . . . one dead, two beaten . . .

VOICE COMMITTEE EXECUTIVE: In Howard Beach . . .

VOICE COMMITTEE SENIOR: . . . with racial epithets smeared in excrement . . .

VOICE COMMITTEE JUNIOR: . . . what do blacks really want . . .

VOICE COMMITTEE EXECUTIVE: Get out . . .

VOICE COMMITTEE SENIOR: Acquittal of four white officers . . .

VOICE COMMITTEE EXECUTIVE: . . . and the masses attempt to rise . . .

VOICE COMMITTEE SENIOR: . . . chanting, Rodney, Rodney, Rodney . . .

VOICE COMMITTEE JUNIOR: . . . in the guise of the Black middle class . . .

VOICE COMMITTEE EXECUTIVE: . . . a gunfight broke out this afternoon . . .

VOICE COMMITTEE JUNIOR: It's no longer about race, it's all economics . . .

VOICE COMMITTEE EXECUTIVE: . . . between Korean merchants and a group of black men . . .

VOICE COMMITTEE JUNIOR: . . . as predicted by Moynihan . . .

VOICE COMMITTEE SENIOR: . . . and more and more upwardly mobile blacks . . .

VOICE COMMITTEE EXECUTIVE: . . . struggled to reconcile those images . . .

VOICE COMMITTEE JUNIOR: . . . in a process labeled purification . . .

(*During the storm* TOD *begins a ritual sacrifice; he holds his wrists out as an offering and slowly cuts them with a razor blade. At the first sight of blood a siren is heard followed by the appearance of his demons,* MARY MARTHA, THE VIRGIN MOTHER; REVEREND JOE, HIS HOLY FATHER; *and* JOHN THE PSYCHIATRIST, THE BEARER OF TRUTH.)

VOICE COMMITTEE SENIOR: . . . a rise in teenage pregnancy . . .

VOICE COMMITTEE EXECUTIVE: . . . re gentrification . . .

VOICE COMMITTEE JUNIOR: . . . beating a black man . . .

VOICE COMMITTEE SENIOR: . . . and looters roamed the streets . . .

VOICE COMMITTEE EXECUTIVE: . . . and drug dependency . . .

VOICE COMMITTEE JUNIOR: . . . just before 7 P.M.

VOICE COMMITTEE SENIOR: . . . two white men . . .

VOICE COMMITTEE JUNIOR: . . . were attacked by a group of 15 black men . . .

VOICE COMMITTEE EXECUTIVE: . . . as racial problems on the nation's campuses . . .

VOICE COMMITTEE SENIOR: . . . struggled yesterday to reconcile those images . . .

VOICE COMMITTEE EXECUTIVE: . . . with societal problems and social backlash . . .

VOICE COMMITTEE SENIOR: . . . acquittal of four white officers . . .

VOICE COMMITTEE JUNIOR: . . . in a process labeled purification . . .

VOICE COMMITTEE EXECUTIVE: cries out from all four corners of the land . . .

ALL VOICES: . . . can't we just get along . . .

The voices of MARY MARTHA, REVEREND JOE, *and* JOHN THE PSYCHIATRIST *become audible as the storm continues. They call* TOD*'s name as if searching through his subconscious.*

VOICE COMMITTEE SENIOR: . . . we've had enough . . .

VOICE COMMITTEE JUNIOR: . . . can't take no more . . .

VOICE COMMITTEE EXECUTIVE: . . . anger ran far deeper . . .

MARY MARTHA: Tod!

VOICE COMMITTEE SENIOR: . . . than reaction to the acquittal . . .

VOICE COMMITTEE JUNIOR: . . . blacks do not count . . .

VOICE COMMITTEE SENIOR: . . . in this country . . .

REVEREND JOE: Tod!

VOICE COMMITTEE JUNIOR: . . . chanting . . .

VOICE COMMITTEE SENIOR: . . . African . . .

JOHN: Tod!

VOICE COMMITTEE EXECUTIVE: . . . American . . .

VOICE COMMITTEE SENIOR: . . . struggled . . .

REVEREND JOE: Tod.

VOICE COMMITTEE JUNIOR: . . . cried out . . .

VOICE COMMITTEE EXECUTIVE: . . . looters . . .

MARY MARTHA: Tod, my son.

VOICE COMMITTEE SENIOR: . . . in a process . . .

REVEREND JOE: My son.

VOICE COMMITTEE JUNIOR: . . . brokc down . . .

VOICE COMMITTEE EXECUTIVE: . . . labeled . . .

MARY MARTHA: I don't understand.

VOICE COMMITTEE SENIOR: . . . gunfight . . .

VOICE COMMITTEE JUNIOR: . . . acquittal . . .

REVEREND JOE: Tod.

VOICE COMMITTEE EXECUTIVE: . . . horrified . . .

VOICE COMMITTEE SENIOR: . . . black . . .

JOHN: The diagnosis . . .

VOICE COMMITTEE EXECUTIVE: . . . beating . . .

VOICE COMMITTEE SENIOR: . . . no more . . .

MARY MARTHA: My son.

VOICE COMMITTEE JUNIOR: . . . illusion . . .

VOICE COMMITTEE SENIOR: . . . backlash . . .

JOHN: The diagnosis is . . .

VOICE COMMITTEE JUNIOR: . . . question . . .

VOICE COMMITTEE EXECUTIVE: . . . Serbian . . .

MARY MARTHA: Suicide?

VOICE COMMITTEE JUNIOR: . . . officers . . .

VOICE COMMITTEE EXECUTIVE: . . . America . . .

VOICE COMMITTEE SENIOR: . . . white . . .

REVEREND JOE: Tod.

VOICE COMMITTEE JUNIOR: . . . dream . . .

VOICE COMMITTEE EXECUTIVE: . . . I had . . .

MARY MARTHA: What has happened to my son?

VOICE COMMITTEE SENIOR: . . . excrement . . .

VOICE COMMITTEE JUNIOR: . . . purification . . .

VOICE COMMITTEE EXECUTIVE: . . . Korean . . .

REVEREND JOE: Suicide.

VOICE COMMITTEE SENIOR: . . . one dead . . .

VOICE COMMITTEE JUNIOR: . . . process . . .

VOICE COMMITTEE SENIOR: . . . two beaten . . .

JOHN: . . . difficult.

VOICE COMMITTEE JUNIOR: . . . anarchy . . .

VOICE COMMITTEE EXECUTIVE: . . . struggled . . .

VOICE COMMITTEE SENIOR: . . . to reconcile . . .

VOICE COMMITTEE JUNIOR: . . . those images . . .

MARY MARTHA: Suicide!

REVEREND JOE: Suicide?

JOHN: Suicide.

MARY MARTHA: Suicide!

REVEREND JOE: Suicide?

JOHN: Suicide.

MARY MARTHA: Blacks don't commit suicide.

REVEREND JOE: Blacks don't commit suicide.

JOHN: Blacks don't commit suicide.

MARY MARTHA: So they say.

REVEREND JOE: That's what they used to say.

JOHN: That's what they want to believe.

MARY MARTHA: Suicide.
Blacks don't commit suicide.
So they say.
At least that was what I was always told.
I don't know how this happened.
It's been a real shock to us all.
Who would've suspected that he was so unhappy.

REVEREND JOE: Suicide, blacks don't commit suicide. That's what they used to say. But those were the days when the threat of death was always near, and there were enough crackers around waiting to do it for you. So you lived in spite of it all. Death existed already. What need there be of suicide. But to-day things are different. Death is still at hand. But it's your own hand that's the greatest threat.

JOHN: Suicide? Blacks don't commit suicide, that's what they want to believe. But I don't think all is lost. He survived, that's the most important thing. That makes it less of a tragedy. We just have to go through the healing process now.

MARY MARTHA: My son's been brainwashed.

JOHN: I think they've all been a little damaged by everything.

MARY MARTHA: All these years trying to be white.

JOHN: But they could see it coming.

MARY MARTHA: Trying to be white.

JOHN: It's a sign of the times.

MARY MARTHA: Has finally affected his brain. Not only does he sound like them, he has to act like them too? Nothing can be so bad that you have to act this way. It's a conspiracy. It's been a conspiracy all this time. There's still time. Now we know. This will help. He will change. We know what we're dealing with now.

REVEREND JOE: I think it all began when they gave religion back to the niggers . . .

MARY MARTHA: Things just got a little out of hand.

REVEREND JOE: . . . the concept of paradise has never been the same since.

MARY MARTHA: But there's still time.

REVEREND JOE: Oh, I don't believe that the great God of Judgment is going to be some starched white spirit. I believe it's going to be the voice of a million bloated pitch black babies sitting regal on their bones, with their heads barely supported for the weight of their knowledge, speaking with the power of the hungry, casting sinners into eternal darkness.

JOHN: Tod has developed a paranoid response to the delusions of his father and the restrained neglect of his mother. They represent two extremes of black militancy and crisis.

TOD: Suicide, suicide, blacks don't commit suicide.

MARY MARTHA: There's still time.

REVEREND JOE: Everything becomes clearer and clearer every day.

MARY MARTHA: I saw this coming.

REVEREND JOE: Cheated death . . .

MARY MARTHA: We're just a little shocked by it all.

REVEREND JOE: . . . we've cheated death.

MARY MARTHA: But things will be different . . .

REVEREND JOE: And now we're alive again.

MARY MARTHA: . . . now that we know the truth.

REVEREND JOE: It's all part of a plan.

MARY MARTHA: We know what we're dealing with, right?

REVEREND JOE: It all becomes much clearer.

MARY MARTHA: Yes, of course.

REVEREND JOE: My faith had faltered.

MARY MARTHA: I wasn't aware that he was hurting so much.

REVEREND JOE: I've allowed temptation to steer me away.

MARY MARTHA: This is just a way to get attention.

REVEREND JOE: But now I'm renewed once again.

MARY MARTHA: I don't think there was much of a crisis.

REVEREND JOE: The enemy has shown their evil hand.

MARY MARTHA: I don't think he really meant to do it.

REVEREND JOE: The battle is in Tod.

MARY MARTHA: He's been depressed lately.

REVEREND JOE: The battle is for the mind of Tod.

MARY MARTHA: A lot of hard decisions to make.

REVEREND JOE: I thought they would come for me first.

MARY MARTHA: It's hard to see clearly.

REVEREND JOE: But he is the one . . .

MARY MARTHA: Clearly . . .

REVEREND JOE: . . . the most vulnerable . . .

MARY MARTHA: . . . for someone like him.

REVEREND JOE: . . . the chosen one.

(*The storm ends as lights go out on* MARY MARTHA *and* REVEREND JOE.)

JOHN: Tod's mother developed a very militant response to a similar pressure. He represents a second generation of compound social crisis, lack of identity, and character conflict due to racial assimilation. He is a perfect example of what the past has created. That's why they're here. He is not what they wanted.

Scene Two—Tod Is the One

(THE COMMITTEE OF SOCIAL REFORM *appears for the first time. The committee consists of three white male executives who sit on top of a ten-foot-high bookshelf; the books on the shelf represent the history of the "Negro problem" in America.*)

COMMITTEE JUNIOR: Then what are we going to do?

JOHN: As of yet, I do not know.

COMMITTEE SENIOR: Such perfection seems to be a terrible thing to waste.

JOHN: I know.

COMMITTEE EXECUTIVE: And this crisis?

COMMITTEE SENIOR: It's a sign.

COMMITTEE JUNIOR: A possible identity rejection?

JOHN: I'm not sure.

COMMITTEE SENIOR: We're too close to fail now.

COMMITTEE JUNIOR: He's unstable.

COMMITTEE EXECUTIVE: Always when we get this close they turn. I thought his assimilation was complete.

COMMITTEE JUNIOR: You're the reason we're in this mess in the first place. Sending off your little alarms.

COMMITTEE EXECUTIVE: I can't control the youth of today, it's unnatural.

JOHN: They've caused him to question his purpose.

COMMITTEE SENIOR: Maybe we've miscalculated the times.

COMMITTEE EXECUTIVE: You can't blame this on me. We've tolerated this situation far too long. The system can no longer support a dying race.

COMMITTEE SENIOR: Our crimes were almost forgotten. If you could have held out for at least another decade, this problem would have been solved.

COMMITTEE EXECUTIVE: It's not my fault liberalism is dead.

COMMITTEE JUNIOR: We must become one, it's the only way to battle the global shift. Tod is perfect.

JOHN: There's one more problem.

THE COMMITTEE: What is that?

JOHN: He still believes in God.

THE COMMITTEE: God? How did that happen?

COMMITTEE EXECUTIVE: I thought their belief in God went out in the 60s.

COMMITTEE SENIOR: Whatever happened to those fine militants, I thought they destroyed their belief in God.

JOHN: They are forgotten like all prophets.

COMMITTEE EXECUTIVE: I loved those pseudo-Marxists. They were so self-destructive.

JOHN: Tod is pure, he was protected from the beginning. His parents hid him away in private school at an early age.

COMMITTEE SENIOR: He is the first?

COMMITTEE JUNIOR: No, he is the last to know legalized oppression in his lifetime.

JOHN: It's not that he remembers, but it still exists in his subconscious. And can be reclaimed.

COMMITTEE EXECUTIVE: He has a claim to the past?

JOHN: He is a very important link.

COMMITTEE SENIOR: He is dangerous.

JOHN: He is unstable.

COMMITTEE SENIOR: His salvation is still intact, that's far too dangerous. It can cause dissension.

COMMITTEE EXECUTIVE: John, it says here that his mother was a Black Panther.

JOHN: She's a corporate executive now.

COMMITTEE JUNIOR: Minority Affairs?

JOHN: No, International Marketing.

COMMITTEE SENIOR: That's progressive.

JOHN: She's quite a wonder.

COMMITTEE JUNIOR: He must hate her.

JOHN: His father is a Baptist minister.

COMMITTEE SENIOR: Oh, John, this should be easy enough, he must hate them both.

COMMITTEE EXECUTIVE: I'm getting nervous.

COMMITTEE JUNIOR: Calm down.

COMMITTEE EXECUTIVE: I'm anxious, I want this thing over.

COMMITTEE SENIOR: I want it over too, but you can't be irrational like the last time.

COMMITTEE JUNIOR: Don't let your bigotry get in the way of progress.

COMMITTEE EXECUTIVE: You haven't lived with this goddamned black menace as long as I have. Hell, I've been everything. I was a conservative, I was a hip liberal before it was in vogue, I've been a reactionary, an abolitionist, nothing seems to work. I'm tired.

COMMITTEE SENIOR: Give it time.

COMMITTEE EXECUTIVE: There is no more time. Can't you see the signs? Tod is the one. He is the link. With his successful assimilation the past will have no meaning and all will be forgotten like a history lesson. We've waited long enough. I should have known to never trust a Jew.

COMMITTEE SENIOR: Sir! There's a way to handle this diplomatically.

COMMITTEE EXECUTIVE: Yes, of course. I'm sorry, John, but you're not really Jewish anyway, you're one of us. I despise ethnicity, it just gets in the way of efficiency and free enterprise. That's why the goddamned Japanese are on our tails. They have no such problems. Those people work for peanuts. Unions and quotas destroy the system, Affirmative Action is a farce, it all destroys the system. We need efficient blacks, not welfare cases.

COMMITTEE JUNIOR: Sir, I believe you've gotten off the subject.

COMMITTEE EXECUTIVE: Yes, yes, of course. I just have so much on my mind. I was almost wiped out today. A billion dollars gone in a flash and then it reappeared. It's a sign, my friends. Nothing's certain. I want this problem solved. I don't have time for race, I've got an economic crisis on my hands.

JOHN: Then what is your decision?

COMMITTEE EXECUTIVE: Destroy his belief in God.

COMMITTEE SENIOR AND JUNIOR: Don't be irrational.

COMMITTEE EXECUTIVE: What do you mean? It's the first step, it's what we've done in the past. It worked before, it will work now. It's all very simple. We used to give the niggers religion until those self-righteous mammies turned God against us. We use capitalism now, it's much more effective. Poverty is immediate, starvation is immediate, salvation takes too long. It encourages endurance. Take away his god, and all he has left is the system, and we're the system. It's so clear. I call for a vote, all in favor . . . (*All three raise their hands.*) Good, none opposed. Tod's belief in God must be destroyed.

JOHN: I'm not sure I can do it.

COMMITTEE EXECUTIVE: Don't worry, we'll be with you. You're an atheist, right? It should be easy.

JOHN: Well, I've been thinking.

THE COMMITTEE: Thinking? Without us? That's not part of the bargain, John.

JOHN: I've been thinking I would like to go home.

COMMITTEE SENIOR: Preparing for Armageddon?

COMMITTEE JUNIOR: What is it that you want?

JOHN: Will you give me back my belief in God?

COMMITTEE JUNIOR: An exchange for an exchange?

COMMITTEE EXECUTIVE: That's one thing I envy about you people, your sense of history. You do nothing for it, yet you still call upon it when you feel betrayed. Yes, we will give you back your Jehovah and your Torah. We're almost through with that anyway, we have no need of your folklore anymore. Just take away our white man's guilt and this great black burden and we'll call it an even trade.

COMMITTEE SENIOR: He's not as perfect as we had hoped.

COMMITTEE EXECUTIVE: But he's close enough. There just isn't any time. The doors of democracy are opening. I want this black problem solved. It's getting in the way of progress. We can't let this follow us into the next century. Either assimilate him or we will be forced to eliminate him. It's the only way.

COMMITTEE JUNIOR: It's all a process for the new age, new life, new freedom, a new deal . . . Show him the way.

COMMITTEE EXECUTIVE: Bring him into the world.

COMMITTEE SENIOR: Make the way clear for him, the end is near.

THE COMMITTEE: You have been chosen.

JOHN: It shall be done.

THE COMMITTEE: Amen.

(*Lights fade out on the* COMMITTEE *as* JOHN *prepares to enter his session with* TOD.)

JOHN: Amen . . . And these were the days of darkness that had been prophesied. And I am a lost voice in the wilderness searching for my home. Much has been lost, yes much has been forgotten. Sold. Sold. Sold my soul and no longer know my people or my reason, all to live in this world. Judaism, what do I know of it, its words, its dates, its salvation.

This was my father's prophecy, not my own, the calling was his. "This is right, the fight for Civil Rights, the fight for justice." Every generation was "the" generation, every new-born was the liberator. Denial, denial, denial, could this be the one?

God will think I'm a Christian even if I don't believe.

I lost the way somewhere, a connection, a purpose. But in Tod's eyes I see myself. In his eyes I see my failure. Have we destroyed the days of bigotry, have we overcome?

There's a voice in the wilderness, I am. Tod is a white man like all white men. This he must accept.

Scene Three—The First Encounter

JOHN: What was college like for you?

TOD: It was in many ways all that I expected. Great buildings, great architecture, history, it was filled with inspiration. But it was very clear that when I arrived something had just died, or was dying.

JOHN: What was that?

TOD: Something had been lost. I could see it on the few black faces who had been there when the spirit was alive. There had been riots there too, you know. But there were no signs of that anymore. There was black unity, but it seemed forced, well, at least to me it did. I thought, "What's the point, I'm here, right?" You see, I was very naive, I still am. Something was dead and I watched it fade away. I even think I was part of its death. They no longer need to go to the inner city for their quotas. There are enough people like me in their little private schools to fulfill any liberal need that might still exist. And they're all very much like me, terribly insane. We recognize it in each other's faces, me and my white friends, them and theirs.

JOHN: Why do you think it was like that?

TOD: It's very hard to say. From the very first day I was there I was challenged. I remember going down to eat and suddenly stepping into what seemed to be a segregated dining hall. There were whites on one side and blacks on the other. I was confused. I thought, "When did this happen?" I thought I had missed something, some special code or instructions.

JOHN: What did you do?

TOD: I sat on the white side like everybody else.

JOHN: And everybody else was white?

TOD: Yes, at the time everybody else was all white. I've never really had any black friends. Do you think that's a sign of some kind of pathology? Maybe I learned something incorrectly somewhere.

JOHN: How did you feel?

TOD: I felt white like everybody else. All the blacks were on the other side. But I kept thinking that I belonged on the other side. I was afraid that I had made some mistake.

JOHN: You made a choice.

TOD: A very ridiculous choice to have to make.

JOHN: Were you angry at the other blacks?

TOD: Why? We all had to make choices for whatever reason. We all had our needs. Whites congregate automatically with other whites and there's no sense of threat. But as soon as you put more than two blacks together there's a rebellion, then your table has turned black and no one white will sit there. And if it's two black men, no one will even consider it. It was all very confusing. I found myself having to defend my race, and to justify how I had gotten to the promised land.

JOHN: Do you worry about not having any black friends?

TOD: Not anymore, now I worry about not having any.

JOHN: What do you mean?

TOD: Something happened somewhere. I can't explain it. I live my life alone now. I am very alone now. My whole world, my whole reason is fading away before my eyes. I have no connection with the people I'm supposed to know. I've lost my sense of purpose. It used to be to succeed. But those games are over now. There are no more written tests. There are no right answers. It's all a lost cause.

(MARY MARTHA *and* REVEREND JOE *slowly enter the scene as* JOHN *fades out.*)

Scene Four—The Conflict

REVEREND JOE: Why are we here?

TOD: It's hard to get a stronghold.

MARY MARTHA: Our son needs help.

REVEREND JOE: Our son needs prayer.

TOD: Everyone is talking about reverse discrimination and even I'm starting to agree.

MARY MARTHA: We've been praying, prayer doesn't stop.

TOD: It's very frightening.

MARY MARTHA: We'll always be praying, I'm getting used to it. I would like a few answers.

TOD: I scream at my parents constantly, they scream back.

REVEREND JOE: Doesn't God give answers? It's in His hands, it's His plan. Wait on the Lord. Don't influence the outcome with your desperation.

TOD: They try to explain, but I don't understand.

MARY MARTHA: And maybe this is part of His plan.

TOD: They want me to be something that they dreamed of long ago.

MARY MARTHA: Prayer doesn't mean you have to sit and wait. You can do. We can move. I thought you would have learned that by now, or maybe you've forgotten.

TOD: They don't want to hear my doubts, they don't want to hear my fears. They want me to be perfect.

REVEREND JOE: Read your Bible.

MARY MARTHA: I'm tired of reading my Bible, all of that "he can't, we can't" shit. That's just another damn puzzle. I want some answers.

REVEREND JOE: And this is where you come for answers?

MARY MARTHA: We didn't have much choice.

REVEREND JOE: Be patient.

MARY MARTHA: You drive me crazy.

REVEREND JOE: You need some faith, trust in Him, "He's never failed us yet."

MARY MARTHA: Nigger, don't preach to me. This ain't Sunday, and I am not in the mood.

REVEREND JOE: You want some answers. I've got your answer. Worry about your own soul and let your son take care of his.

MARY MARTHA: That's not an answer, that sounds like some tired old parable. We're talking about more than salvation. When did you become so complacent?

REVEREND JOE: I think it happened while you were sleeping.

MARY MARTHA: We've both been sleeping.

REVEREND JOE: There's a time for everything.

MARY MARTHA: You're full of shit.

REVEREND JOE: A little respect here, please.

MARY MARTHA: Respect for what, some two-bit preacher who's lost his cause?

REVEREND JOE: Enough of that.

MARY MARTHA: Who would ever know that you were once a rebel, a renegade? No signs from that middle-age paunch and that conservative brow.

REVEREND JOE: Casting stones, Martha?

MARY MARTHA: Can't you tell I'm frightened, man? Don't act like you don't know what I'm talking about. I've seen your failure when our son speaks. You shudder when you hear his thoughts. I see your shame when you hear his ignorance. Who is this stranger in our home? Certainly not the son of one so respected for his fight. It's a tragedy. You're looking at the end. Something died. The words that come out of his mouth sound like they belong to someone else. They sound like words I can't even trust.

REVEREND JOE: That's your son you're talking about.

MARY MARTHA: You're damn right, and I'm not going to lose him without a fight.

REVEREND JOE: Martha, you're not going to lose him, he's exactly what you've made him into . . . perfect.

MARY MARTHA: So that's what allows you to sit there so calm, saying it's all my fault. Well, ain't that just like a black nigger who lost the war long before the battle even started. I guess it's been that way since the beginning. You lost your way the day I met you. There's no need in my feeling sorry for you now. And if he is perfect, I want that shit cured.

TOD: In our lives there has been great absence.

MARY MARTHA: All that is left is talk.

REVEREND JOE: We never talked about the past.

TOD: In our lives there has been unforgivable silence.

MARY MARTHA: Talk, talk, no action.

REVEREND JOE: We never talked about the present.

TOD: In our lives there have been parents who do not talk to their children who do not talk.

MARY MARTHA: No one speaks to me, they say I sold out.

REVEREND JOE: And in our silence, a stranger was born that we fear.

MARY MARTHA: All that I have left is my son.

TOD: History, never taught me, the past, what do I know about the past?

REVEREND JOE: Who is this stranger, my son?

TOD: Are you ashamed of my ignorance?

MARY MARTHA: He is my salvation, but somehow I have failed.

TOD: Are you ashamed?

Scene Five—Lament

JOHN: You mustn't look upon it as failure.

MARY MARTHA: He's dangerous.

JOHN: More dangerous to himself.

MARY MARTHA: We went wrong somewhere.

JOHN: It's not a question of right or wrong. You made choices.

MARY MARTHA: I feel guilty.

COMMITTEE EXECUTIVE: Does part of this guilt have to do with your failure with the Party?

MARY MARTHA: The Party?

COMMITTEE SENIOR: The Black Panther Party, you were once a member, weren't you?

MARY MARTHA: How the hell did you find that out?

COMMITTEE JUNIOR: From your file.

MARY MARTHA: My file?

JOHN: Your corporate file.

MARY MARTHA: Oh, I see. You must have access to a whole lot of shit because of the accident.

JOHN: Suicide is a crime.

MARY MARTHA: I see. Well, yes, I was a member of the Party. I still am, in spirit. The fight is just different. In those days I thought I had found the answer. I dug what the brothers were saying and it was my way of breaking out from my half-white inheritance. But you grow numb after a while. You become a Muslim or you sell barbecue. I mean, you freak when you come that close to true power. The movement ended because blacks are afraid of power, it could mean your death. That's why we're always looking for a savior. Give one dude all the power and when he fails you can save your own neck.

JOHN: It must have been very hard for you to enter the corporate world.

MARY MARTHA: No, it was very easy. I made my move when black was in and we saved the nation just like in slavery. Of course, not being black enough had a few drawbacks then, but I hung in there. Now, once again, I'm almost the ideal. But believe me, on the job I am very black, it's been my edge. You take advantage of every angle you can. I make no mistakes and I record everything.

Most people today are unable to see the faults in the system because they view the world in the same way that white men view the world. Poor Tod doesn't know the difference. He believes everything he's told. Blind faith, that's a curse. He's so damn perfect. I'm going to get that boy to wake up. How the hell did he get that way? My son believes in America and I feel like I've been the butt of some cruel joke. If he were white he wouldn't exist at all.

JOHN: When did things start to change?

MARY MARTHA: I don't know when it started, I only know when I was aware of it. It just happened. I didn't know him, and one day I said it . . .

JOHN: What?

MARY MARTHA: I didn't mean it.

TOD: I couldn't do it.

MARY MARTHA: We got into a fight.

JOHN: About what?

MARY MARTHA: I didn't mean it.

JOHN: What did you say?

TOD: She wanted me to hire some black man at the office.

MARY MARTHA: He had the opportunity to hire someone black at his office.

JOHN: Well?

MARY MARTHA: Well?

TOD: I couldn't do it.

MARY MARTHA: I'm not surprised.

TOD: I thought long and hard. I just couldn't justify it, it wouldn't have been fair.

MARY MARTHA: Fair? What is fair, Tod?

TOD: He just wasn't the best man for the job.

MARY MARTHA: No?

TOD: No!

MARY MARTHA: Was he qualified?

TOD: I guess.

MARY MARTHA: Was he black?

TOD: Yes.

MARY MARTHA: Was he the only black?

TOD: Yes.

MARY MARTHA: Then he was the best man for the job.

TOD: That's not fair, Mother. You have to look at things more deeply than that.

MARY MARTHA: I thought that was pretty deep.

TOD: You can't get away with things like that anymore.

MARY MARTHA: Says who? It's what they do all the time.

TOD: Your age is over, things are different now.

MARY MARTHA: That's when I said it.

JOHN: What?

MARY MARTHA: I said, "You talk mighty bold for someone who'd be out on his black ass if he didn't act so white."

JOHN: You said what?

TOD: She said I was white.

MARY MARTHA: I said he was white.

TOD: What does that mean?

MARY MARTHA: You sound white, you act white, you're starting to smell white . . .

TOD: Can you believe she said that to me? Do I sound white to you? Don't answer that. I think you're going insane.

MARY MARTHA: Yeah, you're driving me crazy.

TOD: You have white men on the brain.

MARY MARTHA: I have one living in my house.

TOD: That's enough of that!

MARY MARTHA: Enough of what, the truth?

TOD: Don't you ever get tired?

MARY MARTHA: No, I never get tired. That's how I've survived.

TOD: Do we have to go through this again?

MARY MARTHA: Untiring, unyielding, Mary Martha!

TOD: Your fight is over, Mother.

MARY MARTHA: This shit ain't over, it's just getting started.

TOD: It deserved its death, let it die.

MARY MARTHA: I fought too long and too hard for you to be so goddamned naive.

TOD: I didn't ask you to fight for me.

MARY MARTHA: You didn't have to. Besides, I didn't do it just for you, I did it for our people.

TOD: Well, then leave me alone and go scream at our people. Go scream at the crackheads, and the welfare cases, and the welfare mothers, and the . . .

MARY MARTHA: Why? You're the biggest case around. You're more dangerous than they are. You have so much to give, Tod, and you're wasting it. It's time to start giving something back.

TOD: What do you want from me?

MARY MARTHA: I want you to fight.

TOD: Fight what? You're living in the past.

MARY MARTHA: This is not the past I'm talking about. We're in a hell of a lot of trouble when everyone's afraid of hiring black people, especially black people.

TOD: I'm here, Mother. What am I if not a sign of your success? You think you failed because I don't hate white people. You want me to agree with everything you have to say, but I can't. Why do you have so much hatred?

MARY MARTHA: I'm a black woman in a racist and sexist society. It doesn't take much. I don't want to fight with you, Tod. I don't want to hurt you. I just want you to understand what's going on. Stop being so trusting.

TOD: You have no faith in me.

MARY MARTHA: That's not true.

TOD: I'm not as naive as you think I am.

MARY MARTHA: You'll see the truth someday. You're not as white as you want to be.

TOD: And I'll never be black enough . . . she said, "white."

MARY MARTHA: I said, "Tod, it's time you stopped trying to be white."

TOD: How can she say that to me, what does she know about it? How does she know how I feel? My mother doesn't know the first thing about being black. She's like some white-assed liberal looking for a cause. No offense.

JOHN: None taken.

MARY MARTHA: I felt guilty.

TOD: She thinks my life's been perfect. I've been destined for failure from the moment I was sent to private school. I was imperfect, I had to become perfect. I had to become white or else I wouldn't have survived.

JOHN: And that was it.

MARY MARTHA: That was something.

TOD: The beginning. We were separate then. I never knew, I never knew that she felt that way too. I thought she was proud. I thought I was doing what she wanted, but now there was something else. There was something that she expected of me, I didn't know what.

MARY MARTHA: We're not bad parents.

JOHN: I didn't say you were.

MARY MARTHA: We're not bad black parents.

JOHN: What about your husband?

MARY MARTHA: Religion does not always acknowledge the need to continue the fight against racism. It's not that he doesn't understand, my husband was once very militant. Let's just say that he's turned the other cheek so many times, he's lost his sense of direction.

REVEREND JOE: My wife doesn't think that I understand the problem, she thinks that I've given up the cause. But do not be deceived by my silence. We must have patience, patience. There is nothing wrong with my son, he is coming into power. A great war has been waged and Tod is the culmination of that war. Our enemy has trained our generals, they have all the knowledge that they need, but they are lost. They are successful, upwardly mobile and lost. We let them battle too long on their own, without our help, without our guidance. But there was a purpose to that as well. The movement did not fail, my friend, but it will have failed if we can't find a way to bring them home again. You see, John, we too have children wandering in the wilderness looking for the promised land. We are close, we are very close to coming together. There are still great risks to take, and great sacrifices. This is where you come in. You must teach Tod how to get back home.

JOHN: I don't quite understand what you expect from me. Analysis is not teaching, there are no guarantees that I will be able to help him.

REVEREND JOE: Help him? Who the hell wants your help!

JOHN: Well, that is why most people come to me.

REVEREND JOE: I want you to teach him and your prejudice will do the rest. You don't understand, Tod has led a sheltered existence for a purpose.

JOHN: Have you tried explaining that to him?

REVEREND JOE: He doesn't understand my language, but he will understand you and your liberalism. So don't try to help, it only gets in the way of purity.

JOHN: What do you want from me?

REVEREND JOE: There is nothing wrong with my son.

MARY MARTHA: The American Dream is a white man's dream.

TOD: The issue is definition that is what I want.

JOHN: I'm sure that there's a way to help.

REVEREND JOE: He needs no help, only knowledge.

MARY MARTHA: It's as if I'm supposed to forget that segregation took place.

JOHN: It's not a question of forgetting . . .

REVEREND JOE: He's coming into power.

TOD: Tell me what it means to be black and that's what I'll be.

JOHN: These matters cannot be so easily answered.

MARY MARTHA: Am I supposed to forget that people spat in my face?

REVEREND JOE: I'm allowing him to do this because he needs to know the language of the enemy.

JOHN: I am not the enemy.

TOD: Extract the goodness from what is white and make it black.

REVEREND JOE: The language of temptation.

TOD: And that is what I'll be.

JOHN: I cannot get personally involved.

MARY MARTHA: Am I supposed to forget my childhood?

REVEREND JOE: And with this knowledge he will lead us to the promised land.

TOD: Destroy the whiteness from what is right and that is what I'll be.

JOHN: This is not logical.

REVEREND JOE: You were selected for a purpose.

MARY MARTHA: Am I supposed to forget the reasons not to trust white people?

TOD: This is what I have become.

JOHN: I am not to blame.

REVEREND JOE: Follow your guilt.

TOD: In their absence.

REVEREND JOE: Your profession.

TOD: In their ignorance.

REVEREND JOE: And not your heart.

JOHN: There's a procedure that we must follow.

MARY MARTHA: Racism still exists, time is running out.

TOD: What is black?

REVEREND JOE: Teach Tod and the truth will reveal itself to him.

JOHN: You must follow the rules.

TOD: What is black?

REVEREND JOE: Tod is waking up.

JOHN: I cannot tolerate ignorance of the process.

MARY MARTHA: What happened to my child?

TOD: Tell me who I am?

REVEREND JOE: The awakening had to be violent.

JOHN: You cannot expect me to solve all of your problems.

REVEREND JOE: The awakening had to be bloody.

MARY MARTHA: What happened to my child?

JOHN: You must follow the rules.

TOD: Tell me who I am.

REVEREND JOE: You know what you must do.

THE COMMITTEE: You people need to learn how to help yourselves!

JOHN: No, no, that's not what I mean. You see . . . you see . . .

(JOHN *removes a book from the shelf and begins reading.*)

> I know that your "obstinate ignorance is merely a defense mechanism against my role in the patriarchal structure." No, I mean, well, look, it's all very simple, here . . .

(*He reads from another book.*)

> "Minority groups in particular may have a culturally induced high level of paranoid belief and this belief may be based upon real discrimination . . ."

(*He begins flipping wildly through many books as the* COMMITTEE OF SOCIAL REFORM *recite quotations from the history of "The Negro Problem."*)

> No, look . . . maybe your answer is here . . . no, maybe here . . . no, maybe here . . . no, maybe here . . . no, maybe here . . . no, maybe here . . .

Scene Six—The Ascension of Books

COMMITTEE EXECUTIVE: In the beginning God created the heaven and the earth . . .

COMMITTEE SENIOR: And he said, "Cursed be Canaan, and servant of servants shall he be unto his brethren . . ."

COMMITTEE JUNIOR: The Negro is the son of Ham, and his inferiority to his white brother is the result of a curse . . .

COMMITTEE EXECUTIVE: . . . in recognizing the Negro as a man and a brother they were compelled to declare man an ape . . .

COMMITTEE SENIOR: When I am told the human race are all from Adam's seed . . .

COMMITTEE JUNIOR: . . . that kinky-headed coons and I are from one common breed . . .

COMMITTEE EXECUTIVE: . . . skin color was affected by the bile . . .

COMMITTEE SENIOR: . . . marks the human species degenerate . . .

COMMITTEE JUNIOR: . . . the cerebral cranium less developed than the white . . .

COMMITTEE SENIOR: . . . characterized by a very strong offensive odor . . .

COMMITTEE EXECUTIVE: . . . believed that Negroes were apes . . .

COMMITTEE SENIOR: . . . that ape-Negro copulation might produce fertile offspring . . .

COMMITTEE JUNIOR: Christianity is the religion of white people.

COMMITTEE EXECUTIVE: Islam is the natural, though false religion of the Negroes.

COMMITTEE SENIOR: The Semites do not possess the harmonious equilibrium . . .

COMMITTEE JUNIOR: With the passing of the need for black laborers . . .

COMMITTEE EXECUTIVE: . . . black people have become useless . . .

COMMITTEE SENIOR: . . . the black man occupies a very special sexual role in American society . . .

COMMITTEE JUNIOR: . . . if you are ever going to have anything like an equal Negro community . . .

COMMITTEE SENIOR: You are for the next thirty years going to have to give them unequal treatment.

COMMITTEE EXECUTIVE: That the American Negro has survived at all is extraordinary . . .

COMMITTEE SENIOR: . . . Affirmative Action is a failure.

COMMITTEE EXECUTIVE: Then you have to wonder if we're ever going to get women and minorities to fit in . . .

COMMITTEE SENIOR: . . . as smoothly as white males did . . .

COMMITTEE JUNIOR: . . . in a system that contained only white males.

THE COMMITTEE: Hello, John. John, the Psychiatrist, John, looking for an answer and a cause.

COMMITTEE EXECUTIVE: There's something that these people have forgotten.

COMMITTEE SENIOR: They were sent here to learn what they could about us, but it seems they've given up that mission.

COMMITTEE JUNIOR: It's sad. They've grown content. They think we define life.

COMMITTEE EXECUTIVE: They think this is all there is to life.

COMMITTEE SENIOR: They dream the same dreams, they have the same ideals, goals.

THE COMMITTEE: It's a great burden on us.

(*The* COMMITTEE OF SOCIAL REFORM *begin a rap.*)

COMMITTEE JUNIOR: They have no hope,
they're filled with dope,
trying to be free.

THE COMMITTEE: They are free,
isn't that a great irony?

COMMITTEE EXECUTIVE: Give them chains
and all they want is freedom.

COMMITTEE SENIOR: Give them freedom
and all they want is equality.

COMMITTEE JUNIOR: Give them equality
and they cease to exist,
tsk, tsk, tsk

COMMITTEE SENIOR: You see, they're just poor,
and now that they're poor,
they can be forgotten.

COMMITTEE EXECUTIVE: America
has no sympathy for the poor.
How can we?

COMMITTEE SENIOR: They lost their cause
in their fight for equality,
we have no sympathy.
How can we?

COMMITTEE EXECUTIVE: Poverty is the foundation of capitalism, everyone knows that.

COMMITTEE SENIOR: It's a shame
but we can no longer
carry the strain
of our white man's guilt.

COMMITTEE JUNIOR: Our greatest defense
is to prove that slavery
was essential to this country.

COMMITTEE EXECUTIVE: Write it like history,
make them forget.

COMMITTEE EXECUTIVE: Forget they were slaves,
make them ashamed to see
what they once were
to what they can be.

COMMITTEE JUNIOR: Train their youth,
make them forget.

COMMITTEE EXECUTIVE: Hell, never teach them.
They won't teach themselves.

COMMITTEE SENIOR: Create a generation
that will never know the reason for their oppression
and we
will never face a revolution.

COMMITTEE JUNIOR: They will just blame
their pain on the shame
of their parents.

THE COMMITTEE: And they'll forget about us.

COMMITTEE EXECUTIVE: We're almost there, John. This generation is the last that has ever known legalized oppression in their lifetime. The Bakke decision was the first sign of the times, the beginning of the end of the myth of racism. We have almost reached the end. Free at last, John, free at last.

THE COMMITTEE: Free at last . . .

JOHN: I remember the first time that I passed . . . the first time that I denied my faith. I thought that was the answer. There was no God, there was no faith, for me this was what it meant to be white. I had no identity, I was like everybody else, I belonged. This was freedom. Yes, Tod, this was freedom.

Scene Seven—The First Lesson

TOD: I have failed somehow. There was something I was working towards. I seem to have forgotten. Maybe I never knew. My parents seem to know but they won't tell me. When I ask, they simply turn their heads in shame. There has never been something I didn't know, or know where to look for the answer. But this . . .

JOHN: What is it?

TOD: I remember the first time I heard the voice. The blacks were there blaming the establishment for not being sensitive to their cause, and I heard someone say, "Then go back where you came from." And it was me . . . Am I a traitor?

JOHN: What?

TOD: Am I a traitor? I've become the enemy somehow by not doing what I was supposed to do, but I don't know what that is. Do you know? Can you tell me what it is, do you know?

JOHN: Tod, you're just battling your parents' expectations.

TOD: No, it's more than that. I shouldn't be this angry.

JOHN: Why are you angry?

TOD: The enemy has eluded me. The face is unclear, but I'm coming closer. I'm getting closer every day. It's a face I almost recognize. I'm afraid.

JOHN: What are you afraid of?

TOD: I'm afraid of what I have become. I'm afraid they'll find me out.

JOHN: Find out what?

TOD: I'm afraid I've become a white man. They'll think it's a conspiracy and that I'm to blame. Can you help me get back?

JOHN: Get back?

TOD: Get back to what I once was.

JOHN: What was that?

TOD: Black, I once was black. I think?

JOHN: Tod, you're still black.

TOD: Are you sure?

JOHN: You look black.

TOD: Looks can be deceiving. People say that I'm not really black. I don't feel black. Is there a way that I'm supposed to feel? I'm not comfortable around blacks. The true blacks, the ones that everyone talks about, the ones who have a purpose and a cause, the ones who call me names and reject me for sounding white.

"Oh, you're not really black." People actually say this to me, still, today, now even more than in the past. Even my mother says it. "You're not really black." What does it mean? What does any of it mean?

They won't accept me, they don't trust me. They treat me like a white man. My mother says I need to wake up, well maybe she better wake up. I won't be blamed for their weakness. Blacks are despised the whole world over. Even the Japanese are racist. Even Africans hate blacks. The true blacks, the people with a purpose and a cause. The race the Americans invented.

JOHN: Tod, please stop.

TOD: Why, do I sadden your liberal soul? Do I disgust you with my honesty? Isn't it sad to see that this is what we've come to.

JOHN: Tod, you haven't become a white man, you've become a racist.

TOD: I'm not a racist, I'm a neoconservative economist who suffers from white liberal guilt, that's a mental disorder. Can it be cured? No? Well, I guess you suffer from it too. I tried working for this nonprofit urban rehabilitation group called PURGE, but that didn't help. I could probably be cured if I went to work for Wall Street. I hear that cures many things. Someone once told me that the best way to cure socialist apathy was to become an investment banker. Is that true?

JOHN: Tod, please . . .

TOD: This is a trial, John. You are the prosecutor, my parents are the victims, and I'm the crime. The creation of Tod was a very dirty crime. He's not a racist, he hates everybody. But he hates himself most of all.

Once Tod believed he had eaten of the tree of knowledge and discovered that he was a nigger. An angel told him of salvation called assimilation and Tod studied and was faithful and waits for his day. But there are times when he sins, and his sins are black, as all sins are. And he bends his knees and begs forgiveness for being what he is.

MARY MARTHA: Why, Tod?

TOD: At that moment, Tod was sitting on the edge of his oppression, and the tempter came and said, . . .

REVEREND JOE: You have tried the white man's way, now try the true way.

TOD: And the tempter looked like Tod's father, and he was black like evil. And this was the first time that Tod ever had any doubts. Everything used to be so clear. Had he reached the end of liberty? And his first taste of oppression invaded him like a plague. Was he a nigger? Where were his white majority friends, and his white majority world, and his white majority liberal arts education when there was no majority acceptance.

What did Tod want, sitting on the edge of his oppression . . . And the tempter said,

REVEREND JOE: Rise up and lead your people to prove that you are chosen.

TOD: But Tod said he would not and overcame temptation, but he was never really sure if he had done the right thing. And it was that uncertainty that grew in him as he waited on the edge for his salvation, but it never came. I just wanted to hear God's voice.

MARY MARTHA: Suicide?

TOD: I just wanted to hear Him say, "Peace be still."

MARY MARTHA: Blacks don't commit suicide.

TOD: I had to free myself. I wanted to walk into the ocean to free my soul. Father, where is the light? Where is the light?

MARY MARTHA: I found him.

TOD: The ancestors cry out from my veins, from my veins.

REVEREND JOE: Come home, Tod, come home.

MARY MARTHA: Forsaken like all Marries. A simple death.

TOD: But I could not answer. I do not speak their language. I look back and there's no recognition. I look forward and there's no light. They do not trust my voice. They say I sound white, sound white, do I sound white to you? Don't answer that. Do I sound white to you? Don't answer that.

MARY MARTHA: Noble in some respect.

TOD: I look forward, the path is dark. Where is the light? Help me find the way. Help me get to the promised land. Hey mister, do you know how to get to the promised land? Do you know the way to the promised land?

MARY MARTHA: He survived a three-day coma.

REVEREND JOE: His survival was a perfect sign.

TOD: Father, speak to me.

(TOD *removes the bandages from his left wrist.*)

Father, speak to me.

(TOD *removes the bandages from his right wrist.*)

But the voice never came. Forsaken.

MARY MARTHA: Not by grace, but by misfortune.

REVEREND JOE: I knew then that my efforts were not in vain.

MARY MARTHA: You would think that such an event would confirm my faith. No, this was a cruel ungodly joke. I don't believe in grace, I believe in Tod. Your world took God away from me. You stole my virginity and now He'll never speak to me again.

REVEREND JOE: Tod is the chosen one.

TOD: God is a coward, I called His bluff and He would not come out from hiding.

There is a battle going on inside of me, a consciously implanted warfare I believe, and I have no choice but to fight. I want a freedom moment before I die. I want to know a freedom moment in my lifetime. Teach me.

THE COMMITTEE: Teach him the way you will have him to go, and he will never stray from it, like trees and streams like slaves . . . Peace be still . . . Peace be still.

JOHN: Come, Tod, and I will show you the way.
Come, Tod, and I will help you justify your past.
Come, and I will lead the way.
Come, I have been chosen . . .
Come and you will see.
Lesson One: God is dead.

COMMITTEE EXECUTIVE: The belief in salvation is what has kept the black masses oppressed for hundreds of years. It is the force which allows them to remain victimized, lost in the illusion of just retribution by a white high holy God.

JOHN: Lesson One: God is dead.

COMMITTEE SENIOR: Religion is an opiate which distracts oppressed peoples from struggling to change their material circumstances. As long as it remains intact, blacks will always be dependent upon white society for their identity and their salvation.

JOHN: Lesson One: God is dead, repeat . . .

COMMITTEE JUNIOR: The most effective way to infiltrate and destroy a society is to replace their pagan gods with an image of the conqueror. This will have the most dramatic effect on the generations still to come. In order for them to overcome this oppression they must destroy the God they have come to love.

JOHN: Lesson One: God is dead, repeat . . .

TOD: God is dead, and my salvation is at hand. Teach me, teach me more . . .

MARY MARTHA: What must we do now, Joe?

REVEREND JOE: We must pray.

MARY MARTHA: What must we pray for?

REVEREND JOE: Mercy, pray for mercy.

MARY MARTHA: I asked God for a child.

REVEREND JOE: Yes, Martha.

MARY MARTHA: My prayers were answered, weren't they, Joe?

REVEREND JOE: Yes, Martha.

MARY MARTHA: We protected our son from the terror, didn't we, Joe?

REVEREND JOE: Through sleepless nights.

MARY MARTHA: Watching over this child. Waiting for the morning to come. Watching and waiting. I lived through nights of terror, and now this.

REVEREND JOE: In time, Martha, in time. We will destroy our oppressors and not lose our souls. In time all will be clear. All will not survive, but a few shall, a few shall be whole again.

MARY MARTHA: When I gave birth to Tod, the lightning glistened across the horizon. When I gave birth to truth and light. I had no life before. My life began with his.

COMMITTEE EXECUTIVE: Oh, stop worrying, John. He's just another educated nigger going insane, you can help prevent the inevitable. You know what happens to insane niggers, the ones who talk of liberation and the war. Don't let things get out of hand this time. We'll be with you. People without gods become apathetic, it's part of the plan. There's nothing we can do about it.

THE COMMITTEE: The final battle has begun, freedom is at hand. Amen.

JOHN: Amen.

REVEREND JOE: And a time will come when your stories will no longer be your own, and your music will be abused, and your soul enslaved, but there is one who will be born of both worlds and he will know, he will know and will lead you, and will suffer greatly, and will prevail. Teach my son, Oh, teach him well . . .

(*There is a flash of lightning. Blackout.*)

(*End of Act One.*)

Act Two

Scene One—Lesson Two

JOHN: Tod.

MARY MARTHA: Tod?

REVEREND JOE: Tod

JOHN: Tod, you don't know.

MARY MARTHA: Tod, you don't know.

REVEREND JOE: Tod, you don't know.

JOHN, MARY MARTHA, REVEREND JOE: What it means to be black in America.

REVEREND JOE: And that is good.

MARY MARTHA: You know nothing about your past.

JOHN: And that is what your parents are responding to.

MARY MARTHA: You think I'm telling you some fucking fairy tale.

REVEREND JOE: Those who say they know have already been defeated.

MARY MARTHA: This shit happened, the stories I tell you are true, they happened to me.

REVEREND JOE: It means nothing.

JOHN: Your apparent lack of knowledge of your culture and your past history. Do you understand what I'm trying to say? In a sense you're not really "black."

MARY MARTHA: Not really black.

REVEREND JOE: Not really black.

JOHN: You've been able to escape those denigrated aspects of your culture which are the only things that people are able to identify as uniquely black.

REVEREND JOE: Uniquely black.

MARY MARTHA: Uniquely black.

REVEREND JOE: For so long we've fought to bring meaning to our existence here. What's the use? There is no meaning to our existence here.

MARY MARTHA: You look at me as if I'm making this shit up.

REVEREND JOE: That's a lost cause.

MARY MARTHA: You look at me with that liberal arts education and I want to slap it off your face.

REVEREND JOE: That's a lost cause.

MARY MARTHA: You think I'm overreacting. It happened. Not like in your fantasy books, why do you think I talk so much about it?

JOHN: My experience is very similar. My Jewish heritage has been greatly diminished.

REVEREND JOE: I know history, Tod, I wrote history. We knew the world. We've explored every vast land. We were the discoverers, we knew about the enemy long before they knew about us. We knew of their savagery, their ignorance, their curse. And we denied the truth for fear of taking on their evil ways.

JOHN: Your hindrance is, of course, your black skin, but most people don't even acknowledge that after a while.

MARY MARTHA: I spent my lifetime fighting.

JOHN: Fighting.

REVEREND JOE: Fighting.

MARY MARTHA: For what you so easily take for granted, as if life has always been like this. As if it will always be this way and never change. As if my life means nothing, has meant nothing.

REVEREND JOE: Nothing.

JOHN: Nothing.

MARY MARTHA: How can I make you understand?

REVEREND JOE: Self-righteous idiots, conquering the world, enslaving every spirit they encountered with their bestiality, stealing land that they claimed to have discovered in the face of men who were already there.

JOHN: Your problem seems to be your inability to reconcile this sense of loss. But to be quite honest, I don't believe there was anything there to lose. You're caught up in a black myth. Tod, Lesson Two: there is no black culture. It does not exist, that is why you cannot find it. There is nothing to find. It's all made up from a failed rebellion that has faded away.

MARY MARTHA: White people cannot be trusted.

REVEREND JOE: And we, blinded by prophecy, by prophecy, knew they were to come, knew we were to be enslaved, knew the evil that they possessed, yet said nothing, did nothing, devoured ourselves, embellished them with riches, sold our souls because of our cursed curiosity and our acquiescent gods.

MARY MARTHA: White people cannot be trusted.

REVEREND JOE: Armageddon has begun. Armageddon is the battle for the minds of the people. It is no longer a question of whether they can love us or not, that would have been the easy way out. It is now a question of whether they can love.

Scene Two—Mary Martha's Lament

(*In the blackout an African beat begins. It slowly turns into the tempo of "The Battle Hymn of the Republic."* COMMITTEE SENIOR *begins humming the melody as the lights come up on the* COMMITTEE *and* MARY MARTHA. COMMITTEE JUNIOR *is wearing a headset and listening to a reel-to-reel tape recorder.* COMMITTEE EXECUTIVE *speaks as the voice of God during* MARY MARTHA's *lament.*)

MARY MARTHA: It all seemed to happen in a moment, a black and white moment.

COMMITTEE SENIOR *begins singing "The Battle Hymn of the Republic."*

We were marching in the movement for freedom, all together, black and white.

Everything around me was black and white, the signs were black and white, the monument, the nuns, and there was singing, and there was chanting, and we marched to the beat, and the dogs, even the dogs were black and white, and the police were white and we were marching and shouting for liberty as the world turned white, then black.

COMMITTEE JUNIOR *begins playing Martin Luther King, Jr.'s "I Have a Dream" speech on the reel-to-reel.*

There was a ringing, a ringing, but I could see nothing in this darkness until a voice spoke to me and from the darkness God appeared in a harsh white light, and He was black, as black as I had thought He would be . . . "Are you God?"

COMMITTEE EXECUTIVE: Yes!

MARY MARTHA: He said, "Yes!" Are you God?

COMMITTEE EXECUTIVE: Yes!

THE COMMITTEE: Yes, yes, He said, "yes."

MARY MARTHA: He said, "Yes!"
God, I want a freedom moment 'fore I die.
I want a freedom moment from my black and white life.
I want a freedom moment in my lifetime,
free from black and white.
I can't wait for salvation.

I can't wait for my Judgment Day.
And God said, "Yes!"

COMMITTEE EXECUTIVE: Yes, this is that moment.

THE COMMITTEE: Yes, this is that moment, yes, this is that moment . . .

MARY MARTHA: And he called me "baby."

COMMITTEE EXECUTIVE: Baby, yes, baby.

THE COMMITTEE: Baby, baby, baby, baby . . .

MARY MARTHA: He said, "Yes!"
And took me in his arms
and held me for a moment
and his love was black.
And I asked him for freedom,
he smiled and I saw stars.
Are you God?

COMMITTEE EXECUTIVE: Yes!

THE COMMITTEE: Yes, he said, yes, he said, yes, he said, yes . . .

MARY MARTHA: He said, yes, and for a moment there was freedom, freedom ringing, sounds so sweet, chanting for some
   justice,
crying for redemption,
marching for freedom in one sweet moment.
And he said, "There will be a child . . ."

THE COMMITTEE: There will be a child, there will be a child, there
   will be a child . . .

COMMITTEE EXECUTIVE: There will be a child of freedom, oh, baby,
   this is freedom, yes, this is freedom . . .

THE COMMITTEE: Baby, baby, baby . . .
This is your freedom, yes,
This is your freedom, yes,
This is your freedom, yes . . .

MARY MARTHA: A child, a child, a child,
from this moment of freedom
and he smiled.

God seemed so pleased
I believed I had made Him happy for a moment.
And he said, "I've never seen anyone as white as you before . . ."

COMMITTEE EXECUTIVE: I've never had anyone white before.
This is freedom.

THE COMMITTEE: Yes, this is freedom.

MARY MARTHA: This is freedom.
White.
A sign of my purity.
White as snow.
And he caressed my skin
with his great black hands.
Are you God?

THE COMMITTEE: Yes, I am God.

MARY MARTHA: He said, "Yes, I am."
And freedom was sweet
and painful
freedom was joy,
washed in his blood,
filled with his love   THE COMMITTEE:
as pure as snow,   Like a dream,
freedom was a moment   like a dream,
in my lifetime   like a dream,
like a dream   like a dream . . .
I once had, forgotten . . .
have I fallen to temptation,
have I lost my salvation . . .
and now they come
to seek us out
and destroy my child.   a child
                                            a child
Rape!   a child
I've been raped   a child
forsaken.   a child
My salvation.   yes
My redemption.   yes
My hope.   yes
Tod.   is
Tod.   is
Tod.   is
My salvation cries out in   Mary Martha
the wilderness   Mary Martha
and I am helpless,   Mary Martha
helpless to save my   poor

own child.   poor
Yes,   poor
yes,   poor
yes,   poor
yes,   poor, Mary Martha
poor, Mary Martha . . .

Scene Three—Power

REVEREND JOE: My wife had a very traumatic experience during the March, she was raped by a black man who thought she was white.

JOHN: Were there any witnesses?

REVEREND JOE: A few, I believe.

JOHN: And you were there?

REVEREND JOE: I found her.

MARY MARTHA: Are you God?

REVEREND JOE: Yes, I'm God's messenger.

THE COMMITTEE: He said, "Yes."

MARY MARTHA: Are you God?

REVEREND JOE: Yes, I'm God's messenger.

THE COMMITTEE: He said, "Yes."

MARY MARTHA: Yes.

REVEREND JOE: She was unconscious for a while. She never seemed to remember anything of what happened.

JOHN: And that was how you met?

REVEREND JOE: Yes.

JOHN: And the marriage followed?

REVEREND JOE: I thought she was the answer.

JOHN: Answer to what?

REVEREND JOE: My prayers, my salvation. I had asked God for a wife, a mate, somehow this seemed . . .

JOHN: Prophetic . . .

REVEREND JOE: It was a day of miracles. There was something we were both searching for, why not this, why not love, and from that a son and our salvation? It was my day of judgment.

JOHN: And the voice of God spoke to you . . .

REVEREND JOE: The voice of God spoke to us all. If you had been there you . . .

JOHN: I was there.

REVEREND JOE: Then you understand.

JOHN: Yes, I'm beginning to.

REVEREND JOE: Why should I waste my time trying to explain this to you? It's useless.

JOHN: Was it you?

REVEREND JOE: Would it make any difference if I said yes?

JOHN: Is Tod your son?

REVEREND JOE: I have never had any reason to doubt that Tod was my son.

JOHN: But your wife believes . . .

REVEREND JOE: What she needs to believe.

JOHN: And you plan to continue to indulge her fantasy?

REVEREND JOE: I plan to continue this journey until the end. I will see that justice prevails.

JOHN: And Tod?

REVEREND JOE: Tod is part of that justice. We all have our part to play.

JOHN: You control your family's lives with these delusions, you're driving them insane with your beliefs. How can you expect Tod to be normal with such expectations, no one should have to live up to your ideals.

REVEREND JOE: The ideology, the ideology is intact. Tod has entered in and will come out clean. He will learn the ways of the enemy and set us free. He is our liberator.

JOHN: You are causing him great turmoil with your beliefs.

REVEREND JOE: No one said it would be easy. Tod is now on the other side. We must work together to bring him back intact . . . whole.

JOHN: Your son is suffering.

REVEREND JOE: At last my son is suffering, as we all have had to do. Millions have lost their lives. He must understand, suffering is part of survival in the land of the enemy. Suffering is the key to his salvation. And ours.

JOHN: I just don't understand how you can continue to uphold these beliefs, it has almost cost him his life.

REVEREND JOE: But he survived, that was the first sign. I cannot explain to you why I believe what I do. Your heart is cold. You do not want to understand. You want to believe in the white man's world. Tod represents another world, the white man's world cannot accept him, it strives to destroy him. Tod's power lies in his complete knowledge of the enemy. He knows so well the ways of white men. That knowledge will be his salvation, and he shall lead us to the promised land.

MARY MARTHA: I met God one day.

JOHN: There was once an alliance.

REVEREND JOE: Those days are over.

MARY MARTHA: It was at the March on Washington.

JOHN: My father fought long and hard for integration.

REVEREND JOE: The world still hates niggers.

MARY MARTHA: I asked God for a child.

JOHN: Blacks demanded too much.

REVEREND JOE: Jews demanded too much.

MARY MARTHA: And He said, "Yes."

JOHN: You shattered our temples.

REVEREND JOE: You betrayed our trust.

MARY MARTHA: Are you God?

JOHN: You betrayed our trust through your negligence.

REVEREND JOE: Through your arrogance.

MARY MARTHA: And God was black.

JOHN: You failed to teach your history.

REVEREND JOE: You were afraid of our power.

MARY MARTHA: Black as I always thought He would be.

JOHN: We were your greatest allies.

REVEREND JOE: You were white like everybody else.

MARY MARTHA: Poor yellow gal, as black as you're ever going to be.

JOHN: Your revolution destroyed the movement.

REVEREND JOE: You never wanted blacks to have power.

MARY MARTHA: So I married the blackest man I could find.

JOHN: You failed to tell the truth.

REVEREND JOE: "The only way we gonna stop them white men from whipping us is to take over."

MARY MARTHA: And put an end to my half white legacy.

JOHN: Tod doesn't trust you.

REVEREND JOE: "We been sayin' freedom for years and we ain't got nothin'."

MARY MARTHA: Rape.

JOHN: You lied to him.

REVEREND JOE: "What we gonna start sayin now is Black Power."

MARY MARTHA: Rape.

JOHN: Live the results of your silence.

REVEREND JOE: Black Power!

MARY MARTHA: I've been raped.

JOHN: You betrayed yourselves.

REVEREND JOE: Black Power!

MARY MARTHA: By America!

REVEREND JOE: Racism is a great evil that has to be extracted from the heart. It shall be ripped out if it must. We have been forced to eat of the tree of knowledge and we know that we were once naked. Lost innocence, raped, we have been raped. Curse the forgotten mythology, curse the forgotten history, curse the forgotten land that we do not know. We do not know how it feels to walk on peaceful soil, native land. All we have are ourselves, the nation, home, Tod.

Scene Four—Am I Black Enough

TOD: What is it?

REVEREND JOE: I want to go home.

TOD: What do they want from me?

REVEREND JOE: Take us there.

TOD: I don't understand what it is I'm supposed to be.

REVEREND JOE: To the promised land.

TOD: I don't understand how I feel.

REVEREND JOE: I want to go back to a time when I was free.

TOD: Am I not black enough for you?

REVEREND JOE: And my language was my own.

TOD: Am I not as black as you think I should be?

REVEREND JOE: My land.

TOD: What do you expect from me.

REVEREND JOE: Take us there.

TOD: I sound white, am I?

REVEREND JOE: We shall remember.

TOD: I sound white, am I?

REVEREND JOE: We must remember.

TOD: I feel it all slipping away.

REVEREND JOE: Do you remember?

TOD: You created me black . . .

REVEREND JOE: To be black.

TOD: . . . and educated.

REVEREND JOE: In America.

TOD: Too black . . .

REVEREND JOE: Doesn't mean . . .

TOD: . . . and too educated

REVEREND JOE: . . . a damn thing.

TOD: . . . for you to understand.

REVEREND JOE: That's all you need to learn.

TOD: Is this what you wanted,
to forget?
You wanted to forget,
but you can't forget.
You wanted to raise
a generation untouched and

unscarred by the pain and
blood of struggle.

I do not know my oppression
I do not know my oppression

Where did you go wrong?
You created me,
but I am not what you wanted,
Am I?
Am I your enemy?
Am I your failure?
Mother, I do not know you.
Father, I do not know you.
Speak to me,
my language . . .
my language

(MARY MARTHA *and* REVEREND JOE *begin a musical minstrel journey
   back to the past.*)

MARY MARTHA: Whatever happened to soul?

REVEREND JOE: Whatever happened to soul?

MARY MARTHA: Soul!

REVEREND JOE: Black as coal!

MARY MARTHA: Soul crossed-over, Joe.

REVEREND JOE: Whatever happened to soul?

MARY MARTHA: We sold our soul.

REVEREND JOE: For gold?

MARY MARTHA: No.

REVEREND JOE: We sold our soul.

MARY MARTHA: For knowledge?

REVEREND JOE: No.

MARY MARTHA: For what?

REVEREND JOE: What did we sell it for?

MARY MARTHA: For salvation?

REVEREND JOE: No.

MARY MARTHA: For freedom?

REVEREND JOE: No.

MARY MARTHA: What did we sell it for?

REVEREND JOE: Acceptance.

MARY MARTHA: Acceptance?

REVEREND JOE: Yes, acceptance.

MARY MARTHA: We got taken.

REVEREND JOE: We got tooked.

MARY MARTHA: We lost our soul?

REVEREND JOE: We sold our soul.

MARY MARTHA: We sold our soul?

REVEREND JOE: Soul crossed over.

MARY MARTHA: Now, it's oversold.

REVEREND JOE: Solid gold.

MARY MARTHA: Solid!

REVEREND JOE: We sold our soul?

MARY MARTHA: We sold ourselves.

REVEREND JOE: For acceptance?

MARY MARTHA: That's all we got?

REVEREND JOE: Not even that.

MARY MARTHA: Not even that?

REVEREND JOE: Am I still a slave?

MARY MARTHA: Am I still a slave?

REVEREND JOE: Am I still a slave?

MARY MARTHA: Am I still a slave?

TOD: I am your monster,
you created me.
But you reject me
you won't accept me

Not black enough,
not black enough,
not black enough

*

I have become what you wanted
me to become
Adaptable.
I am America!
I am your savior
I am your death!

Tod

No struggle
no fight
no history
no heritage
no cause
no culture
no God

I'm afraid.
I'm afraid of what I might do.
I'm afraid I want to slit your throats
and my options are running out.

I'm trying to be fair, but now I have
discovered something dormant in me
that is rising, something rising in me that has
no fear, speaking to me,
the voice of destruction!

Scene Five—The Trial

JOHN: I'm just not certain.

COMMITTEE EXECUTIVE: Just not certain?

JOHN: It may be too soon.

COMMITTEE SENIOR: It may be too soon?

JOHN: Our timing might be off. He seems so volatile.

COMMITTEE JUNIOR: Sounds like cold feet.

JOHN: This is an unpredictable situation.

COMMITTEE EXECUTIVE: Things go differently every day.

COMMITTEE JUNIOR: That is a sign of the end.

COMMITTEE SENIOR: Now, sir, I think we should proceed with caution.

COMMITTEE EXECUTIVE: We've always been cautious with the colored, nigger, Negro peoples of the world, to our disadvantage. We should have wiped them out when they became obsolete.

COMMITTEE JUNIOR: I never realized how old you were.

COMMITTEE EXECUTIVE: Hell, man, I remember the day when you could string up a nigger and that would be the last word on it.

COMMITTEE SENIOR: But you have to give up that memory if we are going to proceed successfully.

COMMITTEE EXECUTIVE: The past is hard to give up.

COMMITTEE JUNIOR: We must make our changes as well. Any sign of your continued bigotry could be detrimental. You've lost Yonkers.

COMMITTEE SENIOR: You lost Forsythe County.

COMMITTEE EXECUTIVE: But I still have Boston.

COMMITTEE JUNIOR: You're losing Atlanta.

COMMITTEE SENIOR: Yes, and your little skinhead Nazis running around are not helping either.

COMMITTEE EXECUTIVE: It's hard to keep things in check, it's unnatural, I can't pretend anymore. They are the youth of today, they say, "Let's go," and I say, "Go!"

JOHN: I think you're going too far. I think we've pushed too hard. We've destroyed him already. We can never get him back now.

COMMITTEE SENIOR: John, John, so naive, we haven't destroyed him, he's perfect.

COMMITTEE EXECUTIVE: History repeats itself, history repeats itself.

COMMITTEE JUNIOR: We've just sped up the process.

JOHN: I don't understand.

COMMITTEE EXECUTIVE: John, this is the moment that we've been waiting for. This generation is far too apathetic to come up with any philosophy of its own. Their ideology is something they have stolen from the past, and the past we know how to correct. Tod is now ready.

JOHN: What must I do?

COMMITTEE EXECUTIVE: It's all so simple, John, love him.

COMMITTEE SENIOR: Love him.

JOHN: Love him? I can't, it's a lie.

COMMITTEE JUNIOR: You have no choice. How else will you fund your trip to Zion?

COMMITTEE SENIOR: You need us, you can't return without your god.

COMMITTEE EXECUTIVE: John, you are broke, you have no cause.

COMMITTEE JUNIOR: You are us, we are the same.

COMMITTEE EXECUTIVE: You have your own niggers now.

COMMITTEE SENIOR: The world has no sympathy for you.

COMMITTEE JUNIOR: Yes, John, how do you plan to resolve Palestine?

COMMITTEE SENIOR: Just like us, John. Just like us.

JOHN: I'm not a racist.

COMMITTEE EXECUTIVE: I'm not a racist.

COMMITTEE SENIOR: I'm not a racist.

JOHN: I've never assimilated.

THE COMMITTEE: I've never assimilated.

JOHN: I am not a part of your culture.

THE COMMITTEE: I am not a part of your culture.

JOHN: I am separate.

THE COMMITTEE: I am separate.

JOHN: I will persevere.

THE COMMITTEE: I will persevere.

JOHN: It is written.

THE COMMITTEE: It is written.

JOHN: It is prophecy.

THE COMMITTEE: It is prophecy. We are one!

COMMITTEE EXECUTIVE: And Tod too shall be, we shall all be one white one.

COMMITTEE JUNIOR: It's the only way to overcome the global shift.

COMMITTEE SENIOR: There was never a revolution and there never shall be. Go fight your own battle. But remember these words, John.

COMMITTEE JUNIOR: Just like us, John. Just like us.

COMMITTEE EXECUTIVE: It was we who were slaves, we who were strangers, and therefore we recall these words as well . . .

JOHN: Stop it. Stop it.

COMMITTEE JUNIOR: You shall not oppress a stranger, for you know the feelings of the stranger.

JOHN: Stop it. You know nothing about me. You have no right.

COMMITTEE SENIOR: Having yourselves been a stranger in the land of Egypt.

JOHN: This is mine, my heritage. My language.

COMMITTEE JUNIOR: When a stranger resides with you in your land, you shall not wrong him . . . You shall love him as yourself.

JOHN: This is not your battle. You abuse culture, you steal culture.

COMMITTEE EXECUTIVE: For you were strangers in the land of Egypt. Love him.

JOHN: I want my belief back.

THE COMMITTEE: As we loved Bobby
As we loved Huey
Love him

JOHN: I want to go back, I want to go back.

THE COMMITTEE: As we loved Martin.
As we loved Malcolm.
Love him.

JOHN: To a time when I was free. Free.

THE COMMITTEE: As we loved Marcus.

As we loved William.
As we loved Frederick.
As we loved them all.
As we loved them all.

JOHN: Free.
THE COMMITTEE: As we loved Mary.
As we loved Fannie.

As we loved Angela.
As we learned to love you.

JOHN: When I was free.

THE COMMITTEE: Love him.

JOHN: Am I still a slave?

THE COMMITTEE: At last he has arrived.
You must make him complete
and he shall disappear forever.
And the rest will defeat
themselves.

JOHN: Am I still a slave?

THE COMMITTEE: There is no defense against love,
acquiesce and accept,
it costs us nothing to concede equality,
it's simply an ideal,
no man can make another man equal.

JOHN: Am I still a slave?
I must answer the call.
I must answer the call.

COMMITTEE JUNIOR: The battle is no longer with us.

COMMITTEE SENIOR: The battle is with the weakness in himself.

COMMITTEE EXECUTIVE: Teach him, John. Teach him well.

JOHN: I would like to do this without guilt, please.

COMMITTEE EXECUTIVE: Very well, we'll see you on the other side.

COMMITTEE SENIOR: The doors are opening to a free world, a new
    society.

COMMITTEE JUNIOR: Be a part of it or be lost forever.

(*The* COMMITTEE *disappears.*)

JOHN: On the battlefield, my friends. On the battlefield. Tod!

Scene Six—The Final Lesson

TOD: I had a dream once that I was at war.
The war seemed to have been going on for quite some time
but I was unaware.
I just appeared,

but I didn't have any armor
and I didn't know what I was fighting for.
But I began to learn how to survive.
I found some books
and they helped a little,
but there was very little time to read
and there was very little air.
Tod, on the edge of oppression, just doesn't care.

JOHN: Come Tod,
I will give you comfort.
Come Tod, I will help you understand
Come Tod, I will explain it all
It is time for your final lesson.

TOD: Have I learned all there is to know?

JOHN: Almost all.

TOD: What is the final lesson about?

JOHN: Love. The final lesson is always about love.

TOD: Will it be a painful lesson?

JOHN: Love is always painful.

(JOHN *positions* TOD *in his chair for the final lesson, the rape of mind,
body, and soul. He slowly removes his belt and walks around* TOD's
chair cracking it like a whip.)

JOHN: Come, Tod. Trust. Think. You must remember.

(*This phrase is repeated throughout* REVEREND JOE *and* MARY MARTHA's
chant. During the chant JOHN *removes* TOD's *belt and lowers his
trousers. He takes* TOD's *belt and fastens it around his neck like a
noose. He inspects* TOD's *body as if he were on the auction block.*)

MARY MARTHA, REVEREND JOE: How to reach that moment,
the selling of ourselves,
the frantic sacrifice of our hearts
to merciless savages . . .

TOD: Are you going to beat me?

JOHN: I'm going to love you.

MARY MARTHA, REVEREND JOE: As we stood and watched with
    horror,
devils, devils,
in their divine right destroy our heritage,
with a single sleight of hand,

the pulling of a switch,
the rape of mind, body and soul,
the poisonous vapors that overwhelm us,
the stench of our dying ancestors,
that haunt us forever . . .

JOHN: Let us take a journey, Tod,
and you will see the truth,
you will know your oppression,
you will feel the pain,
you will see . . .

MARY MARTHA, REVEREND JOE: History,
we must remember,
we must remember,
and wait for one who shall be all powerful,
and shall know the evil that dwells among us,
and shall cast our tormentors away

TOD: And this is knowledge?	MARY MARTHA, REVEREND JOE: History, our history
JOHN: The purest knowledge.	History, our history
	they tied him to a tree
TOD: And this is power?	they strapped her to a stake
	they tied his hands together
JOHN: Power eternal. Do you like it?	they chained their ankles
	they locked the shackles
	they tied the noose
TOD: Yes.	they gathered kindling
	they struck the match
JOHN: Why?	they aimed the rifle
	they branded flesh
TOD: It's the most honest lesson I have learned.	they raped the child
	they held her down
	they cut the flesh
JOHN: Yes?	they chopped his foot
	they sold the child
TOD: Has it always been this way?	they fed the fire
	they yanked the rope
	the alligator smiled
JOHN: From the beginning.	the children screamed
	the man screamed
TOD: And it is never forgotten?	the woman screamed
	the knives fed

JOHN: Civilizations have been born on this knowledge. It's been done for centuries.

TOD: And what will come of this?

JOHN: I give you my white male guilty conscience. I give it to you freely. I give you knowledge. I give you truth to liberate my soul.

As it was given to me so many years ago. Face the beast, Tod. Face the beast and see anew!

the hounds fed
the alligators fed
the fire fed
the ocean fed
the noose fed
the shackles fed
on our flesh
on our flesh
on our flesh
greedily
ravenously
greedily
ravenously
our children as live bait
devoured
a nation
a nation
a nation
fed on spirit
on culture
on flesh
on spirit
on culture
on flesh
on soul
a nation
no nations
on millions
millions
six million
no millions
sixty million
no millions
six hundred million
millions . . .

(*The rape is an exchange of knowledge, the Ascension of Books begins in reverse.* TOD *and* JOHN *recite the passages together as the rape continues.*)

TOD, JOHN: Then you have to wonder if we're ever going to get women and minorities to fit in . . .
Affirmative Action is a failure . . .

THE COMMITTEE (*Reappearing*): Stop, what are you doing?
Stop, you're unleashing demons.
Stop, it is an abomination.
Stop, you cannot teach them.
Stop, you'll destroy the world . . .

TOD, JOHN: . . . the Negro community has been forced into a matriarchal structure . . . That the American Negro has survived at
all is extraordinary . . .

THE COMMITTEE: Stop, they cannot learn. Stop, you cannot teach
them, they are inferior . . .

TOD, JOHN: . . . you are for the next thirty years going to have to
give them unequal treatment . . .

. . . the black man occupies a very special sexual role in American
society . . .

THE COMMITTEE: You are creating a great danger. They cannot
learn, you cannot teach them, they are inferior . . .

TOD, JOHN: . . . black people have become useless . . .

. . . the semites do not possess the harmonious equilibrium . . .

. . . Christianity is the religion of white, white people . . .

. . . the pure blood white is the creature whom God, God destined
should perform the mental labor.

THE COMMITTEE: You are creating your demise. They will de
stroy you.

TOD, JOHN: . . . lower the race of the human species . . .

. . . rigorous tradition of Negro-ape affinity . . .

THE COMMITTEE: Nigger, nigger lover, nigger lover, nigger lover . . .

(*The* COMMITTEE *continues to chant as they gradually disappear.*)

TOD, JOHN: . . . the Negro has the cerebral cranium less developed
than the white . . .

. . . marks the human species degenerate.

. . . skin color was affected by the bile . . .

. . . a people of beastly living without God, law, religion, or common wealth . . .

TOD: Is this oppression?
Is this oppression?
Is this oppression?

JOHN: Yes, Tod, yes, this is how oppression feels. That pain which
you've forgotten, so sweet, the rapes, the lynchings, the sacrifice of life to keep you in your place. A history of hundreds of
years of oppression which for you exist as if they occurred in
a single moment. Rape, pain, oppression is so safe, secure,
the fear.

This I give to you freely, the way it was given to me. My white
man's guilt is yours, take it, take it, take it . . .

TOD: And he said, cursed be Canaan, a servant of servants shall
he be unto his brethren . . .

In the beginning God created the heaven and the earth.
And the earth was without form, and void; and darkness was
upon the face of the deep, and the Spirit of God moved upon
the face of the waters. And God said, "Let there be light: and
there was light."

(*A darkness envelops the stage.* TOD *and* JOHN *are the only characters lit.*)

JOHN: At last I am free. My God, my sovereignty abused and re-
shaped till I no longer felt divine and God no longer spoke
to me. Evil, Tod, the world is ruled by evil and hypocrisy, open
your eyes and see anew.

TOD: What has happened? It seems so peaceful.

JOHN: Yes, they're gone. Freedom is so peaceful and so transient.
They're gone now and I am free for the first time, and see myself for the first time.
Tod, I have sacrificed so much to live in this world. Waiting,
waiting for the call, the trumpet blast, waiting to go home. I
have given you the truth. If the niggers really knew that the
white man never intended to love them, the world would have
ended years ago. Live free or die, Tod, live free or die.
I really have to go now. Freedom is just a suspended moment, Tod, such a fleeting moment. Use it while it lives. Never
let a man tell you what you are, if you do you will always be a

slave. (JOHN *recites as he exits.*) Someone is shouting in the desert, get the road ready for him, make a straight path for him to travel. All low places must be filled up, all hills and mountains leveled off. The winding roads must be made straight, all the rough paths made smooth. All mankind will see his destruction.

Scene Seven—Still a Nigger

TOD: I am the last revolutionary, the only person with a cause that's running out. Was there a revolution before, shall there be? For you will remember that a concession was made and now a debt has to be paid to save your sense of morality. You denied me my humanity and called me beast. And from this you created a world. But now the beast is rising and the debt shall be collected, for your chance to confess has passed, and you have not changed your ways. And there shall be no salvation for you. I your enemy stand and possess the final jewel that you cannot usurp. I am all that you cannot be, I am all that you cannot see. Now, I know all there is to know about you and you barely know me at all.

(*Three panels of the bookshelf begin to open as the* COMMITTEE OF SOCIAL REFORM *appears.*)

COMMITTEE EXECUTIVE. Hello, Tod.

COMMITTEE JUNIOR: Hello, Tod.

COMMITTEE SENIOR: Tod, the boy, Tod.

COMMITTEE EXECUTIVE: Tod, the nigger, Tod.

COMMITTEE JUNIOR: Fighting his way to the 21st century.

COMMITTEE SENIOR: Who would have thought you would make it this far.

COMMITTEE EXECUTIVE: Tod, the boy, Tod.

COMMITTEE JUNIOR: Tod, the nigger, Tod.

COMMITTEE SENIOR: Tod, crying 'cause the system seems so unfair.

THE COMMITTEE: Poor Tod, the boy, Tod.

COMMITTEE SENIOR: He believes in language.

COMMITTEE JUNIOR: He thinks that words will set him free.

COMMITTEE EXECUTIVE: Bound to an image and a sigh.

TOD: Who are you?

THE COMMITTEE: Why, Tod, we're John's white male guilty conscience. We now belong to you.

TOD: I thought you were gone. I thought I was free.

THE COMMITTEE: This is freedom, Tod.

COMMITTEE SENIOR: Freedom carries a great responsibility.

COMMITTEE JUNIOR: Freedom makes strange allies.

COMMITTEE EXECUTIVE: Freedom is a great burden.

COMMITTEE JUNIOR: A burden.

COMMITTEE SENIOR: A burden.

COMMITTEE EXECUTIVE: Feel it.

COMMITTEE JUNIOR: See it.

COMMITTEE SENIOR: Hear it.

COMMITTEE EXECUTIVE: Taste it.

COMMITTEE JUNIOR: Touch it.

COMMITTEE EXECUTIVE: A burden for eating of the tree of knowledge to liberate your soul.

COMMITTEE SENIOR: The road to freedom is dark and narrow.

COMMITTEE JUNIOR: The road to freedom feels something like this . . .

COMMITTEE EXECUTIVE: Everyone has claims to retributions, Tod, what do you want? We gave you forty acres and a mule. We gave the Japanese $20,000 and a smile, will that do?

COMMITTEE SENIOR: I just don't understand you people. You want us to compensate for the crimes of the past. That wouldn't solve anything.

COMMITTEE JUNIOR: We're smarter than that now. We have a better understanding now. We can now extract what is discriminatory from what is idleness.

COMMITTEE SENIOR: The blacks in our society have every opportunity to achieve.

COMMITTEE JUNIOR: Let's face it, there's no better place to go. There are no black Utopias except for the ones you create in your dreams and your false memories of what Africa used to be.

COMMITTEE EXECUTIVE: Don't you remember, I was there. Africa was Hell on Earth. It was no paradise. Savage, barren, with jewels you weren't even aware of, riches, you had no idea.

COMMITTEE SENIOR: Oil, uranium, iron, what use did you have for these things? You had no technology, you now have our technology.

COMMITTEE JUNIOR: Make the best of your situation. I have my own life to live.

COMMITTEE EXECUTIVE: We pretend that we're some modern society that can solve everything diplomatically. Oh, but we're beasts, we ravage and shit on everything in our path.

COMMITTEE JUNIOR: We have not become great men, just more efficient savages.

COMMITTEE SENIOR: You laugh and think that we don't know this. We're not trying to fool ourselves, we know this and accept it.

COMMITTEE EXECUTIVE: You laugh when we pretend not to know that you're still oppressed. What fools. Everything you are, everything you're allowed to be is still in our hands.

COMMITTEE SENIOR: Oh, no, not consciously, we just don't know any better.

THE COMMITTEE: And have no reason to change.

COMMITTEE JUNIOR: Hell, what do you want from us, a piece of paper?

(*All three open their briefcases and take out a folder.*)

COMMITTEE SENIOR: Here, have a guarantee that you are free.

(*They hold out a sheet of paper, then snatch it back.*)

COMMITTEE EXECUTIVE: My freedom isn't guaranteed. Tod, my boy, I wouldn't expect many social reforms in the 21st century, that budget has been cut drastically. You see, even we have our doubts. Life is not as great as it once was. Everything is so easy. We're all so idle. Life was rich when wars were bloody. But now there's very little blood. Just a lot of talk and bombs. Well, we're not as bad as the HUD, but it's still not good. Did you send that memo? Who does the filing now? Oh, here . . . no, see, not good at all. I never thought that I would resent paradise. Hopefully, there won't be much more to re-member. Almost like Black History, wouldn't you say, Tod. A one-week course that you took in the 7th grade and that's all you know. And I know even less. Ignorance is bliss.

COMMITTEE SENIOR: You see, Tod, we wanted to spare you all of this, but you've eaten of the tree of knowledge, and now you have to be cast out.

COMMITTEE JUNIOR: You see, Tod, oppression is the state of peace. Paradise is slavery, without a care in the world. The oppressed know exactly who and what they are, but we fumble around for meaning each day. I mean what can you expect from me, I spend most of the day just trying to cover my ass.

COMMITTEE EXECUTIVE: I almost lost a billion dollars today, one minute it was there, then gone. I got it back, but you can never be certain. Hell, the issue is no longer about race any-more, race is dead, let it die. It's about power, and it always has been. Why should I give up my advantage over you? We fight for advantage, if you want power, goddamnit, then take it!

I'm tired of your apathy, your crying, your welfare. "Am I black?" You better believe your black ass is black, but can you fight, motherfucker?

COMMITTEE JUNIOR: Sir, you're going to ruin everything with your melodrama, calm down.

COMMITTEE EXECUTIVE: I'm tired, I told you, I want this black thing over. I almost lost a billion dollars today! I could be the fucking homeless tomorrow. I'm supposed to care about his simple ass.

COMMITTEE SENIOR: We have to keep him appeased.

COMMITTEE EXECUTIVE: You're just a bunch of chickenshits.

COMMITTEE JUNIOR: Sir, please try to remain professional.

COMMITTEE EXECUTIVE: Chickenshits. You're afraid of niggers, you've always been afraid of niggers. I'm not, bunch of pansy liberals.

COMMITTEE JUNIOR: This is the same attitude that got us into trouble in Simi Valley, let me handle this.

COMMITTEE EXECUTIVE: You little shit, you're going to get us into more deliberations.

COMMITTEE SENIOR: Let him handle it, you've already alarmed everyone with your little neo Nazis, remember Howard Beach.

COMMITTEE EXECUTIVE: Guilty, guilty, yeah, I'm guilty! Who the fuck cares? Take another four hundred years and figure that one out.

(COMMITTEE JUNIOR *walks over to* TOD. COMMITTEE SENIOR *and* COMMITTEE EXECUTIVE *remain behind.*)

COMMITTEE JUNIOR: Tod, I know what you're going through. I know you, I understand. We went to school together, re-member? We lived together for four years. I know your life story.

Look, I'm trying to help you out, Tod, but these two are from the Old School, they believe in the system. They created the system.

Someday we too shall create a system, but there's only so much I can do.

COMMITTEE EXECUTIVE: I'm tired of your apathy, your crying, your welfare. Do something about it. Weak, simple, assimilated, empty, white-assed, nigger . . .

COMMITTEE SENIOR: Sir, please!

COMMITTEE EXECUTIVE: Can he fight? Can he fight?

COMMITTEE JUNIOR: You have to start coming up with some of the answers, the burden's all on you, Babe. Why, you're the first to get this far, so pure and innocent. We're proud of you, but don't let us down, we're counting on you. We've invested a lot in you. Be confident with these people. You know, Tod, I think I've worked with black people more than you have, imagine that. We're with you all the way, just don't turn against us.

Tod, the boy, Tod still hates the world. You used to crack me up you were so naive and innocent. Perfect like a dream. You have the potential to be greater than anything I've ever seen. I envy your oppression, Tod. My idealism is just an ob-session. There's no need for me to be ideal. I believe that you could have been a savior, but you were led astray. You began to believe in your own perfection.

TOD: Wait, I know you. I know you.

COMMITTEE JUNIOR: Yes, Tod, you created me. I followed you like all of your devoted friends who had never met anyone quite like you before. Why, you spoke so well and you were so intelligent. I think we felt betrayed, dumber than a nigger, now that's dumb.

TOD: It was you. I thought you loved me.

COMMITTEE JUNIOR: We all loved you, but did you really think that we could ever vote for you for president? People laughed at us, people called us names as we followed you so perfect and pure. But this is the end, Tod. I'm sorry, but as of now we were never really friends. I can't take the risk of that coming up in some file somewhere. They might think I'm a nigger lover, and then I'd be lost forever. You are the first and the last.

(COMMITTEE JUNIOR *calls over the other members.*)

Yes, here he is, boys, the one I told you about. Tod, the boy Tod. Tod the nigger, Tod, shining black in all his potential. The one who calls himself a savior. The one who performs such miracles. Why, one time he even graduated Phi Beta Kappa right before my eyes. I call for the vote. All in favor say, "Aye."

THE COMMITTEE: Aye!

COMMITTEE JUNIOR: Those opposed. Oh, so sorry, Tod. Still a nigger, Tod, in the 21st century. As I said, I wouldn't expect many social reforms if I were you. What's another four hundred years anyway? You seem to be so good at waiting.

COMMITTEE EXECUTIVE: I'm surprised he even got this far.

COMMITTEE SENIOR: And the book is closed, a tragic chapter in the history of making the American Negro extinct. The anthropologists will say they died from apathy.

COMMITTEE JUNIOR: Sign your name here please.

TOD: I don't remember how.

COMMITTEE JUNIOR: Just make an "X."

COMMITTEE EXECUTIVE: Who's next on the list?

COMMITTEE JUNIOR: Tod Goldstein.

COMMITTEE EXECUTIVE: Sounds like a Jew.

COMMITTEE JUNIOR: No, he still can't be a Jew.

COMMITTEE EXECUTIVE: Why not?

COMMITTEE SENIOR: Check code 517 section 10 under the Tribal Egalitarian Act. We must use the term of "Judaic origin."

COMMITTEE EXECUTIVE: But still a kike!

COMMITTEE JUNIOR: All in favor?

THE COMMITTEE: Aye!

COMMITTEE JUNIOR: None oppose, still a kike.

COMMITTEE EXECUTIVE: Next on the list.

COMMITTEE JUNIOR: Tod Gonzales.

COMMITTEE EXECUTIVE: Come on, what's with you guys, a spic now?

COMMITTEE JUNIOR: But that's our job.

COMMITTEE EXECUTIVE: I hate ethnicity.

COMMITTEE SENIOR: Look here, at least he's from Spain.

COMMITTEE EXECUTIVE: Does Spain still exist?

COMMITTEE JUNIOR: Spain is dead.

COMMITTEE EXECUTIVE: Total reform!

COMMITTEE JUNIOR: All in favor?

THE COMMITTEE: Aye!

THE COMMITTEE: If you turn against us, we will destroy you.

COMMITTEE EXECUTIVE: Next!

COMMITTEE JUNIOR: Tod Gortowski.

THE COMMITTEE: A Polack!
(*The* COMMITTEE *leaves laughing as the bookshelf closes behind them.*)

Scene Eight—Resurrection

TOD: My eyes are clearer now. At last I see, the mystery is gone. No veiled promise, no unseen hand. The truth, the truth at last, not free.

You never really intended for me to survive, did you?
You never intended for me to be equal.
But the road has been made ready. All is clear.

*

Let there be a new language.
Let there be new words.

Elijah said we must have a place to be ourselves, with no contradic-
    tions, and no justifications, and no psychological mandates,
    free to ourselves . . .

And Malcolm said by any means necessary . . .

And Martin said let freedom ring . . .

And Marcus said,

and W.E.B. said,
and Booker T. said,
and Fannie said,
and Angela said,
and Huey said,
and Moses said let my people go . . .

And Tod says, enough's been said.
All it takes is a leap of faith,
the leap of faith.
Do I believe I'm free?
Do I believe I am free?
Do you believe?

And now I know that every moment
is a freedom moment in an act to survive.

I come to bring truth to the word. Haven't you heard this before?
    Do you not see it manifest before your eyes?

Live free or die!

(TOD *raises a Black Power fist.*)
Live free or die!
Live free or die!

(TOD *slowly opens up his fist as a blinding light fills the stage.* TOD *slowly
    lowers his open hand and offers it to the audience.*)

MARY MARTHA (*sings*): Tod opened his black bound fist and found
    his salvation there.
Tod opened his black bound fist and found a new world there.
Tod opened up his black bound fist to lead his people there.
Tod opened up his black bound fist and unleashed the power . . .
Bound was the light.
The blinding light,
for a second
he saw the wonder,
for a second
he saw the future,
for a second
he saw the past.

His hand could bend.
His hand could build.
His hand could take.
His hand could kill.
He was a man.
He has come home.
We all can see,
for a second.

REVEREND JOE: There were no written texts to prophesy his birth.
    Writing is the way of the oppressor. But you see the signs,
    can't you see the signs? The day will come when he will rise
    and the earth shall stand still.

    Tod will say, "this is the end," and it will end. Tod will say,
    "let there be darkness," and the stars will fall from the sky. Tod
    will say, "enough!" and peace, peace in the morning.

TOD: We did not know who we were.
We did not know our richness.
We did not know our beauty.

Until now.

We had to fight for identity.
We had no identity before.
We had to fight for beauty.

Now we know.
And can go home. ·

*

The doors are open.
Won't you come?
Won't you come?

By his hand.
By his hand.
Tod took himself
by his hand and . . .

MARY MARTHA: Tod?

TOD: Yes.

REVEREND JOE: Tod?

TOD: Yes.

MARY MARTHA, REVEREND JOE: Tod.

TOD: I'm alive?

MARY MARTHA: Yes.

TOD: I'm alive?

REVEREND JOE: Yes.

TOD: I'm alive.

(TOD *takes one single step into darkness. Blackout.*)

(*End of Play.*)

SECTION THREE

Reconstructing Black Womanhood

BIG BUTT GIRLS, HARD-HEADED WOMEN

Rhodessa Jones

RHODESSA JONES, performer, writer, lecturer, and teacher, is co-artistic director of Cultural Odyssey, a San Francisco–based nonprofit performing arts organization, and founder of The Medea Project: Theater for Incarcerated Women, a program designed to promote incarcerated women's self-awareness and self-esteem through the creation and production of theater pieces based on their personal histories. Jones's directorial work includes the premieres of *A Taste of Somewhere Else: A Place at the Table* at the Center for the Arts at Yerba Buena Gardens in San Francisco in 1994; *Reality Is Just Outside the Window* at Theater Artaud in San Francisco in 1992; and *Food Taboos in the Land of the Dead* at the Lorraine Hansberry Theater in San Francisco in 1993. Jones annually convenes "Living on the Outside," an intensive theater workshop for women, with Medea Project participants. In 1990 Ms. Jones created *Big Butt Girls, Hard-Headed Women,* a show comprised of a series of monologues based on the lives of women who are incarcerated. It was produced at La MaMa Experimental Theater Club in New York City in 1992, and awarded the 1993 Bessie Award.

Jones's collaborations include Cultural Odyssey's production of *Raining Down Stars,* presented at Theater Artaud in San Francisco; *Perfect Courage,* which premiered at San Francisco's Festival 2000 in 1990 and was awarded Dance Bay Area's Isadora Duncan Dance Award; and *I Think It's Gonna Work Out Fine,* a musical that has appeared at La MaMa Experimental Theater Club in New York City, throughout Europe, and in Japan during 1989–90.

Since 1987 Jones has been commissioned as Artist-in-Residence by San Francisco's City and County Jails, teaching theater to inmates. She has participated in residencies at several major universities, including Yale, Pomona College, and North Carolina State University. Rhodessa Jones lives in San Francisco.

CULTURAL ODYSSEY PRESENTS:
BIG BUTT GIRLS, HARD HEADED WOMEN

Written & Performed By
RHODESSA JONES

Musical Accompaniment & Stage Direction By
IDRIS ACKAMOOR
Additional music by Marvin Gaye & Public Enemy

The Characters

(*In order of appearance*)
Regina Brown
Mama Pearl
Lena Sorrentina
Doris

Time

The Present
(*The performance takes place in one single day*)

The Place

San Francisco City Jail

Performance Notes

In 1987, I was hired to teach "aerobics" at San Francisco's City Jail. My first day it became very clear that something else was called for. I had entered another world, populated by wild, wounded, crazed, cracked, carefree, dangerous, devious, destructive but colorful women: women wading in pain, wearing their displacement like some strange badge of courage; women who had met the Devil and found him to be a very dull dude; misguided women who, with a bit of direction, could be running the world. The work called on all my faculties as an "art teacher." As a creative survivalist, I used everything: aerobics, standup comedy, music, religion, chastisement, sign language, true confession games, improvisational theater, and lots of physical expression, such as hugs and touching (which was against the jail's rules).

It has been exhilarating, painful, outrageous, and frightening, but always alive with honesty, mirth, and generous humor. And, as much as the self-exiled and male-identified females can, they accept me. Some loved me, and others respected me, which came as a surprise to them.

—*Rhodessa Jones*

About the Performance

Big Butt Girls, Hard-Headed Women premiered at the *Women in Theatre Festival*, in Boston, Massachusetts, in 1989. The performance is a series of monologues based on the lives and times of real women who are incarcerated behind bars. The performance utilizes theater, movement, and song to anchor words born out of the silence that is so particular to women who are waiting: women waiting for bail, for mail, for the latest word concerning her child, money from her man, the next visit from her sister, her mother, or the word from her lawyer. The theatrics are based on the question: "Is there a way to retrieve the lives of our sisters and their families?" There are children literally lost between the cracks of our society.

Big Butt Girls, Hard-Headed Women is dedicated to
the memory of Regina Brown, who was murdered in 1989
upon her third release from jail in one year.

The Set:

Center stage is a platform that serves as an aerobics platform. Upstage right is a set of stairs placed against the stage wall that serves as "The Hole." Downstage right, one chair in a pool of blue light; this is the visiting room. Downstage center is washed in stark, harsh light; this is the day room. Center stage left is an altar that depicts various shrines from many cultures. It is a mixture of candles, fruit, found objects, dolls, milk bottles, an African fertility goddess, a huge bouquet of fresh flowers, everywhere there are dried flowers, spices, and Hershey's chocolate kisses.

(Lights go down to come up accompanied by offstage singing.
The ARTIST *continues singing as she enters the stage. The* ARTIST *finishes the song in the altar space; removes gold robe and hangs it on the altar, and robe becomes part of the altar.*
SOUND CUE: "Forest in the Ghetto," a musical collage that depicts monstrous urban reality: horns blowing, tires screeching, babies crying, catcalls, sirens, etc.
The ARTIST *portrays a sound and movement solo, juxtaposed to the soundtrack. She will take us from the innocence of an African-American girlchild to the all too frequent situation/ existence of prostitution that results in incarceration.)*

(In the voice of the girlchild)

Milkshake, milkshake, cream of tartar
Tell me the name of her sweethearter

(A là Aretha Franklin.)

What you want
Somebody got

What you need
You know I got it

> (*She dances suggestively—hands on hips.*)

I got it. I got it. I got it.

Git it, girl! Gon girl!

> (*She freezes into a position of fatherly authority and speaks.*)

Git in the house! Git yo' big butt in the house!!!

> (*The girlchild whines.*)

But I wasn't doin' nothin' . . . nothin', nothin'. I ain't nothin'.

> (*She freezes, then speaks, assuming the
> attitude and posture of an adolescent
> girl trying to be a grown woman.*)

Hey, Tony! Hey, Jerry!

> (*Over her shoulder, conspiratorially.*)

Girl, that looks like Tony and Jerry. Let's go to the sto'.

> (*She circles downstage, ending with her back
> to the audience. She mimes necking, petting, fondling,
> heavy breathing, lustful panting, childish groping.*)

I love you. Nobody does it like you do. Just kiss me.

> (*In a masculine voice.*)

Is it good? Tell me that it's good.

> (*This scenario evolves from passion to labor to childbirth,
> ending with the girlchild facing the audience holding a baby.
> She freezes into a position of motherly authority.*)

Git in the house. Git yo' big butt in the house. Don't be so hard-headed. Haven't you done enough?!

> (*She whines.*)

But I wasn't doin' nothin . . . nothin', nothin'. I ain't nothin'.

> (*She moves into a frenzied dance of self-defense . . . warding
> off blows while holding the baby.*)

You better stop, Jerry. I'ma tell my daddy. Stop!

> (*She mimes being punched in the stomach, knocked to the
> ground, and she's sexually assaulted, ending with her
> legs opened facing downstage. She rolls to her
> side and assumes the voice of authority.*)

Git in the house. Git yo' big butt in the house. A hard head makes a soft ass.

> (*She is rising from the floor. It is painful. It is a struggle.*)

But I wasn't doin' nothin' . . .

> (*Sound of a car horn. She beckons in a pleading voice.*)

Hey, you! You wanna kiss me? Yeah, kiss me, kiss me.

(The sound of sirens, and suddenly
she's handcuffed and struggling, caught.)
Motherfucker, take yo' hands off me. I wasn't doin' nothin'.
Regina, call my mother. Tell her they takin' me to jail, girl.
Lena, they got me on a humbug. Motherfucker, take yo' hands
offa me! Doris, tell my grandmama they takin' me to jail, girl,
and I wasn't doin' nothin'.

(She struggles as though she's being
arrested with handcuffs; the lights
change simultaneously with a musical
interlude of Marvin Gaye's "What's Goin'
On." In the back light we see her change
into blue prison coveralls. After
changing she steps across the aerobics
platform, and comes center stage.)
Good morning. I am Rhodessa Jones from the California Arts
Council. I will be teaching aerobics here every Wednesday morning at 9:00 AM. My pass is newly issued. I have clearance for all the
jails. You got to run a check? Look, Sergeant, why would I want to
break into jail, most folks I know want to break out? Whoa—It's
not that I'm trying to be a wiseass. I just have no great need to
sneak into jail, first thing on a Wednesday morning! Oh, this? This
is my beat box. These are my tapes. Here. What does NWA stand
for? "Niggas With Attitudes." They advocate what? Cop killing!
Look, well, I don't know about all that. The women in my class like
and requested this music. I'd love to discuss it with you, but I've
got a class to teach. I beg your pardon? Read my lips: I have far better thangs to do with my time than sneaking into jail first thing in
the morning. Could I have my pass, please?!

(Light change.
She is on the aerobics platform, overly enthusiastic.)
Good morning, ladies. We're going to begin with some windmills.
Now everybody smile and one . . . two . . . three . . . four . . . C'mon,
Latoya, you too. Alright, good . . . good. And now for all you big-
butt girls, it's time to get another booty for your body. That's right,
we gon do some booty building this morning! What's the use of
having a big ol' butt that you can't use. You know, to express yo'
self. You know, a butt that commands attention . . . One that stands
alone. Let's begin by tightening up with some lunges and press
one . . . two . . . three . . . four . . .

(She freezes. Lights change with a musical interlude.
She steps down from the platform to downstage center.
Addressing the audience.)

In jail. A black woman artist, working in jail. I look out at all those faces. There's my mother's face, my sister's face, and my daughter's face. And I'm wondering how in the *hell* did they get *here* in the first place. And I realize that it is but for a flip of fate that it could be me in here and she out there.

> (*Lights change with musical interlude.*
> *The Falling Woman Dance:*
> *She moves as though she's catching bodies*
> *falling from the air. It is sporadic, and*
> *she calls out simultaneously.*)

Vanessa! Jeanita! Paula! Beverly!

> (*She stops and spouts statistics.*)

85% of all women incarcerated in U.S. penal institutions are women of color.
Donna! Naomi! Paulette! Jessica!
50% are African-American women.
It is a revolving door.

> (*Music . . . She sings, softly, lullaby-like.*
> *The Falling Women's Dance continues throughout the song.*)

Can a body, catch a body?
Can a body, catch a body?
Can a body, catch a body?

> (*She addresses the audience.*)

And how can I, as one woman artist, make a difference, provide a supportive environment in the face of women who know that it's so goddamn hard to live anyway? Women with no jobs, who've lost their children. How do we counter life-threatening situations such as alcoholism, drug addictions, sexual abuse. How do we discuss and explore the reality of AIDS, coming to grips with the fact that screams, "Women die far faster from it."

> (*Lights change. She returns to aerobics platform.*)

Today we're going to work with the mask—in theater your face is the mask. Let's begin by stretching the face. Big face. Little face. C'mon'—it's an anti-aging device. Now, use the tongue. Stretch to the side . . . To the top . . . To the other side . . . All you working girls, pay attention.

> (*Lights and music change.*)

So many faces . . . so many masks . . . so many stories . . . so many songs.

> (*Public Enemy's "Terminator" is heard.*
> *As the music plays, the* ARTIST *portrays*
> *glimpses of many different women.*
> *As the music crescendos,* ARTIST

assumes the character of REGINA BROWN,
who is having sex with two other women.
REGINA *is an African-American woman of about*
thirty. She is strong and aggressive and
appears taller than she is.)

Fuck a bitch. Hit me! Bigger and better bitches than you have hit me. Just because I let you smell my pussy, don't make it your pussy. It's still my pussy. Everybody and anybody will use you so you best get to using first. I learned early, a man or a woman ain't nothin' but a plaything. I tell them all, "It's like the lotto, baby. You got to be in it to win it." Later for all that "Ooh, baby" this and "Ooh, baby" that. I believe in action, so you best get on with the A team. Like Tyrone, he's in love with me, always has been, and I can understand that. But I told him, "I was born a full-grown woman, and it ain't about 'my woman this' and 'my woman that.' I'm my own woman." But, like a lot of men, he don't want to listen. Wanted to control me . . . thought he was my daddy. My daddy is dead, baby. And my mama raised me to be strong and on my own. He got all mad, 'cause he wasn't ready for the real deal. Brought some other girl, some Lily Lunchmeat–lookin' bitch I don't know, home! I told him, "Hey, if sister girl can hang, it's all in the family." Thought he was gonna work my nerves with that shit. And now who's crying? Tyrone. Because I'm carrying another man's baby. And that man ain't even important. The reality check has to do with me, my baby, and my baby's staying with Gerber's. I am a prostitute, straight up. I decided a long time ago, wasn't no man gonna tell me what to do. I'm a full-grown woman, straight up and down. Or my name ain't Regina Brown. WORD! Hit me, bitch . . .

(*She rolls forward with a slap.*
ARTIST *returns to aerobics platform and*
addresses her class again.)

Down on our backs . . . Okay, we're going to stretch up and down through the hands and feet. Now take the feet back over your head. Breathe and stretch. This will make you very popular. You can go home and scare him to death. He'll say, "Damn, baby, I thought you was in the joint." Then you say, "No, baby, I've been at a health spa." Breathe. Work the body, ladies, work the body. You can't sell chicken if it looks like Jell-o. . . . Now because everyone's been working so well, we're going to end with some hand dancing.

(*Addressing the audience.*)

That means you've got to say what I say and do what I do. And I know you're all thinking, "She's from California, anything can happen."

(*The* ARTIST *demonstrates the American Sign Language*
movements for the following words, as the audience mimics.)
Dancing is defined as any movement of the feet with the body in a
standing position. Dance officials will issue a warning if two women
are not dancing. . . . Are not dancing.

(*"As Time Goes By" is played on saxophone.*
ARTIST *addresses the character of* MAMA PEARL.)
Hey, Mama Pearl, I missed you in class today.

(*Artist becomes* MAMA PEARL, *an African-American*
woman who appears to be about 70, though she could be younger.
She is a sage, a crone, and she speaks with the
voice that a velvet rock would have, if a rock could speak.)
Well, I can't always be coming to class now. They done made me a
trustee, you know. That means I get to move around—to work.

(*Artist addressing* MAMA PEARL.)
You look great. I like your hair. But then, Mama Pearl, you always
look spiffy, sharp.

MAMA PEARL:
Baby, that's why they made me the trustee. I take pride in my
appearance. They know they can send me all over this place. Yeah, I
can come and go instead of sitting in that day room with all
that noise and these bitches smoking. Somebody always cussin,'
clownin', or fightin'. But I'm glad you're here, and if you don't do
nothin' else teach them how to have enough self-respect to wash
they funky asses. Here my hand to God, some of them so young
they don't even know how to use a Tampax. I've been in and out of
the joint since 1965 and I ain't never seen it as bad as it is now. The
young women coming and going in this day and time don't have no
sense of theyself. I got three daughters. My older daughter was born
deaf and dumb. She's the reason I went to jail in the first place.

(*She pauses and looks around before*
continuing in a more secretive tone.)
You see, I embezzled some money from the company that I was
working at so my daughter could get special training so that she
could take care of herself, despite her handicap.

These girls need somebody to help them understand that you ain't
got to be in and out of jail to feel important. They got to find a reason to let go of that crack and cut loose these men that pimp them
for drugs, money, cars, even a leather coat. Look at them. Most of
them not even 25 yet and have the nerve to be pregnant up in
here. Like I told you, I got three daughters and I'd rather see these

bitches flush these babies down the toilet than grunt them into the world and treat them the way they do. How? The way they will sell them, lease them to the dope man for some rock. They're flesh and blood, honey. Then the dope man, he gon get busted, and then the baby is lost to child protective services. And these bitches want to cry about they babies. This ain't something I heard; I seen this with my own eyes. You know what I tell 'em? "Take that whining and complaining some place else coz when you was out there fucking and sucking, high out of your mind, I did not get one nut. I did not experience one thrill behind your bullshit. So take all that drama somewhere else."

> (*She pauses and addresses the audience.*)

Here my hand to God, please, I know that it's a hard line, but in this life I've learned you better come with something if you wanna get something.

> (*Lights change.*
> The ARTIST *addresses* MAMA PEARL.)

I'll see you next week, Mama Pearl.

> (ARTIST *returns to the aerobics platform and performs the following lines while doing handstands.*)

The last session of today will be taking the weight. Learning to carry your own weight. So let us begin by pressing up. It's good for you to go upside down. Its a good detox measure. It puts fresh blood in the brain. Come on, LaWanda. Get with the program. I wish Sorrentina was here. She'd be right up here doing all this stuff. But then she's gone home; she's out of here. What did you say? No, she ain't. Are we talking about the same person? A short little Italian sister? Another bitch in the hole? Since when? She's only been gone two weeks. Okay, everybody, that's the end of the session for today. I've gotta check on Lena.

> (*Lights change.*
> The ARTIST *moves from the aerobics platform to the hole.*
> *She becomes* LENA SORRENTINA, *a diminutive Italian-American woman of about thirty. Lena has the tight, muscular build of a former ballerina. She is detoxing and climbing the walls.*)

Hail Mary, full of grace.
The lord be with thee.
Blessed are the fruit of thy womb.
Jesus.
Holy Mary, mother of God.
Pray for us sinners now,
and in the hour of our death.

*

I'm so damn tired. I'm tired of being sick and tired. She's fucking dogmeat, man. Just one little shot. This bitch snitches at Work Furlough. She was getting stoned, too. Piss in a cup. Piss on your family, okay. Fuck you. Count time, my ass. When will this shit end? This is the longest nightmare I have ever had.

> (*She begins a hallucination, addressing an invisible audience of classmates. She is very perky in this address.*)

As valedictorian of the class of '82 I just want to say thanks to my Pop. Daddy. Daddy. We did it, Daddy!

> (*She jumps, waving the diploma.*)

To my guidance counselor, Mr. Carter. Yo! Mr. Carter, I'm up in here. It's me, Lena Sorrentina. I'm up in here. To my dance teacher, Mrs. B., who was always sayin', "Lena Sorrentina, dance witcha hands, you gotta dance witcha hands." Well, I'm doin' it, Mrs. B. I'm dancin'.

> (*She goes into a balletic extension, attempts a relevée, and breaks her foot.*)

No. No. Dr. Karea. I gotta dance it. I been workin' four years for this part. I gotta . . .

> (*Frantically.*)

Mama, Mama, tell him I gotta dance it. Dr. Karea, gimme a shot like they do in sports. Just one shot.

> (*She returns to valedictory speech.*)

I say to you today, class of '82, when we leave these halls this afternoon we are gone forever. I want you to go out into the world and grab it by the collar and give it a big ol' shake. Because we've earned it. We deserve it.

> (*She makes a farewell gesture.*)

Goodbye. Good luck. And God bless you one and all. Remember, this is Lena Sorrentina, and I'll see you all on Broadway. I'll see you all on the big boards.

> (*She falls back into withdrawal, slapping her arm to find a vein. She picks up the needle. Just as she finishes shooting up, she looks up and sees her father.*)

Pop, forgive me, Daddy. I'm so sorry. My friends . . . Pop, you don't understand. It's not my friends.

> (*She becomes incredulous.*)

Move?! Outta your house. Well, fuck you, man. I'm outta your house.

> (*This propels her back into the hole.*)

I choose my friends. I choose my friends. Oh, God, please give me one more shot.

(*Coming out of a dream.*)
Let me go. Let me go.

(*She opens her eyes and, seeing the audience, cries a silent scream. She climbs the walls, sobbing.*)
Let me outta here. I was clean for two whole weeks. I feel like a fucking fish on the line. . . . they're reeling me back in again. Get me outta here. Somebody help me. Let me go. I'm so tired—so damn tired. I'm tired of being sick and tired. Somebody help me, please.

(*The lights go down and come up on the character of* DORIS, *an African-American woman of about 19. The classic girlchild with a child of her own, Doris sucks her thumb as she speaks.*)
Hey, Mama. Hey, Mama. Hey, Brittany. It's Mommy. Hi, baby. Now don't cry. Mama's gonna be home real soon. I promise. Stay with Grandma and be a good girl. Mama, what did Mr. Sullivan say about when I can get out of here? Ain't that some stuff. He know we ain't got no property. Collateral my butt. And anyway, I wasn't doin' nothin'. Resisting arrest?! Mama, I wasn't resisting arrest. I was with Big Willie, and we was on our way to his sister's house when the police stopped Big Willie, ran a check on him, came back to the car and asked for some ID. I asked why. They said I was in the company of a known felon. I said, felon or not, this is my baby's daddy. Then the white police say, "Then your baby must be a felon, too." I say, "Your mama is a felon." Then the black police gets all up in my face and calls me a dope man's bitch. I told him he was the dope, and he could kiss this bitch's butt. Then he gonna try and snatch me out of the car. So by that time you know Big Willie was all over him. So the next thing we know, we down here in jail. Mama, don't worry. Did my job call? This morning? See, that's dumb shit. I'm gonna lose my job behind this mess. And I wasn't doin' nothin'. Mama, call Mrs. Ryan. Tell her I got to reschedule my GED test. Don't cry. I'm a little worried about Mr. Sullivan. He's from the Public Defender's office. So he's gonna make one move for me and two for the state. Mama, how are you feeling? Now, Mama, listen. Don't cry. Remind Aunt Ossie to call Social Services. Tell them that she will keep the kids while you in the hospital, 'cause these people ain't seen no criminal activity until some of them try to take my babies and put them in a home. I love my kids. I love you too, Mama. Don't worry. Pray. Pray for Big Willie. Bye, Brittany. Mommy love you. And you give little Willie a

kiss for Mommy. Be a big girl, you hear? Take care of Grandma. Don't cry. I love you. Bye, Mama. Bye, Mama. Bye.

> (DORIS *walks down over to the day room and proceeds to watch TV with* REGINA *and* MAMA PEARL. DORIS *speaks.*)

Regina, don't turn that. That's my favorite soap. Can't you see I was watching it?

REGINA:

Well, you ain't watching it now. Who gives a fuck about the days of *our* lives.

MAMA PEARL:

Regina, why can't you have respect for other people sometimes? *All My Children* is coming on next and I fully intend to watch it. I need something to calm my nerves after all that excitement we done had around here this morning.

DORIS:

Yeah, ya do. Did that lady really kill her baby, and because of some crack? I just don't understand that.

REGINA:

She did it. Trust me. But it wasn't because of no crack. It was because of that man of hers.

MAMA PEARL:

Yes, if the truth be told, she smothered that baby to get even with him for leaving her.

REGINA:

This is what I heard. Check it out. "Bitch, we through, 'cause you finished. You to the curb. You ass out. You ain't nothin' but a dope fiend and all I care about and want is my baby out of this motherfucker, because you a dope fiend." She da dope fiend, after he brought the shit in the house in the first place.

DORIS:

You mean they was tweakin'?

MAMA PEARL:

Yeah, that's the sin of it. They all out of they minds on cocaine . . . When he decides to leave her, poor thing. I hear she loved him with a hungry love.

REGINA:

Deborah ain't no stupid woman. She got a degree from Berkeley,

had a good job. They used to be happy until they started foolin'
around with that shit.

DORIS:
That's why I don't do no dope. I really love my kids. No man could
ever make me do something like that for all the love in the world.

MAMA PEARL:
Doris, don't ever be sayin' what you won't do. You just keep your
eyes open. Keep on livin', darlin'.

REGINA:
Yeah, 'cause I seen some motherfuckers do some strange things in
the name of love. Fuck love. Love kills.

> (*She punches the television.*)

And it's too bad this shit had to happen, ain't it? Love is the
motherfucker.

> (*Pounds television.*)

I WANT MY MTV!

> (*Lights change and music goes up.*
> ARTIST *addresses the audience.*)

Who are these women? And what are they to you, and you, and you?

> (*She points to audience as she speaks the last line.*
> *She sings the chorus from Bernice Reagon's "Joan Little."*)

They wear my mother's face, my sister, my daughter. And now, if
I'm to believe statistics, my granddaughter? You know, working in
the jails, I don't delude myself and pretend that the time I spend
with these people is gonna make a whole lot of difference.

> (*She mimes struggling under weight.*)

Their problems are too great, too immense. Benign neglect. Alienation. Isolation. Blind rage. Living in some township just outside of
Amerika.

> (*Beatifically, with hands joined as in prayer.*)

But I was raised in a family by a mother and a father who taught
me that when you're called to something too great, too immense,
you can always take it to God. Now the African in my American
teaches me to take it to the Ancestors.

> (ARTIST *begins incantation,*
> *"Take it to the Ancestors."*
> *Building a dance with a chant and a chorus.*)

Take it to the Ancestors.
Build spirit catchers.

This is a spirit catcher for one
Regina Brown, age 27.

Regina: Daughter, Sister, Lover, Mama.
*

Regina Brown, murdered in the
winter of 1989, after her third
release from jail.

Regina: Daughter, Sister, Lover, Mama.

Regina Brown, mother of two children,
left here howling on the ground. A boy
and a girl, left to make it in this hard-luck
place called the world.

Regina: Daughter, Sister, Lover, Mama.

Regina Brown, whore with a heart of gold.

Regina: Daughter, Sister, Lover, Mama.

Regina Brown, who, with a little direction,
could have been running the world.

Regina: Daughter, Sister, Lover, Mama.

Regina Brown, one of my best drama students.

(Dance ends with ARTIST *next to the
altar with the spirit catcher.
She picks up a brass bowl from the altar,
and addresses the audience.)*

I'd like to ask you here tonight to help me complete the spirit
catcher with sound.

*(She reaches into the bowl and begins
sprinkling water on the audience throughout
the following history.)*

This is a bowl of sterilized water. Because I was raised in the house
of one Estella Jones, my mother, who taught me that if we kept a
bowl of sterilized water in all the cupboards, and under all the
beds, we could drown sorrow . . . we could read the weather . . . so

right now I'm asking you to participate in a lullabye written by one Harriet Schiffer. It is a call and response. It goes like this.

> (*The* ARTIST *and audience sing together with musical accompaniment.*)

All women love babies
> All women love babies.

All women love,
All women love,
> All women love babies.

All women love babies.
Regina: Daughter, Sister, Lover, Mama.

> (*Again, addressing the audience.*)

Thank you very much, it's a California thang.

Before I go I'd like to ask you a few questions. Please speak right up. You can talk to me. You'd be amazed at what people have said to me, so speak right up. How many people have ever been mugged? Show of hands, please. Let's keep it simple. Had your bike stolen? Apartment broken into? Car broken into? And in that car was your favorite camera with the best film you ever shot in your life? Had your credit cards misused and abused? Been raped? Know somebody, who knows somebody, who knows somebody, who knows somebody, who knows somebody who's killed somebody?

My point is, we're all involved here. My point is, this ain't no time to be buying dogs and locking doors 'cause you see "them" comin'. 'Cause "they" could be "us" and you may wake up and find that you've locked yourself in and they're sitting at your breakfast table.

Let us not forget to remember that the struggle continues for all of us.

And, you know, when I first made this piece it was for the Women in Theatre Festival in Boston. On returning back home I was approached by the San Francisco Sheriff's Department Work Furlough Program. They asked me to do the work as a way to introduce my workshop "Living on the Outside." And I said fine, I'll do it, but you've got to remember, this is a feminist theatre piece. And they brought me seventy men. The men liked the work and encouraged me to continue speaking on the lives of these women. Soon after I received my first contract to do a run in San Francisco, and it made me nervous, feeling that this was a piece for a particular population. And in the mailbox that day was also this letter from my nephew.

(She moves back toward "the hole.")

My nephew is twenty-five now. He has been serving ten to fifteen years in the state penitentiary in northern California for manslaughter. I love him very much. He writes . . .

(She reads excerpts from the letter.)

Hi Aunt Rho,

I was glad you wrote. How is everyone? (I hope things are well, I haven't heard anything from anyone in my immediate family. I wrote Dad a while back and he sent me a song that he had written, but other than that I haven't heard from anyone.) I hope that my brother is o.k. I was shocked when I found out he had a baby, it made me think once again about how much things will have changed once I get out. Everyone is growing and changing, and so is the world; places that were there when I came in will no longer be there when I get out, and so many other things. On the one hand it's kind of depressing, but on the other hand it is very exciting, the idea of being set free in an old world that's new to me seems appealing. I guess I just like the challenge some things offer. This may sound strange, but a great deal of the time that I am in here I am happy in my own little way. Don't get me wrong, I'll jump at the first chance I get to be free, but I am very content now. I am learning a lot. My music is coming along very well. The truth is, I feel as though a person coming out of the pen should have a better chance at making it than the average person on the streets, but I guess that only applies if the person has used his time wisely while incarcerated. This place can really be a great place to get your mind together. Even the violence and games that people play help you learn and grow, and this place in all reality is just a microcosm of the outside world. So I guess it's up to the individual to use this time the way he or she feels will best benefit her or him. I love you Aunt Rhodessa. Thank you for sticking by me through these times, God's peace be on you.

strawberry thoughts
&
chocolate dreams
forever,

(After reading the letter, the ARTIST *performs a reprise of The Dance of the Falling Woman.)*

Vanessa! Jeanita! Paula! Beverly!

*

Can a body, catch a body?
Can a body, catch a body?
Can a body, catch a body?

Donna! Naomi! Paulette! Jessica!

Can a body, catch a body?
Can a body, catch a body?
Can a body, catch a body?

Doris! Pearl! Lena! Regina!

(As the lights fade, the ARTIST
continues to call for REGINA.)

Regina! Regina! Regina! Regina!

SHAKIN' THE MESS OUTTA MISERY

Shay Youngblood

SHAY YOUNGBLOOD is a playwright, novelist, poet, and screen-writer. Her play *Shakin' the Mess Outta Misery* garnered her an NAACP Theater Award nomination in 1991. *Shakin' the Mess Outta Misery* was produced by TheatreWorks at the Mountain View Center for the Performing Arts in Mountain View, California, in May 1992 and at the Source Theater in Washington, D.C., that same year.

Youngblood's short stories and poetry have appeared in *Essence, Catalyst, Conditions,* and several anthologies. Her collection of short fiction, *The Big Mama Stories,* was published by Firebrand Books. She is the recipient of several grants, awards, and fellowships including the Pushcart Prize XV; the 1993 Astraea Foundation Lesbian Writer's Award for fiction; Colony fellowships to Yaddo in Saratoga Springs, New York, and the MacDowell Colony in Peterborough, New Hampshire; and an artist's grant from the American Aid Society of France. Youngblood has written a screenplay based on *Shakin' the Mess Outta Misery,* to be produced by Sidney Poitier. Shay Youngblood lives in Providence, Rhode Island.

To all my Big Mamas now living
and those whose spirits have passed on.

Acknowledgments

SHAKIN' THE MESS OUTTA MISERY benefited richly from the editing and dramaturgical advice provided by Gayle Austin, Isabelle Bagshaw, and Glenda Dickerson.

Special thanks to Isabelle Bagshaw for her listening ear and loving support.

Characters

Daughter	black woman, mid to late 20s (acts as a child in scenes and as narrator)

Most other main characters are black women
aged fifty-plus and have Southern accents

Big Mama	Daughter's guardian
Aunt Mac	Big Mama's sister
Miss Corine	a hairdresser and professional maid
Maggie	a con woman (also plays Dee Dee and Miss Rosa)
Miss Mary	a maid with unearthly powers (also plays Miss Tom)
Miss Tom	a carpenter and Prayer Circle member (also plays Miss Mary)
Miss Lamama	a maid with an African husband and ways
Dee Dee	Daughter's fast cousin and know-it-all (also plays Miss Rosa and Maggie)
Young Woman	on bus as maid [no dialogue] (also plays Fannie Mae and Miss Shine)
Miss Rosa	runs funeral home (also plays Dee Dee and Maggie)
Fannie Mae	Daughter's blood Mama, a dancing ghost (also plays Young Woman)
Miss Shine	a maid at governor's mansion (also plays Fannie Mae)

Doubling of characters can be reassigned except Big Mama, Daughter, and Fannie Mae.

383

Additional Character Notes

BIG MAMA: Very religious. A healer and storyteller. Sings spirituals with feeling.

AUNT MAE: An independent woman. A sensuous sister. Her clothes and jewelry are flashy. She has a wicked laugh and sexy walk.

MISS CORINE: Wears hair in long braid or wrapped.

MAGGIE: Wears long wig or hairpiece.

MISS TOM: Married to Miss Lily. Only woman in pants.

MISS LAMAMA: Has affected, distinctly African accent.

MISS ROSA: Very proper gossip, dressed in black, perpetual mourning.

TIME:
1920s to present.

PLACE:
A small southern town;
a place where memories and dreams coincide.

Act One

Scene One

AT RISE: DAUGHTER *enters wearing a black coat and hat. She removes her hat and walks around set humming, touching things in a familiar way, remembering, i.e., at* AUNT MAE*'s table, she pretends to pour a drink and toast, at vanity she brushes her hair in mirror, hesitantly sits in* BIG MAMA*'s rocker, closes her eyes and eases into a story.*

DAUGHTER: I was raised in this house by some of the wisest women to see the light of day. They're all gone now. I buried the last one today. Seems like yesterday they was sitting around in this room talking about taking me to the river. I guess they waited to see me steady on my feet before leaving. Those old snuff dippers taught me some things about living and loving and being a woman. I miss hugging them. (*Hugs herself.*) Wrapped up in the warmth of their love, I listened to them all through the years of my childhood, spellbound by their stories of black women surviving with dignity. Big Mama raised me mostly. I didn't call her Big Mama 'cause she was big or even 'cause she was my mama, she wasn't either. She was just regular. An old black woman who had a gift for seeing with her heart.

(DAUGHTER *stands and removes her coat. She is wearing a simple pastel summer dress.*)

(*The* WOMEN *enter humming, forming a circle around the perimeters of the space.* DAUGHTER *is center stage. During their intro each* WOMAN *exchanges places with* DAUGHTER *in center.* WOMEN *sing African ritual song to Yemenjah, Yoruba river orisha to accept their gifts and*

385

answer their prayers. "Yemenjah, Yemenjah olodo, Yemenjah ee ah mee olodo." *Repeat one time.*)

BIG MAMA: Eyes don't see everything only God can do that.

DAUGHTER: Aunt Mae was Big Mama's sister. She taught me how to wear a tall hat on a windy day and how to walk in high-heel shoes. She ran an after-hours liquor business out of her kitchen. She was what you'd call an independent woman.

AUNT MAE: The wine taste sweeter and the berries have more juice when you got your own.

DAUGHTER: And I'll never forget Miss Mary. She knew how to work roots and fix people. Sometimes in the middle of a conversation she would see into your future and start to tell it to you if you didn't stop her.

MISS MARY: I ain't never fixed nobody didn't need it.

DAUGHTER: Miss Corine was one of my best friends. Friday and Saturday evenings she ran a beauty shop outta her kitchen. She had Indian blood in her and was quick to admit to Geechees on her daddy's side. That's why folks said she had fingers that could braid the wind.

MISS CORINE: You got to know where you come from to know where you going.

DAUGHTER: Ooh, and Miss Lamama. Her real name was Jessie Pearl Lumumba. When she was seventeen she married an African and took to wearing African dresses and took on African-like ways. That marriage I heard lasted till Mr. Lumumba brought up the possibility of wife number two.

MISS LAMAMA: What don't kill you, will make you strong.

DAUGHTER: The summer I was twelve I was at a bend in the road and it was scary not knowing what was on the other side. My blood mama Fannie Mae wasn't there anymore and my Big Mamas kept talking about taking me to the river, a strange and mysterious place.

BIG MAMA: Daughter got her blood this morning. We gonna have to take her to the river.

MISS MARY: I could have told you that. I seen the signs.

AUNT MAE: Looks like time done sneaked up on us. She's becoming a woman. We got to keep a sharp eye on her.

MISS CORINE: By the time her mama come to us she was already on the road to ruin.

MISS LAMAMA: Daughter been restless, asking lots of questions.

MISS CORINE: It's about time she got some answers.

ALL WOMEN: Her gifts too.

BIG MAMA: We can give her what we couldn't give her mama. (WOMEN *sing*, "Yemenjah, Yemenjah olodo, Yemenjah ee ah mee olodo." *Repeat one time.*)

ALL WOMEN: Yes.

BIG MAMA: Now, Daughter, on your birthday we gonna take you to the river.

DAUGHTER: (*insolent*): Why I have to go now?

BIG MAMA: Your blood's come. There are some things you need to know and going to the river is a thing you need to do.

DAUGHTER: It's a long way to the river.

BIG MAMA: Don't have to be no river there.

DAUGHTER: Well, what happens at the river?

BIG MAMA: When a girl child get her first blood . . .

MISS LAMAMA: Her mama or one like her mama have to prepare her.

AUNT MAE: Tell her things a woman needs to know.

MISS MARY: Then the women in the family can take her to a secret place for the crossing over.

BIG MAMA: All summer long your Big Mamas gonna be getting you ready.

ALL WOMEN: Your Big Mamas gonna get you ready.

DAUGHTER: There were so many women and so much love, but something was missing. It was my mama. Fannie Mae wasn't really around anymore, not for real, but I could talk to her, and I would ask her about things. Sometimes I'd even talk to God like Big Mama did. "Dear God, please bless Fannie Mae, Big Mama, Aunt Mae, Miss Corine, Miss Tom, Miss Mary, Miss Rosa and anybody else I forgot. If you have time bless my cousin Dee Dee, even if she is mean to me, I'll need somebody to play with in heaven. And God, I been praying for this last thing a long time now and I hope you hearing me, could you please send my mama back? I miss her. I need her to take me to the river. Amen." Mama? Mama, they want to take me to the river, but I told them I don't wanna go. Well, Dee Dee went two years ago and she mean as ever. Mama, I need you . . . why did you leave me?

BIG MAMA: Who you in there talking to?

DAUGHTER: I was thinking, Big Mama.

BIG MAMA: Chile, you suppose to be asleep by now. What you thinking so hard about?

DAUGHTER: About dying.

BIG MAMA: You too young to be thinking 'bout dying, sugar.

DAUGHTER: Not me, Big Mama. I'm scared you might die, then what I do?

BIG MAMA: I ain't goin' nowhere till the Lord is ready for me. Listen, baby, your Big Mama got a whole lot more livin' to do.

DAUGHTER: You not gonna go away like my mama did?

BIG MAMA: I ain't goin' nowhere you can't reach me by calling my name. You my sugarfoot and I wouldn't choose to leave you for all the angels in heaven. Stop worrying unnecessary. You got all your Big Mamas. We all gonna be getting you ready. Now you go on to sleep and don't forget to say your prayers.

DAUGHTER: Yes ma'am. Things be going bad for Big Mama, she would up and go the Bible. She had faith in the power of The Man above to work miracles, and me, I had faith in Big Mama.

Scene Two

DAUGHTER: Colored folks as you know are the most amazing people on this earth. Big Mama raised me in the company of wise old black women like herself who managed to survive some dangerous and terrible times and live to tell about them. Their only admitted vice, aside from exchanging a little bit of no-harm-done gossip now and then, was dipping snuff. They were always sending me to Mr. Joe's grocery store to buy silver tins of the fine brown powder wrapped in bright colored labels with names like Bruton's Sweet Snuff,

Georgia Peach and Three brown Monkies. One time, my mean old cousin Dee Dee told me that snuff was really ground up monkey dust, a delicacy in the royal palaces of Africa.

(DEE DEE *enters with straw in a cup.* DAUGHTER *skips over to her, curious. They begin hand-clapping game, sing-song their responses.*)

DEE DEE: For real, girl! I ain't lying! all you got to do is try it.

DAUGHTER: What? Snuff? That stinky stuff!

DEE DEE: Ain't you got no sense at all? Don't you know nothing?

DAUGHTER: How come you know so much?

DEE DEE: Oh, I forgot you ain't been to the river yet. There's a lot of things you don't know.

DAUGHTER: Have you ever tried it?

DEE DEE: What you think?

DAUGHTER: What it taste like?

DEE DEE: With milk it taste just like a chocolate milk shake. What you do is mix three big spoons of monkey dust in a glass of milk and drink it through a straw, fast. If you drink it all you'll wake up and be real pretty. Like them African dancing girls we saw on TV. They drink it everyday. It'll make your teeth white too. It's a secret though, and you got to swear on the Bible not to tell nobody.

DAUGHTER: All right.

DEE DEE: Go get Big Mama's Bible.

DAUGHTER: Girl, you crazy!

DEE DEE: You want to be pretty, don't you?

DAUGHTER: Yeah. (*Steps back, whispering to* DEE DEE.) She gonna beat my butt! (*Tiptoes towards* BIG MAMA *who is sleeping in her chair.*)

DEE DEE (*whispering back*): Tell her you need it for Sunday School!

DAUGHTER (*reluctantly*): All right.

DEE DEE: Repeat after me. I promise . . . (DAUGHTER *slips Bible away from* BIG MAMA*'s lap. She dashes back to* DEE DEE.)

DAUGHTER: I promise . . .

DEE DEE: ... not to tell nobody ... Not Aunt Mae ... Not Big Mama ... Not Miss Mary ... 'Cause if I do ... I'll turn into a monkey ... You gonna be real pretty.

(*Drinking from* DEE DEE*'s cup,* DAUGHTER *gags.* DEE DEE *hides behind furniture as* BIG MAMA *wakes.*)

BIG MAMA: What's the matter, baby? You get choked on something?

DAUGHTER: I fine, Big Mama.

BIG MAMA: What's all this? Chile, what is going on here?

DAUGHTER: I ain't suppose to tell. I promised on the Bible. Big Mama, I don't want to go to hell.

BIG MAMA (*seizes Bible*): Uh huh! You gonna get me a switch off that bush if you don't tell me what's going on. You ain't going to hell for promising to keep something to yourself that ain't right.

DAUGHTER: Dee Dee said snuff was monkey dust and it make you real pretty.

BIG MAMA: Pretty is as pretty does. It's pretty ways that will get you in heaven. All the monkey dust in the world can't give you a good, kind, honest heart. I'm gonna switch the spite out of that Dee Dee.

DAUGHTER: Big Mama, why you dip snuff? That stuff is nasty.

BIG MAMA: Snuff ain't no worse than them cancer sticks that be killing folks left and right. Ain't never heard tell of snuff harming nobody. 'Cept the one time I recollect. Corine come close as green to a dollar to getting us killed on account of some snuff.

DAUGHTER: What happened, Big Mama?

BIG MAMA: Hold on, chile, I'm getting to it. A story ain't something you just read off like ingredients on a soap box. A story's like a map, you follow the lines and they'll take you somewhere. There's a way to do anything and with a story you take your time. If you wanna hear, you got to listen.

DAUGHTER: I'm sorry. I'm listening, Big Mama.

BIG MAMA: Now, getting back to the story. It was a time when the only place colored folks could sit on a bus was in the back. But the number 99 was known as the Maid's Bus. It arrived downtown every weekday morning at 6 A.M. to pick up the colored domestic workers bound for the rich, white suburbs ninety minutes away. Now on this day, not only was the weather hot, but colored folks was stirred up over the lynching and the killings of colored peoples all over the south. A colored woman had just been found dead. She was raped and sawed open by six white men who made her brother watch 'em ravish her. The whites were getting meaner as the summer got hotter.

(YOUNG WOMAN, MISS MARY, *and* MISS CORINE *march in singing a spirited gospel tune—they stand to wait for bus, fanning in the heat.*)

MISS MARY: Ain't it hot.

MISS CORINE: Too hot to sit in the shade.

MISS MARY: Clothes dried stiff on the line before I finished the breakfast dishes yestiddy.

BIG MAMA: Some awful bloody things happened that summer.

MISS CORINE: It's 5:59 and there come Ralph, right on the dot.

(MISS LAMAMA *rushes in.*)

MISS CORINE: Jessie Pearl, if you have anything to do with it you gonna be late for your own funeral.

MISS LAMAMA: Corine, you know I got to get my grandbabies to school on Friday.

MISS CORINE: I just know you be late all the time.

MISS LAMAMA: Did y'all hear? The young'uns is talking 'bout sittin' in at Woolworth's and boycottin' the buses.

MISS CORINE: I feel kinda proud about what they're doin'.

MISS MARY: Well, we won't have to worry about nothin', 'cause Doctor J. R. Whittenhauser done bought this number 99.

BIG MAMA: Yes ma'am, even if they was rioting downtown, white ladies in Northend were gonna have they meals cooked, babies looked after, and laundry done. That's why they bought the bus. That morning I made the mistake of sittin' in Corine's seat. Now, conversations on the number 99 went something like this . . .

MISS CORINE: Now, shug, you gonna *have* to move. I been riding this bus for thirteen years and I ain't never sit nowhere else, but right here. It's plenty room in the back. This *my* seat and you just gonna *have* to move. (*Other* WOMEN *laugh.*) Well, y'all know this my seat. I always sit here. Oh Lord, my white lady asked me to come in on Sunday afternoon, would you believe, to pour tea for some English foreigners visiting her mama. I told her that her mama was gonna have to pour that tea herself, 'cause I had to go to church on Sunday. The Lord wouldn't appreciate my missing a prayer service to pour tea for the Queen of England.

MISS MARY: My white lady, bless her heart, is as simple as a chile. When the boss man was near 'bout fifty years old, he turn around and left the missus and two grown children to marry this girl right out of college. I knowed it was gonna happen, I seen it in a dream. This chile he married, believe me when I tell you, sends her drawers to the cleaners. Ain't that nothing? A grown woman that can't wash her own drawers.

MISS LAMAMA: Well the rest of us is maids on the job and off, but, Corine, you a professional. You got your training and everything and you ain't shamed to wear your uniform.

BIG MAMA: Nope, Corine wear her uniform just like a policeman. And she ain't no maid. She got them white folks calling her . . .

MISS CORINE: A Domestic Engineer. And my white people pay the price for having a professional in they service. Now Mary, you ought to be chargin' for your services too, 'cause you the one told me I was gonna hit the numbers last week, and told me some other things that come to pass. But now can you tell me where my spit cup is right now?

MISS MARY: Corine, I been telling you this as long as I knowed you and I done knowed you a mighty long time, it'd be highway robbery for me to charge money for a gift give to me by God.

BIG MAMA: Now, we was still in Northend where most of the rich white folk lived, when I took notice of this white Cadillac convertible cruising 'longside the bus. A red-faced white man was driving. A young white woman was sitting up there next to him with her long blond hair just blowing all around her face. Corine . . . you know Corine got to have her a dip of snuff don't care where she is or who she with, she gonna have herself a taste. This day wasn't no different, except that this day

Corine didn't have her spit cup with her. She probably left it at her white lady's house.

MISS CORINE: Lamama, let me use your handkerchief.

MISS LAMAMA: Woman, you lost your mind? This my Ethiopian handkerchief.

MISS CORINE: This a emergency . . .

MISS LAMAMA: No Lord, not this one.

MISS MARY: Use your bag.

MISS CORINE: I can't use my bag. I got them white folks lace table-cloths in here. Shit, y'all, I got to spit somewhere. (*She spits out the window.*)

MISS MARY: Oooh, Corine! You done spit in that white woman's face! (WOMEN *all stare out of window.*)

BIG MAMA: Then we heard a siren and a policeman pulled the bus over. He talked to the white man some, then he got on the bus. Then he say: "Which one of you aunties spit in the lady's face? If don't nobody speak up right now, I'm gonna have to lock every one of you up. All right, I want all you niggers off the bus. That mean everybody. Line up over there." Cars was passing 'long the highway, with folks looking at us like we was from the moon. The white woman was leaning on the Cadillac looking mean and evil as a snake. I thought for sure we was gonna be killed. Then that white man stomp over to where we was lined up against the fence like dogs and hark spit on each one of us. Now Mary was behind me calling on her West Indian spirits and making signs. The white man laughed then he got into his Cadillac with his woman and pulled onto the highway. He drove right into the path of a tractor trailer truck. (*Each* WOMAN *wipes her own face, except for* MISS LAMAMA, *who wipes* MISS CORINE's *face with her Ethiopian handkerchief.*)

MISS MARY: You know the Lord works in mysterious ways.

MISS CORINE: And he sure don't like ugly.

BIG MAMA: I'll never forget it as long as I live. It was a mess of twisted white Cadillac, smoke and burning white flesh. Just a mess. Don't you never forget where we been, or that we got a long way to go.

DAUGHTER: Yes ma'am.

Scene Three

(*Upbeat blues music.*)

DAUGHTER: Wasn't long after Big Mama told me the story about the Maid's Bus that she come home with a woman I ain't never seen before. She was walking behind Big Mama, carrying a grocery sack. She walk real slow and sexy, look like she was smelling roses and time wasn't in her way. (BIG MAMA *has picked up her pocketbook and walks around the stage as if strolling around town. Walking back to* DAUGHTER *followed by* MAGGIE *carrying a grocery sack, they are moving in time with the music.*)

MAGGIE: Can I go now, lady?

BIG MAMA: Sit down.

MAGGIE: I got things to do.

BIG MAMA: You ain't going nowhere. You staying for dinner.

DAUGHTER: Who's that, Big Mama? What's her name?

BIG MAMA: Ask her yourself. She dumb but she ain't deaf.

MAGGIE: My name is Maggie Agatha Christmas St. Clair and I graduated high school and had some college so I ain't dumb.

BIG MAMA: I ain't said nothing 'bout no book learning. You ain't got no common sense and no conscience either. Down there on Kin Folks Corner trying to beat a old woman outta her money. You ought to be 'shamed of yourself. They teach you that in college?

MAGGIE: I was tired of making a living on my back.

DAUGHTER: On your back?

MAGGIE: Ain't nobody ever wanted me for Maggie. They either wanted something from me or they took it without asking. At least now I'm making a living for myself.

BIG MAMA: That ain't no livin'. Jail's full of girls think like that. Ain't no reason for you not to use your God-given potential. Daughter, show Maggie where she can wash up. (DAUGHTER *and* MAGGIE *go to vanity.*) Dinner be ready directly. (*Pause.*) We poor, but I know each piece of jewelry I got, so wash the honey off your hands.

DAUGHTER: You got pretty hair.

MAGGIE: Thank you, 'lil sister. You got pretty eyes.

DAUGHTER: Thank you.

MAGGIE: Can you wink your eyes?

DAUGHTER: No.

MAGGIE: I'm gonna teach you how to wink, 'lil sister. With eyes pretty as yours it'll come in handy.

DAUGHTER: You gonna stay with us now?

MAGGIE: Depends, 'lil sister, on the way the wind blow in the morning.

DAUGHTER: You really do that with men for money?

MAGGIE: I made some mistakes I hope you never have to.

DAUGHTER: Maggie, was you ever in love?

MAGGIE: I been in love too many times to count. If love was a dollar bill, I'd be a millionaire. And if pain was a quarter, it would be triple. (*Extends her hand.*) Do you know what this is?

DAUGHTER: Your hand?

MAGGIE: Look at this, that's my love line. It's broken. And it ain't very long. That should've been my first sign. You want to hear about the first man I fell in love with?

DAUGHTER: Yes ma'am!

MAGGIE: I knowed he was whorish. When I met him he was married and tipping out on his wife. I never figured he'd tip out on me. That was my downfall. His name was Johnny Earl Davis. He would come to the Dew Drop Inn where I was singing and make love to me with his eyes. Chills run up and down my spine when I catch his eyes all over me like that. Pretty soon he was all I could see . . . smell . . . taste . . . or touch. When he asked me to marry him, we almost broke that hotel bed celebrating the engagement. Our lovemaking was like two freight trains meeting head-on—Chile, he was my thunder and honey. A week before my wedding I went shopping for my wedding dress. I bought myself a real expensive white wool suit with pearl buttons and white gloves, shoes, pocketbook and hat to match. I had to admit I looked good—sharp as a tack. I even bought a little see-through nightgown for the wedding night and got some love oil from the hoodoo woman to keep his nature up all night. I was ready. Then, the day of my wedding Johnny Earl Davis call my mama's house and said he had another woman. Say he still loved me but she must have worked a root on him 'cause he just can't help hisself. It like to cut me to the bone. I got in my car and went from joint to joint looking for him. When I found him, he was all dressed up, getting out of a brand new car. I tried to run him down like the dog he was. I heard a few months after I broke his leg and run over his foot, that the woman he was with took all his money and left him. And you know something, 'lil sister, I hope that son-of-a . . . cockroach is still sucking rocks. One good thing came out of it and that was a song. Say, "The Blues Ain't Nuthin' But a Good Woman Feeling Bad." You got to live the blues to sing them, 'lil sister. (*Puts her wig on* DAUGH- TER*'s head.*)

DAUGHTER: You can be my mama if you want to.

MAGGIE: Where your mama?

DAUGHTER: She up north. It's been a long time since I seen her. She's a dancer. If she was here she'd show me how to dance.

MAGGIE: I'm gonna show you, 'lil sister. Gonna show you how to dance. (*Upbeat blues from top of scene.* MAGGIE *teaches* DAUGHTER *dance steps.*) Come on now. Just follow me. That's it. Now put a little something in it. Shake your moneymaker. Yeah, you got it, girl.

DAUGHTER: See, Mama, I can dance! Maggie stayed with us all sum- mer, dancing, cooking, telling stories. Every new moon she used to scrub down the house with hot soapy water mixed with a few drops of holy water she stole from the Catholic church. She was using the holy water to protect the house from evil. One time I asked her why she needed protection. "Don't God hear you when you pray?"

MAGGIE: Yeah, baby, he hears me, but even God needs a back-up.

DAUGHTER: I wasn't a believer at the time so I bust out laughing. But the time Aunt Mae got that growth in her stomach, made a believer out of me. Aunt Mae had a way of keeping Jesus in every conversation. She and Big Mama sure was blood sisters. Them women loved the Lord.

Scene Four

(*Scene:* BIG MAMA *sits in her chair as* AUNT MAE *enters.*)

AUNT MAE: Sister?

BIG MAMA: Good Lord, Mae! If I didn't know better I'd swear you was fixing to have twins. What the doctor say?

AUNT MAE: What them fools know about God's creation? They talking about operating on me!

BIG MAMA: Sis, no!

AUNT MAE: I been with a uncut belly this long, I believe I'll just keep on till Jesus takes me home.

BIG MAMA: Don't talk like that, Mae Francis. Something got to be done.

AUNT MAE: I've been to see Doctor Willie.

BIG MAMA: That man ain't no doctor!

AUNT MAE: He's the best in the business.

BIG MAMA: Where he get his degree, the grocery store? Willie Green sell roots and tree branches . . .

AUNT MAE: What colored folk do before they send these young boys to doctor on us? You'd do well to see Doctor Willie about your high blood pressure.

BIG MAMA: I'm doing just fine, thank you, with my doctor, my medication and the good Lord's will. You'd do well to speak with Lamama about her husband, you so quick to fix things.

AUNT MAE: Otis is a paying customer.

BIG MAMA: It's still a sin, Mae Francis.

AUNT MAE: I give a service to the community. If Otis didn't give his money to me he'd find somebody else to sell it to him. He don't come but once a week.

BIG MAMA: On Sunday! It ain't right no way you look at it. Selling liquor on the Lord's day.

AUNT MAE: Anybody over twenty-one can sit in my kitchen, pay for a drink of uncut liquor and get a little companionship throwed in for free. It's like a social club. Besides, I'm a businesswoman, sister, I got to make a living like anybody else, you know that.

BIG MAMA: I know you do just what you please. Folks talking.

AUNT MAE: They talked about Jesus Christ.

BIG MAMA: You ain't Jesus.

AUNT MAE: And you ain't Mary. Stop acting like you ain't never had a good time. I remember more times than one Daddy had to drag you out of many a juke joint.

BIG MAMA: Never said I was a saint. I've made some mistakes, but that still don't make what you doing right.

AUNT MAE: Don't make it wrong. (*Silence.*) Let's don't fuss, sister, I got too many other things on my mind.

BIG MAMA: We got to take care, sister. You and Daughter all I got. Let's don't fall out over nothing. Time's too short. (BIG MAMA *and* AUNT MAE *hug.* BIG MAMA *starts arranging chairs,* DAUGHTER *begins to pour tea.*)

DAUGHTER: Big Mama being Aunt Mae's closest living kin, called a special meeting of the number 2 Mission Prayer Circle to pray over her. Come dark and just shadows apart, three elder sisters of the church eased in the back door. Miss Mary, Miss Corine, with her spit cup, and Miss Rosa. Miss Rosa was kinda different from other folks, from being around so many dead people. She ran the funeral home down on Front Street. And late as always came Miss Lamama.

(*The* WOMEN *enter one at a time. They talk, take tea and a seat, making a half-circle.*)

MISS LAMAMA: Lord, I had quite a walk here, ladies.

MISS CORINE: Ain't but two block, Lamama. I know you not that old.

MISS LAMAMA: Ain't but two blocks, but I had to stop and talk to Sister Alice. You do know Sister Davis died?

BIG MAMA: Have mercy.

MISS LAMAMA: There's going to be a fight, I can just feel it. Those children of hers will be Rosa's next customers, 'cause they are gonna kill each other over that insurance money.

MISS MARY: Speaking of killing, look here, Lamama, I've been meaning to ask you, is that husband of your sister's still giving her trouble?

MISS LAMAMA: Monday week I come home from church and on my word, sisters, my mama's antique upright piano was missing. Come to find out Henry done pawned it to pay off his gambling debts. Lord, what she gonna do?

BIG MAMA: Have faith and keep praying over it. The Lord will make a way . . . in the meantime, seem to me like she better put a lock on the kitchen sink.

MISS CORINE: Or a knock upside his head, now that'll fix him.

AUNT MAE (*calmly stirring her tea*): A man is only good for a few things and if he can't do them right you don't need him. You can do poorly by yourself. (*Several amens are heard.*)

MISS LAMAMA: If you can keep him at home.

AUNT MAE: That's up to him.

MISS LAMAMA: If he was left alone maybe he could find his way home.

AUNT MAE: All the men I know got a mind of they own and know where they want to be and with who.

MISS LAMAMA (*stands up*): Outside of shut up, I just wanna say one thing to you, Mae Francis . . .

MISS CORINE: It's getting hot in here.

MISS LAMAMA: Leave my husband alone.

MISS CORINE: Otis ain't worth it.

MISS MARY: Ain't no man worth it.

AUNT MAE: You put a lock on him, it ain't my place.

MISS LAMAMA: Don't you talk to me that way.

BIG MAMA: Ladies! Now I want to call this meeting of the number 2 Mission Prayer Circle to order. (*Notices* DAUGHTER.) Chile, what you still doing down here? Go on upstairs so us grown folks can meet.

DAUGHTER: Can I stay for . . . (BIG MAMA *gives her a look.* WOMEN *take their places.*)

BIG MAMA: Is there any old business we need to take care of? All right then, Sister Lamama's gone read her report on the activities of the missionary to the sick.

MISS LAMAMA: Thank you. On Thursday, August the 15th, Sister Mary Joseph and myself called on three sick members of the congregation of the Eighth Street Baptist Church. Now I've already reported that Sister Davis died, God rest her soul. Sister English is recuperating at St. Mother Mary's Hospital in satisfactory condition from her gall bladder operation. She says she appreciates the chewing tobacco and peppermint candies that we took up collection to buy for her. Now Brother Solomon's cataract operation was a success. He says it's scandalous though how short them nurses are wearing they uniforms. He's seeing more now than he ever wanted to. Brother Solomon's sister told me . . .

BIG MAMA (*interrupting*): Thank you for your report, Jessie Pearl. I believe Sister Mary wanna begin her reading of the scripture. (MISS MARY *stands to read with much feeling, a rising fervor. Her last lines are spoken as if she is about to shout. The* WOMEN *saying amens, etc., all the while.*)

AUNT MAE: Thank you.

MISS MARY: Now, I'll be reading today from the fifth chapter of James, verses 13 through 15. "Is any among you afflicted?"

AUNT MAE: Yes, Lord.

Act Two

Scene One

(*SCENE:* DAUGHTER *on stage.* MISS LAMAMA *enters and mimes hanging clothes on the line.*)

DAUGHTER: As time got closer for me to go the river, I started spending more time alone with my Big Mamas, women who gave stories as gifts. Miss Lamama was special in that. Being married to an African, Miss Lamama learned their tradition of storytelling. She wore pink slippers everyday but Sunday when she sang in the choir. I loved hearing her catch notes with her voice and then letting them fly over our heads into the congregation like birds. When Miss Lamama was telling a story her voice was like that too.

MISS LAMAMA: Now, Daughter, I'm gonna tell you about the time Miss Shine got even for a four hundred-year-old wrong, as it was told to me. And 'long as I'm black I'll never forget it.

(MISS SHINE *enters and mimes rolling in tea cart.*)

MISS LAMAMA: Miss Shine lived down the street from us. She had worked in the governor's mansion ever since her husband had died and left her with no insurance and a lot of bills to pay. But Miss Shine caught on quick that the governor and his wife was just simple country crackers. The funniest thing she had to do was pour tea everyday at four o'clock for the governor and his wife. They would sit there in the living room, quiet as two rocks in a river, slurping that sweet tea till suppertime. This particular December, our colored high school chorus

401

was selected to sing at the governor's mansion on Christmas Eve. For weeks that's all folk talked about.

MISS SHINE: You know I'm gonna be there to see our children show out. The governor done asked me already to stay past sundown on Christmas Eve.

MISS LAMAMA: Weeks before the first Christmas pine was chopped, Miss Shine was busy polishing cabinets full of silver and starching closets full of linen. Her biggest job, and one she loved best and saved for last, was cleaning the grand French crystal chandelier that hung in the entry hall to the mansion.

MISS SHINE: It gimme time to think.

MISS LAMAMA: Two days before the singing a strong feeling came over Miss Shine like something bad was about to happen. But, Christmas Eve when she seen them three yellow school buses roll around the circle driveway, Miss Shine's heart was near 'bout busting with joy. She knowed we were gonna do her proud that night. Them little white children was dressed up in blue jackets for the boys and blue skirts for the girls. But we had on long white robes with gold sashes over our shoulders looking just like black angels. The first group of them little white children sang they Christmas carols in high-pitched cut-off notes that didn't sound right to Miss Shine, but she clapped when they was done. The second group wasn't much better, but, Lord, then them colored children broke loose. I led the choir. When we was done there was a deep hush, quiet like even God had stopped what *she* was doing to listen. Then they sent for the children to come inside for hot chocolate. But that governor only invited them white children inside for hot chocolate. Our faces went soft and sad like they was gonna cry. Except for Corine. Her face was hard like she wanted to throw a brick through that mansion window. Your Big Mama looked like she didn't 'spect no less. Shine looked at us, something inside of her broke in two.

MISS SHINE: She was madder than a foam-mouth dog. But what could she do? She left it in the Lord's hands, and he came through. With no warning, the big, round crystal that hung from the middle of the chandelier fell with a loud crash on the marble floor, breaking into a million pieces. It didn't hurt nobody, but Shine took it to be a sign.

MISS LAMAMA: Miss Emmie seen Shine staring and snapped up, "Shine, get a broom and sweep up this mess before one of the children gets hurt."

MISS SHINE: She swept up every piece of crystal she could find. They sparkled like diamonds, but every jagged edge was a dagger in her heart. Folks say things changed, but it's still like slavery times. Miss Shine's mind eased back, way, way back. She heard a chant far off and deep as slave graves and old Africa.

MISS LAMAMA (*beats her calabash in time*): Blood, boil thick, run red like a river, slave scream, wail, moan after they dead. Daddy lynched, Mama raped, baby sister sold downriver. Slaves scream, wail, moan after they dead. The cook knew what to do to save the race, stop the screams.

MISS SHINE: Miss Shine all of a sudden knowed what she had to do to save the race. She was possessed by her power. When she got home she went into her bedroom and she got the wood bowl her mama give her and the iron head of her husband's hammer. She come back to the table spread with all the broke crystal and ground it till sweat dripped off her face into the bowl. And she ground it, and she ground it and she ground it till it was fine as dust. Then she tied it in a corner of her slip. When Miss Shine had to go back to work after New Year's she was ready, almost happy to go.

MISS LAMAMA: Miss Emmie stopped her from washing the lunch dishes to tell her, "Shine, we ready for tea." Miss Shine yes ma'amed her, looking direct in her eyes. Miss Emmie wasn't used to colored making eye contact and she near 'bout run out the kitchen. Miss Shine went on as usual fixing tea. She put the kettle on to boil.

DAUGHTER and MISS LAMAMA: Blood boil thick.

MISS LAMAMA: She kept hearing whispers. She poured the boiling water over the tea leaves and strained it into the big silver teapot.

DAUGHTER and MISS LAMAMA: Run red like a raging river.

MISS LAMAMA: She took down two china cups with a flower pattern and set 'em straight on matching saucers.

DAUGHTER and MISS LAMAMA: Nobody know how the master got sick.

MISS LAMAMA: Miss Shine put everything on the big tea cart.

DAUGHTER and MISS LAMAMA: Nobody know how he die.

MISS LAMAMA: She untied the knot in the corner of her slip and emptied the fine crystals into the sugar bowl and . . .

DAUGHTER and MISS LAMAMA: Stirred it up, stirred it up, stirred it up gooooood. (*Sighs of relief.*)

MISS LAMAMA: Miss Shine kept pouring tea for the governor and Miss Emmie for more than two weeks before she disappeared. Some folks say she moved to an entirely colored town in Texas, other folks say she wasn't really of this world in the first place. Nobody ever see Miss Shine again. From then on, the colored high school chorus started singing Christmas carols at the colored nursing home every year to honor our own folks. Nobody ever talk about wanting to sing for the governor no more. Every time I sing "Spirit of the Living God" solo, I dedicate it to Miss Shine, wherever she is. Daughter, remember, you must always honor your ancestors.

DAUGHTER: Yes ma'am. There are all kinds of gifts you can give and receive, Miss Lamama's was pride. (MISS LAMAMA *exits singing line from mournful gospel.*)

Scene Two

(*Scene*: AUNT MAE *enters straightening up room.*)

DAUGHTER: Miss Lamama's second husband, Mr. Otis, kept Aunt Mae company on Sunday afternoons in her upstairs bedroom. He drove a taxi cab everyday 'cept Sunday, when he would show up at Aunt Mae's and give me a dime to go catch the ice cream truck, making me promise to play on the porch till the street lights came on. That's when he would go home to Miss Lamama. Every Sunday Aunt Mae and Mr. Otis kept the door closed and the gospel singing on the radio turned up loud. Once I asked her, "What ya'll be doing in the room with the door closed?"

AUNT MAE: We be taking care of grown folks business.

DAUGHTER: One Sunday, Miss Lamama come knocking on the front door.

MISS LAMAMA: Tell your Aunt Mae Miss Lamama wanna talk to her.

DAUGHTER: Yes ma'am. Aunt Mae! (DAUGHTER *runs to the bedroom door, scared, and whispers.*) Aunt Mae! Miss Lamama at the door. She wanna talk to you.

AUNT MAE: Tell her I be right there.

DAUGHTER: She coming, Miss Lamama. (DAUGHTER *goes to hide behind furniture.* AUNT MAE *strolls out of the bedroom slowly.*)

AUNT MAE: What you want, Jessie Pearl?

MISS LAMAMA: Want you to know you can have him.

AUNT MAE (*looks at* MISS LAMAMA *stunned, then laughs her rowdy laugh*): Have him?

MISS LAMAMA: I mean it, Mae Francis. Since Otis took up with you, all I had is trouble. Folks talk. Even the pastor know where Otis be on Sunday after church. I'm through.

(*She slaps her hands together and turns away.*)

AUNT MAE: You got the wrong idea, Jessie Pearl. I don't need a husband. I ain't got time to take care of one. What I have is a liquor business.

MISS LAMAMA: Otis ain't bought groceries for over two years. Told me his mama in Ohio needed some operations. I found out she been dead ten years. Tell him his clothes be on the front porch this evening. G'night, Mae Francis, see you in choir rehearsal. (MISS LAMAMA *exits slowly, proudly.* AUNT MAE *is angry.*)

AUNT MAE: Men like that give me a bad name. I try to give married women a break. I don't want to be cause of no major interference like that.

DAUGHTER: Aunt Mae went back upstairs and a few seconds later, Mr. Otis come running out the front door tryin' to catch up with Miss Lamama.

AUNT MAE (*re-enters bedroom and speaks to Otis*): Get out of my house now, you no good lyin' skunk butt and don't come round here no more. That means till hell freeze over.

DAUGHTER: Me and Aunt Mae ran to the living room window, both of us laughing out loud at the sight of Mr. Otis running on drunk legs behind Miss Lamama with his shirttails flying in the wind.

AUNT MAE: Women got to stick together. Now, Daughter, get your cup. (AUNT MAE *pours them both a drink.*) Daughter, please promise me something.

DAUGHTER: What, Aunt Mae?

AUNT MAE: Don't you ever, long as grass is green, go nowhere with a man unless you got some money in your pocket. If you with a man that don't mean you no good, you can always tell him to go to the devil and catch you a taxi cab or a Greyhound bus home. Promise me, baby, will you?

DAUGHTER: Yes ma'am. I promise. Aunt Mae and Miss Lamama were almost friends after that. Aunt Mae didn't seem to miss Mr. Otis none. The things I learned about love. All kinds of possibilities. (*Upbeat blues intro for next scene.*)

Scene Three

DAUGHTER: When the Sunday-after-dark crowd came later that night, Aunt Mae was laughing loud and cussing like it was any other Sunday. Most Sunday evenings after the sun settled down and darkness fell round Aunt Mae's house, she could be found sitting like a queen at the head of her kitchen table pouring short glasses of whiskey for women Big Mama said was loose and men she said was loud. I usually sat on a stool by the refrigerator drinking ginger ale and two splashes in a Dixie cup pretending to be just one of the crowd.

(MISS TOM *and* MISS CORINE *enter.*)

DAUGHTER: Hey, Miss Tom. Hey, Miss Corine. (WOMEN *greet* DAUGHTER *and* AUNT MAE. *Each woman throws a coin into a glass bowl and picks up the drink* AUNT MAE *pours for her.*) Oh, Miss Tom, Billy and Ray Lee got in a fight. I saw 'em out my window last night.

MISS TOM: What you doing up that late?

AUNT MAE: Hey, Tom, where your sister at tonight?

MISS TOM: Lily at the clinic patching up some more Negroes done cut each other up last night.

MISS CORINE (*playfully*): Mae Francis, you know Lily and Tom ain't no sisters. More like man and wife, ain't it, Tom?

MISS TOM: You keep talking and you gonna need patching up. Now get out of my business and take care of your own. If I say she my sister, she my sister. Ain't got to be by blood.

AUNT MAE: Amen. Awoman. Hey, Corine, what you be doing round Kin Folks Corner late at night?

MISS CORINE: Who told you that? I've been working with Doctor Willie as an apprentice.

MISS TOM: You call picking roots and berries, quacking and running numbers work?

MISS CORINE: Doctor Willie didn't pick up root work off the corner, it's a science. Doctor Willie apprenticed with a one hundred percent pure Cherokee Injun medicine man.

AUNT MAE: I got Injun blood in me, too.

MISS TOM: What Negro don't?

MISS CORINE: My great-grandma was pure dee Injun. She live to be 105 years old. She the one took me back to the reservation to meet the medicine man. He taught me some things that can't be found in the history books. The Injuns was doing just fine before the white man come here, living on land that didn't belong to nobody, taking care of business.

DAUGHTER (*trying to get her attention*): Aunt Mae. Aunt Mae. Tell me about the time you was a dance hall girl.

MISS TOM: Lord, Jesus, I don't want to hear that one!

AUNT MAE (*laughs wickedly*): Ain't you heard them old tales enough to tell 'em to me?

DAUGHTER: I wanna hear. You tell 'em better. Tell me 'bout the fat men. Please, Aunt Mae, please. (MISS TOM *dances with* AUNT MAE, *mimes fat man, encourages* AUNT MAE. *Upbeat blues from opening.*)

AUNT MAE: I used to waltz, jitterbug or whatever was called for around the dance floor with customers for a dime a dance. Fat men were the worst. Yes ma'am, they was a curse to us working girls. All they ever wanna do is hug up and grind. So I used to plump myself up with a pillow to keep 'em from getting too close to my privates. Now some of them mens said they wanted to take care of me. They was expecting a compromise on my part that I could not make. I was too independent to take like that without giving. I always have been my own woman. Take marriage, for instance. Now that's a job, darling, and I earned my way dollar for dollar. I put up with other women, drinking and gambling but the one thing I would not tolerate was a liar. I threw Mason Pew out of his own house two days after I married him for lying to me.

DAUGHTER: Did you let him come back, Aunt Mae?

AUNT MAE: No ma'am.

MISS CORINE: Tell the truth now.

AUNT MAE: I'm telling the story. He wasn't too proud to beg. I told him to get up off his rusty knees and out of my face. I didn't want to hear that mess. Wasn't no room in my life for liars, that's all there was to it.

DAUGHTER: What you do when he left?

AUNT MAE: You mean when I put him out. Honey, it was like the Fourth of July, when the smoke cleared I felt free.

DAUGHTER: So why you get married in the first place?

AUNT MAE: Why anybody would, for security. And on top of that, Mason Pew was good looking.

MISS CORINE: He was good looking.

AUNT MAE: Lord knows that was a good-looking man. But his lying took something out of me. I took him back in my house, but I never took him back in my heart. Don't let nobody fool you, sex is something you can live without for a long time. Like my mama told me, if it gets hot, fan it. Love only last till the shine wear off. (*The* WOMEN *toast to that last line.*)

DAUGHTER: When people used to ask me what I wanted to be when I grew up, I'd say, "I wanna be like Aunt Mae. I wanna be independent so every day be like the Fourth of July."

ALL WOMEN: Amen, chile. (WOMEN *exit.* DAUGHTER *and* MISS TOM *walk off to fishing area.*)

Scene Four

(*Scene*: DAUGHTER *and* MISS TOM *sit on stage, apparently fishing.*)

DAUGHTER: Me and Miss Tom were friends, good friends. She taught me how to fish, throw a knife, carve a piece of wood, tame birds and believe in a world of impossibilities. Miss Tom was not a pretty woman, she was handsome like a man. Her hands were big, thick and callused. But she had a woman's eyes, dark and mysterious eyes, that held woman secrets, eyes that had seen miracles and reflected love like only a woman can.

MISS TOM: Let me tell you something, baby. It's people that keep bad luck in your house. That's why I try to keep 'em out of my house and out of my business.

DAUGHTER: What we got to catch with today?

MISS TOM: We got a sardine, some Vienna sausages and canned corn. These old crafty swimmers do like that canned corn. But the fish kinda slow this morning.

DAUGHTER: They slow every time we come here. I don't know why we can't go to the lake? It's a lot of people over there.

MISS TOM: You seen any colored people over there?

DAUGHTER: No ma'am.

MISS TOM: Enough said.

DAUGHTER: Why people different? How come we ain't all the same?

MISS TOM: Wouldn't be as interesting everybody be the same. Be like eating peas and potatoes every day of your life.

DAUGHTER: I eat grits every day.

MISS TOM: Ain't very interesting, is it?

DAUGHTER: No ma'am. (*Silence.*) Miss Tom, you the only lady carpenter I know of. Could I be a lady carpenter when I grow up?

MISS TOM: Peaches, you can be anything you want.

DAUGHTER: Could I marry a woman and live with her like you do with Miss Lily?

MISS TOM: Let me put it to you like this, there's all kind of possibilities for love. I didn't have no choice 'bout who to love, my heart just reached out and grabbed ahold of Miss Lily. She felt the same way I felt, so we lived together. Been together twenty-two years this May. You still got a lot of time to figure out that part of living.

DAUGHTER: How will I know if I'm in love?

MISS TOM: You won't have to ask nobody, you'll know.

DAUGHTER: Was my mama in love?

MISS TOM: I 'spect she must've been. You figure. This slick-talking beauty supply salesman driving a yellow convertible come to call on Corine's shop where Fannie Mae was fixing hair. He offered her a piece of the road, she dropped that greasy hot comb she was holding and they lit out of town in a cloud of fine red dust. You could say she had some kind of feeling.

DAUGHTER: Why couldn't I go with her?

MISS TOM: Your mama didn't just up and leave you out of spite for wanting the high life. She left here intending to make a better life for you and her. Your mama had the courage to reach. Colored folks, as you know, are the most amazing people on this earth. Anything we put our minds to and our hearts into we can get done good, and most times better than that. You'll never know if you can do a thing till you try. And a try has never failed.

DAUGHTER: Yes, ma'am. (*Mimes catching fish*) Oh!

MISS TOM: Hey, look like we gonna have fish for dinner after all.

DAUGHTER: That morning clicked the lock in our friendship, but that was the last time Miss Tom took me fishing. Like she predicted to Big Mama, my interest soon turned to other young folk. But I'll never forget Miss Tom. She and Miss Lily's spirits probably still live in that big, old, white house, loving each other with their eyes wide open.

Scene Five

DAUGHTER: I remember the day that Dee Dee came running into my room all out of breath. "Fannie Mae's dead," she said. I almost asked her who she was talking about. All I could think of to say was: "I guess I don't get to go up north now." I used to hate Fannie Mae for being dead. Big Mama? What cause my mama to die?

(WOMEN *enter in funeral clothes/hats softly singing African ritual song from opening.* "Yemenjah ah say sool, ah say sool Yemenjah.")

BIG MAMA: Hard-headed just like you.

DAUGHTER: Miss Mary, was my mother stubborn?

MISS MARY: Fannie Mae knew her mind and spoke it.

DAUGHTER: Why my mama have to be the one to die?

AUNT MAE: I loved her hard as I love you, but love ain't never saved nobody from dying. (WOMEN *begin to march into scene. Solemn gospel music.*)

DAUGHTER: The only way I can picture her now is asleep at her funeral. I remember sitting on the last pew in the church, all dressed up, with Aunt Mae on one side of me and Miss Corine on the other. The singing that day was sad and I could hear people up in the front hollering and crying. Then they led me up to the front of the church and held me up over the long, white casket surrounded by flowers. Fannie Mae was laying inside looking like she had fallen asleep. She was so beautiful it made my throat hurt to look at her.

AUNT MAE: Do you know who that is?

DAUGHTER: It's Fannie Mae, ain't it?

AUNT MAE: She's in the Lord's hands now. We don't have to worry about her being too pretty no more. She through dancing now.

DAUGHTER: Big Mama say I leaned over that casket and kissed her, right on the lips. Miss Rosa prepared her for burial. She sure did make her look pretty. (ALL WOMEN *except* MISS ROSA *exit.*) Big Mama said Miss Rosa had habits that would drive Jesus to take a drink of whiskey. One Sunday I met up with Miss Rosa on my way to church.

MISS ROSA: Morning, Daughter.

DAUGHTER: Morning.

MISS ROSA: Pretty flowers you have on.

DAUGHTER: Thank you. Big Mama made me wear 'em.

MISS ROSA: Well now, what in the world is wrong with that? It's Mother's Day, isn't it? The red flower is for your living Big Mamas. And that there white flower's so your blood mama know you haven't forgotten her. You know you got to respect the dead as well as the living.

DAUGHTER: Miss Rosa, I do want to thank you for making my mama look so pretty at her funeral.

MISS ROSA: Fannie Mae's passing was a great loss to us all. Sometimes she was the most stubborn creature, wouldn't listen to nothing and nobody. Other times she was sweet as sugar. She was caught in a change. Look like you at that bend in the road now. Pay good attention to the road you travel.

DAUGHTER: Yes ma'am. Grown folks could be so mysterious about certain things. Big Mama and Aunt Mae would bend my ears back about obeying God and my elders. Talk about everybody and everything 'cept my blood mama Fannie Mae. One time I heard somebody say she died from dancin'. Somebody else I heard say she died from an old wound that was too deep to heal. But when I wanted someone to remember my mama to me, all the begging I could manage wouldn't move them to talk much about her.

Scene Six

DAUGHTER: The morning of the day I was going to the river, Big Mama sent me to Miss Corine's to get my hair done. I decided that if anybody was going to tell me about Fannie Mae, it was going to be Miss Corine. She knew everybody's business. Because she ran the beauty shop she was in a position to listen in on everybody's life, first, second and third hand. She was also in a position to give her opinion on a lot of things. Standing over somebody's head for two or more hours does gain their full attention. A crooked hand-lettered sign was stuck in the corner of her kitchen window announcing: "Miss Corine's Beauty Shop, We Curl Up And Dye." Once inside the back door of her kitchen, the strong scent of Sulphur Eight hair grease was like a salve to my soul. I knew I wasn't far from a good feeling. Good morning, Miss Corine.

MISS CORINE: Hey, chile. You ready for your trip to the river?

DAUGHTER: Yes ma'am.

MISS CORINE: C'mon, get up in the chair. Now I'm just gonna grease and plait it up 'cause we gotta wrap it up real special for the crossing over, okay? Lord have mercy, look at this kitchen. I'm gonna have to put the hot comb to this. Hold your ear.

DAUGHTER: Miss Corine, how long you know my blood mama?

MISS CORINE: Chile, I knowed your mama before she was knee-high to a duck. She worked here in my shop for two years.

DAUGHTER: Big Mama and Aunt Mae won't tell me much about her. They say it hurt too much. But I gotta know what happen to her. Please tell me, Miss Corine.

MISS CORINE: Your mama's pride was her long, pretty hair, a good grade and thick, too. Just like yours. Fannie Mae always had her nose stuck in a fashion magazine. If she said it once she said it a thousand times, "Miss Corine, I'm going to New York and wear dresses like that and when I do my dance everybody's gonna scream."

(FANNIE MAE *enters dancing.*)

MISS CORINE: When she turned fifteen she got a scholarship to a little dance school downtown. One day Fannie Mae got to dancing through the park them white folks claimed was theirs. Some white boys ran up behind her. Them boys raped her right there in that park in broad daylight. She fought back, though. When the police come, she carried on so they took her to the mental ward. When they got her in that hospital them animals shaved that poor chile's head clean. (MISS CORINE *wraps* DAUGHTER's *head in a white scarf.*) She bent after that. All your mama ever wanted was to dance. Her dream was to dance all over the world. The closest your mama come to her dream was cleaning up in a dance hall. Now that's all I know. It wasn't a pretty picture but it's the one I saw. If you don't remember nothing else your Big Mamas tell you, I want you to remember this, if you got a dance or dream or anything at all, don't let nothing or nobody get in your way. We ain't saying it's gonna be easy, but we all got a dance to do. You remember this, you hear?

(BIG MAMA *enters.*)

DAUGHTER: Thank you, Miss Corine. (DAUGHTER *with head wrapped, goes to* BIG MAMA.) Miss Corine told me about the bad things that happened to my mama. But she didn't tell me how she died.

BIG MAMA: It was wrong of me not to tell you before now. I been praying for the strength to pass on this part to you. It was like this, Daughter, one morning she called me and told me she dreamed she grew wings. I knew that was a bad sign, so I went up to New York to try to get her to come home so we could heal her. She wouldn't leave New York. I could already see her slipping away. Just before daybreak she tried to fly. Jumped right out that window. I watched her break into a thousand pieces. That's how we lost her. But we still got you and you got all of us. You ever been hungry? You ever need something these women didn't do without to give you? We love you, Daughter. Any woman can have a baby, but it takes a special woman to be a mama. You remember that, you hear?

DAUGHTER: Yes ma'am. (*They embrace and* BIG MAMA *leads* DAUGHTER *around the circle of* WOMEN *singing Yemenjah song.*)

MISS MARY: I love you, baby.

MISS LAMAMA: I love you, peaches.

AUNT MAE: I love you, Daughter.

MISS CORINE: I love you, little mama.

MAGGIE: I love you, 'lil sister. (WOMEN *hum.*)

BIG MAMA: "Welcome, Rita, never fear. We are with you, always near. Close to the river, moon bleed through. We will guide you, guide you through."

DAUGHTER: Mama?

BIG MAMA: I'm here.

DAUGHTER: Mama?

FANNIE MAE: I'm here.

DAUGHTER: Mama?

ALL WOMEN: We here. (ALL WOMEN *circle* DAUGHTER *as they give gifts and sing.* FANNIE MAE *dances to* DAUGHTER *and gives her the sheer silver or white scarf from her waist, then exits.* DAUGHTER *accepts it and begins upbeat 'Yemenjah."* WOMEN *circle and sing then change to "Yemenjah ah say soo."* BIG MAMA *gives* DAUGHTER *her Bible.*)

BIG MAMA: I love you, Daughter. (ALL WOMEN *exit.* DAUGHTER *comes back to present, removes her scarf. Puts on her hat and coat and takes the basket and other gifts, leaves singing,* "Yemenjah ah say soo.")

DAUGHTER: My Big Mamas had well prepared me for the river. I was blessed to have so many women, so much love. I keep their gifts in my heart, and I know to pass them on.

(*Curtain-End*)

COME DOWN BURNING

Kia Corthron

K IA CORTHRON, playwright, is the author of *Come Down Burning*, produced by the American Place Theater in New York City in 1993; *Cage Rhythm*, workshopped at Long Wharf Theater in New Haven, Connecticut; and *Wake Up Lou Riser*, presented by Circle Repertory Company Lab in New York City in 1991. Her plays have received readings at Circle Repertory Company Lab and Playwrights Horizons in New York City; The Philadelphia Theater Company in Philadelphia, Pennsylvania; and at the Voice and Vision Retreat for Women Theater Artists. In 1992 Corthron received the Manhattan Theater Club's first Van Lier Playwriting Fellowship and, under its commission, wrote *Catnap Allegiance*. The winner of the New Professional Theater's Screenplay/Playwriting Festival, she is currently working on new pieces commissioned by Second Stage Theater in New York City and Goodman Theater in Chicago.

Corthron has an M.F.A. in Theater Arts from Columbia University, a degree in communications from the University of Maryland, and is a member of the Dramatists Guild. Kia Corthron lives in New York City.

Characters

Skoolie, 32
Tee, 28
Bink, 32
Evie, 9
Will-Joe, 6

SKOOLIE has legs that don't work. She gets around very ably on her cart, a flat wooden steerable board with wheels. She lives in a shack that she has renovated; the set is the living room/kitchen, and off are the bedrooms. All appliances, cupboards are floor level   a hot plate rather than a range, floor refrigerator, etc. From a standing person's waist level to the ceiling is completely bare.

In the mountains. Skoolie lives on a hill, making more so the difficult task of getting around outside of her own walls, although she does make periodic rolls to the general store, which is just across the path.

At the moment, her sister TEE and TEE's children are staying with SKOOLIE.

Scene i

(SKOOLIE *on the couch,* EVIE *close to her.*)

SKOOLIE: Skoolie take care a ya.

EVIE: My mama take care a me.

SKOOLIE: Skoolie. And your mama.

Who done your hair for ya, huh? Pretty plaits, thick, pretty, who done that, run the comb make it pretty make it don't hurt?

EVIE: Snap went them teeth, my mama yankin' it and fling go them comb teeth, fly 'cross the room. Me cryin', my mama say Why? then see why: us here on the bed, comb teeth there on the dresser. Okay, baby, Don't cry, Don't cry, baby, Sorry, Mama sorry, Mama sorry, baby. Then I don't get nothin' but the brush nine days straight. (TEE *enters, fumble-searches through several drawers of a cabinet.*)

SKOOLIE: No tears I see. Today.

EVIE: You make it pretty and don't even hurt. Not even the comb.

SKOOLIE: How school?

Teacher tell your mama two times two on the board, but you don't care: your eyes out the winda, your mind on wadin' in the crick, tree climbin'.

EVIE: (*Pause.*) She don't like me, Skoolie.

SKOOLIE: Why? (*To* TEE:) Middle drawer.

420

(*Having now glanced at* TEE *for the first time,* SKOOLIE *is startled.* TEE, *oblivious, opens middle drawer and retrieves a jar, pours change out of it.*)

SKOOLIE: (*To* EVIE:) What she say? (*No answer.*) School's cruel. Make ya sit, hours. Write. Listen. But put ya next to the winda, you ain't got nothin' to do but stare out at empty seesaw, slidin' board, basketball hoop. So maybe she likes ya but you don't like her, putcha near that temptation.

EVIE: No.

Likes the other kids.

TEE: She say somethin' to ya, baby? (EVIE *shakes her head.*) She say somethin' tell me. Hear? (EVIE *nods.*) Want peanut butter?

SKOOLIE: I fixed 'em. (*Refers to packed lunches.*)

TEE (*Calls to other room*): Will-Joe.

EVIE: How come we keep our milk money in a jar?

TEE: Gotcher numbers? (*Pause.*) Go on get 'em, keep me up half the night countin' on my fingers not so forget cher homework next day. (EVIE *has already run off into other room.*) Bring your brother.

SKOOLIE: Tee. What did you do to your mane?

TEE: Trim.

SKOOLIE: O my God lemme get my scissors—

TEE: It okay. I like it, Skoolie.

SKOOLIE: I don't, and your boss gonna faint when she see it.

TEE: It okay. (CHILDREN *enter.* WILL-JOE *with very short hair and thumb in mouth.*)

SKOOLIE: Well good mornin', Mr. Will-Joe, how're—(*To* TEE:) Went crazy with them shears last night, didn't ya?

TEE: Grow too fast.

EVIE: See, Mama? See, Skoolie done my hair, make it pretty it don't even hurt, not even the comb.

TEE: I see.

EVIE: How come we keep our lunch milk money in a jar?

TEE: Don't set aside lunch milk money Friday when I get paid, by Thursday ain't be no lunch milk money.

SKOOLIE: Set aside my customer money too.

EVIE: How come?

TEE: Goes, Evie. Money goes, in eggs, butter. In hair ribbons. (*Opens door.*)

SKOOLIE: 'Fore you walk 'em I need a word with ya.

TEE: Ain't walked 'em two days, Ricky's daddy take 'em all in his truck since he got laid off. I jus' watch 'em to the road, down the hill to the other kids 'til he come. What word? (SKOOLIE *looks at her.*) When they's gone. (TEE *opens door.*)

SKOOLIE: Wait. (*She motions for* WILL-JOE *to come to her. He does.*) Uneven, Tee, some places on that boy's head longer than the rest, lemme fix it.

TEE: Can't, Skoolie, twenty to nine, gotta be ready when the pickup come. (*Pause.*) Skoolie. Jazzman wouldn't take my milk last night. Give him half a ounce he spit it right back up.

SKOOLIE: All the kiddies gonna laugh at him, he go in lookin' like a clown. Like that.

TEE: (*Pause.*) Can't. Twenty to nine.

SKOOLIE: Bottle neither? (TEE *shakes her head.*) I'll check. (*Hops down onto her cart and rolls off into other room.*)

TEE: Wait down there, don't cross the road. (*Children exit.*) Don't run, ya slip! (TEE *closes the door, looks out the window.*) I don't stink too much, huh, Skoolie? Not run you out the room. Last night I playin' with Will-Joe, kissin' on him, he pull away. God watchin', though. I say, Gimme this job, eleven to 2:30 lunch shiff, five to 7:30 dinner, I see my kids off in the mornin', pick 'em up between shiffs, three. Perfeck. And not too far a walk to the junior college, bye bye. (*Waves.*) Just a couple miles to the two-year college, what I do ... dirty but ... only food, I jus' scrape off sucked-on meat, I use rubber gloves, no need touch it even. But damn college kids, damn college kids sometime send through cigarette butt stick up outa mash tatas, jus' dirty. They dirty, no respeck somebody else gotta look at it, wipe it off, they know it, why they do it, think they better can do somethin' like that to me, think I used to it, think I like it. My baby okay?

SKOOLIE: (*Rolls in with baby and bottle.*) Vacuum cleaner suckin', I put the nipple in, he whip the milk up. Third bottle in last two minutes.

TEE: Liar. Takin' it though, ain't he?

SKOOLIE: Belly cramps.

TEE: Sure, could see it painin' him soon that milk hit his tummy. Why?

SKOOLIE: Who knows why, why ain't nothin'. What to do about it's somethin', which is rub in the right place, his belly, but also back, his back just above his tushy, on the side. Work for you too, your bad day out the month. Tried it?

TEE: Uh-uh.

SKOOLIE: Guess when you're pregnant much as you, them days you don't got to worry 'bout comin' 'roun' s'much.

TEE: I got kids nine, six, three months, Skoolie. Plenty a periods in between, plenty a pain.

SKOOLIE: Been pregnant more' n three times . . . (*Pause.*)

TEE: Maybe he wanna drink from me.

SKOOLIE: What about our tête-à-tête.

TEE: Maybe he wanna little drink. You talk, I listen.

SKOOLIE: He ain't gonna take it, Tee, he's full.

TEE: Little bit.

SKOOLIE: (*Hands over baby.*) Don't cry, he don't take it. Babies as moody as anybody else. (*Pause.*) See, his belly full, let him sleep.

TEE: Took a sip.

SKOOLIE: Don't give him no more, make his belly thumpin' worse—

TEE: I ain't! I ain't. He jus' took a sip. Went to sleep. (*Pause.*) Skoolie. (*Pause.*)
I the one pay for the lunch milk.

SKOOLIE: You stay here, I charge nothin', you stay free, wanna make a point cuz you pay for the milk.

TEE: Not a point! Not a big point. Little point. (*Pause.*)

Skoolie. Evie say every time she raise her hand, teacher pretend she don't see her, call on somebody else. Or look right at her, call on somebody else.

SKOOLIE: Bad week, teacher got one comin' to her. 'Member you comin' in, baseball cap and coat wide open in the snow, tears, "How come Teacher don't like me no more?" Couple days, yaw's kissin' again. Give her couple days. (*Pause.*)

TEE: Won't stay long.

SKOOLIE: Hmm.

TEE: Won't stay long, Skoolie, we only been here three weeks, gonna move out, save up money get our own place, me/Evie/Will-Joe/Jazzman place.

SKOOLIE: Always schemin'.

TEE: Gonna do it, maybe next week.

SKOOLIE: You ain't never stayed here less 'n six months at a time.

TEE: Do it.

SKOOLIE: 'Til your landlord tell ya three-months-no-rent is plenty enough. 'Til the sheriff knock knock Get out or I get you out. (*Pause.*) You know I count them things. (TEE *looks at her.*) Pads. I been through two rounds now, ain't had to share with no-body. Not one you took since your last time. Fifty-two days ago. (*Pause.* SKOOLIE *rolls to a drawer, pulls out a comb, brush, scissors.*) Come here.

TEE: That all our talk?

SKOOLIE: What been said all needs be said. For now. We do some thinkin' to ourself. Later we resume the conversation. (*Indicates for* TEE *to sit.*)

TEE: Cut it? (SKOOLIE *looks at her.*) I got work eleven, what it don't go right? I'm stuck.

SKOOLIE: When I done it it ain't go right?

(TEE *is still hesitant.* SKOOLIE *"surrenders": tosses scissors back in drawer, shoves it shut.*)

SKOOLIE: Come on. I make it pretty.

(TEE *sits in front of* SKOOLIE. SKOOLIE *begins brushing* TEE's *hair.*)

Scene ii

(SKOOLIE *cornrowing* BINK's *hair, frequently rolling across floor with ease to retrieve a special comb from this drawer, a towel way over there, etc.*)

BINK: What's 'em two humps out back?

SKOOLIE: Two girlies, Markie-Ann was fifteen months toddlin' and J. B. a week and a half, then Markie-Ann down and died and J. B. eight days behind her.

BINK: *O moni O moni Kai Lhita Extridi*—(SKOOLIE *bonks* BINK *on the head with the brush.*)

SKOOLIE: Toldja: No tongues.

BINK: I can't help it, Skoolie, somethin' like that, like buryin' babies, somethin' like that I hear and the Holy Spirit just come down overtake me. They's Tee's?

SKOOLIE: Wa'n't mine.

BINK: Now she pregnant again.

SKOOLIE: Evie then Will-Joe then Markie-Ann then little baby J. B. Then them youngests died, three years later come Jazzman.

BINK: Four months old that baby is, now she pregnant again.

SKOOLIE: I didn't tell ya so's ya tell the town.

BINK: Ain't tellin' nobody.

SKOOLIE: Just tell ya cuz you was here. We's ole friends. Yeah.

BINK: And who's the daddy? I ain't heard 'bout no one 'round Tee.

425

SKOOLIE: Don't ask here, I don't see 'em. I could be a right hand swear the nothin' but the truth witness for immaculate conception, that's how much I know. (*Pause.*)

BINK: Bored, bored, bored, I sure would like to move back. Ow! (*Bonked again.*)

SKOOLIE: Don't wanna hear no Oh-hi-oh neither.

BINK: Just the convenience of it, Skoolie, nice to go shoppin' on Sunday.

SKOOLIE: You know how I feel, I feel Well, guess it wa'n't too important, six days out the week and you forget to buy it all them days. I feel you didn't need it too bad if you couldn't think to buy it on Monday, on Tuesday, on Wednesday, on—

BINK: And wheelchair access, everywhere, you'd like it, Skoolie.

SKOOLIE: I 'on't own no wheelchair, Bink.

BINK: Ramps and stuff, your cart'd work.

SKOOLIE: My cart rolls 'cross the path to the store and back, I got access thereby to my eggs, to my shampoo, to my relaxer kits, to my toothpaste, to my large roller chips, don't need no more access.

BINK: What if ya wanted to go visit somebody sometime?

SKOOLIE: I don't.

BINK: 'Steada make 'em trek up this ole hill all the time.

SKOOLIE: I do the kinda hair job, customers trek up: no complaints.

BINK: Hm. Well I'm complainin'.

SKOOLIE: Then go back to Oh-hi-oh. Why didn't you just stay out there in the city, anyway? I'll tell ya why, money.

BINK: Obligation, Skoolie, Gary's daddy wanted us to come back, take over the hardware store, so we done it. Shoot, coulda done lots better in the city if we wanted to, everything we got here ain't ours, it's the credit card's. But Toledo. Toledo ain't like here, Toledo ain't dependent on no factories, close ya down, lay ya off soon's they find a country got enough protrudin' rib cages to take a dime a day with a smile.

SKOOLIE: Do your own hair! I'm tired a "City's better, City's better."

BINK: Aw come on, Skoolie. (*Pause.*)
Please? (*Pause.*)
I can't cornrow. (*Pause.*)
No one done hair good as you in the city, that's for sure.

SKOOLIE: (*Pause.*) Wouldn't want cher half-baked head walkin' aroun' discouragin' future business. (*Resumes.*)

BINK: How long you livin' on the hill, this shack? Ow, Skoolie, dammit, ya pullin' too hard.

SKOOLIE: Wannit to fall right out? Just what's gonna happen soon's you march out that door, you don't lemme pull it tight. Course what's it matter with you, you gonna pull 'em out in a hour, soon's ya get home.

BINK: I ain't. My head be too sore anyhow.

SKOOLIE: Maybe lived in the city awhile, but you always be too country for the cornrow. Twelve years, I moved up here right after you married and left when we was twenty.

BINK: Done it up right. Wouldn'ta even recognized it was our playshack. Musta bought it cheap, huh? Never used to have a floor, just dirt, soda cans. And no ceilin', nothin' but a few boards on top, half a them missin'. Now it's pretty, now it's warm. Still, (*shudders*) I couldn't live next to that tree.

SKOOLIE: You want beads?

BINK: They cost extra?

SKOOLIE: Whatchu think?

BINK: No thanks, I think I got me some barrettes at home. How long Tee, the kids with ya?

SKOOLIE: Why ya so damn nosy?

BINK: Nothin' else to do. Back three months bored out my mind already.

SKOOLIE: Don't remember ya bein' so bored when we was kids. Always found somethin' when we was kids.

BINK: Always *is* somethin' when ya kids.

SKOOLIE: Out and in, out and in. Started when she's twenty-three, me twenty-seven, Evie four, Will-Joe one plus a month, one a them suckers, Will-Joe's daddy I think, cuts outa town. Wasn't livin' with 'em but did help with the rent 'til he gone. Didn't know 'til the rent due. Three of 'em on my doorstep. She'll stay awhile, leave, get evicted, come back, leave, come back.

BINK: Well that's Skoolie and Tee, when yer daddy die?

SKOOLIE: I was thirteen, Tee nine.

BINK: Well that's Skoolie and Tee, Tee fall down, Skoolie pick her up ever since thirteen and nine, Mr. Jim at the mill catch his arm in that machinery it pull him in, and yaw find out what that mill care 'bout its employees.

SKOOLIE: Thin back here. I got hairpieces, only need two a buck each, fill it in.

BINK: Mr. Jim work twenty years, die, and not enough pension to feed a flea.

SKOOLIE: Twenty-three.

BINK: Then here's Skoolie, thirteen, full-time mama to her baby sister cuz suddenly their mama out cleanin' this house seven to three, that house four to ten.

SKOOLIE: Twenty-three years my daddy work for 'em twenty-three years.

BINK: Me in a fancy pink ruffled thing, and you got me on a pilla on the floor cuz you know the lastest curls to set off my prom look. But a forty-five minute 'do hits a hour and a half cuz every five minutes you rollin' next door to check on Tee's junior high fractions and decimals.

SKOOLIE: My daddy start work when he's fifteen. (*Pause.*)

BINK: Them babies get fever? Or born sick?

SKOOLIE: Hungry. Markie-Ann was doin' okay, three babies was in the budget. But we tried four. Not enough for the last one and put a strain on the other three. Oldest two could take it. Youngest two couldn't. (*Finishes hair.*) Fourteen.

BINK: (*Pays.*) Skoolie. Help me with somethin' else? (*Pause.*)

SKOOLIE: I helped ya with that just 'fore ya left, now back in town and first thing ya need it again?

BINK: Charged me forty then. Got fifty on me now.

SKOOLIE: (*Pause.*) Sixty-five.

BINK: Okay. I gotta go home, get it.

SKOOLIE: How many you had since the one I give ya?

BINK: None.

SKOOLIE: Whatchu got at home?

BINK: Sarah's ten, Jay's eight. That's enough.

SKOOLIE: How you know I still did it?

BINK: Do ya?

SKOOLIE: Not for a couple years, ain't lost my touch though.

BINK: What I thought.

SKOOLIE: Mind if Tee come? I like the help.

BINK: Okay. Confidential though.

SKOOLIE: Well I guess so, Bink, I think I like to stay outa jail.

BINK: Tonight?

SKOOLIE: Naw. Gotta find somebody watch Evie and Will-Joe.

BINK: My Gary watch 'em. He knows it got to be done.

SKOOLIE: Okay, but tomorrow. Need to talk to Tee.

BINK: Okay. Okay.

And I'll make yaw some lemon meringue pie, know ya like
that.

SKOOLIE: Bink. Don't eat nothin' tomorrow.

Scene iii

TEE: C'mere, Evie. (TEE *takes* EVIE's *arm, shows* SKOOLIE, *who groans.*) How you get that big scratch?

EVIE: Went down to lunch and forgot my milk money, Mrs. Shay grab me, say "How many times?" then march me back to my desk, get my nickel and dime.

TEE: (*To* SKOOLIE:) She don't haveta pull that hard.

SKOOLIE: She don't haveta pull at all.

TEE: Mrs. Shay do the white kids like that?

EVIE: Do it to Charlie Wilt, but he cusses.

TEE: She a good girl, Skoolie, no reason do her like that.

SKOOLIE: I know.

TEE: All the teachers before kiss her love her, this 'n mean, nasty, no reason. (*To* EVIE:) Hurt? (EVIE *shakes her head.*) Go play with Will-Joe 'til they come. (EVIE *exits.*) What I gonna do?

SKOOLIE (*going to cabinet*): Cut ain't deep, but p'roxide on it get ridda the sting, keep it don't get infected.

TEE: Done it. What I gonna do 'bout the teacher?

SKOOLIE: Wamme call her? (TEE *shakes her head.*) Whatchu want?

TEE: Want . . . I do somethin'.

SKOOLIE: Wamme talk to her? Ya ain't s'good at talkin', Tee.

I'll call, straighten it out. Think it better I ask Evie first?

TEE: Face-to-face, Skoolie. Oughta be.

430

SKOOLIE: Uh-huh. Well I can't help ya on that, my cart ain't built so to take that hill, plus tomorra my market day, cart will scoot 'cross the path, get my body soap, hair grease, all I need.

TEE: I know.

SKOOLIE: (*Pause.*) You gon' do it? (TEE *nods.*) Go down there, your face 'gainst hers, that teacher? (TEE *nods.*) Okay. Okay. When?

TEE: I do alright, Skoolie. I be fine.

SKOOLIE: Need a babysitter. You requestin' I reschedule my Wednesday market outin'?

TEE: Bink and Gary be here few minutes, maybe I ask she watch Jazzman tomorra. My check come Friday, think she watch my baby I promise her little somethin' enda the week?

SKOOLIE: Keep your pennies, I'll knock five off her fee tonight. (*Pause.*) Tee. You been thinkin'? Boutcher decision?

TEE: Ain't none.

SKOOLIE: Tee, ya can't . . . not think about it. Jus' can't . . . jus' can't have another baby, not think 'bout no options. We's hungry.

TEE: I know, Skoolie, I ain't thinkin' 'bout it cuz I know, cuz I know not much choice. I gonna pull it out.

SKOOLIE: Sure?

TEE: I love my babies, Skoolie, I can't let it incubate, bring it on in here, nothin' happen but it die, it die take another with it, I can't kill my babies, Skoolie. No more. (*Knock at the door.* EVIE *and* WILL-JOE *rush on.*)

EVIE *and* WILL-JOE: I'll get it! I'll get it! (CHILDREN *open door.* BINK, *hair straightened and styled, enters.* CHILDREN *step back, shy.*)

BINK: Yaw's sure Tee's. (*Pause.*)

TEE: (*Pulling coins from pocket.*) Here's some ice cream money, maybe Mr. Gary take ya . . . (*Realizes it isn't enough.*)

BINK: Go on. Think we got some ice cream at home. Yaw like chocolate? (*They stare at her.*) Wanna get a movie?

EVIE: You got a VCR?

BINK: Maybe Mr. Gary swing ya 'round the video store. Pick out whatcha want, one apiece. (CHILDREN *look at* TEE.)

TEE: Go on. (CHILDREN *exit.*)

SKOOLIE: I'll get it ready. (*Rolls off into other room.* BINK *starts slowly moving toward the window, stares out, mumbles indiscernibly except for an occasional "Jesus."*)

TEE: Tonguin', Bink?

BINK: (*Stops*): Sorry. Know yaw hate it.

TEE: Skoolie hate it, I don't. Go on.

BINK: Can't now. Know that tree?

TEE: Oak.

BINK: June. Skoolie and me six, and swingin', swingin'. Then we think we'll race to the top. We almost make it, but get caught up in each other's legs, fall side-by-side. I get up. Skoolie don't. Week later I come back here, by myself, think: We fall the same way, right next to each other, I ain't got a scratch. Skoolie ain't walkin' no more. Then my mouth start movin' in tongues. Ain't been able to stop it since. (SKOOLIE *rolls on.*)

SKOOLIE: Okay.

(BINK *hesitantly moves toward the other room.* SKOOLIE *and* TEE *follow.* BINK *suddenly turns around.*)

BINK: So much bleedin', Skoolie, so much bleedin' and pain, pain the last time, I don't know if I can . . . take it, Skoolie, don't know if I can . . . take it, I jus', I jus' . . . If all the sudden, if all the sudden I start speakin' in tongues, if all the sudden the Holy Spirit come down burnin' me, come down burnin' me, I start speakin' in tongues—

SKOOLIE: Do whatcha have to, Bink.

(*They exit.*)

Scene iv

(TEE *sits cross-legged, stapling all over a single piece of paper.* SKOOLIE *rolls on, pulls herself onto couch.* TEE *continues stapling, then suddenly stops. Looks up.*)

TEE: Appointment at eleven, had for me, I miss mornin' work, good for Mrs. Shay, kids got the music teacher then, she free, so we do it. Meet at the secretary's office, I'm there ten 'til eleven. Wait. Wait, "Ten after, sure she comin'?" "She'll be here," secretary say, nice but fast. Wait. "11:30, she be here soon?" Secretary nod, secretary say "11:30!" call her over the loudspeaker, no answer. Quarter to twelve. Noon. I teary cuz I know music's over now. Secretary check her schedule, "She takin' 'em to lunch now," say she, "Catch her 12:30. She send the kids out for playground break, go back to solitude classroom half a hour." I outside Mrs. Shay door, five after noon, what she lock it for anyhow? I wait, belly growlin', smell cafeteria grill cheese, tomato soup, wait. Eight minutes to one she come, say, "Mrs. Edwards or Mrs. Beck?" cuz she know just two little black kids in fourth grade. I say Beck, she unlock the door, I follow her in, she on and on "Evie a sweet little girl but limited attention span Kids watch too much unsupervise TV Parents always let 'em watch TV Won't tell 'em Read a book Won't tell 'em Do their homework Then come to school, no TV, they's bored." (*Pause.*)

SKOOLIE: Whatchu say? (TEE *shrugs.*) How long she go on?

TEE: Long.

SKOOLIE: How come you don't say nothin'—?

TEE: She got three piles. Papers, she pick up left sheet pick up middle sheet pick up right sheet one staple, clamp, upper left corner, make a fourth pile. She take next one next one next one clamp, fourth pile. Talk all the time clamp talkin' clamp clamp I stare at the stapler clamp She talkin' clamp She talkin' clamp clamp clamp clamp She talkin' clamp She not talkin'. Suddenly she quiet. Wait for me, say somethin'.

SKOOLIE: Whatchu say?

TEE: "Our TV been broke three years."

SKOOLIE: What she say? (*Pause.*) What she say?

TEE: "Oh."

SKOOLIE: Then—

TEE: Then kids clamorin' in and . . . Evie come, Evie see me, run, grab me—

SKOOLIE: Hug ya?

TEE: Uh-uh! Uh-uh! "Don't tell her, Mama! Don't tell her, Mama, I fibbed! Don't tell her, I fibbed!" She tryin' to whisper, but too panicked, so loud enough Mrs. Shay can hear. Then Mrs. Shay tell her Sit down, take me out in the hall, shut the door and lean on it. She say . . . She say . . . "Somethin' a matter with Evie?" I say . . . "Well . . ." I say . . . "Well . . . got this big scratch on her arm." My head look down. Don't know what should say now. Hope she do.

SKOOLIE: Well? (TEE *nods.*) What?

TEE: Pause. Then she say . . . Then she say, "Somebody else at home?"

SKOOLIE: *Huh?*

TEE: I say, *"Huh?"* She say, "Evie's daddy or . . . somebody else? Come back to live with ya?"

SKOOLIE: Aw . . .

TEE: I say, "Uh-uh! Jus' me, my sister."

SKOOLIE: Tee, I hope ya told her she done 'at scratch.

TEE: I say, uh, I say, "Mrs. Shay, I gotta ask you how come that scratch on her arm." She look at me: I nuts. I say, "I think . . . I think maybe one time you pull her too hard." (*Pause.*)

SKOOLIE: She say what?

TEE: She say, "Oh. I'm sorry."

SKOOLIE: What else?

TEE: That all, she look at me, her eyes talk: "What else?" I say "That all, well, I guess that all."

SKOOLIE: That wa'n't all, Tee, she been mean to Evie.

TEE: I didn't cry! She never see me cry. She go back in the class, ten after one, I walkin' fast up and down up and down. Slower. Slow. I halt by the trashbasket sittin' in the hall. It full, I wanna pour it all out, fronta her door, but she gonna know I done it. I stoop by the trashbasket, by the door. If I wait 'til two she ain't gonna figure it's me I think, I think she gonna figure I left figure this done by someone else. So I stay stooped, still. But after 'bout ten minutes this little boy walks by, looks at me, wonderin'. I find the door says "Girls," go in a little stall, sit, my feet up won't no one know I'm here. Quiet 'til two, I wait ten extra, make sure. Tiptoe back, pour real easy, keep my face down case someone walk by. Only thing that make a noise is this stapler tumble out. Surprise. Perfeck condition this stapler and Miss Shay gonna toss it in the trashbasket. I grab it. I run. (*Pause.*)

SKOOLIE: The end?

TEE: We need a stapler, Skoolie. Never had one before.

SKOOLIE: I'll call.

TEE: No! no, whatchu callin' for? I talked to her.

SKOOLIE: Did no good. I'll call. (TEE *staples viciously at* SKOOLIE'*s face.*) You crazy?

TEE: I talk to her! She know I don't take it lyin' down.

SKOOLIE: Took it worse 'n lyin' down, girl, ya started somethin', not finish it. Just make her mad.

TEE: No!

SKOOLIE: Just make her mad, take it out on Evie.

TEE: NO, that a lie, Skoolie! (SKOOLIE *picks up receiver.*) *That a lie, Skoolie!* (TEE *slaps receiver out of* SKOOLIE'*s hand.*)

SKOOLIE: What'sa matter with you?

TEE: I done it myself! I done it myself!

SKOOLIE: What?

TEE: I can take care a my own kids, Skoolie!

SKOOLIE: Well who said you couldn't, Tee—?

TEE: I can take care a myself, Skoolie, don't need you, I can take care a my own kids, take care a myself! myself!

SKOOLIE: Okay—

TEE: Don't need you!

SKOOLIE: Okay! (*Pause. Sound of the operator recording from the receiver.* TEE *hangs it up.*)

TEE: Gonna hurt, Skoolie?

SKOOLIE: Tomorra? (TEE *nods.*) Maybe.

TEE: Bink say she got that pain again, blood again, all night, but now pain gone. She think it worked.

SKOOLIE: Uh-huh.

TEE: Wish we could do it in a hospital, Skoolie. Make sure it done right.

SKOOLIE: Uh-huh. (*Pause.*) Maybe we call the principal?

TEE (*Sits down and staples. Doesn't look up.*): Said she sorry, Skoolie.

SKOOLIE: I know. Good thing you was there, make her say that. But. She didn't say wouldn't happen again. Did she.

TEE (*continues stapling*): Uh-uh.

SKOOLIE: So. Maybe we oughta call her boss. Principal.

TEE: He gonna say we gotta come down though. In person. (*Stops stapling.*) I could carry ya, Skoolie.

SKOOLIE (*Pause*): You can't liff me.

TEE: Yes I can. (*Starts to.*)

SKOOLIE: No! Carry me? Mile and a half? Naw, Tee, we can't. (*Pause.*) Long time I been in school.

TEE: You ain't never been in school. I carry ya.

SKOOLIE: No! I'm heavy, Tee.

TEE: You ain't fat.

SKOOLIE: I'm a big person, I'm a grown woman, I ain't light.

TEE: Easy for me.

SKOOLIE: Naw, Tee, I ain't used to that.

TEE: I can holdja.

SKOOLIE: I'm grown!

TEE: I can holdja. (*Pause.*)

SKOOLIE: Okay. (TEE *starts to lift.*) Careful. Now— Careful, Tee, now— Now watch— Watch my leg, watch my leg!

TEE: Got it.

SKOOLIE: Don't raise me too high now, jus' . . . All right. All right, this all right, this all right. Walk slow, hear? uh . . . don't let no one see.

TEE: Okay.

SKOOLIE: Don't jostle too much, make me dizzy. Watch . . . Watch goin' down to the road, hear? Pretty bumpy on that hill. Now watch—Watch, Tee. Tee, ya drop me, I'm crawlin' right back, hear?

TEE: I hear. You can't crawl.

SKOOLIE: I can pull myself for sure, I sure will pull myself, you . . . you drop me . . . Okay. That's right. (*They are in the doorway.*)

TEE: Skoolie. Pretend like . . . Pretend like all along I plan on bringin' you, tell 'em that. Pretend like we's doin' this together, pretend like you ain't no bigger 'n me.

SKOOLIE: Set me in a chair before any of 'em come, teacher, principal. Make sure my feet pointed in the right direction: heels in the back.

Scene v

(SKOOLIE *holds a flashlight.*)

SKOOLIE: 'S open. (BINK *enters.*)

BINK: Where them kiddies?

SKOOLIE: Tree skippin'. Tee always could separate the spruces from the pines, likes to share them smarts with the babes.

BINK: Tee, Tee, Tee, this I remember 'bout Tee, starin' at a match-box waitin' for it to flip.

SKOOLIE: 'S go.

BINK: Off? (SKOOLIE *nods.*) How come? (*Pause.*) My dress too tight, how come? (SKOOLIE *nods.* BINK *undresses.*) Why you cancelled three o'clock?

SKOOLIE: School. (*Pause.*) Went to school.

BINK (*Pause*): How? (BINK *stands in bra—ragged from use, half-slip, stockings.*)

SKOOLIE: Off.

(BINK *removes stockings and panties, lies supine on couch, knees bent, feet spread. Trembles.* SKOOLIE *rolls to her, clicks on flashlight under* BINK'*s slip. Sudden laughter offstage, then* TEE *and* CHILDREN *enter through outside door.*)

BINK: Skoolie, them babies! them babies!

SKOOLIE: OUT!

(TEE *and* CHILDREN *rush out, never seeing* BINK, *who is blocked by the back of the couch.* SKOOLIE *briefly concludes examination.*)

438

SKOOLIE: You's clean.

(BINK *quickly dresses except shoes, sits on couch, hides face in hands, begins rocking upper body.*)

SKOOLIE: Stop.

BINK (*not stopping*): I needta go out the back door, Skoolie. Aintcha got a back door?

SKOOLIE: They ain't seen ya, Bink.

BINK: Too much coffee, I gotta pee. I gotta pee, I gotta go out the back door.

SKOOLIE: They ain't seen ya. When I call 'em back in they gonna look atcha funny cuz they know somethin' funny's goin' on, but they ain't seen ya. (*To door:*) Come on. (*They reenter.* CHILDREN *run through to other room without stopping.*)

TEE: Wait for me, I run the bath. (*to* SKOOLIE:) Sorry.

SKOOLIE: Toldja wait 'til 8:30, toldja keep 'em half-hour just in case.

TEE: Sorry, Skoolie.

BINK: Skoolie pull the magic again, everything clean, everything fine. I knowed it.

SKOOLIE: Hope you and Gary be wearin' the proper equipment in the future.

BINK: We was always careful, Skoolie, nothin' a hundred percent. How you got to school? (TEE *looks at* SKOOLIE. SKOOLIE *glances at* TEE.)

SKOOLIE: In the principal's office, 3:30, I sittin' comfy and in come Shay with her wristwatch. (*Jazzman starts crying,* TEE *exits.*) With her wristwatch, she glance at her wristwatch, then say I must be Evie's aunt, principal told her I was waitin'. "That I am," say I, tall sittin', erect. Quiet, contest to see who gonna break the quiet. (*Long pause, quiet except for Jazzman's cries.*) "You wanted to speak to me?" Hah! blew it! (TEE *enters with bawling Jazzman.*)

TEE: Won't take my milk, Skoolie, I don't know, won't take my milk.

SKOOLIE: Dummy blew it cuz she showed she was the weaker, showed me, showed her. Leaves me to fight confident. Leaves her to fight compensatin'.

TEE: Skoolie, won't take my milk, he gonna be sick.

SKOOLIE: "Yes, I did," said I, "I wanted to talk to you. You put that scratch on Evie's arm." She all over the room—

TEE: Skoolie, he sick! my baby Jazzman sick! (SKOOLIE *rolls to refrigerator, retrieves bottle of milk, rolls back and slams it down in front of* TEE.)

SKOOLIE: She all over the room! pacin' back and forth. I in chair, don't move. If ever a nervous moment come for me, she don't see it. She see me calm, still. I see her all over the room.

TEE: Won't drink me.

SKOOLIE: "Evie forgot her milk money, Evie always forgettin' her milk money, why go to the lunch room without milk money? I know she's only fourth grade but—. Well I know I mighta pulled too rough but—. Well I got twenty-four kids I gotta look after I try to be patient but—." I say "Chicken butt, I lay it down, you lick it up."

BINK: Naw . . .

SKOOLIE: Naw. I just sit. All I gotta do. My whole body smilin' but she won't never see it.

TEE: Won't drink me!

SKOOLIE: In come principal: Why she so loud? He don't even hear me, I so soft, relaxed. She hysterical. Give that baby some milk!

TEE: Won't take it.

SKOOLIE: He'll take the bottle, Tee! He's hungry, give him some. (*Pause, then* TEE *tries again to give him her breast.*) Give that baby his bottle, Tee, ya wanna starve him?

TEE: Take mine. (SKOOLIE *grabs bottle and baby and begins to feed him.*)

SKOOLIE: Casual I say, "Nothin', Mr. Principal, nothin' goin' on, just me and her havin' a little chitty chat, just me wonderin' how come she gonna scratch our little girl, then lie 'bout it, then claim scratch come from our men, claim we bringin' men in the house claim one of 'em scratch our little girl."

TEE: My little girl.

BINK: What principal say?

SKOOLIE: Blew up.

TEE: My little girl.

SKOOLIE: Notice this, Tee, notice I'm ignorin' your crybaby mood, Tee. Like Shay wa'n't hysterical enough, now the principal's face a hundred ten degrees red. "You said what to her? You said what to her? Don't you never again— I sure am sorry, Miz Beck, sorry 'bout cher little girl please accept my humblest apologies—" (TEE *grabs* SKOOLIE's *cart and begins violently shaking it. Jazzman starts bawling again.* TEE *backs off.*)

TEE: Sorry. I sorry.

SKOOLIE: Ya say that too much, Tee. (SKOOLIE *rocks baby. He quiets.*)

TEE: I hold him?

SKOOLIE: Then she apologize. Don't wanna, but the pupils in the principal's eyes say she better. (*To* TEE:) No. (*To* BINK:) Then I leave.

BINK: What Tee do? Say?

SKOOLIE (*Pause*): Nothin'.

BINK: Nothin'?

SKOOLIE: Nothin', in the bathroom with Evie so Evie don't get upset, seein' my tongue smackin' her teacher around.

TEE: Proteck Evie. She scared. (*Pause.*)

BINK: Aw, let her hold her baby, Skoolie, don't be so mean.

SKOOLIE: Better keep your mind on your business, Bink. (*Pause. Offers baby to* TEE.) Careful, he's asleep.

TEE (*taking baby*): Aw, see 'at little grin on his face. He know his mama come.

BINK: How you leave, Skoolie, how you got there?

TEE: I carry her. (*Pause*). I carry her. (*Pause.*)

BINK: All that way?

TEE: Set her down 'fore them people come: principal, teacher. Pick her up after they's gone.

BINK (*to* SKOOLIE): All that way? (*Pause.*)
      Huh. (*Pause.*) Huh. I gotta pee, Skoolie.

SKOOLIE: We ain't moved the bathroom.

(BINK *exits.* SKOOLIE *looks at* TEE. TEE *looks at Jazzman, whom she has laid on the floor and is rocking. She gradually rocks harder until finally roughly enough that he again starts crying, and she cradles him.*)

SKOOLIE: Tee, stop that! what're you doin' to that baby?

TEE: He take my milk.

SKOOLIE: He don't want it! (*Grabs Jazzman. Now both sisters clutch baby.*)

TEE: Gon' take it.

SKOOLIE: He don't wantcher damn milk, Tee!

TEE: Yes—

SKOOLIE: No! he don't wantcher damn milk, Tee!

TEE: Gon' take it, gon' take it, Skoolie, somethin' wrong! cuz somethin' wrong with baby don't want his mama's milk.

SKOOLIE: No—

TEE: Somethin' wrong—

SKOOLIE: Not with him! Gimme that baby 'fore ya kill him!

EVIE: Mommy! (*She is onstage; stillness.*) Mommy. (*Pause.*) Mommy. (*Pause.*) Mommy, can I give Jazzman a haircut? He need one.

TEE (*Pause*): Tomorra maybe. You remind me, we see. (EVIE *exits.* SKOOLIE *sets Jazzman on couch, rocks.*) I carry you, Skoolie.

SKOOLIE: Why don't you go to the center a town and paint it on the billboard, Tee.

TEE: I could do it again, ya need me. (*No answer.*) Ya need me. (*No answer.*) I could do it, ya want me to or not. You in my way, I could pick you up, move. Nothin' you could do. You bother me, I pick you up, carry you, I carry you someplace else, carry you where you don't bother me.

SKOOLIE: You ever do, Tee, I'll pray God gimme back my legs jus' long enough to kick you. Hard. (BINK *enters.*)

BINK: Gettin' late.

SKOOLIE: You ain't been here ten minutes.

BINK: Gettin' late. Too dark on this hill, Skoolie, how I gonna walk twenty feet down to the road, down to the car not kill myself.

TEE (*with Jazzman*): See, Skoolie! He took a little. Couple drops, now he sleep good. (BINK *looks at her.*) It ain't nothin', Bink.

Sometime he want my milk, sometime he full. (*Pause.*) Whatchu lookin' for? jus' normal.

SKOOLIE: Tee. You hold the flashlight for Bink? (*Moving toward the other room.*) I better go kiss them babies, let 'em know I ain't sore no more. (*Stops.*) Let him sleep, Tee. (*Exits.*)

BINK (*Putting on shoes*): Yaw tree skippin', huh.

TEE: I was a girl scout, Bink, one year, fifth grade. Leader take us on a all-day hike, name this tree, name that plant, hundreds. I remember all, no one else hardly remember one. Easy for me.

BINK: Tee. I come in your house, you sittin' starin' at a matchbox. Skoolie and I be in your mama's bedroom gettin' in real trouble, try on a gown, try on high heels, pinch earrings, come out two hours you still starin' at the matchbox. Skoolie say you waitin' for it to flip. How?

TEE: My mind make it.

BINK: Your mind didn't. (*Pause.*) Hold the light steady at my feet. Move it a inch to the left or the right leaves me in the dark, I miss one step fall in one a them groundhog ditches, you know I'm laid up six weeks.

Scene vi

(TEE, EVIE, *and* WILL-JOE *outside on the stoop.*)

TEE: The whole sky move. Unison. (*Points.*) Big Dipper? Watch it. It stand on its handle now, but wait. Slow slow it flip back, a circle. Couple months, May, it upside down, pour its soup out. Then September, upright again, flat on the burner. Everything shift, everything move together, I see it, I know the map. 'Cept a few lights, they not interested in the rhythm a the rest, got they own mind, never know where they end up. We call them this: (*Points.*) Mars, Venus, Jupiter. I like lookin' up. I like watchin' the change.

EVIE: I wake up to pee, Mama, you whisper us out here, make sure Skoolie don't wake. Why?

TEE: News: We movin'.

EVIE *and* WILL-JOE: Aw . . .

TEE: Lug our suitcase up the slope, 'member I say don't get too comfy?: temporary arrangement.

WILL-JOE: I like the hill! (*No answer.*) Why?

TEE: Cuz we can. Money I make now, and Jane, scrape plates next to me, she say other half her place empty enda the month. Cheap, and two bedrooms: me, Jazzman in one, the second you share. Your own bed. Twins.

WILL-JOE: I like sharin' with you.

EVIE: I like sharin' with Skoolie.

TEE: Gettin' big.

444

WILL-JOE: Skoolie mad at us?

TEE: You think that the reason? (WILL-JOE *nods.*) We not done nothin' make her mad. Have we?

WILL-JOE: (*Meaning* EVIE): Her. She been swingin' on the bad tree. (*Pause. Then* EVIE *swings at him.*)

EVIE: Squeal-mouth! (TEE *intercepts her aim.*)

TEE: That the truth?

EVIE: Tattletale, it ain't nice!

TEE (*Pause*): Skoolie and me nasty to that tree, huh. I change my mind. That tree ain't got the evil eye, it not the devil. Skoolie's thing was a freak, that white oak not housin' the spirits. It old. Earn some respeck. Don't let her catch ya near it though. (*Pause.*)

EVIE: You and Skoolie mad?

TEE: Naw. But two different people. Grownups. Everything Skoolie do not necessarily my business. Everything I do not necessarily hers.

WILL-JOE: We come back to visit?

TEE: Sure.

WILL-JOE: And her visit us? (TEE *looks at him.*) She call, wanna watch our TV, you come pick her up? Carry her down the hill, cross the bridge, cross the traffic light? Like today?

TEE (*considers this*): Yeah. I travel her. (*Sky:*) Funny thing: Uruguay, Australia, Zimbabwe—they ain't got the same map. Their stars ain't ours, down there they got a different sky. I wanna see that. You wanna see that? (*They nod.*) One day, we gonna.

Scene vii

(TEE *sits up on couch. She is slicing an apple.* SKOOLIE *rolls in. As she chatters she makes preparations: water, towels, etc.*)

SKOOLIE: Warm like spring, smell like spring. The babies feel it, they get the giggles whilst we wait on the truck. He just pullin' off, I'm still wavin' and here Irene Halloway come. "Skoolie! Heardja told that Shay off." She had trouble too, said Shay thought both her oldests was dumb, now she worried: her youngest got her in the fall. Well I always thought Irene's boy was dumb, but that big girl was smart enough. I nod, say nothin'. Roll to the store, a hullabaloo—seven at me, grinnin', already got the Bink word. I'm brief: we let her have it. "Dontchu never no more try sayin' they hurt that girl," says principal, "Dontchu never no more lay a hand on that girl." Well, we get the principal to say it, we done the best thing: he signs her paycheck. Tee and me get him to say it, I tell them store people, just shut her up, embarrass her a bit. Make her think. Whatchu doin'! (*Runs to* TEE: *blood all over* TEE's *hand and the apple.*)

TEE: Stomach hurts.

SKOOLIE (*Wiping hand*): Nervous. Normal.

TEE: Salt. My mouth.

SKOOLIE: Better not, toldja not ta eat. And why your hands s'clammy? No draft in here.

TEE: Not eat, my belly clean.

SKOOLIE: Then whatchu got this apple for?

446

TEE: Ain't hungry, just peel it for you. Know ya love 'em, I like to peel.

SKOOLIE: Where's the cut, Tee?

TEE: Peel it, then I wanna cut it, fours. Then cut again. Again, sixteen. Again—

SKOOLIE: I don't see the cut, all this blood can't be from your hangnail-suckin'.

TEE: Wish I slice it off, whole hand. Then I be better. Like you.

SKOOLIE (*back to preparations*): Nasty talk, Tee. But you got stuff to go through today, so no dwellin' on it. (*Pause.*)

TEE: Skoolie. I think . . . time to go.

SKOOLIE: Where we goin'?

TEE: Us. Me, my kids. I found a place. It in the budget, my new money.

SKOOLIE: Well. I won't be rushin' in no new boarders. Just in case your budget don't hold up two months down the road. When we's done, remind me to dunk your hand in alcohol. Not now, I don't like chemicals in the vicinity 'til things all patched up.

TEE: You like my place, Skoolie. It got a basement.

SKOOLIE: Here? Or the other room? (*Pause.*) You better not mess up my couch. (SKOOLIE *exits into the other room.*)

TEE: You know that video store jus' open? My new house right round the corner. You gon' come visit, Skoolie. And I make a pot a spaghetti. Hot bread. (*Pause.*)

Skoolie. (*Pause.*) Skoolie, I think I made a mistake, sorry.

(SKOOLIE *rolls in, her back to* TEE. *She has a wire hanger, and proceeds to untwist it.*)

TEE: I sorry, Skoolie, I think . . .

I think I yanked the wrong thing.

(TEE *will pull from under the blanket another straightened—and bloodied—hanger. Eventually* SKOOLIE, *absorbed in her task and ignoring* TEE, *turns around. Stillness. Then* SKOOLIE *rushes to lift blanket. Blood all over* TEE's *groin, legs, the couch.*)

SKOOLIE: NO! (*Rushes to phone.*) Tee! Tee, what'dju do? Need the clinic, need the emergency room. S'pose ta wait for me, toldja wait for me! This a emergency, we live on the hill, my sister, my sister got blood, my baby sister got a lotta blood, come from her vagina. We live on the hill, shack on the hill, right 'cross from the general store, know it? Fast, please, cuz, lotta blood, lotta, big . . . pool . . . (*Hangs up. Rushes back toward* TEE *but falls off cart.*) Dammit! wheresa goddam clean towels?

TEE: Belly hurt—

(SKOOLIE *finds towels, rushes back to* TEE, *positions towel between* TEE's *legs.* TEE *shivers.*)

SKOOLIE: Cold?

(SKOOLIE *puts a towel over* TEE, *rolls, falls off cart again. Screams in frustration. Gets back on cart, goes to cabinet and retrieves blanket. Starts to go back to* TEE *but cart gets stuck.*)

SKOOLIE: *I hate this thing!*

(SKOOLIE *gets off cart, pulls herself to* TEE, *covers her. Quiet.*)

SKOOLIE: Don't go to sleep! Don't go to sleep!

TEE: Will-Joe do his readin' last night, he come ask for help. I say better if he get Evie. Or you. (*Pause.*)

SKOOLIE: Say somethin'!

TEE: Nothin' else.

SKOOLIE: There is, you gonna talk to me. (*Pause.*) *Hear?* Tell me 'bout . . . uh . . . Tell me 'bout that time ya steal my cart, Mama catch ya, fan yer heiny. How come ya done it? (*Pause.*)

How come ya done it?

TEE: Don't know—

SKOOLIE: Say!

TEE: Jus' mean—

SKOOLIE: How come ya steal that cart, Tee?

TEE: Because. It was you.

SKOOLIE (*Pause*): Talk! (*Pause.*) Aw. Aw, don't cry, don't cry, honey. Just talk for me, please? Jus' say somethin', Tee.

TEE: How come "Skoolie"?

SKOOLIE: How come, ya think?

TEE: Cuz ya never went to school.

SKOOLIE: Uh uh. Uh uh, probably toldja that cuz I like ya to believe it, was a lie. Me and Bink . . . Me and Bink fall outa that tree June before first grade. All summer I bein' carried. To the bed. To the couch. Out the door. *Hate* it. September Daddy carry me to his truck, drive me, set me at my desk, leave. Everyone see it. No one play with me. Not come near, but watch all the time, point. One day, I start pullin' out. Teacher turn her head, I pull myself out the door. I rollin' you over, hear? (*Starts to.*)

TEE: *Hurts* . . . Skoolie, *hurts—*

SKOOLIE: Okay, just yer face. Needta see yer face. Ambulance here soon. (*Pause.*) Kids giggle, they like I get away, won't tell. She find me in the hall, or the playground, carry me back, tell Daddy, he gimme a beatin',' take me back next day, I do the same. Just too many kids, always could find a time to make my break, she couldn't watch all us and she couldn't tie me up and she wanted to. Year over, beatin' every day, Daddy say he gonna give 'em to me harder I start doin' it in second grade. Well I start doin' it in second grade, but guess what? 'Steada harder, they gettin' softer. Finally, Thanksgivin', Daddy say, "You done the effort, girl, guess it ain't your pleasure. You ain't gotta go back to school, no more." Round then I get my name. And he build me a cart, no more bloody cut legs from pullin' 'em, ugly for everybody else, I didn't care, I couldn't feel 'em nohow. Now I go where I please, no more carryin', I go where I want. So "Skoolie" ain't cuza no school. Cuz I did taste school. Spit it out. (*Pause.*)

TEE: Skoolie, when you fall out that tree—it hurt?

SKOOLIE (*Pause*): Me and Bink fall out. I hear a big funny crack. From me. Felt somethin'. If it hurt I never knowed it—over too quick. Then we start to gigglin'. Cuz the crack noise was so weird, cuz the whole thing's so funny, us flip out the tree. Then we push our palms down, gonna pull ourselves up. Bink's up the first try, not me. I push again—nothin' movin'. Look up at her. Push a third. Nothin'. Look up at her. I start to get scared. (*Looks at* TEE. TEE *is dead.* SKOOLIE *rolls to cabinet and gets a brush, rolls back and starts stroking* TEE's *hair.*) Not so bad a haircut you give. Just stroke it right. (*Pause.*) Shoulda got a pitcher a us yesterday, Tee, both us, you takin' me down the hill, not bump me once. Smooth ride. I ain't been carried in a long time, Tee.

(*End*)

SECTION FOUR

The Black Family in Crisis

CRYING HOLY

Wayne Corbitt

Clarissa Bell Armstrong	Mother Bell's youngest daughter, age 35
Loretta Cordon	Mother Bell's foster daughter, quiet and mannish, age 50
Waters Hardy	Mother Bell's oldest son, poet, age 40, flamboyant
Merideth Stoller	Waters's friend, dreadlocked English woman, anthropology professor, age 35
Mother Charlotte Beatrice Bell	"Mother" is a religious title used in the Sanctified church. A large proud woman, age 70

WAYNE CORBITT, writer and performance poet, is the author of the performance pieces *Blackbirds Boogie in the Black Moonlight* and *The Gospel According to Wayne: Waves of Gravity and Time*. The latter piece was produced at Josie's Cabaret and Juice Joint, New Langton Arts, and The Marsh, all in San Francisco, as well as nationally and internationally at the Gay and Lesbian Theater Festival in Seattle in 1991 and the Good Vibration Film Festival in Germany in 1992. Corbitt's full-length autobiographical play, *Crying Holy*, was produced by Theater Rhinoceros in San Francisco, California, in 1993. He appears in Marlon Riggs's final film, *Black Is, Black Ain't*, winner of the 1995 Sundance Award for Best Documentary. His most recent work, *A Fish with Frog's Eyes*, a performance poem inspired by the life and death of Jean-Michel Basquiat, was presented by the Lorraine Hansberry Theater in San Francisco in February 1995. Wayne Corbitt lives in San Francisco.

Act One

Scene 1

(*Stage dark except for a special* WATERS *walks into.*)

WATERS: At such a place and time
    the spirit fell down
is how my family believed
so do I
only differently

I have rarely let things be
and with the state of my life on this planet
I do tend to rant and rave
as well as turning pouting sulking and depression
into an art form

I am a poet
and that is my excuse

It's not all my fault
My mother spoiled me
My skin is black
I am male and queer

It doesn't matter
that my Mother did the best she could
or that racism in America makes my skin color
    an issue
or that my gender is happenstance

or that I am queer in spite of what I was
    told to be

I am an arrogant poet
cheated out of the certainty of future
by HIV disease

I needed (*hesitantly*)
to go home
and—
rest in the bosom of my family
a family of women
for 1,000,005 reasons
I have always identified with women
and I wanted to rest in their bosom

It was a long weekend after Labor Day
I'd been on the road three weeks
I was looking forward to rest

(*Short pause.*)

Accepting things the way they are
is something I don't do very well
That long weekend after Labor Day

My family and me
were tested humbled and put through the fire
Maybe we came out of it stronger
Maybe not

But I love them still
no matter what
We love each other
We're family

Scene 2

(*Gospel music on the radio. Large crowded kitchen, where* CLARISSA *and*
    LORETTA *are parceling out work. They are wearing pretty summer*
    clothes.)

CLARISSA: I don't really want to do anything
But I guess I'll do the baked beans
(*Referring to radio.*)
Turn this down so I can hear myself think

LORETTA: What'd you mean
don't want to do nothin
It's your party
Guurrrl, you better get on the stick
After you get them beans
You can help me with the potato salad

CLARISSA: Chile, cookin for my big brother can get scary
He likes all that gourmet stuff
lobster ravioli and frog grass

LORETTA: Frog grass?

CLARISSA: You know
that French chopped liver
That's what Winnie calls it

LORETTA: Yo husband sho is crazy
Frog grass

CLARISSA: Anyway, Waters is picky
Momma said he liked to drive her crazy
lookin for clean food

LORETTA: Clean food
What he grow up on
Dirty food?

Skinny as he is
don't look like he's eatin' much of anything to me
But he sho look a lot better than I expected
You know
like those
you know like
those
        victims
you see on the news

I guess all we can do is pray

CLARISSA: I love the way he looks

*

Seems like he gets more handsome
older he gets

But honey chile
all that jewelry!
And girl
I hope he keeps his shirt on
Especially in front of Momma

LORETTA: What's wrong with his chest?!

CLARISSA: Honey it makes that hair look normal

LORETTA: Gurrl did you see that hair on his friend?!

CLARISSA: That's dreadlocks
Waters' tryin to grow those too

LORETTA: Dreadhocks?

CLARISSA: No girl, dreadlocks

LORETTA: Look like a burrhead to me

CLARISSA: Lo', less you wanna hear the speech
'bout natural beauty
I wouldn't mention his or her hair

LORETTA: Now what in the world did he do to his chest

CLARISSA: Believe me, you don't want to know

LORETTA: That hair is enough for me
but girl you got to tell me 'bout his chest
He got a tattoo or something

CLARISSA: No girl
that's on his arm
On his chest he got more jewelry

LORETTA: Hush

CLARISSA: Nette saw it
That time he came to see her
When she lived in Fort Wayne
She called me up and said Water's gone wild honey
He done pierced his titties

LORETTA: What?! (*Grabbing her breast and grimacing.*)

CLARISSA: You heard right
Pierced nipples

*

Now, you know Momma will worry me to death
    if she sees that
They don't understand
Something like that

I will get no rest

LORETTA: What on earth

CLARISSA: I'm tellin' you

Nette's in Chicago
poppin in and out so fast you hardly notice

Bobby at least comes up for a weekend now and then

And Waters blows into town like a hurricane
Know what I'm sayin'

LORETTA: He don't even have to come
He mails the hurricane
Member that letter?

CLARISSA: I will never forget it
and he got upset 'cause Momma sent it back
If one of my children sent me somethin like that
I'd send it back too

LORETTA: Waters sho do stir it up
and we pick up the pieces
Now why ain't Nette here?

CLARISSA: I don't know
She and Waters were so close
Now, look like they make a point of avoiding each other
Waters said he was thru after that last visit
Poor thing, she just don't know how to entertain

LORETTA: Same treatment you and your Momma got

CLARISSA: Worse according to Waters
With a month's notice
She couldn't get lunch together

LORETTA: What!

CLARISSA: Waters told her a full month ahead of time
he was stoppin drivin cross country
for lunch

and Miss Ann-ette
says her kitchen is being remodeled
so they got to bring their own
Waters thinks its cause
he got what he got
What you want me to do for the potato salad

LORETTA: You can peel them eggs
Most of that's for Waters's deviled eggs

You think she's worried 'bout that?

CLARISSA: I don't know—
My guess is she's not mean or that mean
just dizzy

        Sometimes I wish
there was something like a familyec-tomy
        Nothing permanent mind you
        Just a break

'Cause sometimes they all work my nerves
Momma spoiled Waters rotten
let Annette run wild
ignored Bobby
and I'm the only one in town

They all ran away
and whenever somethin's up
I'm the one they all come running to
Just your average American dysfunctional family
        coordinator here

LORETTA: Just don't coordinate yourself in the State Mental
        Hospital

CLARISSA: Maybe thats what I ought to do
Go off
Way off!
Just like Waters use to do

LORETTA: You don't want that kind of attention
I remember your Momma
You know how he could turn everything every which way
Next thing you know
its Waters singin and Waters draws

and this that and the other
And you just watch Waters gone be preachin one day

CLARISSA: To hear her talk
She didn't have no other children but him

LORETTA: What about his friend?
Her name Merideth, right
She from the West Indies?

CLARISSA: No, she from England
but her people come from there
Sweet girl

LORETTA: That where he gets all this Afrocentric mess from?

CLARISSA: Couldn't tell you that
she's anthropology professor
And for a while
she got Momma's hopes up
then she turned out to be that way too
Studied in Africa
She's a real Doctor, Ph.D. and all
But real home folks

LORETTA: You know what Sistah Brown say
All this Afrocentric mess is driving people away from God

CLARISSA: Now I don't know about all that
Sistah Brown don't know what she's talkin' about

LORETTA: Well, Mother Bell said amen

CLARISSA: M'deah and Sistah Brown
would say the light bulb is driving people away from God
if it was new
It's either driving people away from God
or the work of the devil

Sometimes I wonder
what about love?!
Everything is the work of the devil

For all that talk of the devil in church
You'd think we go to praise him
What about love?!

LORETTA: Now you know God is love
But Sistah Brown say . . .

WATERS (*entering with* MERIDETH): Did I hear the name of the
    woman I love
that paragon of delight
that infinitely desirable
silk slick and satin Sistah Brown

CLARISSA: You'd better watch it boy
talkin' about the saints that way

MERIDETH: Who is Sistah Brown?

WATERS: She's a love goddess
a wild woman
bitch in heat

CLARISSA: Hush that!

LORETTA: Boy, you better watch how you talk about the saints
Sistah Brown libeled to walk through that door any minute

CLARISSA: No, she had to drive to Muncie for Sistah Peters' funeral

WATERS (*to* MERIDETH): I have never met Sistah Brown
She is a complete mystery to me
But honey
every time I come home
Sistah Brown is either in the hospital
visiting the hospital
or going to a funeral
Chile, I cannot
for the life of me
remember who she is
but her name is always mentioned
in connection with funerals and hospitals
With a reputation like that
Sistah Brown is the last person
I wanna see visiting me in the hospital

LORETTA: Well, Merideth
What do you think of this brood
Ain't they somethin'
Remind you of home

MERIDETH: Everything but the accent
Yours is a bit strange

(*Laughter.*)

WATERS: Oh really! (*With affected British accent.*)

CLARISSA: Girlfriend just make yourself right at home

WATERS: Don't get too comfortable Miss Thing
M'deah ain't here yet

LORETTA (*to* CLARISSA): I forget to tell ya
Mother Bell called and asked if she could bring anythin

WATERS: Oh Lord, I hope you told her no
or at least something simple
Like salad or something

LORETTA: I told her we got everything

WATERS (*to* MERIDETH): I love my mother dearly
but cooking is not exactly her forte

LORETTA: Well she said she'd be over around six o'clock
and to call her if ya'll needed anything

CLARISSA: I'd better call her
otherwise she feels left out
(*Picks up the telephone and dials.*)

WATERS (*as* CLARISSA *dials*, imitating MOTHER BELL): "I just wanted
to make sure it was alright to come over."

Honey, I can hear her now

CLARISSA: Momma, Clarissa. . . .
Ain't nobody tryin' to leave you out . . .
We ain't doin' nothin' you can't be part of. . . .

WATERS: She will create some great drama

CLARISSA: Momma, will you come on over
we just hangin out and cooking
Well . . .

WATERS: Tell her to bring some ginger ale

CLARISSA: She wants to know what kind
She know how picky you are

WATERS: Schweppes

CLARISSA: He said Schweppes
(CLARISSA *turns the receiver away from her face and returns it, frowning.*)
Just bring anything you can find

WATERS (*exasperated*): It doesn't matter all that much

CLARISSA: He said it don't matter
So come anytime you feel like it
(*Hangs up the phone, frowning.*)
Dag, she always got to make everything so complicated
But she's comin as soon as she take Aunt Serene home

WATERS: Aunt Serene ain't comin'?!

CLARISSA: No, she ain't feelin so good

MERIDETH (*to* WATERS): Your favorite

WATERS: Aunt Serene is aptly named, oh yes, she one of my favorite
    people

CLARISSA: Grab that pan of ribs, Merideth

MEREDITH: At your service Ma'am. (*To Waters.*) You're alright?

WATERS: Um-hum.

CLARISSA: I got the chicken
and I'll introduce you to my not so aptly named brothers-in-law,
my husband's brothers, Bugger and Doodoo

Fair warning. Winnie, Bobby, and my boys been imitatin' you
so aint no tellin' what Bugger and Doodoo picked up.

(CLARISSA *and* MERIDETH *exit.* WATERS *and* LORETTA *continue to
    make food:* WATERS *deviled eggs,* LORETTA *potato salad, quietly for
    a long pause.*)

LORETTA (*awkwardly*): Well . . .
your Momma tells me
uh
that you writing poetry now

WATERS: Trying

LORETTA: Well
every time you send her something
She's callin everybody in Indianapolis
to read it to us

WATERS (*surprised*): Aw how nice

She told me she liked it
tho I'm surprised she understand it

LORETTA: Your Momma understands
a whole lot more than she gets credit for

*

She's proud of you children
(WATERS *looks at* LORETTA, *surprised. Sounds of laughter and male voices offstage.*)

WATERS: Sounds like they're having a good time out there

LORETTA: You don't have to stay up in here with me

WATERS: I know
But I don't get to spend much time with you

Why is it you always
Why is it you always say
"Your Momma"

(*They continue to work quietly, with no reply from* LORETTA, *who acts as if she didn't hear the question. Sound of laughter offstage.*)

WATERS: Why don't we finish up in here
and both go out together
Don't you know you're as much a part of this family
as anybody
Seem to me even more so now
You're around her more than anybody

LORETTA (*pause to consider*): I've always been a little bit afraid of you

MOTHER BELL (*offstage*): Hey, where is everybody

LORETTA: We back here

(MOTHER BELL *enters.*)

MOTHER BELL: Hi baby (*Kissing* WATERS.)
Ooooh, everything sho smells good
Merideth make any of that bar-b-que she talked
    about last night

(*To* LORETTA)

She was tellin' us about some fancy African sauce
Jerky or something like that
What was that stuff?

WATERS: She was talkin about groundnut stew
it's an African dish

MOTHER BELL: Well it sho sounded good
Whew, I'm gonna sit and rest a minute

Your ginger ale is in that bag
I hope its alright
They didn't have no schepp, speps scheps
Whatever you call it
That some kind of gourmet ginger ale?

WATERS: Why is it
every time I get specific about food or drink
ya'll use the "g" word
I don't really care what kind of ginger ale it is

MOTHER BELL: What's my baby makin

(*More loud laughter offstage.*)

WATERS: Deviled eggs
taste some

MOTHER BELL: Umm, umm.
Loretta, taste this

(LORETTA *has a bite.*)

LORETTA: Boy, you sho ain't lost your touch

MOTHER BELL: I want you to make me smothered chicken and
    biscuits
(*To* LORETTA:) Chile
When I was out there in California
biscuits melt in your mouth
and that gravy
Boy you ain't gonna leave here
till I get me some of that fried chicken
biscuits, and gravy—
Everybody outside?

LORETTA: Yes, Ma'am

MOTHER BELL: Well, what ya'll sittin' up in here for
(*To* WATERS:) We never could get you outside
to play with the other children
always sittin' up with the grown folks

WATERS: Except when you threw me out
I remember one time when
it had snowed
and you had company
can't remember who

but I was righteously indignant
at not being allowed to stay inside

I remember banging so hard on the door
My hands bled—

MOTHER BELL: Now you know you ain't had no bleedin' hands

WATERS: It was on Thirty-first Street
and I was seven years old

MOTHER BELL: Yo daddy always said
I should have left you out there more often
If I had
well maybe. . . .
Did ya'll go up to see yo daddy today

WATERS (*hesitantly*): Yeah
Clarissa, Bobby and me

Its so hard to see him that way
and remember the way he was

MOTHER BELL: All we can do is pray . . .

    You know
I don't know if I want you t' make me fried chicken
or liver and onions
Lo, he made liver
Melt in your mouth

(WATERS *looks at* MOTHER BELL *incredulously.*)

WATERS: I'll make you anything you want

MOTHER BELL: That's my baby
Of all my children
I know I can count on you
(*To* LORETTA:) Loretta, get me some water
no, give me some of that ginger ale
Waters, you don't mind if I have some of your ginger ale
do you?
You used t' drink Perrier
Oh, after I came back from California
I started drinkin' a glass of that Perrier Water

after I eat
and get a good belch, 'hind that Perrier

WATERS: You can get the same kind of action
from soda water
and it's a lot cheaper
I've become an expert on cheap style

MOTHER BELL: Is ginger ale cheap style
Loretta, put some more ice in this for me

WATERS: No
ginger ale is ginger ale
I drink it cause I like the taste

MOTHER BELL: I'm getting on your nerves
talkin' too much
But I'm just so glad to see you

(MOTHER BELL *tears up. More laughter offstage as* CLARISSA *and*
    MERIDETH *enter laughing.*)

CLARISSA (*to* MERIDETH): I warned you about my brothers-in-law

(*Pause.*)

What happened in here

WATERS: Just reminiscing about the good old days

CLARISSA: And what funerals were you discussing
(MERIDETH *and* CLARISSA *burst out laughing.*)
Ya'll ought to hurry up in here
The party's out there
(*To* WATERS:)
Winnie said you recited a poem for him and the boys
Now you got to do one for us

MERIDETH: Go on Waters, do "Night Blindness."
Your Mum would love that one
'ello Mother Bell
Go on Waters, do "Night Blindness."

MOTHER BELL: Both Waters and Annette learned speaking in
    school but Waters is the only one who did anything with it

WATERS: Arbitrary vision round midnight
doncha move too fast
    but don't stop
What?
fly blind bird   fly

feel your way thru the sky
                    Why?
comin' up on Sunday
maybe moon's gonna glow on a starry sky
and I
don't mind if you can hardly see
unless you do
then I cry
        like a baby
Why?
        'cause the moon's gonna shine on a starry sky
and you could be free
even though you can't see
        who?
Might be comin' at you
        between the sparklin' stars
        behind the moon
soon
        The world will turn and
        mornin's gonna break
        Wait!
blind birds don't see
even when the moon is full on a starry sky
and fly 'till day breaks on orange sunrise
        Wise?
in the surreal beauty of a cloudless night sky
wings stretch across a full moon blind and free

MOTHER BELL (*smiling*): Same as you did for the boys?

WATERS: Yes Ma'am

MOTHER BELL (*closed eyes*): Oh I can see it
so plain
Wearin a black satin robe
and red velvet streamers

(*Open eyes.*)

The lord's callin you

WATERS: But maybe for something else Momma
Maybe for somethin' else

MOTHER BELL: Maybe

(*Pause.*)

CLARISSA: Hey ya'll the party's outside
Grab that potato salad and them deviled eggs
and let's get to it

(*All exit except* MOTHER BELL. MOTHER BELL *sits and grimaces, closing her eyes.* WATERS *comes back and offers his arm.*)

WATERS: I'm glad you liked my poem

MOTHER BELL (*Taking* WATERS'S *arm.*): And you recite it so well

(*They both exit.*)

Scene 3

(MOTHER BELL'S *house. Sofa and 2 chairs on either side with TV facing sofa left of center. Raised on a platform behind stage right, a bed and sofa made up for sleeping. Front stage right, a single bed and chair. Far stage left are a table and three chairs.* MOTHER BELL *lies asleep on the sofa in front of the TV wearing a ruffled bedcap and an open Bible laying across her chest. There is an electric fan near the TV, which is on, tuned to a religious program.* WATERS *and* MERIDETH *are offstage, both shushing the other as they enter, attempting to be as quiet as possible.* MOTHER BELL *stirs.*)

MOTHER BELL: Ya'll have a good time

WATERS: Yes Ma'am
We stayed at Clarissa's 'till about 10:30
then we went out

MOTHER BELL: Where'd ya'all go to

WATERS (*hands on hips*): We went to a . . .

MERIDETH: We went to a club on Massachusetts Avenue
Though we had the hardest time locating it
Your downtown is very much like San Francisco
rather difficult to understand
Turned out we'd been driving around in circles
trying to find the place
eventually making a wrong turn
And there it was

MOTHER BELL: Well, I'm glad ya'll enjoyed y'self

Whew look at the time
I should have carried these old bones to bed
long time ago
Gotta pick up my riders 9:30 for Sunday School
You know where everything is

(MERIDETH *grabs her things and goes to the bathroom.*)

I made up your bed

(*Whispers to* WATERS.)

I hope she don't mind sleeping on the couch

WATERS: She's slept in village huts in Africa
Believe me she won't mind sleeping on the couch

Thank you for having her

MOTHER BELL: Why you're so very welcome
You know any of your friends are welcome here

WATERS: Wish Donald could have visited
He and Winny would have been a hoot
I miss my partner

(*Pause.*)

Ya'll do me proud

MOTHER BELL: Well I'm glad

(*Pause as* MOTHER BELL *looks at the TV.*)

WATERS (*awkward*): Remember that corsage?

MOTHER BELL (*smiling*): Oh yes

WATERS: I was so weird on that trip (*after thought*)
but really happy you came to visit us

Donald told me about giving it to you
he said
he said he gave it to you
and um
when he gave it to you
You started to cry
He didn't know what to do
He had such a confused look on his face

when he told
when he told that story
He really loved you
Oh how I miss him
(*Pause.*)

MOTHER BELL: He was a real gentleman
I was so sorry and sad when he passed
Yes sir
a real gentleman

WATERS: What did you do after you got home tonight

MOTHER BELL (*watching TV*): Well my prayer partner came over
he's goin' thru some trials
But I just pray with him
give it over to God
and I'm through

Folk get all upset over things they can't do nothin' about
I just give it over to God
Put it in His hands
and leave it alone

WATERS: Ym-hum
What's takin Miss Thing so long in that bathroom

MOTHER BELL: Be a little patient
She's probably takin' care of women's business

WATERS: Well I got to take care of some men's business
(*Yelling to the bathroom.*)
So she better get her skanktidy butt out of there

MOTHER BELL (*laughing*): You sound like you used to
talkin' bout your sisters
They'd be in that bathroom primpin'
and you'd be out here sayin'
Ya'll better get your skanktidy butts outta there
I gotta pee
ya'll used t' tickle me . . . . . .

WATERS: Sometimes

I wonder what you remember

(MERIDETH *enters as* WATERS *goes to bathroom, wearing a T-shirt and a
    wraparound skirt of African fabric.*)

MERIDETH: It was a lovely day

MOTHER BELL: Sometimes
I think Waters is ashamed of us

MERIDETH: Oh no, quite the contrary
He often says
"I could introduce my family to the Queen of England
and the Queen would be honored."
He's very proud of you
But . . .
I think he's a bit frustrated
by the differences

MOTHER BELL (*dropping her voice*): What differences?

MERIDETH: Different points of view
Particularly the way you deal with—
Stop me if I'm intruding

MOTHER BELL: No Baby, go right on (*With attitude.*)

MERIDETH: Umm, well
the matter of his illness
There's been no mention of it since he's been here
He's a bit frustrated by that

MOTHER BELL: I don't believe he got it
Faith is the evidence of things not seen
and the substance of things hoped for
Dogs bark,
but that don't mean somethin's out there
Dogs bark at nothing but wind blowin leaves in the dark

(WATERS *enters slowly, listening quietly.*)

Dogs bark
trained out of the necessity of evil
It is dangerous prophesy
      false
They bark at nothing

WATERS: But they bark Momma
the dogs bark

(*Long pause as* MOTHER BELL *looks at the TV with a stoic frown and* WA-
      TERS *and* MERIDETH *stare at* MOTHER BELL.)

MOTHER BELL: Well, I'm off t' bed.

(MOTHER *goes to her bedroom and sits on her bed reading the Bible,* WA-
TERS *and* MERIDETH *go to the top bedroom.* MERIDETH *sits on the
bed while* WATERS *changes into a similar outfit.* MERIDETH *is
thumbing thru some photo albums laid out on the bed.*)

WATERS (*changing into T-shirt and skirt*): So sistah girl
Still trying to save the world from the windy city?

MERIDETH: I'd be happy to save just one brilliant student from herself.

WATERS: Your Toni Morrison lookalike?

MERIDETH: Yeah
She's so angry
and unreachable no matter how I try

WATERS: You know
Some people don't want to be saved

MERIDETH (*taking offense*): That's defeatist

WATERS (*soothing*): I know, but realistic
Not everybody is willing to follow you on the path of enlighten-
ment
Can't save the world, dahlin'
She still rollin' her eyes—

MERIDETH: Every time I speak directly to her
It's only a month into the semester
and already I seem to have lost her

WATERS: Now who's being defeatist
and after only a month too

MEREDITH: You're right
Temporary insanity
I'm not giving up on 'er
He sums up the peculiar joy
teaching all black students

WATERS: What's different

MEREDITH: I think we expect more of each other

WATERS: Families do expect so very much of each other
And colored folks is family out of necessity

MEREDITH: It's the same all over the world, isn't it

WATERS: Such a family

MEREDITH: Always dividing
always so far away . . .
It's never easy coming home when you've been gone so long

WATERS: And I've been gone so long.

MEREDITH: Your Mum's lovely

WATERS: Everybody likes my mother except her children
and we'd probably like her if she wasn't our mother
I don't trust people who don't like my mother

MERIDETH: She's awfully grand

WATERS: Mother Bell is a diva, true diva

MERIDETH: Certainly knows how to get your attention

I do wish you'd change your mind
and go to church tomorrow
I'd love to see it

WATERS: See Momma preach

MERIDETH: Yeah

WATERS: You just did girlfriend—
What is this,
Some sort of anthropological study?

MERIDETH: Everything's an anthropological study, darling

WATERS: Oh really!
and what brought up the dogs bark?

MERIDETH (*whispering*): She says she doesn't believe you really
   have it

WATERS: Aw shit

Is this contagious?
Say the fucking word Miss thing, Puleease
AIDS AIDS AIDS!

MERIDETH: Shhh! She'll hear you

WATERS: Momma hears what she wants to hear

MERIDETH: Fascinating analogy

WATERS (*imitating* MOTHER BELL*'s preaching style*): Very useful

*

Dogs bark
at nothing
but wind blowing leaves in the dark

ferociously
they bark

What faces turn
two sides
wrong and right and right and wrong

Someone weeps terror
fear repeating fear
ghosts of bad dreams
children have after midnight horror movies

barking dogs
fenced and battle-ready

Wind whispered leaves signal growling
dangerous prophesy

Dogs bark
trained out of the necessity of evil
and the demands of duty

listen to the dogs bark
       they bark
       at nothing

Momma wrote that
and every time she has a point to make
she takes the part that suits her argument
and says no more
So dahlin
Wanna see the history of my sex life

MERIDETH: These look more like family pictures to me

WATERS: Honnney, we'll get back to these
The good stuff is in this one
Dis be da convention book!
Chile,

I worked those conventions
especially that youth convocation
from the time I was 13

(*Pointing to a picture.*)

Girlfriend, don't he look like a screaming queen?
Evangelist Bobby Hope
my first conventioneer
He eventually got married
and had four or five rugrats

MERIDETH: He got married to a woman?
The Lord does move in mysterious ways
doesn't he?!

WATERS: You ain't seen nothin yet
Check out the Mass Choir
(*Pointing*) that one and that one and that one

MERIDETH: You're kidding

WATERS: And honey, that was before I was sixteen
We'd shout and fall out at the Saturday night musical
Fuck our brains out the rest of the night
and those same queens said amen the loudest
when the preacher said the abomination line on
Sunday morning

MERIDETH: What hypocrisy

WATERS: What behavior modification
Everybody knows too—
except the sho-nuff sanctified Holy Ghost–filled saints
the deaf, mute and blind . . .
and the children

MERIDETH: You were only a child at thirteen

WATERS: No honey
I lost that at seven
to a straight upright deacon
At least the Evangelist Bobby Hope gave me a choice
Aw shit
this ain't so fun anymore

(WATERS *closes the album, drops it on the bed and shakes his fingers.*)

Why don't I narrate these

(*Picking up another album as* MERIDETH *climbs on the bed and puts her
arms around* WATERS *from behind and looks over his shoulder.*)

Our history
My heritage

MERIDETH: How lovely

WATERS (*seriously*): No, beautiful
We are very beautiful people

(*Pointing out a photo.*)

    Momma
on her wedding day
When the preacher asked
"do you take this man"
she answered, "I reckon"
I'd love to have this one
They're so handsome

Its hard to remember seeing him today
looking at this picture
so good-looking and strong
You can see a simplicity in my daddy
of goodness
and in all seriousness
a gentle man
still

MERIDETH: He's not your blood father

WATERS: He was/is my father
The sperm donor is a 40-year-old secret
that my mother still keeps quite secret

MERIDETH: Never easy to watch infirmity
You love him very much
the man who raised you I mean

WATERS: Yes I do

MERIDETH: Why don't you ask for——

WATERS: Can't give that
    that's Granny-grand, my grand mother
She looks like a dyke here

MERIDETH: Was she

WATERS: I always wondered
never knew any man in her life, after Granddaddy
I was never quite sure of her story
    But honey,
these sanctified sisters
I am convinced, often do without
    Grand-daddy, Granny's one and only
Here he is
was married five times
and Momma has a half-brother somewhere
    They say
When they rolled him out of the nursing home
in an ambulance going to the hospital that last time
he copped a feel off a nurse's behind
and when Momma scolded him
saying, "Daddy, you ought to be shamed"
he said, "Just a taste for the road."

I never liked him

MERIDETH: Why?

WATERS: He was such a man. (*Said with disgust.*)

MEREDITH: For a queer you have . . .

WATERS: Have a major problem with the male sex?
    Grand-daddy sure was fine tho'
I wouldn't mind growing old looking like him

MERIDETH: You might grow old after all

WATERS (*irritated*): Don't do that
She does that!
Been doing that ever since I got here!

MERIDETH: What did I do?

WATERS: Pretend—
This is Aunt Jo

MERIDETH: One of your favorites

WATERS: Everybody's favorite . . .
(*New photo.*) Aunt Serene and Granny
(*New photo.*) Momma, Aunt Ceil, and Aunt Ree
(*New photo.*) Aunt Willie

MERIDETH: So many aunts
and Mother Bell has a brother

WATERS: Half brother

MERIDETH: But no sisters

WATERS: Only child of her mother, Granny
The Aunts are mostly cousins and friends
Very complicated family tree

MERIDETH: Uncles?

WATERS: I guess so. . . .
(*New photo.*)
Loretta, now she *looks* like a dyke

MERIDETH: You keep projecting lesbianism on these women
Any truth to the rumor?

WATERS: Just wishing I weren't so alone I guess
(*New photo.*)
and these are her boys
good boys and her no good ex-husband
(*New photo.*)
Bobby when he was a baby, so cute
(*New photo.*)
Miss Annette in high school . . .

(*Fade to black. Fade up on* MOTHER BELL *sitting on the bed with her back
to the audience, gently rocking and softly moaning. She turns and
falls to her knees.*)

MOTHER BELL: This evening and once again as I lay my head down
to sleep
Lord Jesus
I thank you for one more day
with an able body and clothed in my right mind
I thank you for the hot sun and the evening breeze
I thank you for my trials and tribulations
(*Moaning.*)
Thank you for my trials and tribulations
Thank you for my children all around me
Thank you for keepin' 'em safe, well and prosperous
Lord, I thank ya
You been so good
I just can't thank you enough
Lord, you let me see my babies together
All grown

All grown up
Lord, where went the time
Where went the time, Lord Jesus
We saw a road up a hill
So busy climbin'
and You keep takin' me higher
Hey, higher Lord
  Higher Lord
Keep takin' me higher
  in Your word
  in Your grace
Keepin' me Lord
Keep me Lord
You only know
only you know
  they heavy burdens I carry
Rebuke that demon
Ain't nothin' but a demon
The devil is busy Lord Jesus
Satan the Lord rebuke you in the name of Jesus
I know you
and you can't have 'em
not one of 'em
Lord God you brought me out
saved me
kept me
filled me
Now Lord I'm humbly in your care
on my knees
givin' it over to you
Lift it Lord
Lift this weight
  So heavy
  so heavy on my shoulders
Take it away
I know you're able
I know you're able
Doctor said I was barren
Could'n have no babies
Lord you heard 'em tell me I wasn't a woman
You heard 'em laugh and backstabbin'
But I was weak
lost faith

and in my sin
In my sin
You look pity Lord
You looked down with pity on my wretched soul
    preachin' your gospel
    wearin' Your white robe
    with a scarlet heart
You pitied me in my sin
and you gave me my heart's desire
You blessed me with my baby
You blessed me with a son
Oh Lord I thank you
They said I wasn't a woman
They said I couldn't have no babies
But you made 'em liars
    Liars all
    the doctors and the women
    the gossips and the backstabbers
I know I know
I know where you brought me from
Childless
You gave me a child
In my sin
With somebody else's man
You gave me a child
Lord I thank you
even when I gave up
You gave me my heart's desire
Oh bless Your name
I'm sorry Lord
I'm so sorry Lord
I just couldn't see how you blessed me
I was shamed in my sin
But Lord I know it's all on the altar
Lord I've repented
Lord I know you've forgiven me
You gave me a husband
You blessed me with a good man
    took me as his wife
    and my sin as his own
And Lord I thank you
You've been so good so good so good
I just can't tell it all

Thru it all Lord God
Thru it all
     On the highways and byways down yonder
     kept us safe from the crackers
put food on the table
when I didn't have but fifty cents in my pocket
the rent got paid
Haven't failed me yet
You haven't failed me yet
I know you to be a healer
I know You to be a miracle worker
I know Your power Lord
Send it Lord
Send it send it send it
Rebuke the devil from hell
You made liars of 'em before
     long ago
     You made me a woman
     When they said I wasn't
     You made me a woman
     I had him
     but You gave him to me
I'm believin' and trustin' in your word
You said if I live Holy
Holy Holy Holy
You said if I walk in the light
You'd guide my footsteps
They told him a lie Lord Jesus
I know IT TO BE A LIE
It's got to be a lie
I'm believin' and trustin' in You
     to lift my burden
TAKE IT AWAY
It's a lie
It's a lie from a devil's hell
It can't be true
I waited so long
Prayin' and waitin'
Prayin' and waitin'
and you answered my prayer
even after I lost faith
even in my sin
even as they laughed and talked about me

Out of the depths
like the woman at the well
        Like Lazarus
You raised me up
A new creature in Christ Jesus
I've stayed so long
Tryin' to walk this narrow road
Please Sir Jesus
Please Sir Jesus
Hear my plea
My first born
My favorite
Lord I know You're able
I know You're able
Fix it Jesus
fix it fix it fix it
Whatever it takes
In your will
make it alright alright alright
I know You're able
Worry him Lord worry him Lord worry him Lord
Your will be done
Call him to repentance
Bring him to your bosom and make everything alright
Save him Lord
Heal and save him Lord Jesus
you gave him to me
Now I'm givin' him over to You
Make him over
Make him over
Wash him clean
Everything everything that's not like You
take it away and make him whole
Make him whole and holy
HOLY LORD HOLY HOLY HOLY
Have your way
Have Your way Lord Jesus Your will be done
I know it's your will
You wouldn't
You wouldn't
        give me my heart's desire
Just to take it away
I'm . . . (*Moaning.*)

I'm putting it all in Your hands
All of it
in Jesus' name
Hey, bless Your name
In Jesus' name
In Jesus' name
Oh Lord please don't take my baby . . . . . .

(*Moans.*)

These blessins we ask in Jesus' name. . . . Amen

(*Fade to black.*)

Act Two

Scene 1

(*Stage dark as wide spotlight comes up down center.* MERIDETH *and* LORETTA *walk into the light from opposite sides of the stage and face the audience.*)

MERIDETH: If Waters had stayed here, he'd be dead or crazy

LORETTA: Waters was born
and ain't been nothin' but trouble since

(CLARISSA *walks into the spot between* LORETTA *and* MERIDETH.)

CLARISSA: Everybody takin' sides
and nobody's on mine

MERIDETH: If I hadn't come along
Heaven only knows what they would have put him thru

LORETTA: I don't understand it
Never understood it
Pout and sulk was all he ever did
and M'deah could always find an excuse
There'd be nobody else but him
He came along out of the blue, mind you
and I turned into M'deah's personal slave girl

MERIDETH: I'm not quite comfortable leaving
He'll be alone with them
and no one to protect him

CLARISSA: I once chased Waters with a knife
We were teenagers
Only four years older than me and
he was walkin' round like he was my lord and master

Gonna make me clean the kitchen
"How you expect me to cook in this mess," he said
"Get in here and clean this up"

I told him to kiss my ass
He gets the broom
I get a knife
Momma took his side

(CLARISSA *continues after short pause.*)

He went off about a year later
There was blood all over
like he was tryin to cut away somethin

I loved him again
not cause I felt sorry for him
But because he'd illustrated for me the pain of being different
Especially his kind of different

MERIDETH: The longer we're here
I see him losing himself
and me losing him
I know I will one day
the thought of that day frightens me
I depend on him, you see
We queers must make our own family
Blood family tends to desert
or oppress us
Waters, Donald and I made a family
We lost Donald
I don't know how I'll bear losing Waters
He's so far away now
Seeing him here is like not seeing him at all
Why is our blood so oppressive?

LORETTA: He'll go home
Bea will need me again
everything will go back to normal

until he dies
Then nothin'll be the same
He'll leave this world
like he came into it
Messin with the rhythm of life
Before he was born, she was my Momma
I want my Momma back!
She been gone forty years

CLARISSA: I got two boys
Wonder what I'd do if . . .
I try to be a good mother
and I know I've made mistakes
like Momma knows
and you just don't know how hard it is
until you try to do it y'self

Waters
Momma
I'm reminded of that old warhorse of a sermon
Ezekiel 37th chapter
and Ezekiel had a vision
of a valley of dry bones
and the Lord asked him
"can these bones live"
And Ezekiel answered
O Lord God thou knowest
and God told Ezekiel
to call them up
Momma
Waters
Why can't you just love one another
Life is too short
Time don't stop
I'm remembering Ezekiel's vision
when when when
there was a rumble
I can feel a rumble
like a rock to and fro
and something's ready to blow
rumblin like a rock
rumblin like a rock

MEREDITH—CLARISSA—LORETTA: rumblin like a rock

CLARISSA: Come together or explode!

(*Blackout.*)

Scene 2

(*The kitchen of* MOTHER BELL*'s house.* MERIDETH *(wearing T-shirt and skirt) is in the kitchen making egg and chips.* WATERS *is in bed and* MOTHER BELL *is in the bathroom. It is early Sunday morning.* WA-TERS *gets up groggily and puts on his skirt and T-shirt and goes to kitchen.* WATERS *walks past the TV on which is a religious program.* WATERS *looks briefly at the TV and rolls his eyes upward and goes to the kitchen.*)

MERIDETH: I thought you'd be sleeping in

WATERS (*yawning*): I don't sleep well away from home
How'd you sleep girlfriend?

MERIDETH: The sofa was actually quite comfortable

(*Whispering.*)

Interesting tho'
Mother Bell letting us sleep in the same room
She's in the bathroom by the way

WATERS: I can tell by the TV
(*Yelling toward the bathroom.*)

Momma, can I turn the TV off
and turn on the radio?
I'll turn on the gospel station

MOTHER BELL (*offstage*): Play what you want
I got to be gone in ten minutes

WATERS: Thanks (WATERS *goes to turn off TV and turn radio on.*)

MERIDETH: Clarissa said she's be by for coffee before church
Pour you a cup

WATERS (*taking a bag of pill bottles from the refrigerator, opening them one by one and taking one or two from each bottle*): After breakfast——
These don't sit so well with coffee

(*Pouring orange juice.*)

Thanks for coming along (*Busses* MERIDETH *on the cheek.*)
Every time I come here
I'm haunted by this frightened little sissy
and they just don't understand——
        Anyway
thanks for rendezvousing

MERIDETH (*whispering*): Shhh, she's going to hear you

WATERS: Thanks for coming down
It's really nice having my families meet

MERIDETH: No problem—sorry I'm leaving this afternoon
but I honestly enjoy your family

WATERS: I'm sorry you're leaving too
Wish I honestly enjoyed my family
(MERIDETH *shhhs* WATERS *and gestures toward the bathroom.* WATERS
        gestures in a limp-wristed blowoff way.)
I guess they're alright
Its just I wish
Chile I just wish they'd deal with it more
        head on
All this cheerful positive shit
is getting on my last nerve

MERIDETH (*whispering*): At least wait until she leaves for church

WATERS: Then Clarissa will be over
She's a lot easier than (*whispering*) Momma

But at least I have wonderful friends (*in a little boy voice*)
like a certain nappy-headed overeducated professor

MERIDETH: I don't think my hair goes over well here
But we won't talk about that

WATERS: Let's talk about overeducated professors
so much more interesting

(*Waters scratches his head.*)

MERIDETH: No, new subject

WATERS: No, let's stick with overeducated professors
"Little Momma" (*Little-boy voice.*)

MERIDETH (*giving* WATERS *a serious mocking glare*): I'm not so sure I
        want to be cast in that role
and I still want to change the subject

WATERS: And the subject was hair
Wasn't it?

MERIDETH: No, we don't have one

WATERS: Looks like you've got a fine head of hair, Miss Thing

MERIDETH (*suppressing laughter*): Stop

Will you please stop!

WATERS: Miss Thing, Miss Thing
Will you please choose a subject?
Hair or education nappy or overbred

MERIDETH: Will you get off it!

WATERS: Yes, Little Momma

MERIDETH: Waters

WATERS (*teasing*): Little Momma

MERIDETH (*bored and annoyed*): Whenever you're finished

WATERS: Wrong line

MERIDETH: Wrong line?
What line do I have here

WATERS: I just hate it
When people are patient with me

(MOTHER BELL *enters dressed for church, no makeup, no jewelry except for
    a brooch.*)

MOTHER BELL: Ooooeee!
Lawd have mercy, that sho' looks good
Ya'll got enough for me?

(*There is a knock at the door.*)

MERIDETH: Yes ma'am
Why, don't you look nice

WATERS (*going to answer the door*): That must be Clarissa

MERIDETH: Just egg and chips

(CLARISSA *enters dressed for church carrying a purse and Bible.*)

CLARISSA: Good mornin brother dear
Merideth
Motha'deah

(CLARISSA *busses each one on the cheek.*)

WATERS (*smiling with pride looks at* MOTHER BELL *and* CLARISSA)
    Mother Charlotte Beatrice Bell
and the good Sistah Clarissa Rose Bell Armstrong
Dressed and I do mean Dressed
for Sunday to meetin' service
Um um um
Ya'll gonna have them brothers jumpin in that prayer line
"Lawd have mercy
Make them Bell women stop lookin' so good
so I won't lust in my heart so much
Help me Lawd—"

MOTHER BELL (*laughing*): Boy don't you be mockin' the Holy
    Ghost

WATERS: Ain't nobody mockin' the Holy Ghost
I was trying to pay ya'll a compliment
Is that allowed? (*Teasing.*)

MOTHER BELL (*suppressing laughter*): Yes Sir
Just don't put the Holy Ghost in it

(WATERS *stands behind* MOTHER BELL *and mimes strangling her.*)

MERIDETH: Coffee Clarissa, Mother Bell?

CLARISSA: Thanks Merideth.

MOTHER BELL: Yes, baby

WATERS (*to* MERIDETH, *leaning against a counter conspiratorially, arms
    folded, legs crossed at ankle*): A long time ago
When I came home to visit
Annette, Clarissa, and Momma
me, Winnie and it was just Arthur then, Clary's boy,
Anyway they took me on
    What would be my last visit to a shopping mall
At a certain point on this excursion
Winnie, Arthur and I were walking behind the three Bell
    women
and Winnie elbows me and points
to three sets of major hips swayin' to and fro in perfect sync

Va voom Va voom Va voom

(WATERS *makes a swaying dipping gesture. Everybody laughing.*)

CLARISSA: My hips ain't nowhere near
big as Annette's wide track pontiac
and my booty cain't touch Momma's
            all due respect M'deah
And anywho
my husband ain't complainin'

WATERS: Well I ain't so sure about that
Winnie said your wide track was wid-en-ing

MERIDETH: You shouldn't be telling tales

(*To* CLARISSA:) I'll bet he said nothing of the sort

CLARISSA: Like I said
I get no complaints

MOTHER BELL: Well I come by my walk natural
They use't say I was switichin
But baby when you got a certain amount of equipment
Things just gonna move a certain way

MERIDETH: And you just can't help that
Can you Mother Bell?

(*A knock at the door.*)

WATERS: I'll get it (*Starts to walk and stumbles, then answers the door,
    limping and shaking his feet while mumbling under his breath.*)

Damit damit damit

MOTHER BELL: No Ma'am, I can't

(LORETTA *enters. Attempting a peck on the cheek, they bump heads and try
    again.* WATERS *turns ignoring* LORETTA*'s presence and walking
    quickly toward* MOTHER BELL.)

WATERS: Yeah, right!
Those hips and that butt just have a mind of their own

(*Putting his arm around* MOTHER BELL.)

and they just don't behave (*He kisses her on the cheek.*)

MERIDETH: Very much like your feet Waters

MOTHER BELL (*to Loretta*): Lo', what you doin here

LORETTA: I came t'get you for church

CLARISSA (*to* WATERS): What's wrong with your feet
They go off walkin' by themself (*Laughing.*)
Mornin' Loretta

MERIDETH: Morning Loretta

MOTHER BELL (*to* LORETTA): I was gonna get you

WATERS (*to* CLARISSA *and disengaging himself from* MOTHER BELL *matter-of-factly*): No, they just do dead sometimes

MOTHER BELL: Poor circulation
(*to* LORETTA)
So whose car we gone take
cause I got riders

LORETTA: We can take mine
I got a full tank

WATERS (*in a silly voice*): No Ma'am, its HIV
Sometimes
my feet go dead
And I should take short cool showers
be-cause
in people of color with HIV
the skin gets ashy dry
then there's funguses and—

MERIDETH: Fungi

WATERS: I beg your pardon
Fungi and bacteria etc. . . . . . .

(WATERS *smiles a wide strained smile.*)

And there's a pill for everything

(WATERS *and* MERIDETH *sadly giggle while* MOTHER BELL, CLARISSA *and* LORETTA *are stone-faced.*)

MOTHER BELL (*to* MERIDETH): Girl, you know who you favor?
Linda Blunt
You remember her? (*To* WATERS)
She use't baby-sit for ya'll
Not for long tho'
I had trouble getting baby-sitters to come back
Those young'uns use't chase 'em out of the house with
baseball bats
I never did have the trouble those baby-sitters had with my

children
'Cept for some of the Mother's Board
Mother Thompson and Mother Whitlock especially
They just loved Waters
Oh, after church
Waters rush to the front pews,
that's where they all sat,
and kiss 'em one by one
They all thought he was so sweet
    Why . . .

WATERS (*obviously pissed off*): Excuse me,
I'm gonna take a dump
(WATERS *goes to the bathroom and slams the door. Long pause as* CLARISSA *frowns and shakes her head.*)

MERIDETH (*to* MOTHER BELL): You know, he really needs your sup-
    port in this

MOTHER BELL: I just don't believe he got it, I'm claimin the victory
and I'm believin' and trusting in God
that its a lie from a devil's hell

CLARISSA: But Momma . . .

MERIDETH: Well he does have it
and he needs the counsel and support of his family

MOTHER BELL: He's got our support
We just ain't the kind of people
that talks about it all the time
We thought it be better to keep cheerful
positive

CLARISSA: But Momma
Maybe he needs more than that
You should have—

MOTHER BELL: He needs to trust in God
He needs to believe God will heal him

MERIDETH: He doesn't

MOTHER BELL: We keep prayin . . .
Oooo look at the time
I better get goin'

(MOTHER BELL *collects her things and knocks on the bathroom door. To* WATERS.)
I'm gone baby

See you at Clarissa's this evening
(*To* CLARISSA.)
I'll see you at Sunday School
Come on Loretta let's get going

CLARISSA: I might skip Sunday School this morning

MOTHER BELL: Suit y'self (MOTHER BELL *busses* CLARISSA *on the
   cheek.*)
Now let me get a big hug from my Merideth
Professor Merideth (*She hugs* MERIDETH.)
Now don't you be a stranger
and have a safe drive back to Chicago

MERIDETH: Thank you. . . .
Um . . .
I really had a nice time

MOTHER BELL: I'm glad
Well, I'm gone
Come on Loretta
You gone make me late
We better take my car . . .

(MOTHER BELL *exits with* LORETTA, *waving bye-bye. Short pause as*
   MOTHER BELL *exits.*)

MERIDETH: My oh my—

CLARISSA: That's one way of puttin' it

(*Yelling toward the bathroom.*)

Waters, she's gone
you can come out now

(WATERS *enters and angrily sits at the table as* MERIDETH *sits down with
   them.*)

WATERS: Do you believe that!

CLARISSA: She was rude

WATERS: No, more than that
It's like she only wants so much information—
or she doesn't care

CLARISSA: Now wait a minute
You're not being fair

WATERS: Fair!
Life ain't fair
I do have HIV disease
The love of my life is dead from it
Since 1984, I've been watching my friends die
Life ain't fair

CLARISSA: Merideth, could you please excuse us

MERIDETH (*looks at* WATERS): You're alright

CLARISSA: He's alright, excuse us please

MERIDETH: I'll just go pack (MERIDETH *exits.*)

CLARISSA: Thanks
(*To* WATERS.)
You and Momma
Ya'll act like you're in a race
a race to die
And after my pastor's wife
and Mother Wilson
I'm very aware of how old Momma is
and she's as close to death as you are

WATERS: This ain't about that
this is about this family's denial!
Listen sistah woman
I don't expect trumpets to sound
or an announcement in the Sunday bulletin—

CLARISSA: Momma was rude
but you know how she is
it doesn't mean she don't care
We just don't know what you expect from us
I don't understand

WATERS: Neither do I. . . .
Momma . . .

CLARISSA: I'm telling you I won't hear talk about Momma
You and Annette

WATERS: Don't compare me with Annette

CLARISSA: I don't know why . . .
Long time ago
She wrote a letter to M'deah
just like yours
Momma knows she wasn't the best mother in the world

She didn't need ya'll to remind her
Annette said the same thing

WATERS: She can't say the same thing
Its not the same issue

CLARISSA: What's the issue—
Momma won't bend

WATERS: Or acknowledge that . . .

CLARISSA: Momma won't bend
You are just visiting

WATERS (*pause*): You think this is a visit?

CLARISSA: Ya'll come home
drop a bomb
and leave me to deal with the fallout

WATERS: Maybe I'm just being weird
but I've been here five days
And with the one exception of my brother-in-law
Nobody's talked about it
or asked me how I'm doin
or even asked me how's it's goin'
don't ya'll see your own denial?

CLARISSA: We're just tryin to keep positive
But you gotta know we care

WATERS: I know you care
But sometimes that's not enough
No . . .

CLARISSA: We pray
Momma and I
We get together at my house
Sometimes with Dolly and Loretta

Sometimes
It's just me and Momma
That's what we know to do
That's how we care

(*Long pause as* CLARISSA *and* WATERS *sip coffee quietly.*)

WATERS: That kind of caring isn't enough

CLARISSA: How we supposed to care?

I know this woman who has a gift
The gift of healing
and laying-on hands

WATERS: I know you mean well
but no

CLARISSA: I don't know what else to do

WATERS: You and Momma

CLARISSA: Don't start

WATERS: If you'd let me talk
If you'd listen
Nobody's listening
        That's the problem
Nobody is listening
Momma don't want to talk about it
You don't want to talk about it

CLARISSA: Now you can't say that
You've never talked to me
(*Pause. Pleadingly.*) And I do ask questions
(*Pause.*)
Maybe they're not the right questions
You just assume

WATERS: I assume
my family will love and support me
I speak more freely with my friends
than my family
        Look
I am honored by your prayers
truly honored
Prayer is a wonderful thing
        But baby sistah
this is something we can't pray our way out of

I'm scared
and I can't put it into words
What I need
I just know it ain't here

CLARISSA: If you don't know
then how you expect us to know

*

If you need it
Then you ought to know what it is

WATERS: There are things
I believe
things

That ought to be natural

Showing
hear me now
Showing concern when someone you love has trouble
ought to be natural

CLARISSA: A whole lot of things ought to be natural

Why did you come home
Why are you here?
(*Pause as* WATERS *stares at her angrily.*)
I'm sorry
I'm glad you're here
but it looks like to me
you come a long way to have a lousy time
and I don't know what to do to make you happy

WATERS (*very angry*): Life is not about happy!
I have never been happy
I've been Black, male and queer all my life
I figure
the most I can hope for is content
with a purty now and then
Not too many parties these days
outside of the farewell kind!

(*Pause to cool down.*)

I was content with Donald
and when he got sick
That contentment kept me sane
I have survived something
I thought would kill me
I had no vision of life without him
I am strong, I am invincible, I am woman

CLARISSA: What?

WATERS: Bad joke

CLARISSA (*singing*): You can bend but never break me
cause it takes too much to make me
(MERIDETH *enters and joins in.*)
more determined to blah blah blah
I am strong, strong yeah, yeah
(MERIDETH, CLARISSA *and* WATERS *together clowning it up.*)
I am invincible, invincible
I am woman oh yeah

CLARISSA: Chile, you ought to quit

MERIDETH: I heard the singing
and figured you were all talked out

CLARISSA: I am, anyway
I'm gonna be late for church
if I don't get outta here now—
Motha'deah will be rollin her eyes at me 'til next Sunday
(*Busses* WATERS *and hugs and busses* MERIDETH.)
Merideth, you have a safe trip home
and come down for a visit sometimes
You don't have to come with Waters
You're family
Bye—

(CLARISSA *exits.*)

WATERS & MERIDETH: Bye-bye　　　Thanks for everything

(MERIDETH *begins to pick up around the kitchen.* WATERS *goes to the living room.*)

WATERS: Girlfriend
leave shit alone
I'll get to it later
We don't have much time before you have to go
Come on in here
We may not get to see each other before Christmas
And I miss having you around
Seems like everybody I get close to
either moves away or dies

(MERIDETH *joins* WATERS *on the couch in a friendly cuddle.*)

MERIDETH: We'll see each other before Christmas
and there's always the phone

So you must get over your phonaphobia
and let me know how you're doing

How are you doing?

WATERS: You know?
I'd nearly accepted the way they deal with things
But this morning was too much

MERIDETH (*thoughtful pause*): Deep down
and you're not going to like this
But she must be in incredible pain

WATERS: Mother Charlotte Beatrice Bell can't or won't
let you see it
But oh how she pisses me off
Diva Diva Diva (*Broad gesture and leans forward like Rodin's* "Thinker.")
What gets me is the nerve
"no the sun will not shine today
Because it is not my pleasure."
and she's still the most interesting person I know
Damit damit damit
I wonder how I survived that shadow
     the comfort and the shade
     smothering and cold

She thinks the world turns just because she's on it
problem is
So do I

MERIDETH: So do you what?

WATERS: Think the world turns because she's on it
and I'm just like her, La Grand Diva (*A small laugh.*)

MERIDETH: You are sooo much alike

WATERS: I do do a major imitation
don't I
but I'm not such a steamroller
"Merideth—you know who you look like?" (*Imitating* MOTHER BELL.)
said cheerfully as she plunges a stake thru my heart

(*High drama.*)

MERIDETH: Now that's a bit overdone

WATERS: Drama is something I can't help honey
it's in the genes

*

What was she thinking Miss Thing?!?
I know
if she doesn't acknowledge it
it don't exist

MERIDETH: She's really convinced you don't have it
How'd she put it
"I'm believing and trusting in God
that's a lie from a devil's hell"
Nearly had me convinced

WATERS: In my wildest daydreams I had as a child
gazing out the window at the leaves
turning from green to gold and gone
I was a plump girl with long coarse hair and brown skin
      living in a house by a river
      a long way from the projects where we lived

So in my wildest daydreams I had as a child
it was all different
I wasn't a sissy boy
or lonely
or skinny
or poor
But an elegant brown girl
regal as Momma

Why couldn't she just sit down and shut up (*angry*)!?!?

MERIDETH: You're not going to like this, either
But give her a break
She's 70 years old
And her oldest son has AIDS
It's not something I'd want to discuss over breakfast

WATERS: Girlfriend, feels like I'm always giving her a break
Not this time
Not this time

MERIDETH: What are you going to do

WATERS: I have to say something
and I don't know what
(*Looking off, talking to* MOTHER BELL *as if she were there, breathlessly, fearful and pleadingly.*)

"Momma, you were rude . . .
Momma I need you to just hold my hand sometimes
and say nothing . . .
Momma I need my tears to fall on your breast
when I cry sometimes. . . .
Momma tell me you're as scared as I am
Momma you're as much my miracle as I am yours
Momma all I want sometimes is you
Momma why is this so hard
Momma I hope I die before you do
'cause sometimes I need you to just hold my hand
and I don't know what I'd do if you weren't here"
(*Wiping tears away.*)
I'm a forty-year-old Momma's boy

MERIDETH (*puts her arm around* WATERS): I was never quite sure what
    I would do with my life
I just went along with the moment
never really committing to anything
but fascinated by everything
not understanding that everything
has a name
It's called culture

(*Both* MERIDETH *and* WATERS *are crying.*)

WATERS: And honey, you still can't

MERIDETH: I take great pride in my groundnut stew
Its nearly as good as me mum's

WATERS: Girlfriend, if I were you
I would talk about my Momma that w . . . Wait a minute
I don't think this is an ideal time to play the dozens

Scene 3

(*Late Monday evening. Living room set of* MOTHER BELL's *house.*
    MOTHER BELL *is seated stage left* [*big cushy chair*] *hands folded.*
    LORETTA *is half reclining on the sofa. TV flickering in the dark as*
    MOTHER BELL *and* LORETTA *watch* Wheel of Fortune *with great
    seriousness.*)

LORETTA: Now she know
she didn't have to buy no vowels

(MOTHER BELL *nods as if only half hearing.*)
"n" fool
"Dancing in the dark"

MOTHER BELL: You got it
That's it

LORETTA: Ain't nothin' but three vowels in the whole thing

MOTHER BELL: I thought "n" was one of the letters you choose first

LORETTA: I bet Waters could clean up on this show

MOTHER BELL: He wouldn't do that

(*Pause, watching TV.*)

LORETTA: See I told you
"Dancing in the dark" . . .

He ought to try getting on this show

MOTHER BELL: He think he's too good

LORETTA: Like his daddy's folks

MOTHER BELL: Robert Bell's folks be on that show in a New York
   minute

LORETTA: I ain't talkin 'bout that daddy

(MOTHER BELL *gives* LORETTA *a stinging glare out of the corner of her eye.*
   LORETTA *takes note and flashes a small smile that quickly fades.*)

While this commercial's on
I'm goin to the john

MOTHER BELL: Um

(*As* LORETTA *leaves for the bathroom* MOTHER BELL *throws her head back
as if to surrender. Then she is alone.*)

So many times
My children disappoint me
I don't say so
Never did
'cept for Bobby
that poor child practiclly raised hisself
and he's as good as gold
   my baby
But Waters was the first
My favorite

So much joy he was
All those gifts
Wasted to the world

Clary was a hellion
Annette was so fast
I never could figure out what to do with my girls
You could have knocked me over with a feather
if somebody told me
things would turn out so

Waters was a good boy
Still is
He just ain't my boy no more
(*Looking out of the corner of her eye to the bathroom, frowning.*)
She ain't talkin' bout *that* daddy

Lord Jesus, Lord Jesus (*Sadly whispered. Pause as she softly moans with eyes closed.*)

LORETTA (*entering slowly*): Bea, you want a cold drink

MOTHER BELL: No baby

Lord I just don't know
Keep prayin

LORETTA: That's all we can do
Keep prayin

Aw, shoot
I missed that last puzzle
you notice what it was

MOTHER BELL (*chuckling*): No baby—

Waters ought to be back soon

LORETTA: Where he off to

MOTHER BELL: Didn't say
Pouted all night at Clarissa's
Mad with me 'bout somethin'
I don't know what

LORETTA: Well he's goin back to California tomorrow

MOTHER BELL: My children
my children

(*Long pause as* LORETTA *shakes her head and both stare at the TV deep in their own thoughts—note the sound of the TV is garbled.*)

LORETTA: That black girl had her chance yet

MOTHER BELL: No
That woman painted like a clown
took all that time with "Dancing in the Dark"
Nobody else got to play yet

LORETTA: You know who she look like?
Sister Munnerlynne

MOTHER BELL: Yeah, they do favor
'cept this chile ain't so fat

LORETTA: Lord, you 'member when she fell out
right on top of Brother Williams

MOTHER BELL: Now you know the Holy Ghost don't act like that
Po' man could've been crushed to death

LORETTA: Now look at that!
You know, sometimes
I think that "lose a turn" is rigged up for black folks

MOTHER BELL: Um-hum
Just like life

LORETTA: Now here come that painted-up woman
Stupid heifer

MOTHER BELL: Loretta (*Laughing.*)
its just a TV show
Ain't no need to go round callin folk heifers

LORETTA: Now you just watch
that black girl gonna get "lose a turn" or "bankruptcy"

MOTHER BELL: Oh Lord!
She got that $5000 panel
What is it Lo'?

LORETTA: I don't know
ain't enough consonants yet

MOTHER BELL: Lord Jesus
You know that girl need that money

LORETTA: Six words

"How to _e"
that'll be "be"
"_er_ _er _ _o _ _la _"
I know, if she don't hit "lose a turn" or—

Choose a "U" or a "P" (*At the TV.*)

MOTHER BELL AND LORETTA: See, I told you

MOTHER BELL: Prayer changes things

LORETTA: Well, she almost hit bankrup—
"U" or "P" (*At the TV.*)

MOTHER BELL: What is it Lo' (*Excitedly.*)

LORETTA (*calm and cool.*)
"How to be very very popular"
and if she ain't fool enuf to spin again,
she got it!

MOTHER BELL: You talk about Waters—
You the one

LORETTA: I'd turn into Lot's wife
in front of those cameras
What Waters mad with you about?

MOTHER BELL: I don't know
Waters never would say what was upsettin him
He'd either hide in his room
or throw a fit
All I'd know was he'd be mad

LORETTA: Never sayin' why?
How old Waters?

MOTHER BELL: You know he's forty

LORETTA: When he gonna start acting like it

Here's the last one
"p _ _st _ _ . . ."
"Plastic"

(WATERS *enters.*)

MOTHER BELL: Hey hey
look who's here

WATERS (*sits in chair opposite* MOTHER BELL): How ya'll doin

LORETTA (*with a cursory glance*): Alright

So you on your way
back to California tomorrow

WATERS: Yes ma'am, back home. . . .

Loretta, I need to talk to Momma alone

MOTHER BELL: Now you know Lo is family

WATERS: If she were Clarissa, Annette or Bobby—
I need to talk to you alone
This is really important

You understand, don't you Loretta

(LORETTA *looks to* MOTHER BELL.)

MOTHER BELL: You go on home
get some rest
We got to get up early

LORETTA: What time you pickin' me up

WATERS: I don't have to be at the airport 'til 7

MOTHER BELL: I guess we'll be gettin' you
oh, six-thirty

(LORETTA *goes to kiss* WATERS *and he, reaching up, bumps heads with her.
They smile and gently buss each other embarrassedly.* LORETTA *exits,
with* MOTHER BELL *letting her out.*)

You be careful out there
Honk when you get in the car

LORETTA (*offstage*): See ya'll six-thirty in the morning
(*Pause, honk.* MOTHER BELL *sits back in her chair and continues to
watch TV.*)

WATERS: Can we turn this off?

MOTHER BELL: You don't like *Family Feud*

WATERS (*frustrated*): Can we at least turn it down

(MOTHER BELL *picks up remote, turns sound down.*)
I need to talk. . . .

*

This is ridiculous
I'm sittin here watching some stupid game show
tryin' to start a serious discussion
This is too weird

MOTHER BELL: I'm listening

WATERS: Okay, here goes
Yesterday morning . . .

MOTHER BELL (*watching TV*): Yes

WATERS: We were hangin out
jokin and whatnot
I started talkin about my ailments

MOTHER BELL: Uh huh

WATERS: and you completely changed the subject

MOTHER BELL: Uh huh

WATERS: Do you realize how abrupt it was?

MOTHER BELL (*indignant*): Abrupt?

WATERS: Yes abrupt
The way you changed the subject was abrupt
to put it politely
It was rude, if you want to know the truth

(WATERS *glances at the TV with more frequency, increasingly irritated.*)

I don't want apologies
I . . .

(MOTHER BELL *sits stoic and still, hands folded straight ahead.*)

Will you give me some attention here
I'm talking to you

MOTHER BELL: Well I'm listening

WATERS: No
You're not
You're sitting there watching *Family Feud*

MOTHER BELL: Go head, I'm listening

WATERS: I don't believe this . . .
Momma turn it off, please

MOTHER BELL (*picks up remote, turns TV off, turns on lamp*):

Ok, you have my complete attention
Well I'm sorry if I was rude

WATERS: Momma, it was more than that
and "I'm sorry" just don't get it

MOTHER BELL: Well all I can say is I'm sorry
What else did you have to say

WATERS: Please (*hissing.*)
Momma, my health is on my mind most of the time
I don't want to talk about it all the time
but I do talk about it sometimes
It just comes up

MOTHER BELL: I said I'm sorry
I abruptly changed the subject
that was rude
What else do you want me to do

WATERS: Will you listen to yourself
We are not talking about abrupt or rude
Hear me
Why are you always leaving . . .

MOTHER BELL: I repented of that
and like I sent your letter back
I won't hear this in this house

WATERS: You don't know what I was gonna say
Not for want of a variety of complicated subjects
But unless God has endowed you
With powers to read minds . . .

MOTHER BELL (*quietly authoritative*): Don't blaspheme in this house
    either

What do you want me to say

WATERS: Can't I have my own faith?

(MOTHER BELL *looks at* WATERS *incredulously. Begging.*)
Can't you and I talk

We never talk
You tell me things
You don't listen when I speak
Momma . . .
It still fees like you're always leaving

MOTHER BELL (*uncomfortable*): You the one gone
What do you want me to do
Cry and scream, woe is me
    I don't do that
Give it over to God
That's what I do

WATERS: And what do I do?

MOTHER BELL: You know what to do

WATERS: No Momma
I don't know what to do
You tell me what to do

MOTHER BELL: You know

WATERS: No I don't

MOTHER BELL: Yes you do

WATERS: What then
you tell me
TELL ME

MOTHER BELL (*quietly threatening*): Don't raise your voice to me

WATERS: Then tell me what to do

MOTHER BELL: You know
Some people
wouldn't let you in the house
I'd think you'd be grateful to be welcome here

WATERS: Why thank you for letting me thru the door
Now tell me what to do
Don't go

MOTHER BELL: I ain't goin noplace

WATERS: You keep tryin Momma but it ain't that easy
Tell me what to do
I will not leave it alone
You tell me what to do

MOTHER BELL: Dogs bark
ferociously
they bark

WATERS: At what Momma
at what

MOTHER BELL: Nothin

WATERS: No Momma
They barkin at somethin

The dogs be barkin at hard wind
a cold hard wind that's comin
Momma
tell me what to do!

MOTHER BELL (*frowning*): I don't have to tell you
What you already know

I raised you in the Church
You know what to do

WATERS (*head rushing*): Sometimes my feet go numb
I sleep a lot
Most of my old fag buddies are dead
My doctor treated my lover too
I feel guilt being alive

Sometimes my feet go numb
in people of color the skin is ashy dry
coffee and tea don't go well with my medication
I remember sexual freedom

Sometimes my feet go numb
it takes one to two days to get a prescription filled at San Francisco
    General
I heard two guys making a speed deal at the Food Bank once
My thumbnails are blue from the AZT
Bruises that don't heal quickly worry me
    Sometimes my feet go numb
My sweat smells medicinal
My urine stinks
Television commercials make me cry
The news makes me angry
I'm tired all the time

*

Sometimes my feet go numb
I take an antidepressant and other drugs to scare my voices away
I hate pity
The very idea of wearing diapers is humiliating
I wonder if the acupuncture is doing any good

Sometimes my feet go numb
and I don't notice until I try to walk
then I stumble
swear
shake them awake
and move on

Tell me what to do Momma

MOTHER BELL (*tears running down her face*): You must repent
You must come back to God
I don't
I won't believe you got what they say you got
I've claimed the victory
But be warned
You've got to come to repentance

WATERS: What?!

MOTHER BELL (*composed*): You made me say it
So you listen
No way around it
You must be born again
You know that
You know that
I raised you right
I wasn't perfect
but I raised you right

WATERS: You raised me the best you knew

MOTHER BELL: Can't do no better than my best
I raised you the way you should go
like the Bible say—

WATERS: In the last fifteen or twenty years
it all comes down to
"like the Bible say
like the Bible say"

You 'member the last time I went to church with you?
Do you?
It was Mother's Day, the day after Clarissa's wedding
This woman gets up to the pulpit
purportedly to read a Mother's Day poem
Which made my stomach turn, by the way
But not before quoting some television evangelist
that her Jesus was not a homosexual
lookin dead at me

I got no quarrel with Jesus
I've never thought of him having sex
But religion
Organized religion
That is a very different story
That woman's judgment is from the same poisonous vine
responsible for more war slavery prejudice suffering and
persecution than you and I together could imagine

Momma, look at me
I'm not some cute little white boy on the six o'clock news
I'm your eldest son
I am queer
I did not choose it
I do not choose to hide it
or sneak around or pretend or lie
I will let no self-righteous zealot, book, or religion condemn me

MOTHER BELL: How can it condemn you
When you know the truth
You condemn yourself

WATERS: There is no "the truth"
A whole lot of people claim to know
"the truth"
I worry about those people

MOTHER BELL: You can't deny the truth

WATERS (*very angry*): What?!!
Honey, I can't do this—

What is right wading in this water?!
that baptizes souls with excuses to hate
or wear blinders

Take 'em off Momma
I have
The truth is for fifteen years
I was a self-hating Black slut
The truth is I came by it naturally
I was so dumb
I really thought you were praying with those brothers
I took off the blinders Momma
and realized you was prayin
just like me
at those conventions
and believe me I wasn't prayin

MOTHER BELL (*coldly angry*): Don't be bringin that mess up
I sent your letter back
and I won't hear that in this house

WATERS: Yes
You
Will
You apologized
We forgave
but nobody forgot

MOTHER BELL (*very angry and controlled*): God forgave me
I apologized to my children
that is all I can do
You don't want to hear it but—

WATERS (*interrupting*): No I don't

MOTHER BELL: But you will
Yes
You
Will
The word is there
always been there to justify our faith
Roman 1:26–28
". . . God gave them up to vile affections: for even there women did
change the natural use into that which is against nature:

And likewise also the men, leaving the natural use of the women,
burned in their lust one toward another; men with men working
that which is unseemly . . .

*

And even as they did not like to retain God in *their* knowledge, God
gave them over to a reprobate mind."

You are on dangerous ground, boy

WATERS: Yes ma'am
I am
I have HIV disease
It has baggage
and sometimes it weighs me down
in muck and mire so thick
I might sink if I dare stop moving

I cannot go home as who I am
        it seems
unredeemed by what blood
unsaved by what grace
unnatural by whose standard

MOTHER BELL (*frowning*): Have mercy

WATERS: They say
this is not true
        manifold wonder
they say
hold tight
and oh yes my my my sweet Lord
and cry
try I try I try
I cannot go home as who I am

        Past
other notions
        Past
what was
        Past
camouflage closets quietude assimilation patience
        all past
still
I cannot go home as who I am

but want and want and want
some homebody to hold me and

*

(MOTHER BELL *gets up from her chair and crosses to sit on the arm of* WATERS's *chair and cradles his head to her breast.*)

MOTHER BELL: You're mine, I had you
but God wants your mind

(*Said simultaneously as* WATERS *continues to recite his poem, repeating the phrase till the end of the poem.*)

WATERS: Rock me with
heat musk salt and sweet

Sweet home
longing to share
my joy in knowing who and what I am

    Now and then
familiar breezes blow
    Now and again
a whistling wind is haunting
honeychile!
Say what to laughing me oh my
    oh my oh my
and I cannot go home as who I am

(MOTHER BELL *rises and crosses to the TV and turns it on, sitting on the couch.*)

MOTHER BELL: Well it's late and you got an early plane
We'd better get to bed

(*Fade to black. Cross-fade shaft spotlight center stage, which* WATERS *walks into.*)

WATERS (*singing*): I cannot go home as who I am
    it seems
unredeemed by what blood
unsaved by what grace
unnatural by whose standard

MOTHER BELL (*walking into the light singing, standing beside* WATERS):
    I dreamed I went to the City called Glory
so bright and so fair

WATERS (*taking* MOTHER BELL's *hand tenderly*): They say this is not
    true

   manifold wonder
they say
hold tight
and oh yes my my my Lord have mercy
and cry
try I try I try
I cannot go home as who I am

MOTHER BELL: When I entered the gates cried holy
the angels all met me there
They carried me from mansion to mansion
and oh the sights I saw

WATERS: Past
other notions
      past
What was
      past
remembrance
      past
camouflage, pretence, quietude, assimilation, patience
      all past
still
as who I am I cannot go home

But want and want and want
some homebody to hold me and

MOTHER BELL: I cried I want to see Jesus
the one who died for all

WATERS: Rock me with
heat musk salt and sweet

MOTHER BELL: I bowed down on my knees and cried Holy

WATERS: Sweet home
longing to share
my joy in knowing who and what I am

MOTHER BELL: HOLY!

WATERS: Now and then
familiar breezes blow
      Now and again a whistling wind is haunting

MOTHER BELL: I cried HOLY!
I clapped my hands and cried HOLY! (*Claps her hands and embraces* WATERS.)

WATERS: Honeychile
Say what to laughing me oh my oh my oh my

MOTHER BELL: Holy is His name

WATERS (*holding* MOTHER BELL *tightly*): and I cannot go home as who I am

(*Curtain*)

BEFORE IT HITS HOME

Cheryl L. West

CHERYL L. WEST, playwright, is a former human services counselor. Her first major play, *Before It Hits Home*, was produced by the Arena Stage in Washington, D.C., in 1991 and subsequently at the Second Stage Theater as part of the New York Shakespeare Festival in New York City in 1992. *Before It Hits Home* won the prestigious Susan Smith Blackburn Prize, an international award given to a woman who has written a work of outstanding quality for the English-speaking theater. It also received the Multicultural Playwright's Festival Award in 1989 and the 1992 Helen Hayes-Charles McArthur Award for outstanding new play produced in Washington, D.C. Filmmaker Spike Lee has optioned the play's film rights.

West's plays include *Jar the Floor*, produced at Northlight Theater in Evanston, Illinois, in 1992 and at several regional theaters in 1993; *Puddin n' Pete*, which premiered at Chicago's Goodman Theater in 1993; *Getting Right Behind Something Like That*; and *A Mistake & a 1/2*. West's *Holiday Heart* premiered in a three-way coproduction with Syracuse Stage in Syracuse, New York, the Cleveland Playhouse in Cleveland, Ohio, and Seattle Repertory Theater in Seattle, Washington, during the 1993–94 season. It was then produced by the Manhattan Theater Club in New York City and the Arena Stage in 1995.

West's credits include the PBS *Great Performances* dramatic miniseries, *Trials*, and pilot development for 20th Century-Fox. She is writing a screenplay for Oprah Winfrey's Harpo Studios. Cheryl L. West lives in Champaign, Illinois.

This play is dedicated to those who have to hide
and to those who refuse to

Characters

WENDAL, Black male in his early 30s
REBA, Black woman in her 50s, Wendal's mother
BAILEY, Black man in his late 50s, Wendal's father
MAYBELLE, Black woman in her 50s, Reba's best friend
SIMONE, Black woman in her early 20s, Wendal's lover
ANGEL PETERSON, Black woman in her early 20s, woman in clinic
DOUGLASS, Black man in his early 40s, Wendal's lover
JUNIOR, Black male in his late 20s, Wendal's younger brother
DWAYNE, Black boy, 12, Wendal's son
DOCTOR, White woman in her 40s or 50s
NURSE, a middle-aged Hispanic or Asian woman

**   The following part is played by the above:
ANGEL PETERSON (should be played by whomever plays Simone)
TWO ATTENDANTS (Attendants can be used as part of the crew, but
their primary actions are to assist Wendal on stage.)

Property List

Act One

Saxophone with case (WENDAL)
Kitchen table
Cigarettes (DOUGLASS)
Matches/lighter (DOUGLASS)
Tablecloth (REBA)

Magazine (ANGEL PETERSON)
Small table and chair (NURSE)
Appointment book (NURSE)
2 other chairs
Bag (WENDAL)
Book (*Tao Te Ching*) (WENDAL)
Clipboard with medical forms
Pen
Big bag (ANGEL)

Gift box with red dress (MAYBELLE)
Table and chairs
2 suits in dry cleaner's bags (BAILEY)
Nail polish (MAYBELLE)
Emery board (MAYBELLE)

Chair
Stethoscope (DOCTOR)

Phones
Speech cards (BAILEY)

Chairs (DOUGLASS, SIMONE)
Papers (DOUGLASS)
Pen (DOUGLASS)
Lotion (SIMONE)
Beer (DOUGLASS)
Receipt (SIMONE)
Brochure (DOUGLASS)

Futon cushion
Sheet
Cigarette and lighter (WENDAL)

Cassette (jazz) (DOCTOR)
Hospital bed
Nightstand
Dressing
IV hookup and stand
Surgical tape (that does not rip hair)
Intercom buzzer (hand held)
Gifts: flowers (DOUGLASS)
        books: Bible
                When Bad Things Happen to Good People
        candy
Speech cards (BAILEY)

Duffel bag (JUNIOR)
Small box with bracelet (JUNIOR)
Box with watch (JUNIOR)
Plaque
Jacket for Dwayne (JUNIOR)

Suitcase (WENDAL)
Wheelchair (NURSE)
Sax case (WENDAL)

Act Two

Dining table
6 chairs
Table setting for six
Purse (MAYBELLE)
Fork/spatula (JUNIOR)

Covered platter (WENDAL)
Pot with sauce (DWAYNE)
Casserole dish (WENDAL)
Covered dish (JUNIOR)

Medicine/pillbox (WENDAL)
Glass of water

Suitcase (REBA)
Beeper (WENDAL)
Pillbox (WENDAL)
Pills (WENDAL)
Milk carton (JUNIOR)

Hospital bed
IV unit and stand
Wood (BAILEY)
Saxophone with case
Towel (BAILEY)
Rubber gloves (BAILEY)
Newspapers (BAILEY)
Oven mitts (MAYBELLE)
Plate with tin foil (MAYBELLE)

Author's Note

There is a tendency to be seduced by the Bailey family, thus having the focus of the play be on them. This is not my intention. Wendal's two worlds—before he gets home and after he gets home—are equally important and at times, equally fractured. Douglass and Simone are not "social" characters and should not be portrayed as such. The action shifts frequently and the pacing between scenes should be quick, and in some scenes (as noted), action juxtaposed. To expedite this, whenever possible, actors should remain on stage while other scenes are taking place and remain true to the overlapping dialogue in the play.

Prologue

(WENDAL *is in a bar playing his saxophone.* WENDAL *is into it, feeling the power, his power. Each note punctuates how "bad" he is. He's one fine confident specimen.*)

(*Sound cue of audience clapping.*)

WENDAL: Thank you. Thank you. I dedicate that song for a special lady, Mrs. Reba Bailey, and since today is her birthday and I can't be with her . . . that one's for you Mama. You know we talk about first love, but we got it wrong. I'm here to tell you, your first love connection is Mama, that first love journey is with her. And usually it's the one kinda love that outlasts the test of time. Homeboy over there says I heard that. (*Chuckles.*) I know that's right. Don't get me wrong, I love my woman, I ain't no Oedipus or some sick shit like that, but I ain't shamed to tell you, I got one of them Sadie Mamas. Can't touch her. Yeah, you know what I'm talkin' 'bout. So happy birthday Mama . . . (*Coughs.*) This next tune, a ballad. We're gonna play it deep, deep as your Mama's soul . . . (*He plays saxophone again.*)

SIMONE (*crosses*): Baby I told you that cough is getting worse. Flu doesn't hang on this long. Do I need to call the doctor for you? Is that what you're waiting on? Ok, Simone's going to call the doctor for her big baby. Make him an appointment . . . but mister baby better take his sick behind down there. No more excuses Wendal. Ok? (*Suggestively.*) Hey baby it's been a while. . . . Do I have to start hanging my panties out to dry on your horn? (*Simone exits.*)

WENDAL: For those of you who don't know, I'm Wendal Bailey and we're Sojourn. We're glad you came out tonight. Fellas and

531

me gon' take a short break. So, have another drink, don't forget to tip the ladies and we'll be right back at you. (*Just then* DOUGLASS *strikes a match, lights a cigarette.* WENDAL *crosses to* DOUGLASS *and takes a drag off of* DOUGLASS*'s cigarette, silence for a moment. The silence is not awkward; instead these are two people used to communicating in whatever form, even abbreviated, if and when their environment dictates to do such.*)

DOUGLASS: You have any time later?

WENDAL: I don't know. I promised Simone I'd be home early. Break's over. You gon' wait around?

DOUGLASS: Probably. I liked that last song. What's the name of it?

WENDAL: Hell if I know. The shit defies a title. If you knew my old girl, you'd know what I mean. (WENDAL *starts to play; his sound is eerie in its need, its desperation.*)

Act One

(*Clinic reception area. Sound of* WENDAL *singing before lights. Waiting is a very pregnant* ANGEL PETERSON. *A half-finished lunch is at her side. She is tired-looking, haggard. Nurse is sitting at the desk.*)

ANGEL (*slamming the magazine*): How long she gon' be? I can't be sitting up here all day.

NURSE: Like I told you before Ms. Peterson, the doctor will be with you as soon as possible.

ANGEL: That's what you said two hours ago. (*Grumbling to herself.*) All day sittin' up in somebody's f'ing clinic, with nothing to look at but you white folks.

NURSE: Ms. Peterson, first of all I'm not white.

ANGEL: Same difference. (WENDAL *enters loudly singing; so cool—so full of himself.*)

WENDAL (*to* NURSE): Excuse me, I have an appointment with a Dr. Weinberg. Bailey . . .

NURSE: Yes . . . you can fill out this medical history form (*hands him a clipboard*) and the doctor will be with you in a few minutes.

ANGEL: She lying.

WENDAL (*to* ANGEL): What's up? How you doing?

ANGEL: Hangin'. (WENDAL *sits, works on the clipboard, starts humming and singing again. After a moment, to* WENDAL.) Hey. (*Louder.*) Hey. Yeah, I'm talking to you cutie pie. This first time here?

WENDAL: Un-hum.

533

ANGEL: Could tell. You too damn happy to be in the family. (*Pause.*) Taurus!

WENDAL: What?

ANGEL: Naw don't tell me. Sag, Cancer, Gemini . . . Gemini! You's a Gemini if I ever saw one. My old man was a Gemini. All you fine mutherfuckers are Geminis. Can tell by the way you walk. You think yo shit don't stink.

WENDAL: Scorpio. And I been told my shit smells better than most colognes, 'specially them expensive kind.

ANGEL: (*laughs*): Umph! I heard that. (WENDAL *laughs too.*) Man, what's your name?

WENDAL: Wendal. Wendal Bailey.

ANGEL: My name Angel. Angel Peterson.

WENDAL (*eyeing her stomach*): So when's the big day?

ANGEL: Soon. Just holdin' on till it gits here, then I'm gittin' on board, catching the first thing smokin' 'tween this hell and heaven's door. (ANGEL *has a coughing fit,* WENDAL *hands her a handkerchief. She wipes her mouth, then takes out a compact and lipstick, applies makeup, a little too much, which gives her a garish appearance. She continues while looking in the compact mirror.*) I don't know what I'd do without this shit. (*Re: Makeup.*) How I look?

WENDAL: Fine.

ANGEL: You ain't a good liar Wendal Bailey. See the secret is they don't seem to find as much wrong with you when you look pretty. (*Holds out the compact to him.*) You wanna try some?

WENDAL: I'll pass.

ANGEL: So Mr. Shit-smell-better-than-cologne, what you here to see the AIDS doctor for?

WENDAL: Who said who I was here to see? What I'm here for ain't really none of your business. . . .

ANGEL: Oh-oh. Got me a live one here. I love you first-time boys. Some indignant mutherfuckers. Well you better come offa that pride Mr. Bailey, 'cause you gon' git your feelings hurt . . . (*Yelling to* NURSE.) Tell this sick mutherfucker he's got AIDS and put him out of his misery . . . so he can stop walking around foolin' himself . . .

NURSE: Ms. Peterson . . . we do not discuss a patient's medical history with another patient.

WENDAL: You got a nasty mouth on you, you know that?

ANGEL: Un-hun . . . it finally caught up with the rest of me.

WENDAL: Well I don't appreciate it.

ANGEL: Me neither. (*A beat.*) Solid. I was just trying to help you out brother. Welcome you into the family.

WENDAL: What are you talking about? What family?

ANGEL: You'll see . . .

NURSE: Ms. Peterson, you can come in now . . .

ANGEL: I'll see you around . . .

WENDAL: I doubt it. . . .

ANGEL: Oh yeah, we'll see each other again . . . just like the train . . . there's always a new one coming in and another one going out . . . (*She exits singing the same song* WENDAL *was singing when he entered.* NURSE *looks at* WENDAL. WENDAL *starts to laugh. It is an uneasy laugh.*)

WENDAL: She's a trip. (*Laughs again.*) I don't think the chick's playing with a full deck. Kept calling me part of some family. (*Laughs again as his laugh fades into* REBA's *and* MAYBELLE's *laughter. Fade in to Bailey household.* MAYBELLE *is in the mirror trying to see her backside.* REBA *is standing behind her.*)

MAYBELLE: I don't see what you talkin' about Reba . . .

REBA: That's because you don't wanna see . . .

MAYBELLE: That ain't nothing . . . nothing but a curve.

REBA: Well that curve is ten pounds with dimples. You oughtta get here early so you can get on the floor with me and do some exercise.

MAYBELLE: That floor is hard.

REBA: And so is your head.

MAYBELLE (*pouting*): I don't 'preciate you talking 'bout me like this. You done gone an' hurt my feelings. I oughtta keep what I brought over for myself.

REBA: What you done made now, Maybelle?

MAYBELLE: Nuttin'. It don't concern you. It's got my name on it now.

REBA: Come on. (*Tickles her.*) You ain't mad at your Reba now, are you?

MAYBELLE (*giving in, laughing out loud*): Stop, stop Reba, you know I'm ticklish. Stop Reba.

REBA (*stops tickling her*): I ain't got time to be carrying on like this. I got work to do. You pick some beans for me?

MAYBELLE: Yeah, but don't you want your surprise now?

REBA (*absentmindedly*): What surprise?

MAYBELLE: Where's your mind Reba?

REBA: I don't know.

MAYBELLE: I told you I had got you something . . . wait till you see what . . .

REBA (*not really listening to her*): Don't say nothing to Bailey but I had me one of those dreams again. My child was playing Maybelle, playing his horn, I declare he was, playing it like his life depended on it.

MAYBELLE: He's fine Reba. You would've heard if something was wrong. But wait . . . wait till you see what I got. It'll cheer you right up. (*Takes out a big box, hands it to* REBA.) Voilà.

REBA: You didn't. I thought you brought something to eat. (*Stomps her feet.*) I know you didn't.

MAYBELLE: Well you know more than I know. Go 'head, open it up.

REBA (*excited like a child, goes through a ritual of balling her fists and stomping her feet, wanting to take the box, but holding back*): I . . . I can't. I can't. I just can't. I know you didn't get it. You didn't, did you? Well, did you? I just can't. I know what it is . . . I told you I didn't need it. You did it, didn't you? You got it? I can't stand it. Naw, don't tell me . . .

MAYBELLE: Half the joy of giving you a present Reba is watching you go through this stupid-ass ritual. You ain't changed since you were five years old.

REBA: Oh shut up.

MAYBELLE: Go 'head, take the box.

REBA: Well, give it here. (*Takes the box.*) Maybelle, you shouldn't spend your money on me like this.

MAYBELLE: And miss this? (REBA *opens the box, it's a beautiful dress.*)

REBA: Oh Maybelle.

MAYBELLE: Yeah, it's the same one. Told you to buy it but you was too cheap. I had the girl put it on layaway. Go on, slip it on. (REBA *takes off her housecoat and slips on the dress.*)

REBA: It's beautiful.

MAYBELLE: Lord, it was meant for you. That dressmaker knew what she was doing! Go look in the mirror. (REBA *looks in the mirror.*)

REBA: I'm ready. (*Sings.*) "Put on your red dress baby 'cause we going out tonight. . . . Put on your high-heeled sneakers . . ." (MAYBELLE *joins in, they sing and do an old-time dance with silly sequential steps. After a moment and unbeknownst to the two,* BAILEY *and* DWAYNE *enter.* BAILEY *is carrying two suits in a cleaning bag, which he makes a big deal about hiding from* MAYBELLE. *They watch* MAYBELLE *and* REBA *a moment, enjoying the show.*)

MAYBELLE: Whew, I done worked up a sweat. That's my exercise for the day.

REBA (*kisses her*): What would I do without you?

MAYBELLE: Well, I never plan for you to find out. (REBA *takes off the dress and slips back into her housecoat.*)

BAILEY (*gruffly, for he is always jealous witness when it comes to the intimacy between the two women*): For once I'd like to walk through this door and not find you sittin' up in my house.

MAYBELLE: You know I brighten up your day Luke Bailey . . . (MAYBELLE *takes out fingernail polish and an emery board, starts doing her nails.*)

REBA (*folding up the dress and putting it in the box*): Bailey, call the Center. They called 'bout an hour ago.

DWAYNE (*overlapping, kissing her*): Hi Aunt May.

MAYBELLE: Hi baby.

DWAYNE: Aunt May, you need me to cut the grass again this weekend?

MAYBELLE: Well, I don't know.

DWAYNE: How about trimming the hedges?

MAYBELLE: Boy, you sure is enterprising. (BAILEY *is almost comical as he attempts to hide the suits from* MAYBELLE *while getting* REBA *to notice them.*)

BAILEY (*to* REBA): Which one?

DWAYNE: I'm going to see my Dad if he doesn't come home soon.

BAILEY: If your father wanted you to come, he'd send for you.

REBA: Bailey!

BAILEY: Well he would. Now Reba which . . .

DWAYNE: Can I be excused?

REBA (*busying herself straightening up the house*): Where you going?

DWAYNE: Watch TV.

BAILEY (*overlapping, whispering*): Reba, which suit?

REBA: You do your homework?

DWAYNE: It's Saturday.

REBA: What, you don't learn nothing except Monday through Friday?

BAILEY: Boy, get it over with.

DWAYNE: But, Daddy, I can do it tomorrow.

BAILEY: Well, I was thinking that tomorrow a certain young man might want to go with his Daddy fishing.

DWAYNE (*excited*): Really?

BAILEY: Yeah really, really. Reba which one? You know I got this thing coming up, you know, which suit?

REBA: I don't know Bailey. You decide. (*To* DWAYNE.) And Mister, you ain't going nowhere if I don't see you crack a book before the day is out. I mean that Dwayne. Maybelle, did you know that Bailey got nominated . . .

BAILEY: Reba.

REBA: . . . as volunteer of the year . . .

BAILEY: Reba don't . . .

REBA: . . . down at the Boy's Club.

BAILEY: Reba! Shit! (*Throws the suits on his chair, pouts.*) You getting to be just like her, can't keep nothing to yourself.

REBA: Well it ain't no secret Bailey. He's got to give a speech.

MAYBELLE (*crossing to* BAILEY): Well, that's good Bailey. That's why you been trying to hide them two suits looking silly? Ain't that one your funeral suit?

BAILEY: Leave me alone.

MAYBELLE: Wish that husband of mine would volunteer at something.

REBA: He just enjoying his retirement.

MAYBELLE: Wish he'd do it some other kinda way. All he wants to do is eat and sleep and pat on me, makes me sick. Let me get on out of here. Been up in here all day.

BAILEY: Today ain't no different than any other. Don't know why you pretending you in a hurry now. Don't know how you keep a husband . . . 'cause if you was my wife. . . .

MAYBELLE: I wouldn't wish that on nobody. No offense Reba.

BAILEY: Un-humm. Keep on talkin'.

MAYBELLE: Bailey, I bet you didn't hear 'bout Thelma Butts? Heard tell her husband put her out on the corner . . .

BAILEY (*clearly interested*): On the corner? Say what?!

MAYBELLE: That's right. And she ain't passing out leaflets either. Passing out something else though. . . . And cheap!

REBA (*overlapping, sharply*): Maybelle, don't start that mess. I don't allow that kinda talk in my house, you know that. Need to stay out of other people's business, 'specially somebody nasty and trifling like that.

MAYBELLE (*taken aback, sputtering*): I was . . . I . . .

REBA: I mean it.

BAILEY (*conspiratorially to* MAYBELLE): Tell me later.

REBA: I heard that Bailey.

BAILEY: Anybody else call?

REBA: No, but I thought we'd hear from . . . (*Catches herself.*)

BAILEY: From who?

REBA: Nothing.

BAILEY (*annoyed*): You on that again?

REBA: On what Bailey?

BAILEY: We ain't callin' him. Hear me? I mean that. If he got a dime to his name, Wendal can pick up the damn phone and call us . . .

REBA: Dwayne, what I tell you 'bout listening around grown folks talking? That's why you too grown now.

DWAYNE: I wasn't listening.

BAILEY: Boy, what your Grandma tell you? You better get them feet to marching. (DWAYNE *exits.*)

REBA: Wish you wouldn't talk about his father like that in front of him.

BAILEY: Why not? Call a spade a spade, son or no son. His father is worthless. Playing in two-bit clubs, talking that funny talk.

REBA: He's a musician and if he's happy . . .

BAILEY: Happy! How you know he's happy? He don't bother to call here and tell you he's happy. (*To* MAYBELLE.) He rather play somewhere in a juke joint than make an honest living, he could've helped me down at the store . . .

REBA (*angry*): That store ain't everything Bailey.

BAILEY: It puts food on this table and in that boy's mouth upstairs. Ain't no damn music feedin' him . . . ain't seen a horn blow no food this way . . .

REBA: Hush Bailey, he'll hear you.

BAILEY: I don't give a damn. I don't want him growing up pretending that Wendal is something he's not . . . making excuses for him all the time. You do that enough for everybody.

MAYBELLE: Well sir . . . like I said I guess I better be getting on out of here . . .

BAILEY: Hey, hey Maybelle, Reba tell you Junior coming home?

REBA: I forgot.

MAYBELLE: Really? Can't wait to see my boy.

BAILEY: Yeah, I'm gonna have him come down to the store and help me get those new shelves up. Think we gon' expand to that back room, start selling small appliances . . .

REBA: He's only going to be here a few days Bailey. He's on leave, not work release.

BAILEY: Little hard work never hurt nobody and Junior, that boy, ain't never been scared of hard work. Not like Mr. Music Man.

REBA: Crossing the line Bailey. I'm not in the mood today to be tangling with you about them boys.

BAILEY: Thirty years and you still don't see that boy for what he is. (*Exits in a huff.*)

REBA: I get so sick of him comparing Wendal to Junior.

MAYBELLE: Well Reba, honey, you know a man don't like softness in his sons.

REBA: Well, a man gets what he makes! (*Lights down on Bailey household and up on* WENDAL *sitting on examination table.*)

WENDAL: Lord Jesus. God . . . I ain't got no words. Just need a little favor. I know I'm in no position to bargain, but just let this one be different. I need it to be negative. So why don't you help me out here. . . . Oh shit. (*The* DOCTOR *enters and starts listening to his lungs. Nervous and with forced humor.*) It's just a little cough. You know, between you and me Doc, I don't believe that test was right, somebody in that lab must have screwed up. Should've had it redone, but me and the band was on the move. You know how that is. We don't stay in one place too long.

DOCTOR: How long have you been seropositive?

WENDAL: You mean when did I test?

DOCTOR: Yes.

WENDAL: About seven months ago. It wasn't here. I think it was in Florida. Don't know why I'm even here. You see I can't have AIDS. Look, I got a woman . . . we thinking about getting married . . .

DOCTOR: Any history of IV drug use?

WENDAL: What?

DOCTOR: I'm trying to ascertain Mr. Bailey if you have engaged in any risk behavior.

WENDAL: Smoke a little weed every now and then. . . .

DOCTOR: So if I understand you correctly, you believe you contracted the virus through sexual intercourse?

WENDAL: No, you don't understand me correctly . . .

DOCTOR: I know this is uncomfortable Mr. Bailey. . . .

WENDAL (*putting on his shirt*): All you doctors are alike. You my fourth one and every one of you trying to make me believe I'm dying.

DOCTOR: I didn't say anything about dying. . . . If you would just sit . . .

WENDAL: You know this whole AIDS thing is some kind of conspiracy. Some more of ya'lls genocide. . . . Try and lay everything on us, cancer, drugs, whatever y'all think up. Well I'm here to tell you, y'alls AIDS better take a number, get in line. And you might as well wipe that silly grin off your face 'cause this is one nigger that ain't goin' lay down and die. Call it what you want, but I ain't sick. (*Yelling.*) You hear me? I'm fine . . . (*Collapses with a coughing spell.*) I'm fine . . .

DOCTOR (*after a moment*): Mr. Bailey, I think you and I both know that you are not fine . . . now if we . . .

WENDAL: Ya'll some cold mutherfuckers.

DOCTOR: Who do you think you're talking to?

WENDAL: All you had to do was tell us, didn't cost you nothing . . . not a damn thing . . .

DOCTOR: I'm not responsible for . . .

WENDAL: Then who is? Now let me see if I got this right. You telling me I got bad blood . . . well now . . . remember ol' Tuskegee? I recall you told 'em they had bad blood too . . . and then watched 'em rot to death. Ya'll got a history of this bad blood shit, don't you?

DOCTOR: Hey, hey time out. I tell you what, it's the end of the day . . . the end of a very long day . . . I've seen more patients today than most doctors see in a week so why don't you do us both a favor and cut the shit. You've seen four doctors, if you want I'll refer you to a fifth. I've been working in this epidemic for a long time and it's not because I have an affinity for your suffering or for that matter, my own. You understand? The bottom line: you screwed somebody, you didn't protect yourself, and that's your responsibility, not mine. Your partners will have to be notified. You can do it or you can have the state do it. Which will it be?

WENDAL: Just tell me how long I've been infected.

DOCTOR: I can't. Were any of your partners gay or bisexual men?

WENDAL: Naw. I don't mess with no men. (*Getting up, putting on his shirt.*) Time's up Doc, I gotta go.

DOCTOR: Wait. What about your girlfriend? I know it's difficult, but you have a responsibility to inform your partners. (*Loud.*) Mr. Bailey, you have a responsibility to inform your partners . . . (*Repeats until* WENDAL *phones home; he is using a public phone. It's a difficult conversation for him. Lights up on the Bailey household. He is practicing his speech. Phone rings,* BAILEY *crosses to answer, carrying speech cards.*)

BAILEY: I'll get it. Hello. (WENDAL *hesitates, is tempted to hang up.*) Hello?

WENDAL: Hello.

BAILEY: Speak up. I can hardly hear you. (*The following exchange is much talking at once and escalated voices as each tries to be heard.*)

WENDAL: Hello. Hello Dad.

BAILEY: Wendal?

REBA (*crowding near the phone*): Is that Wendal?

DWAYNE (*overlapping on the upstairs extension*): Daddy?

BAILEY (*yelling in the phone*): Boy, what are you doing up?

REBA: He's a grown man Bailey.

BAILEY: I'm talking about Dwayne. Dwayne's on that phone upstairs.

REBA: He's supposed to be sleep.

WENDAL: Dad, you still there?

BAILEY: Yes. (*Phone.*) Wendal where are you?

DWAYNE: Hi Daddy. How you doing? . . .

WENDAL: Hey man, I thought you'd be sleep.

BAILEY: He should be. Get off that phone Dwayne.

REBA: Let the boy talk to his father.

DWAYNE: I almost got enough money to come . . . I wanna come see you.

REBA: Is he ok? Is he coming?

WENDAL: I may be coming there. Dad, you still there?

BAILEY (*to* REBA, *irritated*): Yes. Yes.

REBA (*whispers to* BAILEY): Be nice. Try to get along.

BAILEY (*in phone*): Wendal? (*Irritated, quickly before interrupted again.*) I'm here, got this dinner to go to, got to give a speech

. . . getting honored . . . volunteer of the year . . . all the boys voted for me . . . role model . . .

REBA: Bailey, you ain't got to shout, he ain't hard of hearing. Let me talk.

BAILEY: And Dwayne and I going fishing.

DWAYNE: I'm getting straight As, except for a few Cs and couple of Bs.

BAILEY: I can't hear myself think. DWAYNE GET OFF THAT PHONE NOW.

WENDAL (*overlapping*): I want you to know that I love you Dwayne.

BAILEY: Didn't I tell you to hang up? It's past his bedtime. HANG THAT PHONE UP DWAYNE. (DWAYNE *hangs up.*)

WENDAL (*overlapping*): Did you hear me Dwayne?

REBA: Let me talk Bailey.

BAILEY: Just a minute. Well, you sound good. Your brother coming home.

WENDAL: I was thinking about coming home . . . I'd like to see you . . . Dad I. . . .

BAILEY (*overlapping*): Coming home a sergeant. Service made a man of him. I always did say that boy was gonna 'mount to something.

WENDAL: Yeah, you always did. Dad . . .

BAILEY: Yeah, I'm real proud of him. You don't sound right. You in some kind of trouble?

WENDAL: Why do you always ask me that? Why do I always have to be in some kind of trouble to call home?

BAILEY: So you not in trouble. You working?

WENDAL: Yeah. We're trying to get a record deal. Looks like it might come through. Supposed to have a meeting with this producer.

BAILEY (*obviously disgusted*): Your mother is here. She's right here. Let me let you talk to her.

WENDAL: Dad wait.

BAILEY (*overlapping*): Wait. Wait just a moment. Here she is. (*Hands the phone to* REBA, *clearly exasperated, exits.*)

REBA: Before you say a word, Mama's gon' tell you what's waiting on you. Fried corn, candied yams. Your mouth watering? Chicken and dressing, greens that'll make you shout, beef so tender the butcher wanna buy it back. Then we gon' finish it all off with some 7-Up pound cake and Neapolitan ice cream, trim it with Maybelle's sweet potato pie.

WENDAL: Have mercy!

REBA: You just say when. I'm a get that guest room dolled up for Simone. Dwayne done moved most of your stuff from the attic in his room so you can probably bunk in with him. . . . Lord, the house is gon' be full again. . . . I can't wait. Simone cooking any better?

WENDAL (*Starts coughing uncontrollably*): I gotta go. Talk to you later Mama. (*He hangs up, she exits. Lights to* DOUGLASS *and* SIMONE *area.* DOUGLASS *is sitting at a desk.* SIMONE *enters singing. She has just bathed and is wearing* WENDAL's *robe. She surveys the house with pleasure, maybe puffing up the pillows, straightening things for the umpteenth time.* WENDAL *watches both of them for a minute, clearly debating who he should approach first. The following scene should be paced so that the dialogue and action overlap.* WENDAL's *world is literally split between the two relationships.*)

DOUGLASS: How did you get in?

WENDAL: The door was open. I saw her leave.

DOUGLASS: I thought we agreed . . .

SIMONE: Finally! What do you think? Pretty proud of myself. What do you think about the color? I got this serious vision about wallpapering the whole place.

DOUGLASS: Wendal, did you hear me? We've been through this before. I thought we agreed . . .

WENDAL: This couldn't wait. (*Kissing him, holds on.*)

DOUGLASS: Well, I'm glad to see you too.

SIMONE: How 'bout a kiss? Lay one on me. (*She kisses* WENDAL.)

SIMONE and DOUGLASS: You ok?

WENDAL: Yeah. You smell good.

DOUGLASS: Yeah, I thought I'd try a new scent.

SIMONE: Just got out the shower. Boy, where did you get that cologne? I like it.

DOUGLASS: I went by the club last night. Where were you?

WENDAL: Somebody was supposed to sit in for me. I went away for a few days. Needed to think.

SIMONE: How come you didn't call?

WENDAL: We got through late every night. I thought you'd be studying.

SIMONE: How considerate. (*Hands* WENDAL *the lotion.* WENDAL *kneels and starts applying the lotion and massaging her feet.*) I thought we could fix up a spare room for Dwayne when he comes to visit. . . . Hello in there, a spare room for Dwayne, your son. . . .

DOUGLASS: What's her name go with you?

WENDAL: You know her name.

SIMONE: I may have some good news. A teacher is leaving. They're going to recommend me to replace her. My own classroom! Isn't that great?

WENDAL: How long is she gon' be gone?

DOUGLASS: I don't know.

SIMONE: It's a big class, but I'll have an aide.

WENDAL: Where's the kids?

DOUGLASS: She let them go to some concert that I suspect will give them permanent hearing damage.

SIMONE: Of course I might not get it. But think positive, that's what you're always telling me . . . (*She moans with pleasure.*) That feels good. Nobody has hands like you.

DOUGLASS: I just found out today that Alison needs braces. At her age! I told Beth maybe we should try a pair of pliers . . .

WENDAL: Pliers! That's cold-blooded Douglass. (DOUGLASS *laughs;* SIMONE *laughs at the same time.*) What? What is it?

DOUGLASS: You're right.

WENDAL: I have something to tell you.

SIMONE (*overlapping*): Oh, just that the kids were teasing me about you today. You were a big hit with them. You should see them strutting around, they all think they're sax players now . . . and of course the girls all want to grow up and marry you. (SIMONE *laughs again, is bubbling over with excitement.*)

DOUGLASS: Beth is taking the kids to see her mother. I'll be a free man for a week, one whole glorious week with no demands.

WENDAL: I have something to tell you. There's something else. Come on Simone, what's up?

DOUGLASS: I have to see a few clients in the morning. Why people wait to the last minute to file. . . . You could tell *Simone* you had a gig. . . . Thought maybe we could go somewhere . . .

WENDAL: Will you shut up for a minute?

DOUGLASS: What did I say?

SIMONE: Touchy. Touchy.

WENDAL: Nothing . . . I just . . .

DOUGLASS: Let me fix you a drink.

WENDAL: How about a beer?

DOUGLASS and SIMONE (*both exit to get a beer*): Ok.

WENDAL: But I can get it.

SIMONE: That's ok.

DOUGLASS (*off*): You want something to eat? You've lost weight.

SIMONE (*off*): Dwayne called but it was a strange message. He said your father said to call your mother but not to tell your mother . . . something like that. You see the doctor before you left on Friday? Did they find out what's wrong with you?

DOUGLASS: I cooked. The roast would melt in your mouth.

SIMONE: I tried a new recipe, but I took pity on you and threw it out.

DOUGLASS: You sure I can't tempt you?

WENDAL (*irritated*): No.

DOUGLASS (*entering, hands him a beer*): It was just a simple question?

SIMONE (*entering*): No?

WENDAL: They want to run some more tests.

SIMONE: Sorry, we're out of beer.

WENDAL: That's ok.

SIMONE: More tests?

WENDAL: What's with the silent treatment? You know how I feel about her. And you're the one that said it was just a good time. . . . And for seven years, we've been having a real swell time, haven't we? . . . You ever get the seven-year itch Douglass?

SIMONE: You telling me everything?

WENDAL (*sharply*): You think I'm lying?

SIMONE: Is that a challenge or an answer?

WENDAL: No.

DOUGLASS: You could have spared me this dark mood you're in. . . . Why don't you take it on home to Simone.

SIMONE (*snuggling*): I'm glad you're home. I missed you.

WENDAL: I needed to talk to you.

DOUGLASS: My back's been bothering me again. Will you do my shoulders? (WENDAL *massages his shoulders.*)

WENDAL: How's that?

DOUGLASS: Good. You really ought to go in business. (DOUGLASS moans with pleasure.)

WENDAL: You wanna hear a joke?

SIMONE: My sister may stay with us for a few days. That husband of hers is acting up again.

DOUGLASS: Not particularly.

WENDAL: What's the differences between a black man and a fag.

DOUGLASS: I can hardly wait for this punch line.

SIMONE: I don't know why she doesn't leave him. I keep telling her she can do better.

WENDAL: One doesn't have to tell his mother. (*Laughs, seeing* DOUGLASS *didn't get it.*) You don't get it?

SIMONE: I have another surprise for you. (*Dramatically opens her robe, revealing a sexy nightgown.*) Voilà! (*In a Dracula voice, she parades around him.*) I want to make love to you my sweet.

WENDAL: Be still my heart.

DOUGLASS: Wendal?

SIMONE (*in the same Dracula voice*): Your heart can be still, but I was hoping something else would get to moving. (*Continues to parade around and tease him.*)

WENDAL: What am I going to do with you?

DOUGLASS: Now can we talk about something else? I can make reservations . . .

SIMONE: I can think of something my sweet.

WENDAL: See, my mother is not the only one I have to tell. I'm trying to tell you. . . .

DOUGLASS: Tell me what Wendal?

SIMONE: Tell me.

WENDAL: What?

SIMONE: Go 'head tell me. When were you planning to ask me? The answer is yes, yes, yes, yes.

WENDAL: I don't think we should see each other anymore. At least . . . not like . . . you know what I mean . . .

DOUGLASS: No, I don't know what you mean.

SIMONE: I found it. You know. . . .

WENDAL: Don't be dense.

DOUGLASS: Well, talk English.

SIMONE: I wasn't snooping, not exactly. I was just straightening out your nightstand and I just happened across. . . .

DOUGLASS (*pause*): I knew this day was coming. Trust you to be creative in breaking the news. Fag jokes, no less. So, you decided to marry her, huh?

SIMONE: It's a tad expensive, but I'm sure it's really beautiful. (*Hugs him.*) I love you so much. All weekend I've been on cloud nine. When were you going to ask me?

WENDAL: Marry? I got AIDS Douglass.

SIMONE: When?

WENDAL: Well, this certainly wasn't what I had in mind.

DOUGLASS: Where did I put that brochure?

WENDAL: I can't believe you went rummaging through my things.

DOUGLASS: I figured we could go to that same place . . . maybe even get the same room. . . . Now, where did I put it?

WENDAL: What?

SIMONE: I wasn't rummaging . . . I was looking for a number . . . this ring, it's on layaway for me, isn't it?

WENDAL: Who else?

DOUGLASS (*looking somewhat frantically for the brochure*): Remember how we jumped on that bed so it would look like you slept in it. . . .

WENDAL: We broke it. But Douglass what's that got to do . . .

SIMONE: I know it was supposed to be a surprise. If you want, I'll be surprised again . . . over and over again. . . .

DOUGLASS: I felt like a kid again. The maid, what was her name again?

WENDAL: Why do you always have to push?

SIMONE (*annoyed*): 'Cause somebody needs to jump-start your ass.

DOUGLASS: What was her name?

WENDAL: I don't know Douglass . . . I'm really not in a mood for a trip down memory lane. . . . Didn't you hear what I said? I tested positive . . .

SIMONE: You're right, maybe I am pushing. I just don't understand this. What's happening to us Wendal?

DOUGLASS: She was a doll. I think she knew. I'm sure she knew. Two black men traveling alone together . . .

SIMONE: I live with you. I sleep with you. I used to make love with you, at least until you started shutting me out.

DOUGLASS: "You boys sure know how to mess up a room. Look like you been riding the devil in here."

SIMONE: I moved in here because that's what you said you wanted . . .

WENDAL: Douglass . . .

DOUGLASS: Jasmine. That was her name. Jasmine.

WENDAL: It was what you wanted.

SIMONE: I thought it was what we both wanted. I've tried not to push, tried like hell but you always knew I wanted more . . . I never made that a secret . . . I have no desire to be somebody's trial wife or trial roommate or trial nothing . . . understand? It's either shit or get off the pot baby.

DOUGLASS (*finding the brochure, crosses to* WENDAL *with it*): Here it is. I found it.

WENDAL: I can't. I'm sorry . . .

SIMONE: I'm sure there's some humor in this somewhere.

WENDAL: This virus is kicking my ass Douglass . . . I guess it's a test of my faith . . . I know death is a part of life . . .

SIMONE: Can't you at least be a little more original? You're sorry. That's all you can say is you're sorry.

DOUGLASS: When'd you find out?

WENDAL: A couple days ago.

SIMONE: I don't believe you. Why did you buy the ring in the first place?

DOUGLASS: And you're just now telling me?

WENDAL: You have to believe me. I wanted things to work. I love you. I wanted you to be my wife. With you I thought I had a future.

DOUGLASS: I don't believe you.

SIMONE: Past tense?

WENDAL: No. But you're the one who set the rules, way in the beginning. No strings, no commitment.

SIMONE: I want a commitment.

WENDAL: Me too. But everything has changed.

DOUGLASS: This can't be happening.

WENDAL: I knew I had to tell you and I'm still trying to find the right words to tell Simone . . .

DOUGLASS: Well, you didn't seem to have any problem finding the right words to tell me . . .

SIMONE: Prove it.

WENDAL: She has no idea.

SIMONE: I said prove it. Make love to me.

WENDAL: I'm scared, real scared Douglass.

SIMONE: I need you.

WENDAL: I need you too. (SIMONE *starts to undress him.* DOUGLASS *slowly tears the brochure into little pieces.*)

DOUGLASS: You know I'm not sick. I've been gaining weight. Just this morning Beth told me I was getting fat.

WENDAL: I can't do that to you.

DOUGLASS: You think I gave you this shit, don't you?

WENDAL: I just want to settle down.

DOUGLASS: You think it was me?

SIMONE: You are my best friend.

WENDAL: You know you're my best friend.

DOUGLASS: Don't use that word. I am your lover!

WENDAL: I need a friend.

DOUGLASS: And I didn't give it to you.

WENDAL: Right now Douglass that's the least of my worries. It really doesn't matter . . .

SIMONE: I'm not letting go.

DOUGLASS: It most certainly does matter.

SIMONE: I can't let go. Hold me Wendal.

WENDAL: Simone, baby don't. I can't. (WENDAL *and* SIMONE *kiss deeply.*)

DOUGLASS: I trusted you.

WENDAL: God, give me strength. I'm . . . so scared. . . .

DOUGLASS: I trusted you.

WENDAL: That goes both ways.

DOUGLASS: I'm the one with the family . . .

SIMONE: I want to be your family. (*He struggles, they struggle, but ultimately need and passion win out.* WENDAL *and* SIMONE *lie back on the bed or floor.*)

DOUGLASS: We were careful . . . (*Softer to himself.*) We were, weren't we Wendal? (*Lights shift to* SIMONE *and* WENDAL *in bed. At lights,* SIMONE *is sitting in bed, clutching the sheet for protection, for comfort.* WENDAL *is smoking a cigarette. Neither looks at the other. Silence for a moment, clearly they're both in pain, however* SIMONE's *pain is more obvious in its physical expression.*)

SIMONE: I wanted you so bad . . . I've been waiting weeks . . . for this? You've never . . .

WENDAL (*reaching to touch her*): Simone, I . . .

SIMONE (*recoils at his touch*): There's this little boy in my class— Raymond. I don't know if you remember him. He stutters, so he's real shy. The kids make fun of him, even the teacher loses patience, but every time I see him I just want to take him in my arms and hold him, protect him because I know no one sticks around too long with somebody who can't communicate. Not enough love in the world that can withstand that kind of stinginess, that kind of terror. You hear what I'm saying Wendal? The teacher says I'm not helping him by not making him speak, but the real message always seems to come through when the words are moved out of the way . . . don't you think? Like now, how I heard you, for the first time loud and clear . . . it's been good Wendal, but I can do better. You know what I'm saying? . . . I can do better with someone, someone who cares, at least even tries to stutter. (*Waits, no response.*) Hope you can get your money back on the ring. (*She exits while we watch* WENDAL *come to grips with what has just happened.*)

WENDAL (*to himself*): What have I done? Simone, forgive me. (*Lights shift to* WENDAL *in hospital. Hospital intercom sound.* WENDAL *is hooked up to IV and oxygen. As much as his strength allows, he's having a full-fledged tantrum, knocking things off his bed table, pushing intercom buttons.*) I'm sick of this. Wendal you getting out of here today. Where's the fucking nurse? (*Into the bedside intercom.*) Will one of you devil's angels get in here and get this shit out of my arm? I want out of this fucking hell hole.

NURSE'S VOICE: Mr. Bailey, now we've been through this before. Relax. You're not well enough to be discharged . . . just relax, the doctor is on her way . . .

WENDAL (*pulls the cannula out*): I don't want to see the fucking doctor, I want my fucking clothes. (DOCTOR *enters.*)

DOCTOR (*firmly*): WENDAL STOP. RIGHT NOW.

NURSE'S VOICE: Mr. Bailey, do you want a shot? (WENDAL *collapses in the bed.*) Mr. Bailey. . . . Do you need something to relax you?

DOCTOR (*into intercom*): It's ok nurse. It's Dr. Weinberg. (*To* WENDAL *as she readjusts the cannula.*) I see we're in a good mood today. (*No response.*) Such a charming patient. . . . It does my heart good to see you every day.

WENDAL: I wish I could say the same. (DOCTOR *laughs.*) It doesn't take much to get you people to laugh, does it?

DOCTOR: Wendal, I do believe you're getting better . . .

WENDAL: I bet you say that to all the guys . . .

DOCTOR: Try and have a little more patience . . . (*Takes a jazz music cassette out of her pocket.*) I'll just leave this right here.

WENDAL (*brightening considerably*): You got it?

DOCTOR: Yes.

WENDAL: You didn't have to do that Doc.

DOCTOR: I know. But music has a way of soothing the soul, making one more patient, a little less likely to throw things around a room, don't you think? . . .

WENDAL: Just tired Doc, that's all. Soon's I think things are getting better, ya'll find something else . . . tired of these tubes and I'm real tired of them nurses talking to me like I'm two. I hate feeling so . . . (*Pause.*) I don't know . . .

DOCTOR (*touches him*): You'll be out of here soon, after we isolate what's causing this recent bout of diarrhea. Until then, give the room and the nurses a break. Ok? (WENDAL *nods yes.*) Have you told anyone you're in here? What about your family? (DOUGLASS *appears laden with gifts.*)

WENDAL: I told him.

DOUGLASS (*whispering*): I brought you a few things. Some flowers. I thought you might want some candy . . . a Bible . . . I won't stay long. I have to pick up Alison from school.

DOCTOR: Sir, this is a hospital, not a mausoleum. You can speak up.

WENDAL (*to* DOUGLASS): Fuck you.

DOCTOR: Right now, Wendal, I don't think you're able. (*Laughs loudly, no response from* WENDAL *or* DOUGLASS.) Well, it was just a little doctor humor. (*Extends her hand to* DOUGLASS.) Hi, I'm Dr. Weinberg.

DOUGLASS (*hesitates, not sure if he should reveal his name*): Dennis . . . Dennis Smith.

DOCTOR: Smith did you say? We see a lot of Smiths in here. I was beginning to wonder if our buddy here had any friends. Well, good to meet you Dennis. (*To* WENDAL.) Check on you later Wendal. (*Exits.*)

WENDAL: Dennis? Dennis Smith? You couldn't be a little more creative, like Dennis "Coward."

DOUGLASS: I would've come sooner. I just came by to tell you I was negative.

WENDAL: Haven't seen you in weeks . . . and the only reason you here now is to deliver me a Bible and a bulletin about you being negative. Well, who cares?

DOUGLASS: Maybe I shouldn't have come.

WENDAL: Bingo. So, you're negative. Maybe your antibodies are a little on the slow side.

DOUGLASS: Just came by to see how you were doing.

WENDAL: Now you've seen.

DOUGLASS: Where's Simone?

WENDAL: It's over.

DOUGLASS: Is she . . . Is she ok?

WENDAL: Haven't heard from her.

DOUGLASS: I mean . . . you know . . . does she know?

WENDAL: We all know what we want to know.

DOUGLASS: But . . .

WENDAL (*defensive*): But nothing. Now if you came in here to inquire about Simone I suggest you . . . (WENDAL *gags, spits up in pain.*)

DOUGLASS (*wiping his brow*): I'm sorry. I didn't mean to get you so upset.

WENDAL: You tell Beth? (*No response, pause.*) I didn't think so. So what's all that?

DOUGLASS: I stopped by the bookstore, picked up some books for you. I know how much you like to read and I thought . . .

WENDAL (*reading one of the titles*): *When Bad Things Happen to Good People* . . .

DOUGLASS: See, I think Wendal the secret is thinking positively. . . . You really got to change your attitude . . . meet this head on . . . that's how my father beat cancer . . . he never gave up . . .

WENDAL (*irritated*): And where is he now? Six feet under, still thinking positive. Don't bring that shit in here. I don't get it. Everybody talking 'bout positive attitude, like people ain't still dying. What the fuck is wrong with you people? Guess if you die it's 'cause you didn't have enough positive attitude. Well I'll grin all day long but the bottom line is I'm still gon' die. And if I wanna be pissy about it along the way, that's my right.

So why don't you take that jolly attitude shit down to the morgue, maybe they can use your ass down there.

DOUGLASS: I'd say something if I could think of something redeeming . . .

WENDAL (*suddenly starts thrashing with his feet and moaning*): Shit . . . dammit . . .

DOUGLASS: What's wrong?

WENDAL: My feet. Shit. Goddamn! (DOUGLASS *removes the covers, for a moment is taken aback by the sight, but then starts to massage* WENDAL's *feet.*) They hurt so bad sometimes, other times I can't feel them at all. Look like little ape feet, don't they? Done turned blue black. Think I'm dying from the bottom up. That feels good. It's nice to be touched with a hand instead of rubber gloves. (*A beat.*) I need a favor. Can you buy me a train ticket?

DOUGLASS: A what?

WENDAL: I'm going home, to my parents' home. If I'm going to beat this thing . . .

DOUGLASS: That's it. Now you're talking. . . . You got to fight Wendal . . .

WENDAL: I believe I could get stronger at home . . . Mama would feed the fight back in me and my father, well . . . he don't take no for an answer . . . (BAILEY *appears either through the audience or on the other side of the stage. He is dressed in one of the suits we saw earlier. He has some yellow pad papers in his hands. He delivers the following to the audience. For the following exchange,* WENDAL *and* BAILEY's *speeches overlap on line end words. Light focuses tighter on just* WENDAL.)

BAILEY: Fathers, men, you have to take up time with these here boys. If they don't turn out right you don't have nobody to blame but yourselves.

WENDAL: I want to take the train.

BAILEY: I took my son on a train ride once . . .

WENDAL: When I was a kid, I loved the train. My father took me once to Mississippi on it . . .

BAILEY: I was born in Mississippi. All my people's from there . . .

WENDAL: We were going to see his folks . . .

BAILEY: That was when my mother and father was still living . . .

WENDAL: Just the two of us. Junior stayed home with Mama . . .

BAILEY: It was just me and him . . .

WENDAL: I can't tell you how much I loved having him all to myself.

BAILEY: It was our time. Wendal needed to come to some understanding . . .

WENDAL: Everybody knew him. I was so proud of him . . .

BAILEY: To know my roots, if you will. You see he was spoiled, not by me . . .

WENDAL: Let me eat, drink as much pop as I wanted . . .

BAILEY: His Mama. . . . The two of them was some kind of special together . . .

WENDAL: He was so excited, showed me every sight along the way, wouldn't even let me sleep . . .

BAILEY: You kids have it easy. I wanted Wendal to see what hard work was about . . .

WENDAL: Soon's I'd drift off, he'd wake me up and say, look Wendal. Look at that Wendal . . .

BAILEY: You see I love my son, both my sons . . .

WENDAL: Sometimes it wouldn't be nothing but a field . . .

BAILEY: They and their Mama is what I works hard for. . . . See, I didn't really want him working at the store. Wendal was special, different from Junior. That boy, from day one, was destined for bigger things . . . you could see it in his eyes . . . by the time Wendal was in grade school, shoot, he was reading better than me . . . I just knew he'd be an astronaut or some kind of scientist . . .

WENDAL: I don't think he ever thought I'd amount to anything. Now I gotta tell him this . . .

BAILEY: Fathers have to set an example for their children, 'specially them boys. . . . My father was everything to me . . .

WENDAL: Wish I'd told him how much I enjoyed myself. . . . Soon's we got there, I started crying, told him I wanted to go home and never go back . . .

BAILEY: He had so much fun when it was time to leave, he told me naw, he was staying. Ain't that something? (*Folds up the paper.*)

It was our time. (*Walking off.*) I'll have to ask Wendal one day if he remembers when we took the train that time . . . (*Blackout on* BAILEY. *Broad lights on hospital scene.*)

DOUGLASS: You're tired. I'll get you that train ticket.

WENDAL: Thank you. (*Closes his eyes.*) They're waiting on me.

DOUGLASS: Who?

WENDAL: My family. (*Lights to* BAILEY *household.* BAILEY *and* JUNIOR *enter laughing loudly.*)

DWAYNE (*hugging him; immediately works at monopolizing* JUNIOR'S *attention*): Uncle Luke.

JUNIOR: Boy, you ain't nothing but a bean sprouting. Look at this head. Ouch!

REBA (*overlapping*): Junior.

BAILEY: Don't he look good, Reba? A sergeant.

REBA: Yes indeed.

JUNIOR: Where's Wendal, Mama?

REBA: He's not here . . . not yet.

BAILEY (*irritated*): Reba.

REBA: Don't Reba me, Luke Bailey.

DWAYNE: He's coming. He promised this time.

BAILEY: (*to* JUNIOR): That brother of yours did it again. Called weeks ago making his empty promises, he's coming home and gets your mother all upset . . .

JUNIOR: Whoa, I didn't mean to start another world war.

REBA: You oughta stop acting like you don't get disappointed too. Every time that phone ring, you jumping.

JUNIOR: So, is he coming?

REBA: He said he was. It'll be so good to have both of you home.

JUNIOR: Well, I got presents for everybody.

BAILEY: Oh, you didn't have to do that.

JUNIOR: (*overlapping*): I didn't have time to wrap anything. This is for you Mama. (*Gives her a small box.*)

REBA: Oh Junior, you shouldn't have. I . . . I . . . You didn't have to buy me . . .

JUNIOR: Mama, before you start, I know I didn't have to, b
'bout saving us a little time and taking the present a
(*Retrieves a windbreaker for* DWAYNE.) See if it fits little
Mama, you can open the box now.

REBA: Ok, ok. (*Takes out a bracelet.*) Oh Junior. It's beautiful.

JUNIOR: Put it on.

REBA: I' try it on but I have to put this up for safe keeping.

JUNIOR: Mama, I didn't buy it for you to keep it in a box under the bed.

REBA: Well, maybe I'll wear it to church . . .

JUNIOR: Why don't you wear it tonight so I can see it on you.

BAILEY: You know your Mama ain't gon' change. Under our bed
still look like a department store, don't throw nothing away.
Thirty years I been buying for this woman and she still act like
she ain't never had nothing.

REBA: Ya'll can laugh if you want, but I appreciate everything I get in
this life. Ain't nothing promised. . . . When you been poor . . .

JUNIOR: Before you start preaching Mama, what you cook?

REBA (*laughs in spite of herself*): Ok boy.

DWAYNE. Thanks man. (*Tries it on.*) It fits.

REBA: That's nice. The color really suits him. This boy gets more
handsome by the day. Don't he put you in mind of Wendal
when he was this age?

BAILEY: I don't see it myself. Um . . . Junior, son, it don't seem like
you brought enough clothes. Is that all you brought what's in
that bag? You know, this time of year the weather can be
tricky.

JUNIOR: I'm set. Got plenty of clothes Dad.

BAILEY: Oh I see. Just didn't look like much in that bag.

JUNIOR: Yeah, I got something in there for Wendal and Auntie May,
too. (*Deliberately teasing* BAILEY, *stretches out, loosens his clothes.*)
Dad, you got any beer? (REBA *and* DWAYNE *look over at* BAILEY
who is making a big deal about hiding his disappointment.)

BAILEY: What ya'll looking at me like that for?

JUNIOR (*laughs*): Old man, you know I got you something.

BAILEY: Well, it wasn't like I was looking for something. . . . You k
don't put much store in getting presents. It ain't even Chr

JUNIOR: Here. (*Hands him a box.*) Try this on for size.

BAILEY: What is it?

JUNIOR: Open it up and see.

BAILEY: (*opens the box*): A watch.

JUNIOR: A watch that ain't cheap. It's got an alarm and the date. . . .

BAILEY: Is this diamond real?

JUNIOR: They told me it was.

BAILEY: Look Reba.

DWAYNE: Boy, that's sharp.

REBA: It sure is. Junior, you shouldn't spend all your money on us like this.

JUNIOR: Always make some more money Mama. They ain't nothing much.

BAILEY: Good-bye Timex! Ain't gon' be able to hit me in the butt with a red apple.

JUNIOR: I'm glad you like it Dad.

REBA: What you get your brother?

JUNIOR: A chain and I got this box of candy for Auntie May.

BAILEY: That's one thing Maybelle don't need is candy. Anybody wanna know what time it is?

DWAYNE: Three o'clock.

BAILEY: Who asked the question Dwayne?

JUNIOR (*noticing the plaque for Bailey*): What's this?

BAILEY: Oh just something else I got from them boys.

REBA: Your father won . . .

BAILEY: It was no big thing, you know something like being, oh I don't know . . . father of the year . . . no big thing.

JUNIOR: That's great Dad.

REBA: He had to give a speech.

JUNIOR: You did? I bet you got a standing ovation.

BAILEY: Naw, but they clapped real hard. Reba tell him.

REBA: Tell him what Bailey?

DWAYNE: And they was hooting. (*Starts making a hooting sound.*)

BAILEY: You know, about my speech.

REBA: Bailey, you can tell him. (*Moving to the phone.*) Let me call Maybelle. She'll be sick if she ain't included. (*Starts to dial.*)

JUNIOR (*overlapping*): Maybe I'll go down there while I'm here . . . shoot some hoops. Me and Wendal used to practically live down there.

BAILEY (*overlapping, looking for a beer in the refrigerator.*): It ain't changed much. Different boys, same stink, but I'll take you down there. You'd be a good example to them boys. You know, while you're here I want you to help me finish some cabinets . . . (*Fade to hospital waiting area.* WENDAL *is sitting, looks around hopefully, yet impatiently, clearly he's been waiting for a while. Next to him is his suitcase and his sax case. There's something pitiful about the change in him, the weakness, the unsteady deliberation.*)

DOUGLASS (*enters*): What are you doing in here? I went to your room first. Am I late?

WENDAL: Yes.

DOUGLASS: You said noon. It's only a few minutes after.

NURSE (*enters*): Here's your medicine Mr. Bailey.

DOUGLASS: Why don't you just send him home with the whole pharmacy?

NURSE: I'll be back in a few minutes with your wheelchair.

WENDAL: Not necessary.

NURSE: Hospital rules. (*She exits.*)

DOUGLASS: I don't know why you insist on boarding a train today. You sure this trip is ok with your doctor?

WENDAL: Yes Douglass.

DOUGLASS: I wish you wouldn't go until you're feeling stronger.

WENDAL: I'm going Douglass.

DOUGLASS: I can get you a hotel room for a few days . . .

WENDAL: Douglass I'm going. I can't wait. Few home-cooked meals, my family, be good as new.

DOUGLASS: Maybe you're expecting too much Wendal.

WENDAL: I have to.

DOUGLASS: Just don't want to see you hurt . . . (WENDAL *laughs.*) What's so funny?

WENDAL: AIDS done already hurt my feelings Douglass. I don't know how much more hurt I can get. (*Pause.*) Appreciate you taking care of things . . . figure you ain't such a bad guy, outside of my family, you the longest relationship I've had . . . that oughtta count for something . . . (*Hugs him.*)

DOUGLASS: Hey, I hope you aren't getting sentimental on me. I'm trying my damnest to be butch here. (*They both laugh a moment while they grapple with the loss.*) And look at you, you got your shirt buttoned all wrong. (*Re-buttons his shirt.*)

WENDAL: Thought it looked funny. You know, you'd make somebody a good husband.

DOUGLASS: Real cute. (*Finishing the buttoning.*) There. (*Pause.*) I may never see you again.

WENDAL: Don't.

DOUGLASS: Don't what?

WENDAL: Come on let's get out of here. I don't need a wheelchair. (WENDAL *picks up the suitcase.*)

DOUGLASS: Don't try to lift that. I can get it.

WENDAL: I can get it.

DOUGLASS: I said I would get it.

WENDAL: I'm not helpless Douglass.

DOUGLASS (*they struggle*): Would you let me carry the damn suitcase?!!!

WENDAL: Yeah, I'll let you carry it and I love you too. (*A moment as they both struggle with the loss, regrouping, teasing.*) Just psyching you out. Carry the damn thing so I can strut out of here looking like my old fine cute self. Who knows, somebody may look my way, give me a little play . . .

DOUGLASS (*laughing with him*): Nigger please, not hardly . . .

NURSE (*rolling the wheelchair*): Time to go home Mr. Bailey.

DOUGLASS (*helping* WENDAL *in the chair*): That's right Mr. Bailey, time for you to go home. (*They exit.*)

(*End of Act One*)

Act Two

(*Lights up on Bailey household.* WENDAL, JUNIOR *and* DWAYNE *are in the kitchen preparing dinner.* REBA, MAYBELLE *and* BAILEY *are in the living room;* REBA *is dressed in her gifts, the red dress, the bracelet.*)

REBA: I feel so useless. You all don't need any help in there?

DWAYNE, WENDAL and JUNIOR (*off, in unison*): No.

WENDAL (*off*): That's the third time Mama.

MAYBELLE: It sure is good to have them home. And they got the place looking so good.

REBA: They got most of the upstairs painted and they supposed to paint in here before Junior leave out.

BAILEY (*mumbling*): I still got them cabinets down at the store I want done.

MAYBELLE (*overlapping*): Wendal helping out too?

REBA: Oh yeah.

MAYBELLE: He don't look too well to me.

REBA: Trying to fatten him up a little.

BAILEY: He look OK. Don't you all start borrowing trouble with all that fussing over him. (DWAYNE *enters, starts setting the table.*)

MAYBELLE (*to* DWAYNE): How's it going in there? (*To* REBA *and* BAILEY.) Whatever they cooking, I hope we gon' be able to eat it. (*To* DWAYNE.) Honey, do it look edible?

DWAYNE: I don't know. It look OK.

BAILEY: Junior's a pretty good cook. It's Wendal ain't never learned his way 'round a kitchen.

REBA: Father like son.

MAYBELLE (*laughs*): You got that right. She got you there Bailey.

BAILEY: I can cook. Reba know I can cook, she just don't let me.

REBA: Bailey please. (DWAYNE *moves* MAYBELLE*'s purse on the floor,* MAYBELLE *screeches.*)

MAYBELLE: Un-Un. Un-Un child. Don't put my purse on that floor. That's bad luck. Put a woman's purse on the floor and she'll never have any money.

DWAYNE: Sorry.

MAYBELLE: Just hand it here. (DWAYNE *hands her her purse.*)

BAILEY: I don't know why you clutching that purse so, you know you ain't got nothing but a dollar in it. All your money if you got any is up between them bosoms.

REBA: Bailey!

BAILEY: Why you Baileying me. I ain't never seen Maybelle pull money from no purse. Maybelle need money she going between them pillows up there.

MAYBELLE: I got my money where I know it's safe. You just jealous. Some fool steal your wallet, you's a man without a dime. Somebody steal my purse, (*cups her breasts*) I'm still loaded.

REBA (*laughs out loud*): Now that's the truth.

MAYBELLE: And you oughtta be complimenting your wife on how nice she looks instead of worrying 'bout where I put my money. She look real sexy in that dress, don't she?

BAILEY: Little flashy, I think, for Reba.

WENDAL (*enters, has overheard the last comment*): I think she looks beautiful, real special tonight.

REBA: Well thank you son.

BAILEY (*defensive*): I didn't say she didn't look beautiful. (*To* REBA.) That bracelet Junior bought you, now it look nice with that dress. (*To* WENDAL.) Did you see the bracelet your brother bought your Mama?

WENDAL: No. (*Admires the bracelet.*) That's nice.

BAILEY: And he got me this watch. Did I show it you? It's got a real diamond.

WENDAL: Yeah. You showed it to me when I first got home.

BAILEY: And he got Dwayne a little jacket. Did you show your father your jacket Dwayne?

REBA: He can show him later Bailey.

BAILEY: Oh. OK. That's fine with me. Junior just bought us home such nice things . . . I just thought Wendal might like to see 'em.

DWAYNE: Daddy's buying me some skates.

BAILEY: I don't know nothing 'bout that.

WENDAL: (*his arm around* DWAYNE): That's because I'm buying 'em.

BAILEY: Oh.

JUNIOR (*enters with a big fork and spatula, deadpan serious*): We got a fire extinguisher?

REBA: What?

MAYBELLE: Lord. Lord. I knew I should have eaten before I left home.

JUNIOR: Wendal kinda set fire to the chicken.

WENDAL (*laughing*): Quit lying on me man. (BAILEY *realizes* JUNIOR's *kidding, starts to laugh.*)

JUNIOR (*laughing out hilariously*): And the potatoes . . .

BAILEY: I ain't surprised.

WENDAL: Man stop . . .

JUNIOR: And the pot holder . . . the kitchen curtains . . .

WENDAL: He's lying Mama. He's lying . . .

REBA (*getting up, on her way to the kitchen*): What have you all done to my kitchen?

JUNIOR (*stopping her*): I'm kidding. I'm kidding. Everything's cool.

REBA: Get out of my way Junior. I don't know what made me take leave of my senses, letting ya'll cook.

JUNIOR: Come on Mama. I'm kidding. The kitchen still in one piece. This your party, you shouldn't have to cook. All you supposed to do is sit right down here and enjoy this masterpiece or burnt pieces your two sons and grandson have concocted. Wendal's specialty this evening is a la crisp.

WENDAL: OK man.

MAYBELLE: That's OK. Wendal's a star. He ain't meant to do common labor, ain't that right baby? (*Kisses him.*)

WENDAL: Yeah. That's right. Thank you Aunt May.

BAILEY *and* JUNIOR: Shit.

MAYBELLE: So, what's the entertainment this evening? I know you and Junior gon' sing.

JUNIOR: Well . . .

REBA: Maybe you can play something on your horn for us.

BAILEY: That horn'll wake up the whole neighborhood this time of night . . .

MAYBELLE: Ya'll come on and sing a song, sing the song that used to make me wanna holler. Ya'll gon' do that for your Auntie May?

WENDAL: Well, I don't know. My throat's been bothering me.

BAILEY: I thought that's how you made your living boy. How you gon' work playing music when you complaining about your throat bothering you?

REBA: Ya'll sing a little bit. It would do me good to hear ya'll sing together.

MAYBELLE: It'll do me good too.

JUNIOR: OK. How 'bout it man?

WENDAL: OK.

JUNIOR: What's the song Auntie May?

WENDAL: Start us off.

MAYBELLE: OK, I'll help you out. (MAYBELLE *starts humming a blues song such as "Kiddeo."* WENDAL *joins in and takes the lead.* JUNIOR *accompanies, then everybody joins in. Bailey gets up and starts dancing a wild exaggerated dance, maybe the funky chicken.*)

REBA: Go on Bailey. Go on now . . .

BAILEY: Come on Maybelle. Come on here.

MAYBELLE (*getting up and dancing with him*): What are you doing Luke Bailey? You better sit down before I embarrass you. You know you can't keep up with a young woman like me. Come on and dance with me Junior.

BAILEY (*dancing with* DWAYNE) Come on boy. (WENDAL *dances with his mother; clearly everybody is enjoying themselves;* MAYBELLE *becomes winded from* JUNIOR *spinning her around, sits down exhausted.*)

MAYBELLE: Oh Lordy . . . ooh . . .

BAILEY: What's wrong Maybelle, you can't keep up with the old man? I thought you was gon' embarrass somebody this evening.

MAYBELLE: I know when to stop making a fool of myself, something you oughtta learn Luke Bailey. You know you ain't gon' be able to move in the morning.

JUNIOR: I ain't sang that in years.

MAYBELLE: It still sound good.

JUNIOR (*to* WENDAL): Man, I see you ain't lost your touch. Still know how to croon.

BAILEY: Yeah, sound pretty good if I say so myself.

WENDAL (*surprised, pleasantly*): Thanks Dad.

BAILEY: Yeah, sound damn good. Never said you didn't have a voice. You know we having this program down at the Center on the twenty-first. Maybe you can sing at it. People down there always asking me 'bout you, wanting to know when you gon' make a record, you know how people are, wanna make you out more than you is. You don't have to answer me now, just think about it. . . . They may have me do another speech . . . I told you 'bout my speech . . .

JUNIOR: Man you been telling us 'bout that speech . . .

MAYBELLE: Yes Jesus!

WENDAL (*seeing that* BAILEY *looks a little hurt*): I'd like to hear you speak Dad. Never heard you before an audience. It can be tricky.

BAILEY: You got that right.

WENDAL: Let me know what you want me to sing.

JUNIOR: Well, what about me? Maybe I can do a little background. (*Starts doing some rifts; clearly carrying a tune is not* JUNIOR*'s strong point.*) Do wah do wah . . .

BAILEY (*cutting him off*): I want you to do a solo, it ain't gon' be but a few minutes . . .

REBA (*noticing how much* WENDAL *is sweating*): Wendal, you ok?

BAILEY: He's fine. Now Wendal . . .

WENDAL (*overlapping*): Fine Mama, just need a little water. Better change my shirt too. Be right back. (*He exits.*)

MAYBELLE: Oh Lord, look now how this knee done swole . . .

BAILEY: That knee ain't swole, that's just fat Maybelle! (*Falls out laughing.*)

JUNIOR: (*trying to conceal his laughter*): Nothing like a woman with a little flesh on her bones, though, ain't that right Auntie May?

MAYBELLE: That's right and I wanna thank you Junior. Your father eyesight just failing him. And you know what they say . . . every time a fat woman shakes, a skinny woman loses her home.

REBA: Please, don't you two get started.

MAYBELLE: I ain't getting nothing started. I feel too good this evening. My boys are home.

BAILEY: They's mens Maybelle, face it. You getting old.

MAYBELLE: They'll always be my boys. I don't make no difference between them and my own four.

WENDAL (*enters, he has changed his shirt*): How they doing?

MAYBELLE: Got 'em all married off. They, they wives' problems now. Speaking of wives, you and that child looking to get hooked up? What's her name again?

WENDAL: Simone.

MAYBELLE: Yeah. Pretty black thang.

WENDAL (*a little uncomfortable*): Well right now she's back there and I'm here. I just wanted to come home for a while. Didn't realize how much I missed everybody.

REBA: Well, we missed you too. Didn't we Bailey?

BAILEY: Yeah, I'm glad he's here. Now that you sleeping through the night again maybe I can finally get some decent shut-eye.

MAYBELLE: Yeah, Wendal, having you home does this house good. This place needed livening up. All Auntie May need now is a little sustenance. Junior, ain't there no cheese slices or bread sticks? Ain't seen no dinner party without no hor-de-derves.

WENDAL: Won't be long. (*Exits to the kitchen.*)

BAILEY (*overlapping*): Maybelle, you can't even pronounce the word.

MAYBELLE: Aw shut up Bailey.

JUNIOR (*overlapping*): You have to talk to Wendal. This his thang, I'm just following orders.

WENDAL (*enters with fancy folded napkins which he places on the table*): Everything's almost ready. We'll seat you now. (*With much formality,* WENDAL *seats his mother at the table,* JUNIOR *seats* MAYBELLE *while* DWAYNE *attempts to seat* BAILEY.)

BAILEY (*to* DWAYNE): I can manage my chair on my own, thank you.

WENDAL (*switches the forks around*): Table looks nice Dwayne.

MAYBELLE: Where you learn how to do all this?

WENDAL: I've done my share of waiting tables. First course: shrimp cocktail. (*Snaps his fingers in the air for* JUNIOR *and* DWAYNE *to follow him.*) Gentlemen, if you please . . .

JUNIOR (*grumbling good-naturedly as he exits*): Now Mr. Head Waiter, I didn't know you snapping your fingers at me was part of the deal. I don't see why we can't eat buffet style, should've set up a soup kitchen . . . (DWAYNE *and* JUNIOR *exit behind* WENDAL.)

MAYBELLE (*shaking her head*): Umph, that's not a good sign. Whenever the service is too fancy, the food ain't worth shit. I bet we gon' get one shrimp.

BAILEY: You lucky to have that. Now you eat everything else and you gon' eat what these boys done cooked with a smile on your face. Ain't that right?

MAYBELLE: Yes sir massa.

BAILEY: Think it's kinda nice they giving their Mama a break.

REBA: That's more life I've seen in Wendal since he been here. And I love to hear my boy sing.

BAILEY: Yeah. Kinda put me in mind of the old days. Every Saturday, remember how he used to put on them little shows for us . . . ?

REBA: Yeah.

MAYBELLE: And that sorry James Brown act ya'll used to do. I used to have to drag my boys over here so ya'll would have a little audience.

REBA: Honey, yeah, Bailey and that cape.

MAYBELLE: Wendal falling down to the ground squealing like a pig and there come Bailey trying to get on the good foot with that toilet paper roll. . . . 'Member that Bailey? How you'd drape Wendal? When you was younger you used to have a lot more spirit.

BAILEY: I still do. (*Getting excited.*) Maybe after dinner I'll see if Wendal still remember our little routine we used to do . . .

MAYBELLE: Oh Lord we gon' be subjected to that again. (REBA *suddenly reaches over and kisses* BAILEY.)

BAILEY: What's that for?

REBA: Nothing. I'm just so damn happy.

MAYBELLE: Reba, honey, did you say damn?

REBA: Yes. Damn. Damn. Damn. Damn happy!

JUNIOR (*enters carrying a covered platter, sets it down in the middle of the table*): Un Un Un. Don't touch. Wendal says no unveiling till he's present. Forgot how bossy he is. Been leading me around all day, shopping and practicing . . . made me read every label, on every can, on every aisle . . . took us three hours . . . three hours in somebody's grocery store . . . I'm 'bout to fall out and he's whistling Dixie . . .

WENDAL (*off*): Junior. Hey bro' . . .

JUNIOR: See? I got to get on back to the Army so I can get me some rest. (*He exits.*)

MAYBELLE: That boy know he love his brother. (*Reaches for the cover of the platter.*) Shoot. I need to prepare my stomach.

BAILEY (*smacks her hands*): Wendal wants us to wait so we gon' wait. (WENDAL *brings in another dish.*) Everything smells good son.

WENDAL: Hope it tastes good. I don't know if Junior read the recipes right. (*He exits.*)

MAYBELLE: Umph! Did you hear that? They got to read while they cook. Lord, maybe I got a candy bar in my purse.

BAILEY (*laughing*): I ain't got a candy bar but I got some peanuts in the basement. (*They all crack up laughing.*)

WENDAL (*enters*): What's so funny?

MAYBELLE and REBA: Nothing.

BAILEY (*overlapping*): Nothing son. Nothing. Just enjoying ourselves in here. (DWAYNE *comes out carrying a pot with sauce dripping, he's soiled the front of his shirt.* WENDAL *is behind him carrying
a casserole dish.*)

REBA: Dwayne you done spilled something on your shirt.

DWAYNE: Oh.

MAYBELLE: You have to be careful. Watch what you doing.

BAILEY: Leave the boy alone, it'll wash out.

WENDAL: I'll get him something.

REBA: Maybe you should've cooked in some old clothes.

JUNIOR (*enters with another dish*): Last one. Ready to dig in?

WENDAL (*enters with an apron, a frilly type*): No, remember, we're
serving 'em.

MAYBELLE: We getting served? Well can I make me a special order?

REBA: Maybelle.

WENDAL: Here Dwayne. Put on Mama's apron while you serve.
(*Ties apron around* DWAYNE.) There.

BAILEY: Now he looks like a little sissy faggot. (JUNIOR *laughs loud,
everybody snickers except* WENDAL *whose whole demeanor has changed.*)

REBA: I think he looks kinda cute.

WENDAL: I don't see anything funny.

DWAYNE (*with much disdain*): I don't look like no fag. (*Takes the
apron off.*)

WENDAL (*trying to control his rage*): What you say? (DWAYNE *looks
scared, knows his father is angry, is confused and embarrassed. Grabbing him.*) Answer me. I said what did you say?

DWAYNE (*slightly indignant*): I said I didn't look like no fag.

WENDAL: I don't ever want to hear you say something like that
again. You understand me?

BAILEY: I don't know why you jumping all over the boy. They call
theyselves that.

WENDAL: So! We call ourselves nigger, but that don't mean we are
one. You don't allow him to use that word in this house. Do

you? Go on Dwayne say nigger to your grandfather. Say nigger like you said fag. . . . Go on, say it . . .

BAILEY: Dwayne you bet not say one word . . .

WENDAL: Why the silence now? Dwayne, I told you . . .

REBA: I'd like to talk about something else, like this dinner . . .

JUNIOR: Yeah man, I don't know why you all upset, ain't nobody called you a fag. It was just a joke.

MAYBELLE: I sure am ready to eat this food.

WENDAL (*overlapping*): You'll never change. I guess it's just a joke you raising him like you tried to do me . . . with the same small-minded . . .

BAILEY: At least I'm raising him.

WENDAL: Is that what you call it?

REBA: Wendal!

JUNIOR: Whoa! You need to back up man. (JUNIOR *sits at the table.*) Come on. Everybody let's eat.

BAILEY (*angry*): I don't know why in the Sam hell you come home. You ain't satisfied unless you upsetting everybody. Gotta defy me no matter what. Thank God I got me one son that's got some sense, but you, you wanna ram that crazy shit down my damn throat every time I turn around, well who needs it? This is my house . . . you hear me? Mine. And the door swings both ways. If you don't like it Mister, then let the door hit you where the good Lord split you. You can take your narrow ass back where . . .

REBA: Bailey! That's enough.

DWAYNE: I'm sorry Dad. I didn't mean to make you mad.

WENDAL: I'm not mad at you Dwayne.

DWAYNE: You not getting ready to leave again, are you?

REBA: No. Your Dad is gon' be right here. Now everybody let's eat. We letting the food get cold. (*Puts on the apron, starts serving, in silence everybody passes food.*) Dwayne sit down. (DWAYNE *hesitates, looks at his father expectantly.*) I said sit down Dwayne. (DWAYNE *takes his seat at the table.*) What part of the chicken you want Bailey?

BAILEY (*still angry*): I don't care.

JUNIOR: Old man, you better care. Me and Wendal went through a lot of trouble. Ain't that right Bro? Wendal had me inspecting every chicken in the store.

MAYBELLE: Wendal, baby you and Junior done cooked a feast here. Yes Lord! I may have to hurt myself.

REBA (*looks up at* WENDAL *who's still standing away from the table*): Wendal?

WENDAL (*looks at all of them for a moment, hesitates*): Sorry Mama. I think I lost my appetite. (WENDAL *exits. Lights. Later on that night.* WENDAL *comes downstairs. He's sick. With much effort, he moves to the kitchen and gets ice water from the refrigerator. Takes his medicine, moves back to the living room.* REBA *enters wearing a robe.* WENDAL *quickly hides the medicine.*)

REBA: I didn't know anyone was down here. You feeling any better?

WENDAL: A little.

REBA: How 'bout some ginger ale? I don't know why, I just woke up and had a taste for some pop. You want some?

WENDAL: No.

REBA: Sorry everything didn't work out like you planned this evening. (*Pause.*) Everything was going fine. Why'd you have to fight with him?

WENDAL (*moving to the couch*): Why don't you ask him that question?

REBA (*walking around the room*): I'm glad you and Junior gon' paint in here. I'm a help. Since you all been here I feel kinda useful again. Lately, I seem to have a lot of time on my hands. Sometimes I catch myself sitting all day right there on that couch and Lord this house can get so quiet. With Dwayne not needing me as much . . . don't get me wrong, I'm not complaining. He's got a mind of his own, just like you did. Scares your father. Sometimes a father can't see his son for his own failings. You ever think about that?

WENDAL: Oh Mama. Why do you always defend him?

REBA (*as if she didn't hear him*): Oh me and Maybelle go but sometimes I think about what if . . . what if something happened to your father . . . he never wanted me to work. I ain't never been nothing but somebody's mother. And today I wondered if I had even been good at that. (WENDAL *looks at her directly and she at him.*) I defend him for the same reason I defend you . . . because you both a part of me. Now why don't you tell Mama what's bothering you. I let it go for a week but something's eating you alive, I saw it when you first walked through that door.

WENDAL: Nothing.

REBA (*firmly*): I asked you a question. Don't let me have to ask you twice.

WENDAL: I haven't been well Mama. Been a little under the weather.

REBA (*relieved*): Well, we'll just have to get you better. It's probably one of them flu bugs going around . . .

WENDAL: It's not that simple.

REBA: I'll make an appointment the first thing in the morning with Dr. Miller and . . .

WENDAL: Has he ever treated an AIDS patient?

REBA (*not registering*): Oh, he's treated all kinds of things. (*What he said sinking in.*) A what?

WENDAL: I have AIDS Mama.

REBA: Well, we'll just get you there and have him check you out.

WENDAL: Mama, do you ever hear what people really say? Did you hear me say I have AIDS?

REBA: No Wendal. AIDS, I don't know nothing about it. You ain't got that.

WENDAL: I do.

REBA: What I just say? I don't know nothing about no . . .

WENDAL: I'm sorry.

REBA: Oh my God, tell me you kidding Wendal.

WENDAL: I wish.

REBA: Bailey . . .

WENDAL: I haven't figured out how to tell him.

REBA: How? How did you get something like this?

WENDAL: I don't know.

REBA (*her anger and fear out of control, loud*): What do you mean you don't know? You come home and you're dying of some disease and you don't know how the hell you got it.

WENDAL: I'm not dying. I have . . .

REBA: Did you have some kind of surgery and they gave you bad blood?

WENDAL: No. What difference does it make how I got it?

REBA: You been lying to us. You been home here and you ain't said a word . . .

WENDAL: Every day I tried to tell you . . . I practiced this speech . . .

REBA: I don't want to hear no damn speech. I want to hear how the hell you got this? You're not one of them . . . that why you got so mad at dinner?

WENDAL: Mama.

REBA: No. No. I know you're not. You've been living with Simone . . .

WENDAL (*carefully choosing his words*): Mama, you know that I never was quite right like Daddy used to say . . . (*No response from* REBA.) Try to understand Mama. I have relationships with women and sometimes with men.

REBA: No you don't, un-un. No you don't. You're my son, just like Junior . . . you're a man. You're supposed to . . .

WENDAL: Supposed to what? Be like Daddy. His world don't stretch no farther than this couch . . .

REBA: Boy, who the hell are you to judge anybody?

WENDAL: Mama, it's not much different than you and Auntie May.

REBA: What you say?

WENDAL: It's not so different than how you feel about Auntie May . . .

REBA: How dare you? How dare you twist me and Maybelle's relationship into this sickness you talking. That woman is like a sister to me. You hear me? A sister!

WENDAL: A sister that might as well live here. You closer to her than you are to Daddy.

REBA (*enraged*): You shut up. Shut your mouth. Shut your filthy mouth. Don't be trying to compare that shit . . . my life ain't the one on trial here.

WENDAL: I'm sorry. I just thought you might understand Mama.

REBA: UNDERSTAND! How can a mother understand that? How can I understand that you're one of them people, that I raised a liar for a son . . . I was so happy . . .

WENDAL: Mama, forgive me. I would've done anything to spare you . . .

REBA: Is that why you don't come home?

WENDAL: It's hard pretending.

REBA: You don't have to pretend with us. We're your parents . . .

WENDAL: Yeah, right. Dad can't stand to hear anything about my life and where does he get off having Dwayne call him Daddy?

REBA (*his last words lost on her*): Couldn't you have given us a chance? Maybe we would have . . .

WENDAL (*softly, tries to touch her*): I am now Mama.

REBA (*shudders at his touch, sharply*): Don't you tell your father. You hear me? I'll tell him. It'll kill him if it came from you. (*More to herself.*) I should've never let you leave here. Bailey told me . . . said I kept you too close, wasn't no room left over for him . . . he told me no good would ever come to you . . . he told me . . . (*Yelling.*) You better get down on your knees right now boy and you better pray, beg God's forgiveness for your nasty wicked ways . . .

WENDAL: Pray! Mama, what in the hell you think I've been doing? I've prayed every night. I laid in that hospital bed thirty-two days and thirty-two nights and all I did was pray. You know how lonely it is Mama to lay in a bed that ain't even your own for thirty-two days, nothing but tubes and your own shit to keep you company; what it is to bite into a pillow all night so people can't hear you screaming? No TV, I didn't even have a quarter to buy myself a paper. I tried to get right with your God, I asked him for some spare time, to keep me from pitching my guts every hour, to keep me from shitting all over myself, to give me the strength to wipe my ass good enough so I didn't have to smell myself all night. I prayed that they would stop experimenting on me, stop the rashes, the infections, the sores up my ass. I prayed Mama for some company. I prayed that somebody would get their room wrong and happen into mine so I could talk to somebody, maybe they would even put their arms around me 'cause I was so damn scared, maybe it would be somebody who would come back, somebody who would want to know me for who I really was and I prayed harder and I prayed to your God that if I could just hold on, if I could just get home . . . I'm not going to apologize Mama for loving who I loved, I ain't even gonna apologize for getting this shit, I've lived a lie and I'm gonna have to answer for that, but I'll be damn if I'm gon' keep lying, I ain't got the energy. I'm a deal with it just like you taught me to deal with everything else that came my way . . . but I could use a little help Mama . . .

REBA: No more. You hear me Wendal? No more. I never thought I'd see the day I'd be ashamed of you, that I wouldn't even want to know you. (*She exits.*)

WENDAL (*quietly to himself*): Well, welcome home Wendal. (*Lights. The next morning.* WENDAL *is still asleep on the couch.* DWAYNE *enters from the kitchen.*)

DWAYNE (*nudging Wendal*): Daddy. Daddy. You woke?

WENDAL: Hmm.

DWAYNE: Daddy, you woke?

WENDAL: I am now.

DWAYNE: You want to watch videos?

WENDEL: It's a little early, isn't it? (DWAYNE *turns on the television.*)

BAILEY (*coming down the stairs*): I don't see why we have to go to church today, it ain't even Sunday.

WENDAL: Morning Dad.

BAILEY: Morning. You feeling better this morning?

WENDAL: Yeah.

REBA: DWAYNE!!!!

BAILEY: I don't know what's gotten into that woman this morning.

WENDAL: Go see what your Grandma wants.

DWAYNE: Ok. Granddaddy, I made you some toast. I left it on the table.

BAILEY: Thanks, 'cause if it's up to your Grandma, I'm not getting nothing this morning. She in some kind of state. (DWAYNE *exits, a moment.*)

WENDAL: Sorry 'bout last night. You've done a good job with him.

BAILEY: I tried.

WENDAL: It shows. (*Neither speaks for a minute.*) Dad.

BAILEY (*overlapping*): Son. (*They laugh.*)

WENDAL: Age before beauty.

BAILEY (*playfully*): All right boy, I can still take you out. Only reason I ain't is 'cause I don't wanna mess up my Sunday-go-to-meetin' clothes.

WENDAL: Dad, you'll never change.

BAILEY (*more than a hint of seriousness*): Do you want me to?

WENDAL (*a moment*): I try not to want for things anymore, 'specially things I have no control over.

BAILEY: Yeah, I guess that's probably wise. (*Another pause.*)

REBA (*yelling from upstairs*): Bailey!!!

BAILEY (*yelling back*): What? What Reba?

REBA: Are you ready?

BAILEY: Yes woman. Yes. I been ready. (*To* WENDAL.) Now where were we? What were we talking 'bout?

WENDAL: You were 'bout to tell me you glad I'm home.

BAILEY (*looks at him for a moment*): Why you trying to pick around inside me boy?

WENDAL: I wasn't. I was just . . . forget it.

BAILEY (*pause*): You know my offer still stands. If you ever want to come work for me . . . I got a lotta plans for the store. Did I tell you I'm thinking about expanding?

WENDAL: Yes.

BAILEY: Not interested, huh?

WENDAL: I didn't say that.

BAILEY: Yeah.

REBA (*coming down the stairs carrying an overnight bag, overlapping*): Look how nasty this tablecloth is. (*Whisks the tablecloth off the table, looks around trying to figure out where to put it.*)

BAILEY: Reba, the tablecloth wasn't that dirty. Leave it on the chair, we can get it when we get back.

REBA: I said it was nasty. I want it out of my sight.

BAILEY: Sugar, I don't know why you so upset but . . .

DWAYNE: And I don't understand why I have to go to Aunt May's. I can stay here, clean out the basement. Dad and I can clean it out and get it done by the time you get back. Right Dad?

BAILEY: That basement is filthy. Reba, if he's not going to church, then why can't he stay here?

REBA: FINE. WHATEVER YOU SAY IS FINE BAILEY. WHAT DO I HAVE TO SAY ABOUT ANYTHING AROUND HERE ANYWAY? WHAT HAVE I EVER HAD TO SAY ABOUT ANYTHING?

BAILEY: I didn't mean it like that Reba. I just thought the boy might wanna . . .

WENDAL: Dwayne, why don't you go start on the basement while your grandparents and I talk.

DWAYNE: But am I staying home?

WENDAL: Yes. Now go. (DWAYNE *exits*.)

BAILEY: What's going on here?

WENDAL: Dad . . .

REBA (*cutting him off*): Nothing. Bailey, I wanna talk to Wendal. Alone. Please wait for me in the car. Please.

BAILEY: Somethin' I should know?

WENDAL: Yes.

REBA (*overlapping*): No. Bailey please. Please honey. And take the suitcase with you.

BAILEY (*picks up the suitcase, mumbling to himself*): A suitcase to church . . . it ain't even Sunday . . . all morning 'bout to take my head off, now I gotta go wait in the car like some child. (*He exits.*)

WENDAL: Mama, I should tell . . .

REBA: Shut up. Just shut up. Don't say a word. I heard enough from you last night to last me a lifetime. I'm about to walk out that door and try and explain to that man out there why I don't have a home no more. I hate what you've done to my house Wendal. Spent my life here, inside these walls, trying to stay safe, keep my family safe . . . didn't know any better, maybe if I had, I could deal with what you done brought in here. See this slipcover, I made it. And that afghan, I made that too, these curtains . . . I made this tablecloth, see this lace. I made you. My son! And I took such pride . . . but last night you made me realize I hadn't made nothing, not a damn thing . . . been walking around fooling myself. . . . It's hard to look at something . . . I mean I look around here and it's like somebody came in and smeared shit all over my walls . . . I'm scared to touch anything . . . you hear me Wendal, scared to touch anything in my own house. . . . Nothing. Maybe if I could get outside these walls I could . . . I can't stay here and watch it fester, crumble down around me . . . right now I can't help you . . . I can hardly stand to even look at you . . . I can't help your father . . . what good am I? I don't know anymore. I just know this house is closing in on me and I got to get out of here.

WENDAL: But Mama I can go.

REBA: Wouldn't make no difference. This ain't a home no more.

WENDAL: Mama, can we at least talk? I need you . . . if you would just let me . . .

REBA: You need?! Hmph! You need?!! I don't give a damn about what you need Wendal. Did you give a damn about us?

WENDAL: You act like I got this just to hurt you. . . . Don't leave Mama . . . I . . .

REBA: I can't help you right now. You understand? Mama can't help you. (*Starting to exit.*)

WENDAL: But where are you going? (REBA *exits.* WENDAL *throws something, maybe hits the door behind her as his beeper goes off, he retrieves his pillbox, gets ready to take his medicine but instead throws the pills across the room, after a moment.*)

DWAYNE (*enters*): Dad, you OK? (WENDAL *jumps.*)

WENDAL (*snaps*): Man, don't come up behind me like that.

DWAYNE: I'm sorry. Can I ask you something? (WENDAL *nods yes.*) I only need 'bout forty more dollars. School's almost out and I thought I could go back with you for the summer. Simone said it was OK.

WENDAL: You talked to Simone?

DWAYNE: Yeah we were gonna surprise you. She said she was fixing me up a room.

WENDAL: Dwayne, Simone and I ain't together no more. So you don't have to pack up, your Dad plans to be around here.

DWAYNE (*excited*): Really? Wow, then we could go places, go to all the games . . . Daddy, I mean Granddaddy, he takes me to the games and he tries to play ball . . . don't tell him I said this, but he's kind of old . . .

WENDAL: You don't have to worry, I won't tell him that. (*Pause.*) There's so much I want to say to you, like be careful how you judge people, weigh a man carefully, you never know when you may get on the same scale . . .

DWAYNE: You don't want me to be like Granddad.

WENDAL: What I want is for you to think for yourself, make your own choices, you know the kind you can defend, not with your fists but in your heart.

DWAYNE: I got it. So what we gon' do today?

WENDAL: Why don't you go work in the basement for a while. I'll take a shower, then we'll go somewhere, maybe to the Center or take in a movie . . .

JUNIOR (*entering*): How come nobody woke me up?

DWAYNE: 'Cause you were snoring. Granddaddy say you sound worse than Amtrak.

JUNIOR: Ok man. I don't want to have to bust no head today. Have to do you like I used to do your Dad.

WENDAL: Why you wanna lie to the boy? Wasn't a day in the week that somebody wasn't going upside your head. Your Uncle always had a lotta mouth Dwayne.

JUNIOR: Don't let him lie to you. Your Uncle spent all his time defending your Dad.

WENDAL (*obviously there's some truth in* JUNIOR'S *statement*): Dwayne, the basement's calling you.

DWAYNE: OK. But I wanna hear . . .

JUNIOR: I'll tell you if you wanna hear some stories . . .

WENDAL: The basement Dwayne. You can listen to your Uncle's tales later.

DWAYNE: OK. You gon' call me when you ready to go? (WENDAL *shakes his head yes;* DWAYNE *exits.*)

JUNIOR: Where's the folks?

WENDAL: Church.

JUNIOR (*looking for food in the kitchen*): Wait a minute. It's not Sunday. Well, maybe it's some type of social. Mama didn't cook? (*Takes the milk carton out and drinks from it.*)

WENDAL: I don't think so. Why did you have to say that shit in front of him?

JUNIOR: What?

WENDAL: Defending me.

JUNIOR: What in the hell is wrong with you Wendal? I was just kidding. What happened to your sense of humor? And I did have to kick ass because of you. I know what it is. You must not be getting none? Is that your problem?

WENDEL: Drop it man.

JUNIOR: Hey, I was just trying to make conversation. I can take my black ass back upstairs.

WENDAL: Junior wait. I'm just a little uptight.

JUNIOR: I can see that.

WENDAL: OK already. Next subject. Service seems to agree with you. You look good. Going back to school when you get out?

JUNIOR: Nah, I don't think so.

WENDAL: Don't they pay for it?

JUNIOR: Yep.

WENDAL: So what's stopping you?

JUNIOR: Correct me if I'm wrong, but I don't remember you going back to school.

WENDAL: I know I didn't, that's why I'm trying to talk to you knucklehead. Man, look at you, you got a lot going for you . . .

JUNIOR: Guess who you starting to sound like? Reason you can't get long 'cause you two are too much alike. And I sure as hell wish you'd stop using me in ya'lls battles. . . .

WENDAL: Man, what you talking about?

JUNIOR: I'm not the favorite Wendal. Just your stand-in. God forbid you ever get your life together.

WENDAL: I'll look over that last comment and deal with your initial silly-ass statement. Dad's been throwing you up to me ever since I can remember. If Junior did it, why didn't I figure out a way to do it better . . .

JUNIOR: Hit the nail on the head. Only time I count is when brother Wendal is fucking up . . .

WENDAL: I don't want to talk about him. I was just trying to tell you something for your own good. Junior you oughtta finish your education . . .

JUNIOR: My own good is just that, my own good.

WENDAL: Man, your problem is you don't listen.

JUNIOR: Look who's talking. Seem to me, I listened better than you.

WENDAL: Not from where I'm sittin'.

JUNIOR: Well, you need to go sit somewhere else then. Look, I ain't trying to be you. Ain't into making no big inroads. Call me Joe-Regular. Go to work, have a family, retire. Simple. I don't fault you for your life, so get up offa me 'bout mine.

WENDAL: I didn't mean no harm.

JUNIOR: Yeah right. As long as we straight.

WENDAL: Guess I was just playing big brother. Didn't mean no harm.

JUNIOR (*pause*): Want you to be my best man.

WENDAL: Say what?

JUNIOR: Yeah. Yeah. When the right woman comes along . . . what can I say? She teaches school, one of them fine churchgoing women. Her name is Anita and she loves my dirty drawers and Lord knows I can smell hers all day long, you hear me?

WENDAL: Man you crazy. (*They both laugh, it's a needed tension release.*) Congratulations Junior. (*Goes to hug him.*)

JUNIOR: Go on Wendal, you still ain't learned 'bout hugging up on men . . .

WENDAL: I love you man, that's all.

JUNIOR: I know that . . . we brothers. Man you been smoking some funny shit this early . . . (WENDAL *starts coughing uncontrollably.*) What's wrong with you Wendal?

WENDAL: Junior . . .

DWAYNE (*enters*): I need some garbage bags. Dad, I thought you were gon' take a shower. If we don't get to the Center early . . . (BAILEY *enters, it's obvious he's trying hard to control himself.*)

JUNIOR (*to* DWAYNE): I don't think your father feels too well . . .

DWAYNE: What's wrong?

BAILEY: Come here.

WENDAL: What?

BAILEY: I said come here. Bring your ass over here and look me in my face.

WENDAL: Dwayne, go finish what you were doing.

BAILEY: No, you don't. Stand right there. Don't you move.

WENDAL: Dad, please, not in front of him.

JUNIOR: Can somebody tell me what's going on here? Wendal come on . . . let me help you . . .

BAILEY (*overlapping*): Little late to be ashamed. (BAILEY *roughly grabs and examines* WENDAL'*s arms.*) Where's your marks? Where you hiding 'em?

WENDAL: What marks?

BAILEY: You know what I'm talking about. You been doing drugs.

WENDAL: Dwayne, get outta here.

BAILEY: No. It's time he know the truth. . . .

WENDAL: I don't know what you talking about. Dwayne . . .

BAILEY: You don't know what I'm talking about? You don't know what I'm talking about!!! I'm one step off your ass boy . . .

JUNIOR: Dad, please he's sick.

BAILEY: He's sick alright. Tell him. Let me hear you tell your brother, hear you tell your son, tell 'em you's a junkie. . . . Tell them why your mother was ashamed to stay in the same house with you. Tell 'em Mr. Junkie . . .

WENDAL: I'm not a junkie . . .

BAILEY: Then what the hell are you? (*The question hangs in the air, recognition, finally.*) I never laid a hand on you but you better get out my sight before I kick you straight to hell's door.

JUNIOR: Will somebody clue me in?

WENDAL: Dad, if you'd let me explain . . . I'm not sure how I got it . . .

BAILEY: I don't wanna know how you got it. The sight of you breaks my heart. I oughtta kill you. (*Shoves him.*)

DWAYNE: Granddaddy, what's wrong?

WENDAL: It's OK Dwayne. Go on now. Your grandfather is just upset about something.

JUNIOR (*overlapping*): Man stop it. Can't you see he's sick? I don't know what's going on here, but you gon' have to come through me 'cause I ain't gon' let you lay another hand on him . . .

BAILEY: Boy get out of my way. I'll go through you and anybody else. He won't need the AIDS when I get through. . . .

JUNIOR: What you say?

BAILEY: AIDS. That's what I said.

JUNIOR: Naw Wendal. It can't be. You ain't got that. Tell me you ain't got that.

DWAYNE: Dad?

WENDAL: Dwayne . . . I'm sorry. If you all would just let me explain . . . I didn't know if you'd understand. . . .

BAILEY: You right. I don't understand. You no son of mine. In my house. . . . Did you hear me? (*Violently throws* WENDAL *on the floor, who attempts to crawl away from him.*) Take your sissy fairy ass and get the hell out of my house.

JUNIOR: What the fuck you doing? He's sick. Look at him.

WENDAL (*reaches out for* DWAYNE): Dwayne . . . (DWAYNE *backs off, exits.*)

JUNIOR. Wendal why? Naw, I can't deal with this. . . . Can't deal with this right now . . . I looked up to you . . . I looked up to him . . . I can't deal with this . . . I . . . I . . . can't . . .

BAILEY (*to* JUNIOR): Boy, stop that whining. (JUNIOR *is crying, turns his back, walks away to exit.*) Did you hear me? Stop all that whimpering. (*Just before* JUNIOR *is almost out the room.*) Where you think you goin'? You just gon' turn your back? Raised you to turn your back on your brother? (JUNIOR *stops, but doesn't turn around.*)

JUNIOR: Don't do it Dad . . .

BAILEY: I'm talking to you Junior. You a man or not? Are you a man or not?

JUNIOR (*pause, finally turns around, he's crying*): It's not gon' work this time. You hear me? It's not gon' work Dad. You got what you always wanted. Right there. He's all yours. (*Turns around to exit.*)

BAILEY: Boy, don't you turn your back to me. Don't you ever turn your back to me.

JUNIOR: Fuck you. Is that man enough for you? There's your son Dad. There's the man you always wanted. (*He exits.*)

BAILEY (*pause*): Get up. I said get up. Get up Wendal.

WENDAL: I can't Daddy.

BAILEY (*a beat as the anger is replaced by grief*): If you could've just told me. Wendal, if you could've just told me. If you could've just told me . . . you my son . . . what we gon' do? (*Eventually he drops to his knees, scoops up* WENDAL, *maybe rocks him, cries.*) You my son . . . don't cry Wendal . . . don't cry, we gon' get through this . . . we Bailey men don't give up, do we? . . . just you and me now. Oh Wendal I been waitin' . . . waitin' so long for you to grow into somethin' . . . you my son . . . God help me . . . what I got to wait on now? . . . (*Lights dim as attendants wheel hospital bed into the* BAILEY *living room.* WENDAL *is placed in the bed, maybe* BAILEY *helps. IV is hooked up.* BAILEY *exits. A passage of time—it's weeks later.* BAILEY *enters carrying wood. He is a changed man: gone is the neat appearance, the sense of order and control. He drops the wood, then opens* WENDAL*'s saxophone case, crosses to the kitchen, retrieves a towel, forgets why he has the towel . . . looks over at* WENDAL, *retrieves and puts on rubber gloves . . . cleans him up.*) You woke?

WENDAL: Where's Dwayne?

BAILEY: Maybelle's bringing him.

WENDAL: Mama?

BAILEY (*an untruth*): She asked about you. (*Turning him to check the bed pad.*)

WENDAL: Really?

BAILEY: Yeah.

WENDAL: She coming home?

BAILEY: Yeah. And she'll be sending your dinner after a while . . .

WENDAL: I was gon' take him on the train with me. Remember when we took the train.

BAILEY: Yeah. I remember. Look. I brought the wood in . . . member for the cabinets? We can sand a little after you have your supper.

WENDAL: Look Wendal, you see it? That's red dirt . . . sweet Missis-sippi dirt. I see it Dad. Mama, you see it? Mama?

BAILEY (*helpless, but with forced cheerfulness*): You hungry? Maybe a little something. It was something else I was 'bout to do. Now what was it. . . . Oh I know. I was gon' clean up your horn for you. Shine it up, so you'd be real slick when you start playing again. Got to get this place cleaned up before your Mama gets home. She'll have my head on a platter, letting this house go like this. (*Starts to pick up a little: maybe strewn newspapers, mail.*) How 'bout a little soup? Couldn't get off to sleep last night, that couch ain't that comfortable, so I got up 'bout three with this bright idea. Thought I'd make you some soup . . . cut up a lot of vegetables in it. (WENDAL *moans.*) I know the sores hurt, (*losing control*) but how the hell you gon' get well if you don't eat somethin'? (*Recovers, less harsh, starts shining the saxophone.*) Yeah, I'll get this shined up for you. (*Blows a note or two on the horn.*) You wanna give it a try? (*Takes the horn to the bed, waits for* WENDAL *to take, no response.*) Well, maybe a little later. Later on maybe you'll feel like playing, a little something. (*Places the horn on the table.*) Yeah it's a beautiful day outside. I wish you could see it. (*Crosses to the window, to himself.*) Your Mama likes days like this, she'd be out there in that garden right now wearing that funny hat with the fruit on it . . . I got to figure out what I should put on to go over there. What you think? My blue suit or the black one? You wait a minute and I'm a go get 'em . . . then we can decide. (*Just then* DWAYNE *and* MAYBELLE *enter.* MAYBELLE *wears a hooded rain poncho, a wool scarf wrapped around her face and on her hands are oven mitts.* DWAYNE *has a large bruise on his face; gone is the innocence, the sweetness; he's an angry little boy who doesn't know what to do with his anger, with any of his feelings.*) Hi. I'm glad ya'll got here . . . just getting ready . . . Maybelle, what in the hell do you have on? It must be ninety degrees outside. If you don't look ridiculous . . .

MAYBELLE: I didn't want to take any chances. (*Looks around at all the things down in the house.*)

BAILEY: Maybelle, if it wasn't for ignorance, you wouldn't have no sense at all. And Dwayne what you hiding back there for? Come over here. (*Reluctantly* DWAYNE *crosses.*) Get over here! (*Notices the bruise.*) You been fighting? (*No response from* DWAYNE *who looks at him defiantly.*) Did you hear me ask you a question?

MAYBELLE: Them kids making that boy's life miserable.

DWAYNE: I can handle myself.

BAILEY: You try handling yourself some other kinda way. You speak to your Dad? (*No response from* DWAYNE.) Boy get over there before that ain't the only bruise you sportin'.

DWAYNE (*crosses to the bed, has a hard time looking at* WENDAL; *begrudgingly*): Hi.

BAILEY (*takes* MAYBELLE *to the side*): How's Reba today? (*Now that* BAILEY *isn't looking* DWAYNE *moves away from the bed.*)

MAYBELLE: The same. Driving me nuts. Bathing all day and when she ain't in the tub she's somewhere changing clothes. I swear she ain't never been a vain woman, but now she hangs in that mirror for hours . . . I don't know what she sees . . . I wish she'd cry or yell or do something . . . 'cause right now I can't reach her . . . every day she slipping a little further away from me. (*Whispers.*) Spends half the night watching Dwayne sleep. That's right, I'm telling you the truth, she sits straight up in that chair and watches that boy sleep, and then she goes in the room and the rest of the night she's walking and talking, to who I don't know, to herself or God one. . . . She misses you.

BAILEY: Then she oughtta come home.

MAYBELLE (*pause*): Today's menu: chicken and fried corn. I tried to get Reba to help . . .

BAILEY (*taking the tin foil off the plate*): This looks good. Wendal likes fried corn. Look Wendal.

MAYBELLE: Bailey you know he can't eat that.

BAILEY: How you know what he can eat? How do any of y'all know what he can eat? I been in this house with this boy for weeks and has anybody come by? Has anyone bothered to come and see what he can eat?

MAYBELLE: I'm doing the best I can. I cook every day for you . . . I don't know what else you expect . . . I'm taking care of Reba and that boy. Come on Dwayne let's go.

BAILEY: What you mean? Ya'll just got here. I was hoping you'd stay with him so I could go sit with Reba a while . . . (WENDAL *grunts, moans.*)

MAYBELLE (*timidly, waves*): Hi Wendal. It's Maybelle, Auntie May. I can't stay . . .

BAILEY: What's wrong with you? Even if he wanted to, he ain't got the strength to bite your ass.

MAYBELLE: It ain't no cause for you to talk to me like that.

BAILEY: And it ain't no cause for you to be afraid of him like that. Why don't you touch him . . .

MAYBELLE: Have you gone nuts?

BAILEY (*the cost of all the weeks of holding it together, he explodes; there's an edge of madness, grabs her, forces her to the bed*): I said touch him. You used to rock him and sing to him, just like he was your own. . . . I want you to touch him . . . right now . . .

MAYBELLE: Bailey let go of me. You scaring me.

BAILEY: Good. Touch him. That's my son you treating like some leper. I said touch him.

MAYBELLE (*terrified, crying*): Let me go Bailey. Let me go. I can't. Please.

BAILEY: What if it was one of your sons? Huh?

MAYBELLE: I wouldn't touch them either. I wouldn't have no AIDS in my house.

WENDAL (*overlapping*): Dad, it hurts.

BAILEY (*quickly letting go of* MAYBELLE, *who retreats*): I'm right here Wendal.

WENDAL: I wanna go. Help me. It hurts. I gotta go see Simone . . .

BAILEY: Now hold on Wendal, Dwayne's here. (*To* DWAYNE.) Say something to him.

DWAYNE (*still defiant*): What?

BAILEY: Tell him you love him. (*No response from* DWAYNE, *pleading.*) Please Dwayne. Tell him something. Anything. He's still your father. You may not get another chance. . . . He's still . . . (DWAYNE *doesn't move.*)

WENDAL (*overlapping*): You see that plot of land, that's where your old man first started kicking . . .

BAILEY (*panicking*): Fight Wendal. Remember what I told you 'bout fighting. Don't let him take you out. Stay on the ropes son. . . . You can't give up. Come on. Don't give up. I'm in there with you. Ain't gon' let you go yet. . . . Come on son, fight now.

MAYBELLE: I got to get out of here. I'll send Reba. Come on Dwayne. (DWAYNE *doesn't move.*) Wendal, Auntie May love you. I'm sorry Bailey. I'm so sorry. (*She exits.*)

WENDAL (*overlapping*): I'm riding Dad. I'm on the train. I see you . . . Junior. I see Dwayne . . . Mama . . . (SIMONE *enters in profile on the other side of the stage, a special light.*) Simone . . . (*Gasping for breath.*) She's pregnant. Oh my God no . . . I'm so sorry Simone . . . I'm sorry . . .

BAILEY: I'm right here Wendal, but don't die on me. Please, don't leave me. . . . (BAILEY *screams.*) NO. . . . (*Sobbing.*) Don't take him. Don't take him. God, give me some more time with him . . . just one more day, please don't take him. (*Lights on* SIMONE. SIMONE *takes off her earrings, then her wig and then the robe and transforms into* ANGEL PETERSON *from Act One.*)

SIMONE (*fully transformed*): God don't have nothing to do with it. Time to get on board Wendal Bailey. Welcome to the family . . . (*As lights go down,* ANGEL *sings the same song* WENDAL *was singing in the first scene in the reception area.*)

(*The End*)

IMPERCEPTIBLE MUTABILITIES IN THE THIRD KINGDOM

Suzan-Lori Parks

SUZAN-LORI PARKS is a playwright and screenwriter. Her works include *Imperceptible Mutabilities in the Third Kingdom,* originally produced by BACA Downtown in Brooklyn in 1989 and awarded the 1990 Obie Award for Best Play; *Betting on the Dust Commander,* produced by Theater Row Theater in New York City in 1991; *The Death of the Last Black Man in the Whole Entire World,* performed at Yale Repertory Theater's 1992 Winterfest in New Haven, Connecticut, and originally produced by BACA Downtown in Brooklyn in 1990; *Devotees in the Garden of Love,* premiered at Actors Theater of Louisville's 1992 Humana Festival; and *The America Play,* which premiered in 1994 at the Yale Repertory Theater in New Haven, and was later produced at the Joseph Papp Public Theater in New York City in 1994 as part of the New York Shakespeare Festival, Yale Repertory, and Theater for a New Audience.

Other plays include *Venus,* commissioned by the Women's Project and Productions, New York City, *The Sinner's Place,* and *Fishes.*

Parks is the recipient of two National Endowment for the Arts Fellowships for Playwrights and has been awarded grants by the Rockefeller Foundation, Ford Foundation, New York State Council on the Arts, and New York Foundation for the Arts. She is also a recipient of a Whiting Foundation Writers Award. For her newest play, *Venus,* she received grants from the W. Alton James Foundation and the Fund for New American Plays. Her credits include work for radio, television, and film. Parks wrote her first feature-length screenplay, *Girl 6,* for Spike Lee's company, Forty Acres and a Mule.

Parks is an associate artist at the Yale School of Drama and a member of New Dramatists. She lives in New York's Greenwich Village.

Distorted mirror

naturalist watches

they watch animal kingdom

Part One: Snails

The Players:
MOLLY/MONA
CHARLENE/CHONA
VERONICA/VERONA
THE NATURALIST/DR. LUTZKY
THE ROBBER

Part Two: Third Kingdom

The Players:
KIN-SEER
US-SEER
SHARK-SEER
SOUL-SEER
OVER-SEER

Part Three: Open House

The Players:
MRS. ARETHA SAXON
ANGLOR SAXON
BLANCA SAXON
CHARLES
MISS FAITH

Third Kingdom (Reprise)

The Players:
KIN-SEER
US-SEER
SHARK-SEER
SOUL-SEER
OVER-SEER

Part Four: Greeks (or The Slugs)

The Players:
MR. SERGEANT SMITH
MRS. SERGEANT SMITH
BUFFY SMITH
MUFFY SMITH
DUFFY SMITH

Part One: Snails

A.

Slide show: Images of Molly and Charlene. Molly and Charlene speak as the stage remains semi-dark and the slides continue to flash overhead.

CHARLENE: How dja get through it?

MOLLY: Mm not through it.

CHARLENE: Yer leg. Thuh guard. Lose weight?

MOLLY: Hhh. What should I do Chona should I jump should I jump or what?

CHARLENE: You want some eggs?

MOLLY: Would I splat?

CHARLENE: Uhuhuhnnnn . . .

MOLLY: Twelve floors up. Whaduhya think?

CHARLENE: Uh-uh-uhn. Like scrambled?

MOLLY: Shit.

CHARLENE: With cheese? Say "with" cause ssgoin in.

MOLLY: I diduhnt quit that school. HHH. Thought: nope! Mm gonna go on—go on ssif nothing ssapin yuh know? "S-K" is /sk/ as in "ask." The little-lamb-follows-closely-behind-at-Marys-heel-as-Mary-boards-the-train. Shit. Failed every test he shoves in my face. He makes me recite my mind goes blank. HHH. The-little-lamb-follows-closely-behind-at-Marys-heels-as-Mary-boards-the-train. Aint never seen no woman on no train with no lamb. I tell him so. He throws me out. Stuff like this happens every day y know? This isnt uh special case mines iduhnt uh uhnnn.

CHARLENE: Salami? Yarnt veg anymore.

MOLLY: "S-K" is /sk/ as in "ask." I lie down you lie down he she it lies down. The-little-lamb-follows-closely-behind-at-Marys-heels. . . .

CHARLENE: Were you lacto-ovo or thuh whole nine yards?

MOLLY: Whole idea uh talkin right now aint right no way. Aint natural. Just goes tuh go. HHH. Show. Just goes tuh show.

CHARLENE: Coffee right?

MOLLY: They—expelled—me.

CHARLENE: Straight up?

MOLLY: Straight up. "Talk right or youre outta here!" I couldnt. I walked. Nope. "Speak correctly or you'll be dismissed!" Yeah. Yeah. Nope. Nope. Job sends me there. Basic skills. Now Job dont want me no more. Closely-behind-at-Marys-heels. HHH. Everythin in its place.

CHARLENE: Toast?

MOLLY: Hate lookin for uh job. Feel real whory walkin thuh streets. Only thing worse n working sslookin for work.

CHARLENE: I'll put it on thuh table.

MOLLY: You lie down you lie down but he and she and it and us well we lays down. Didnt quit. They booted me. He booted me. Couldnt see thuh sense uh words workin like he said couldnt see thuh sense uh workin where words workin like that was workin would drop my phone voice would let things slip they tell me get Basic Skills call me breaking protocol hh-hhh! Think I'll splat?

CHARLENE: Once there was uh robber who would come over and rob us regular. He wouldnt come through thuh window he would use thuh door. I would let him in. He would walk in n walk uhround. Then he would point tuh stuff. I'd say "help yourself." We developed us uh relationship. I asked him his name. He didnt answer. I asked him where he comed from. No answer tuh that neither. He didnt have no answers cause he didnt have no speech. Verona said he had that deep jungle air uhbout im that just off thuh boat look tuh his face. Verona

she named him she named him "Mokus." But Mokus whuduhnt his name.

MOLLY: Once there was uh me named Mona who wanted tuh jump
ship but didnt. HHH. Chona? Ya got thuh Help Wanteds?

CHARLENE: Flies are casin yer food Mona. Come eat.

MOLLY: HELP WANTEDS. *YOU GOT EM?*

CHARLENE: Wrapped thuh coffee grins in em.

MOLLY: Splat.

B.

*Lights up onstage with canned applause. At the podium stands the
Naturalist.*

NATURALIST: As I have told my students for some blubblubblub
years, a most careful preparation of one's fly is the only way by
in which the naturalist can insure the capturence of his subjects
in a state of nature. Now for those of you who are perhaps not
familiar with the more advanced techniques of nature study let
me explain the principle of one of our most useful instruments:
"the fly." When in Nature Studies the fly is an apparatus which
by blending in with the environment under scrutiny enables
the naturalist to conceal himself and observe the object of
study—unobserved. In our observations of the subjects subjects
which for our purposes we have named "MOLLY" and "CHAR-
LENE" subjects we have chosen for study in order that we may
monitor their natural behavior and after monitoring perhaps—
modify the form of my fly was an easy choice: this cockroach
modeled after the common house insect *hausus cockruckus* fashioned entirely of corrugated cardboard offers us a place in which
we may put our camera and observe our subjects—unobserved—.
Much like the "fly on the wall."

C.

Molly and Charlene onstage.

MOLLY: Once there was uh me named Mona who wondered
what she'd be like if no one was watchin. You got the Help
Wanteds?

CHARLENE: Wrapped thuh coffee grinds in um.—Mona?

MOLLY: Splat. Splat. Splatsplatsplat.

CHARLENE: Mm callin thuh ssterminator for tomorrow. Leave it be for now.

MOLLY: Diduhnt even blink. I threatened it. Diduhnt even blink.

CHARLENE: Theyre gettin brave. Big too.

MOLLY: Splat!

CHARLENE: Mona! Once there was uh little lamb who followed Mary good n put uh hex on Mary. When Mary dropped dead, thuh lamb was in thuh lead. You can study at home. I'll help.

MOLLY: Uh-uhnn! I'm all decided. Aint gonna work. Cant. Aint honest. Anyone with any sense dont wanna work no how. Mm gonna be honest. Mm gonna be down n out. Make downin n outin my livelihood.

CHARLENE: He didnt have no answers cause he didnt have no speech.

MOLLY: Wonder what I'd look like if no one was lookin. I need fashions. "S-K" is /sk/ as in "ask." The-little-lamb-follows-Mary-Mary-who . . . ?

CHARLENE: Once there was uh one Verona named "Mokus." But "Mokus" whuduhnt his name. He had his picture on file at thuh police station. Ninety-nine different versions. None of um looked like he looked.

MOLLY: Splat! Splat! Diduhnt move uh muscle even. Dont even have no muscles. Only eyes. Splat! Shit. I woulda been uhcross thuh room out thuh door n on tuh thuh next life. Diduhnt twitch none. Splat! I cant even talk. I got bug bites all over! I need new styles.

CHARLENE: Once there was uh one named Lutzky. Uh exterminator professional with uh Ph.D. He wore white cause white was what thuh job required. Comes tuh take thuh roaches uhway. Knew us by names that whuduhnt ours. Could point us out from pictures that whuduhnt us. He became confused. He hosed us down. You signed thuh invoice with uh X. Exterminator professional with uh Ph.D. He can do thuh job for $99.

MOLLY: Mm gonna lay down, K?

CHARLENE: Youre lucky Mona.

MOLLY: He thuh same bug wasin thuh kitchen?

CHARLENE: Uh uhnn. We got uh infestation problem. Youre lucky.

MOLLY: He's watchin us. He followed us in here n swatchin us.

CHARLENE: I'll call Lutzky. Wipe-um-out-Lutzky with uh Ph.D. He's got uh squirt gun. He'll come right over. He's got thuh potions. All mixed up. Squirt in uh crack. Hose down uh crevice. We'll be through. Through with it. Free of um. Wipe-um-out-Lutzky with thuh Ph.D.. He's got uh squirt gun. He'll come right over.

MOLLY: Uh—the cockroach-is-watching-us,-look-Chona-look! Once there was uh me named Mona who wondered what she'd talk like if no one was listenin.

CHARLENE: Close yer eyes, Mona. Close yer eyes n think on some-uhn pleasant.

D.

The Naturalist at the podium.

THE NATURALIST: Thus behave our subjects naturally. Thus behave our subjects when they believe we cannot see them when they believe us far far away when they believe our backs have turned. Now. An obvious question should arise in the mind of an inquisitive observer? Yes? HHH. How should we best accommodate the presence of such subjects in our modern world. That is to say: How. Should. We. Best. Accommodate. Our subjects. If they are all to live with us—all in harmony—in our modern world. Yes. Having accumulated a wealth of naturally occurring observations knowing now how our subjects occur in their own world (*mundus primtivus*), the question now arises as to how we of our world (*mundus modernus*) best accommodate them. I ask us to remember that it was almost twenty-five whole score ago that our founding father went forth tirelessly crossing a vast expanse of ocean in which there lived dangerous creatures of the most horrible sort tirelessly crossing the sea jungle to find this country and name it. The wilderness was vast and we who came to teach, enlighten, and tame were few in number. They were the vast, we were the few. And now. The great cake of society is crumbling. I ask us to realize that those who do not march with us do not march not because they will not but because they cannot. . . . I ask that they somehow be—taken care of for there are too many of them—and by "them" I mean of course "them roaches." They need our help. They need our help. Information for the modern cannot be gleaned from the primitive, information for the modern can only be gleaned through ex-per-i-men-tation. This is the most tedious part of science yet in science there is no other way. Now, I will, if you will, journey to the jungle. *Behavioris distortionallus-via-modernus.* Watch closely:

E.

During this part the Robber enters, steals the roach and attempts an exit.

CHONA: Verona? Hey honeyumm home?

VERONA: Chona Chona ChonaChonaChona. Mona here?

CHONA: Laying down.

VERONA: Heart broken?

CHONA: Like uh broken heart. Thuh poor thing. I'll learn her her speech. Let's take her out n buy her new styles.

VERONA: Sounds good.

CHONA: She wants fashion.—We got roaches.

VERONA: Shit! Chona. Thats uh big one. I got some motels but. I got some stickys too—them little trays with glue? Some spray but. Woo ya! Woo ya woo ya?! They gettin brave.

CHONA: Big too. Think he came through that crack in thuh bathroom.

VERONA: Wooya! Wooya! Shit. You call Lutzky? Thuh Ph.D.?

CHONA: On his way. We'll pay. Be through. He's got uh squirt gun.

VERONA: We'll all spit thuh bill. He gonna do it for 99?

CHONA: Plus costs. Mona dunht know bout thuh Plus Costs part. Okay?

VERONA:—K. Maybe I can catch uh few for our Lutzky shows.

CHONA: Once there was uh woman who wanted tuh get uhway for uhwhile but didnt know which way tuh go tuh get gone. Once there was uh woman who just layed down.

VERONA: Traps. Place um. Around thuh sink corner of thuh stove move move yer feet threshole of thuh outside door. Yeauh. Mm convinced theyre comin in from uhcross thuh hall—slippin under thuh door at night but I aint no professional—see?! Lookit im go—movin slow-ly. He's thuh scout. For every one ya see there are thousands. Thousands thousands creepin in through thuh cracks. Waiting for their chance. Watchim go. Goinsslow. We gotta be vigilant: sit-with-thuh-lights-out-crouch-in-thuh-kitchen-holdin-hard-soled-shoes. GOTCHA! Monas got bug bites on her eyelids? Mmputtin some round her bed. Augment thuh traps with thuh spray.

CHONA: Once there was uh woman was careful. Once there was uh woman on thuh lookout. Still trapped.

VERONA: Vermin free by 1990! That means YOU!

CHONA: *Wild Kingdoms* on.

VERONA: YER OUTTA HERE!

CHONA: Yer shows on.

VERONA: Great. Thanks.

CHONA: Keep it low for Mona. K?

VERONA: Perkins never shoulda uhlowed them tuh scratch his show. Wildlife never goes outta style. He should told em that. Fuck thuh ratings. Oh, look! On thuh trail of thuh long muzzled wildebeest: mating season. Ha! This is uh good one. They got bulls n cows muzzles matin closeups—make ya feel like you really right there with em. Part of thuh action. Uh live birth towards thuh end. . . .

CHONA: You want some eggs?

VERONA: They got meat?

CHONA: —Yeauh—

VERONA: I'm veg. Since today. Kinder. Cheaper too. Didja know that uh veg—

CHONA: Eat. Here. Ssgood. Ssgood tuh eat. Eat. Please eat. Once there was uh one name Verona who bit thuh hand that feeds her. Doorbell thats Lutzky. I'll get it.

VERONA: Mona! Our shinin knights here!

MONA: THE-LITTLE-LAMB-FOLLOWS-MARY-CLOSELY-AT-HER-HEELS—

VERONA: Wipe-um-out Dr. Lutzky with uh P uh H and uh D. Baby. B. Cool.

MONA: B cool.

CHONA: Right this way Dr. Lutzky. Right this way Dr. Lutzky Extra-ordinaire Sir.

LUTZKY: I came as quickly as I could—I have a squirt gun, you know. Gold plated gift from the firm. They're so proud. Of me. There was a woman in Queens—poor thing—so dis-traught—couldn't sign the invoice—couldn't say "bug"—for a moment I thought I had been the unwitting victim of a prank phone call—*prankus callus*—her little boy filled out the forms—showed me where to squirt—lucky for her the little one was there—lucky for her she had the little one. Awfully noble scene, I thought. You must be Charlene.

CHONA: Char-who? Uh uhn. Uh—It-is-I,-Dr.-Lutzky,—*Chona*.

LUTZKY: Ha! You look like a Charlene you look like a Charlene you do look like a Charlene bet no one has ever told that to you, eh? Aaaaaaah, well. I hear there is one with "bug bites all over." Are you the one?

CHONA: I-am-Chona. Mona-is-the-one. The-one-in-the-living-room. The-one-in-the-living-room-on-the-couch.

LUTZKY: What's the world coming to? "What is the world coming to?" I sometimes ask myself. And—

CHONA: Eggs, Dr. Lutzky?

LUTZKY: Oh, yes please. And—am I wrong in making a liveli-hood—meager as it may be—from the vermin that feed on the crumbs which fall from the table of the broken cake of civilization—oh dear—oh dear!

CHONA: Watch out for those. We do have an infestation problem. Watch out for those.

LUTZKY: Too late now—oh dear it's sticky. It's stuck—oh dear—now the other foot. They're stuck.

MONA: THE-LITTLE-LAMB—

VERONA: SShhh.

CHONA: Make yourself at home, Dr. Lutzky. I'll bring your eggs.

LUTZKY: Can't walk.

CHONA: Shuffle.

LUTZKY: Oh dear. Shuffleshuffleshuffle. Oh dear.

VERONA: Sssshhh!

LUTZKY: You watch *Wild Kingdom.* I watch *Wild Kingdom* too. This is a good one. Oh dear!

MONA: Oh dear.

CHONA: Here is the Extraordinaire, Mona. Mona, the Extraordinaire is here. Fresh juice, Dr. Lutzky Extraordinaire?

LUTZKY: Call me "Wipe-em-out."

MONA: Oh dear.

VERONA: SSSSShhhhh.

LUTZKY: Well. Now. Let's start off with something simple. Who's got bug bites?

MONA: Once there was uh me named Mona who hated going tuh thuh doctor. —I-have-bug-bites-Dr.-Lutzky-Extra-ordinaire-Sir.

LUTZKY: This won't take long. Step lively, Molly. The line forms here.

CHONA: I'll get the juice. We have a juice machine!

LUTZKY: I have a squirt gun!

VERONA: He's got uh gun—Marlin Perkinssgot uh gun—

MONA: Oh, dear. . . .

LUTZKY: You're the one, aren't you, Molly? Wouldn't want to squirt the wrong one. Stand up straight. The line forms here.

CHONA: I am Chona! Monas on the line! —Verona? That one is Verona.

LUTZKY: ChonaMonaVerona. Well well well. Wouldn't want to squirt the wrong one.

VERONA: He's got uh gun. Ssnot supposed tuh have uh gun—

MONA: "S-K" IS /SK/ AS IN "AXE." Oh dear. I'm Lucky, Dr. Lutzky.

LUTZKY: Call me "Wipe-em-out." Both of you. All of you.

CHONA: Wipe-em-out. Dr. Wipe-em-out.

LUTZKY: And you're "Lucky"?

VERONA: He got uh gun!

MONA: Me Mona.

LUTZKY: Mona?

MONA: Mona Mokus robbery.

CHONA: You are confusing the doctor, Mona. Mona, the doctor is confused.

VERONA: Perkins ssgot uh gun. Right there on thuh Tee V. He iduhnt spposed tuh have no gun!

MONA: Robbery Mokus Mona. Robbery Mokus Mona. Everything in its place.

CHONA: The robber comes later, Dr. Wipe-em-out Extraordinaire, Sir.

LUTZKY: There goes my squirt gun. Did you feel it?

VERONA: I seen this show before. Four times. Perkins duhnt even own no gun.

CHONA: Once there was uh doctor who became confused and then hosed us down.

LUTZKY: I must be confused. Must be the sun. Or the savages.

MONA: Savage Mokus. Robbery, Chona.

CHONA: Go on Mokus. Help yourself.

LUTZKY: I need to phone for backups. May I?

VERONA: He duhnt have no gun permit even. Wait. B. Cool. I seen this. Turns out alright. I think. . . .

CHONA: Juice? I made it myself!

MONA: I am going to lie down. I am going to lay down. Lie down? Lay down. Lay down?

LUTZKY: Why don't you lie down.

MONA: I am going to lie down.

CHONA: She's distraught. Bug bites all over. We're infested. Help yourself.

LUTZKY: You seem infested, Miss Molly. Get in line, I'll hose you down.

MONA: MonaMokusRobbery.

LUTZKY: Hello Sir. Parents of the Muslim faith? My fathers used to frequent the Panthers. For sport. That was before my time. Not too talkative are you. Come on. Give us a grunt. I'll give you a squirt.

VERONA: Ssnot no dart gun neither—. Holy. Chuh! Mmcallin thuh—That is not uh dart gun, Marlin!!!

MONA: Make your bed and lie in it. I'm going to lay down.

CHONA: Lie down.

MONA: Lay down.

CHONA: LIE, Mona.

MONA: Lie Mona lie Mona down.

CHONA: Down, Mona down.

MONA: Down, Mona, bites! Oh my eyelids! On-her-heels! Down Mona down.

VERONA: Call thuh cops.

LUTZKY: That will be about $99. Hello. This is Dr. Lutzky. Send ten over. Just like me. We've got a real one here. Won't even grunt. Huh! Hmmm. Phones not working. . . .

VERONA: Gimmie that! Thank-you. Hello? Marlin-Perkins-has-a-gun. I-am-telling-you-Marlin-Perkins-has-a-gun! Yeah it's loaded course it's loaded! You listen tuh me! I pay yuh tuh listen tuh me! We pay our taxes, Chona?

CHONA: I am going to make a peach cobbler. My mothers ma used to make cobblers. She used to gather the peaches out of her own backyard all by herself.

LUTZKY: Hold still, Charlene. I'll hose you down.

CHONA: Go on Mokus. Help yourself.

VERONA: HE'S SHOOTIN THUH WILD BEASTS!

MONA: Oh dear.

VERONA: He-is-shooting-them-for-real! We diduhnt pay our taxes, Chona.

LUTZKY: Here's my invoice. Sign here.

CHONA: X, Mona. Help yourself.

MONA: Splat.

CHONA: Cobbler, Dr. Lutzky? Fresh out of the oven????!!!

MONA: Splat.

LUTZKY: Wrap it to go, Charlene.

MONA: Splat.

LUTZKY: What did you claim your name was dear?

MONA: Splat.

CHONA: I'll cut you off a big slice. Enough for your company. Youre a company man.

LUTZKY: With backups, Miss Charlene. I'm a very lucky man. Molly's lucky too.

MONA: Splat. Splat. Splatsplatsplat.

VERONA: Cops dont care. This is uh outrage.

LUTZKY: Here's my card. There's my squirt gun! Did you feel it? I need backups. May I?

VERONA: Dont touch this phone. It's bugged.

LUTZKY: Oh dear!

CHONA: Cobbler, Verona?

LUTZKY: Well, good night.

VERONA: We pay our taxes, Chona?

LUTZKY: Well, good night!

VERONA: We pay out taxes Chona??!!!!?

MONA: Tuck me in. I need somebody tuh tuck me in.

F.

Verona speaks at the podium.

VERONA: I saw my first pictures of Africa on TV: Mutual of Omahas *Wild Kingdom.* The thirty-minute filler between Walt Disneys wonderful world and the CBS Evening News. It was a wonderful world: Marlin Perkins and Jim and their African guides. I was a junior guide and had a lifesize poster of Dr. Perkins sitting on a white Land Rover surrounded by wild things. Had me an 8 x 10 glossy of him too, signed, on my nightstand. Got my nightstand from Sears cause I had to have Marlin by my bed at night. Together we learned to differentiate African from Indian elephants the importance of hyenas in the wild funny looking trees on the slant—how do they stand up? Black folks with no clothes. Marlin loved and respected all the wild things. His guides took his English and turned it into the local lingo so that he could converse with the natives. Marlin even petted a rhino once. He tagged the animals and put them into zoos for their own protection. He encouraged us to be kind to animals through his shining example. Once there was uh me name Verona: I got mommy n dad tuh get me uh black dog n named it I named it "Namib" after thuh African sands n swore tuh be nice tuh it only Namib refused tuh be trained n crapped in corners of our basement n got up on thuh sofa when we went out n Namib wouldnt listen tuh me like Marlins helpers listened tuh him Namib wouldnt look at me when I talked tuh him n when I said someuhn like "sit" he wouldnt n "come" made im go n when I tied him up in thuh front yard so that he could bite the postman when thuh postman came like uh good dog would he wouldnt even bark just smile n wag his tail so I would kick Namib when no one could see me cause I was sure I was very very sure that Namib told lies uhbout me behind my back and Namib chewed through his rope one day n bit me n run off. I have this job. I work at a veterinarian hospital. I'm a euthanasia specialist. Somcone brought a stray dog in one day and I entered "black dog" in the black book and let her scream and whine and wag her tail and talk about me behind my back then I offered her the humane alternative. Wiped her out! I stayed late that night so that I could cut her open because I had to see I just had to see the heart of such a disagreeable domesticated thing. But no. Nothing different. Everything in its place. Do you know what that means? Everything in its place. Thats all.

(*Lights out*)

Part Two: Third Kingdom

KIN-SEER: Kin-Seer.

US-SEER: Us-Seer

SHARK-SEER: Shark-Seer.

SOUL-SEER: Soul-Seer.

OVER-SEER: Over-Seer.

————.

————.

KIN-SEER: Kin-Seer.

US-SEER: Us-Seer.

SHARK-SEER: Shark-Seer.

SOUL-SEER: Soul-Seer.

OVER-SEER: Over-Seer.

————.

————.

————. . .

KIN-SEER: Last night I dreamed of where I comed from. But where I comed from diduhnt look like nowhere like I been.

SOUL-SEER: There were 2 cliffs?

KIN-SEER: There were.

US-SEER: Uh huhn.

SHARK-SEER: 2 cliffs?

KIN-SEER: 2 cliffs: one on each other side thuh world.

SHARK-SEER: 2 cliffs?

KIN-SEER: 2 cliffs where thuh world had cleaved intuh 2.

OVER-SEER: The 2nd part comes apart in 2 parts.

SHARK-SEER: But we are not in uh boat!

US-SEER: But we iz.

SOUL-SEER: Iz. Uh huhn. Go on—

KIN-SEER: I was standin with my toes stuckted in thuh dirt. Nothin in front of me but water. And I was wavin. Wavin. Wavin at my uther me who I could barely see. Over thuh water on thuh uther cliff I could see my uther me but my uther me could not see me. And I was wavin wavin wavin saying gaw gaw gaw gaw eeeeeee-uh.

OVER-SEER: The 2nd part comes apart in 2 parts.

SHARK-SEER: But we are not in uh boat!

US-SEER: But we iz.

SOUL-SEER: Gaw gaw gaw gaw eeeee—

KIN-SEER: Ee-uh. Gaw gaw gaw gaw eeeee—

SOUL-SEER: Ee-uh.

US-SEER: Come home come home dont stay out too late. Bleached Bones Man may get you n take you far uhcross thuh waves, then baby, what will I do for love?

OVER-SEER: The 2nd part comes apart in-to 2.

SHARK-SEER: Edible fish are followin us. Our flesh is edible tuh them fish. Smile at them and they smile back. Jump overboard and they gobble you up. They smell blood. I see sharks. Ssssblak! Ssssblak! Gaw gaw gaw eee-uh. I wonder: Are you happy?

ALL: We are smiling!   *Slaves?*

OVER-SEER: Quiet, you, or you'll be jettisoned.

SOUL-SEER: Duhduhnt he duhduhnt he know my name? Ssblak ssblak ssblakallblak!

OVER-SEER: Thats your *self* youre looking at! Wonder #1 of my glass-bottomed boat.

KIN-SEER: My uther me then waved back at me and then I was happy. But my uther me whuduhnt wavin at me. My uther me was wavin at my Self. My uther me was wavin at uh black black speck in thuh middle of thuh sea where years uhgoh from uh boat I had been—UUH!

OVER-SEER: Jettisoned.

SHARK-SEER: Jettisoned?

KIN-SEER: Jettisoned.

US-SEER: Uh huhn.

SOUL-SEER: To-the-middle-of-the-bottom-of-the-big-black-sea.

KIN-SEER: And then my Self came up between us. Rose up out of thuh water and standin on them waves my Self was standin. And I was wavin wavin wavin and my Me was wavin and wavin and my Self that rose between us went back down in-to-the-sea.

KIN-SEER: FFFFFFFFF.

US-SEER: Thup.

SHARK-SEER: Howwe gonna find my Me?

KIN-SEER: Me wavin at Me. Me wavin at I. Me wavin at my Self.

US-SEER: FFFFFFFFF.

SOUL-SEER: Thup.

SHARK-SEER: I dream up uh fish thats swallowin me and I dream up uh me that is then becamin that fish and uh dream of that fish becamin uh shark and I dream of that shark becamin uhshore. UUH! And on thuh shore thuh shark is given shoes. And I whuduhnt me no more and I whuduhnt no fish. My new Self was uh third Self made by thuh space in between. And my new Self wonders: Am I happy? Is my new Self happy in my new-Self shoes?

KIN-SEER: MAY WAH-VIN ET MAY. MAY WAH-VIN ET EYE. MAY WAH-VIN ET ME SOULF.

OVER-SEER: Half the world had fallen away making 2 worlds and a sea between. Those 2 worlds inscribe the Third Kingdom.

KIN-SEER: Me hollering uhcross thuh cliffs at my Self:

US-SEER: Come home come home dont stay out too late.

SHARK-SEER: Black folks with no clothes. Then all thuh black folks clothed in smilin. In betwen thuh folks is uh distance thats uh wet space. 2 worlds: Third Kingdom.

SOUL-SEER: Gaw gaw gaw gaw gaw gaw gaw gaw.

KIN-SEER: May wah-vin et may may wah-vin et eye may wah-vin et me sould.

SHARK-SEER: How many kin kin I hold. Whole hull full.

SOUL-SEER: Thuh hullholesfull of bleachin bones.

US-SEER: Bleached Bones Man may come and take you far uh-cross thuh sea from me.

OVER-SEER: Who're you again?

KIN-SEER: I'm. Lucky.   *Refers to Godot?*

OVER-SEER: Who're you again?

SOUL-SEER: Duhdduhnt-he-know-my-name?

KIN-SEER: Should I jump? Shouldijumporwhut?

SHARK-SEER: But we are not in uh boat!

US-SEER: But we iz. Iz iz iz uh huhn. Iz uh huhn. Uh huhn iz.

SHARK-SEER: I wonder: Are we happy? Thuh looks we look look so.

US-SEER: They like smiles and we will like what they will like.

SOUL-SEER: UUH!

KIN-SEER: Me wavin at me me wavin at my I me wavin at my soul.

SHARK-SEER: Chomp chomp chomp chomp.

KIN-SEER: Ffffffffffff—

US-SEER: Thup.

SHARK-SEER: Baby, what will I do for love?

SOUL-SEER: Wave me uh wave and I'll wave one back blow me uh kiss n I'll blow you one back.

OVER-SEER: Quiet, you, or you'll be jettisoned!

SHARK-SEER: Chomp. Chomp. Chomp. Chomp.

KIN-SEER: Wa-vin wa-vin.

SHARK-SEER: Chomp chomp chomp chomp.

KIN-SEER: Howwe gonna find my Me?

SOUL-SEER: Rock. Thuh boat. Rock. Thuh boat. Rock. Thuh boat. Rock. Thuh boat.

US-SEER: We be walkin wiggly cause we left our bones in bed.

SOUL-SEER, US-SEER, SHARK-SEER, KIN-SEER and OVER-SEER: Gaw gaw gaw gaw gaw gaw gaw gaw gaw gaw gaw gaw gaw gaw gaw gaw—

OVER-SEER: I'm going to yell "Land Ho!" in a month or so and all of this will have to stop. I'm going to yell "Land Ho!" in a month or so and that will be the end of this. Line up!

SHARK-SEER: Where to?

OVER-SEER: Ten-Shun!

SOUL-SEER: How come?

OVER-SEER: Move on move on move—. LAND HO!

KIN-SEER: You said I could wave as long as I see um. I still see um.

OVER-SEER: Wave then.

Part Three: Open House

A.

A double-frame slide show. Slides of Aretha hugging Anglor and Blanca. Dialogue begins and continues with the slides progressing as follows: (1) they are expressionless; next (2) they smile; next (3) they smile more; next (4) even wider smiles. The enlargement of smiles continues. Actors speak as the stage remains semi-dark and the slides flash overhead.

ARETHA: Smile, honey, smile.

ANGLOR: I want my doll. Where is my doll I want my doll where is it I want it. I want it now.

ARETHA: Miss Blanca? Give us uh pretty smile, darlin.

BLANCA: I want my doll too. Go fetch.

ARETHA: You got such nice white teeth, Miss Blanca. Them teeths makes uh smile tuh remember you by.

ANGLOR: She won't fetch the dolls. She won't fetch them because she hasn't fed them.

ARETHA: Show us uh smile, Mr. Anglor. Uh quick toothy show stopper.

BLANCA: She won't fetch them because she hasn't changed them. They're sitting in their own filth because they haven't been changed they haven't been fed they haven't been aired they've gone without sunshine.

ANGLOR: Today is her last day. She's gone slack.

BLANCA: Is today your last day, Aretha?

ANGLOR: Yes.

ARETHA: Smile for your daddy, honey. Mr. Charles, I cant get em tuh smile.

BLANCA: Is it? Is it your last day?!

ANGLOR: You see her belongings in the boxcar, don't you?

BLANCA: Where are you going, Aretha? You're going to get my doll!

ARETHA: Wish I had me some teeths like yours, Miss Blanca. So straight and cleaned. So pretty and white.—Yes, Mr. Charles, I'm trying. Mr. Anglor. Smile. Smile for show.

BLANCA: Youre going away, aren't you? AREN'T YOU?

ANGLOR: You have to answer her.

BLANCA: You have to answer me.

ARETHA: Yes, Missy. Mm goin. Mm goin uhway.

BLANCA: Where?

ARETHA: Uhway. Wayuhway.

ANGLOR: To do what?

ARETHA: Dunno. Goin uhway tuh—tuh swallow courses uh meals n fill up my dance card! Goin uhway tuh live, I guess.

BLANCA: Live? Get me my doll. My doll wants to wave goodbye. Who's going to sew up girl doll when she pops?!

ANGLOR: Who's going to chastise boy doll? Boy doll has no manners.

BLANCA: Who's going to plait girl doll's hair?! Her hair should be plaited just like mine should be plaited.

ANGLOR: Who's going to clean their commodes?! Who's going to clean our commodes?! We won't visit you because we won't be changed! We'll be sitting in our own filth because we won't have been changed we won't have been fed we won't have been aired we won't have manners we won't have plaits we'll have gone without sunshine.

ARETHA: Spect your motherll have to do all that.

BLANCA and ANGLOR: Who!??!

ARETHA: Dunno. Smile, Blanca, Anglor, huh? Lets see them pretty white teeths.

(*Camera clicking noises*)

B.

Onstage, Mrs. Aretha Saxon.

ARETHA: Six seven eight nine. Thupp. Ten eleven twelve thirteen fourteen fifteen sixteen. Thupp. Seventeen. Eighteen nineteen twenty twenty-one. And uh little bit. Thuuup. Thuup. Gotta know thuh size. Thup. Gotta know thuh size exact. Thup. Got people comin. Hole house full. They gonna be kin? Could be strangers. How many kin kin I hold. Whole hold full. How many strangers. Depends on thuh size. Thup. Size of thuh space. Thuup. Depends on thuh size of thuh kin. Pendin on thuh size of thuh strangers. Get more mens than womens ssgonna be one number more womens than mens ssgonna be uhnother get animals thuup get animals we kin pack em thuup. Tight. Thuuup. Thuuuup. Mmmm. Thuuup. Count back uhgain: little bit twenty-one twenty nineteen eighteen seventhuup sixteen fifteen fourteen twelve thuup eleven then uh huh thuuup. Three two thuuup one n one. Huh. Twenty-one and one and one. And thuh little bit. Thuuup. Thup. Thirty-two and uh half.

MISS FAITH: Footnote #1: The human cargo capacity of the English slaver, the *Brookes*, was about 3,250 square feet. From James A. Rawley, *The Transatlantic Slave Trade*, G. J. McLeod Limited, 1981, page 283.

ARETHA: $32^1/_2$ Thuuup! Howmy gonna greet em. Howmy gonna say hello. Thuup! Huh. Greet em with uh smile! Thupp. Still got uh grin. Uh little bit. Thup. Thuuup. Thirty-two and uh little bit. $32^1/_2$. Better buzz Miss Faith. Miss Faith?

MISS FAITH: Yeahus—.

ARETHA: Thuup. Sss Mrs. Saxon. 2D.

MISS FAITH: Yes, Mrs. Saxon. Recovering? No more bleeding, I hope.

ARETHA: You wanted tuh know thuh across.

MISS FAITH: Holes healing I hope.

ARETHA: 32 and uh half.

MISS FAITH: Is that a fact?

ARETHA: Thup. Thatsuh fact. 32 feets and uh half on the a-cross! Thats uh fact!

MISS FAITH: Thank you, Maam!

ARETHA: You say I'm tuh have visitors, Miss Faith! You say me havin uh visitation is written in thuh book. I say in here we could fit—three folks.

MISS FAITH: Three. I'll note that. On with your calculations, Mrs. Saxon!

ARETHA: On with my calculations. Thuup.

MISS FAITH: Mrs. Saxon? I calculate—we'll fit six hundred people. Six hundred in a pinch. Footnote #2: 600 slaves were transported on the *Brookes*, although it only had space for 451. *Ibid.*, page 14.

ARETHA: Miss Faith, six hundred in here won't go.

MISS FAITH: You give me the facts. I draw from them, Maam. I draw from them in accordance with the book. Six hundred will fit. We will have to pack them tight.

ARETHA: Miss Faith—thuup—Miss Faith—

MISS FAITH: Mrs. Saxon, book says you are due for an extraction Mrs. Saxon an extraction are you not. Gums should be ready. Gums should be healed. You are not cheating me out of valuable square inches, Mrs. Saxon, of course you are not. You gave me the facts of course you did. We know well that "She who cheateth me out of some valuable square inches shall but cheat herself out of her assigned seat aside the most high." We are familiar with Amendment 2.1 are we not, Mrs. Saxon. Find solace in the book and—bid your teeth goodbye. Buzz me not.

ARETHA: Thup. Thup. 2:1.

MISS FAITH: Footnote #3: The average ratio of slaves per ship, male to female was 2:1.

ARETHA: "Then she looketh up at the Lord and the Lord looketh down on where she knelt. She spake thusly: 'Lord, what proof canst thou give me that my place inside your kingdom hath not been by another usurpt? For there are many, many in need who seek a home in your great house, and many are those who are deserving.' " Thuuuuup! Thuup. "And the Lord looketh upon her with" Thuuuup! "And the Lord looketh upon her with kind azure eyes and on his face there lit a toothsome—a toothsome smile and said, 'Fear not, Charles, for your place in my kingdom is secure.' " Thup. Thuuup! Charles? Miss Faith?

MISS FAITH: Buzz! BUZZZ!

(*Buzzer*)

C.

Dreamtime: Charles appears. Blanca and Anglor hum the note of the buzz.

ARETHA: And she looketh up at the Lord—

CHARLES: And the Lord looketh downeth oneth whereth sheth knelth—

ARETHA: What proof can yuh give me, Lord? I wants uh place.

CHARLES: A place you will receive. Have you got your papers?

ARETHA: Thuh R-S-stroke-26?[4]

CHARLES: Let us see. It says "Charles." "Charles Saxon."

ARETHA: Had me uh husband names Charles.

[4]A common form from the Division of Housing and Community Renewal.

CHARLES: Funny name for you, Mrs. Saxon. "Charles"?

ARETHA: My husbands name. We's split up now.

CHARLES: Divorce?

ARETHA: Divorce?

CHARLES: The breakup of those married as sanctioned by the book. Illegal, then. Non legal? I see. Were you legally wed, Charles? Wed by the book? Didn't—"jump the broom" or some such nonsense, eh? Perhaps it was an estrangement. Estrangement? Was it an estrangement? Estrangement then? You will follow him, I suppose.

ARETHA: He's—He's dead, Mister Sir.

CHARLES: I'll mark "yes," then. Sign here. An "X" will do, Charles.

ARETHA: I dunno.

CHARLES: There is a line—

ARETHA: Mehbe—

CHARLES: —that has formed itself behind you—

ARETHA: Mehbe—do I gotta go—mehbe—maybe I could stay awhiles. Here.

CHARLES: The book says you expire. No option to renew.

ARETHA: And my place?

CHARLES: Has been secured.

ARETHA: Where?

CHARLES: Move on.

ARETHA: Where to?

CHARLES: Move on, move on, move on!

(*Humming grows louder*)

D.

Humming is replaced by buzzer buzz. Miss Faith appears to extract Aretha's teeth with a large pair of pliers.

ARETHA: How many—extractions this go, Sister Faith?

MISS FAITH: Open up. ALL. Don't look upon it as punishment, Mrs. Saxon, look on it as an integral part of the great shucking off.

The old must willingly shuck off for the sake of the new. Much like the snakes new skin suit, Mrs. Saxon. When your new set comes in—and you will be getting a new set, that the book has promised—they will have a place. We will have made them room. Where would we go if we did not extract? There are others at this very moment engaged in extracting so that for us there may be a place. Where would we go if we did not extract? Where would they go? What would happen? Who would survive to tell? The old is yankethed out and the new riseth up in its place! Besides, if we didnt pluck them we couldnt photograph them. To be entered into the book they must be photographed. Think of it as getting yourself chronicled, Mrs. Saxon. You are becoming a full part of the great chronicle! Say that, Mrs. Saxon. You dont want to be forgotten, do you?

ARETHA: Thuup! I was gonna greet em with uh grin.

MISS FAITH: An opened jawed awe will do. Open? Yeauhs. Looks of wonder suit us best just before we're laid to rest. AAAh! Open. Hmmm. Canine next, I think. Find solace in the book. Find order in the book. Find find find the book. Where is the book. Go find it. Find it. Go on, get up.

ARETHA: Thuuuuup.

MISS FAITH: Read from it.

ARETHA: Thuuuuuup?

MISS FAITH: Now.

ARETHA: Thup. Thuuuuppp! "The woman lay on the sickness bed her gums were moist and bleeding. The Lord appeared to her, as was his custom, by dripping himself down through the cold water faucet and walking across the puddle theremade. The Lord stood over the sickness bed toweling himself off and spake thusly: 'Charles, tell me why is it that you. . . .'" Thuuuuuup! "Charles" uhgain. Thup. Wonder why he calls her "Charles," Miss Faith? Now, I had me uh husband named Charles wonder if it says anything uhbout Retha Saxons husband Charles in thuh book. Still. Havin uh husband named Charles aint no reason for her tuh be called—

MISS FAITH: Open! She is named what her name is. She was given that name by him. The book says your Charles is dead. Sorry. Never to return. Sorry. That is a fact. A fact to accept. The power of the book lies in its contents. Its contents are facts. Through examination of the facts therein we may see what is to come. Through the examination of what comes we may turn to our book and see from whence it came. Example: The book has let us know for quite some time that you expire 19-6-65, do you not, Mrs. Saxon. You expire. (Footnote #5: "Juneteenth," June 19th in 1865, was when, a good many months after the Emancipation Proclamation, the slaves in Texas heard they were free.) You expire. Along with your lease. Expiration 19-6-65 with no option to renew.

ARETHA: Thuuup?

MISS FAITH: You expire. Yes, Maam!

ARETHA: Yahs Maam.

MISS FAITH: Yes, Maam. 19-6-65. That's a fact. And now we know youre to have visitors. And now we know that those visitors are waiting on your doorstep.

ARETHA: Naaaa?

MISS FAITH: Now. 32.5, 19-6-65? Now. Open! Now. Close!

ARETHA: Now. Howmy gonna greet em? Was gonna greet em with uh smile. . . . Awe jawll do. I guess.

MISS FAITH: Youre expiring. It's only natural. Thats a fact. Amendment 1807,⁶ Mrs. Saxon. A fact. You sit comfortably. I'll buzz them in.

(*Buzzer*)

E.

Dreamtime: Charles appears.

CHARLES: You know what they say about the hand that rocks the cradle, don't you, Aretha?

ARETHA: Nope.

CHARLES: Whats that?

ARETHA: No suh. No Mr. Charles suh. I dont.

CHARLES: Well well well. "No suh. I dont." Well well well well thats just as well. How about this one, eh? "Two hands in the bush is better than one hand in—"

---

⁶In March of 1807, England's slave trade was abolished.

ARETHA: Sssthey feedin time, Mistuh Charles.

CHARLES: —Go on. Feed them. Ooooh! These will make some lovely shots—give the children some wonderful memories. Memory is a very important thing, don't you know. It keeps us in line. It reminds us of who we are, memory. Without it we could be anybody. We would be running about here with no identities. You would not know that you're my—help, you'd just be a regular street and alley heathen. I would not remember myself to be master. There would be chaos, chaos it would be without a knowledge from whence we came. Little Anglor and little Blanca would—well, they would not even exist! And then what would Daddy do? Chaos without correct records. Chaos. Aaaah. You know what chaos is, don't you.

ARETHA: No suh. I dont.

CHARLES: He he he! Aaaaah! Ignorance is bliss! They say ignorance is bliss—only for the ignorant—for those of us who must endure them we find their ignorance anything but blissful. Isn't that right.

ARETHA: Yes suh.

CHARLES: "Yes suh Yes suh." Heh heh heh heh. Hold them up where I can see them. Thaaaat's it. You will look back on these and know what was what. Hold em up. There. Thaaaaaat's just fine. Smile. Smile! Smile? Smiiiiiile—

(*Clicking of camera*)

F.

Clicking of camera is replaced by buzzing of door.

ANGLOR: Very nice!

BLANCA: Very nice!

MISS FAITH: As the book promised: very well lit, views of the land and of the sea, a rotating northern exposure—

ANGLOR: Very very nice!

BLANCA: Oh yes very nice! Blanca Saxon—

ANGLOR: Anglor Saxon.

ARETHA: I'm Mrs. Saxon.

MISS FAITH: —Expires 19-6-65.

ANGLOR: Very nice.

BLANCA: We're newlyweds.

ARETHA: I'm Mrs. Saxon.

BLANCA: Newlyweds. Newly wedded. New.

ANGLOR: Very new.

MISS FAITH: Very nice.

BLANCA: Blanca and Anglor Saxon.

ARETHA: Thuup! I'm—

MISS FAITH: Very nice. 32.5, 19-6-65. By the book. As promised.

BLANCA: We read the book. The red letter edition. The red her-ring.[7] Cover to cover. We read the red book.

ANGLOR: We're well read.

ARETHA: You ever heard of Charles? He's in thuh book—

MISS FAITH: Five walk-in closets. Of course, theyre not in yet.

BLANCA: Does she come with the place?

MISS FAITH: She's on her way out.

BLANCA: She has no teeth.

ANGLOR: Haven't I seen her somewhere before?

BLANCA: Anglor Saxon!—He's always doing that. When we met he wondered if he hadn't seen me somewhere before. And he had! We had to make an Amendment.

MISS FAITH: The closets will go here here there and thar. We will yank her out to make room for them.

ANGLOR: Thus says the book. Amendment 2.1. Always liked that amendment. It's very open—open to interpretation.

MISS FAITH: We will put in some windows, of course.

BLANCA: Of course.

ANGLOR: Yanking out the commode?

MISS FAITH: Commodes just for show.

ARETHA: Just for show.

---

[7]Red herring. In co-op apartment sales, a preliminary booklet explaining the specifics of sale.

BLANCA: We might like to have a bathroom. We're planning to have a big family.

ARETHA: A family. Had me uh family once. They let me go.

ANGLOR: Meet our children: Anglor and Blanca. They're so nice and quiet they don't speak unless they're spoken to they don't move unless we make them.

MISS FAITH: This is where we plan the bathroom.

ANGLOR: You'll never guess where we met.

BLANCA: Love at first sight.

MISS FAITH: Plenty of room for a big family.

ANGLOR: Guess where we met!

MISS FAITH: We'll rip out this kitchen if you like leave it bare youll have more space.

ARETHA: Charles got you tuhgether.

ANGLOR: Close. I told you we know her, Blanca.

MISS FAITH: We'll put in the commode and rip it out then put it back again. If you so desire.

BLANCA: Guess!

ANGLOR: We're going to need someone to mind that commode. We're going to need help.

ARETHA: I raised uh family once. I raised uh boy. I raised uh girl. I trained em I bathed em. I bathed uh baby once. Bathed two babies.

BLANCA: We're childhood sweethearts. From childhood. We met way back. In the womb.

ANGLOR: We need help.

BLANCA: We're twins!

ARETHA: That iduhnt in thuh book.

ANGLOR: We're related. By marriage. It's all legal. By the book.

MISS FAITH: We will put the commode closer to the bath. Put the commode in the bath. Youll have more space.

ARETHA: We got different books.

ANGLOR: We have the same last name! Saxon! Blanca Saxon—

BLANCA: Anglor Saxon. Blanca and Anglor Saxon—

ARETHA: I'm Mrs. Saxon. Howdeedoo.

ANGLOR: Mrs. Saxon, we need help.

BLANCA: We're going to have children. We're going to breed. Weve bred two and we'll breed more.

MISS FAITH: Its all a part of the great shucking off—

ARETHA: You wouldnt know nothing uhbout uh Charles, wouldja? Charles was my husband. Charles Saxon?

MISS FAITH: The old must willingly shuck off to make way for the new. Much like the snakes new skin suit. The new come in and we gladly make them room. Where would they go if we did not extract?

ANGLOR: I don't suppose youve nowhere to go? We need help. You seem like a sturdy help type. I suppose you can shuffle and serve simultaneously? Wet nurse the brood weve bred? A help like you would be in accordance with the book. Make things make sense. Right along with the record. More in line with what you're used to. I would be master. Blanca: mistress. That's little master and little missy. Yes, that's it! Give us a grin!

MISS FAITH: Shes on her way out.

ANGLOR: Give us a grin!

BLANCA: Anglor, she's toothless.

ARETHA: Charles sscome back! I see in down there wavin—no— directin traffic. Left right left right left—he remembers me right right he's forgiven me right left right right he wants tuh see me.

MISS FAITH: Charles is dead.

ANGLOR: Thus says the book?

ARETHA: Make uh amendment. Charles ssdown thuh street. On thuh street down thuh street.

MISS FAITH: Not in my book.

BLANCA: We've got different books.

ARETHA: We got differin books. Make uh amendment. I'm packin my bags. I left him. Had to go. Two babies to care for.

ANGLOR: We know her from somewhere.

ARETHA: Had tuh go. He gived me his name. Make uh amendment.

BLANCA: We've got the same name.

ANGLOR: WE KNOW HER FROM SOMEWHERE! Too bad she can't grin.

ARETHA: Had to go. Have tuh go. Make thuh amendment, Sister Faith, Charles is back.

MISS FAITH: You need help. She comes with the place. She can live under the sink. Out of mind out of sight.

BLANCA: She's toothless.

ANGLOR: Not a good example for the breed. Make the amendment.

ARETHA: Miss Faith? Make uh uhmendment. Charless waitin—

MISS FAITH: Charles is dead! Never to return. Thus says the—

ARETHA: Buchenwald! Buchenwald! I—I showed em my blue eyes n they hauled me off anyway—

BLANCA: Stick to the facts, help! She's bad for the brood. Make that amendment.

MISS FAITH: An amendment.

ARETHA: Nine million just disappeared![8] Thats uh fact!

BLANCA: Six million. Six! Miss Faith? The amendment! I would like another child. I would like to get started!

ARETHA: They hauled us from thuh homeland! Stoled our clothes!

MISS FAITH: Amendment! Amendment XIII.[9] you have been extracted from the record, Mrs. Saxon. You are free. You are clear. You may go.

ANGLOR: Free and clear to go. Go.

MISS FAITH: Go.

BLANCA: Go.

ARETHA: Oh. How should I greet him? Should greet im with uh—

BLANCA: GIT! Wave goodbye, children! That's it. That's it! They're so well mannered.

ANGLOR: Wife? Brood? Isn't this a lovely view? And the buzzer! It works!

(*Buzzer*)

---

[8]An estimated 9 million Africans were taken from Africa into slavery (Rawley, *The Transatlantic Slave Trade*). An estimated 6 million Jewish people were killed in the concentration camps of WWII.

[9]Amendment XIII abolished slavery in the United States.

G.

Dreamtime: Charles appears.

CHARLES: You let them take out the teeth you're giving up the last of the verifying evidence. All'll be obliterated. All's left will be conjecture. We won't be able to tell you apart from the others. We won't even know your name. Things will get messy. Chaos. Perverted. People will twist around the facts to suit the truth.

ARETHA: You know what they say bout thuh hand that rocks thuh cradle?

CHARLES: I didn't rock their cradles.

ARETHA: You know how thuh sayin goes?

CHARLES: "Rocks the cradle—rules the world," but I didn't rock—

ARETHA: Dont care what you say you done, Charles. We're makin us uh histironical amendment here, K? Give us uh smile. Uh big smile for thuh book.

CHARLES: Historical. An "Historical Amendment," Ma'am.

ARETHA: Smile, Charles.

CHARLES: Where are you going, Miss Aretha?

ARETHA: Mmm goin tuh take my place aside thuh most high.

CHARLES: Up north, huh?

ARETHA: Up north.

CHARLES: Sscold up there, you know.

ARETHA: Smile, Charles! Thats it!

CHARLES: Chaos! You know what chaos is?! Things cease to adhere to—

ARETHA: SMILE. Smile, Charles, Smile! Show us them pretty teeths. Good.

CHARLES: I can't get the children to smile, Ma'am.

ARETHA: You smile.

CHARLES: They're crying, Miss Aretha!

ARETHA: Smile! Smile! SMILE! There. Thats nice.

CHARLES: They're crying.

ARETHA: Dont matter none. Dont matter none at all. You say its uh cry I say it uh smile. These photographics is for my scrapbook.

Scraps uh graphy for my book. Smile or no smile mm gonna remember you. Mm gonna remember you grinnin.

(*Whir of camera grows louder. Lights fade to black*)

Third Kingdom (Reprise)

OVER-SEER: What are you doing?

US-SEER: Throw-ing. Up.

KIN-SEER: Kin-Seer scz.

SHARK-SEER: Shark-Seer sez.

US-SEER: Us-Seer sez.

SOUL-SEER: Soul-Seer sez.

OVER-SEER: Over-Seer sez.

KIN-SEER: Sez Kin-Seer sez.

SHARK-SEER: Sezin Shark-Seer sez.

US-SEER: Sez Us-Seer sezin.

SOUL-SEER: Sezin Soul-Seer sezin sez.

OVER-SEER: Sez Over-Seer sez.

KIN-SEER: Tonight I dream of where I be-camin from. And where I be camin from duhduhnt look like nowhere like I been.

SOUL-SEER: The tale of how we *were* when we *were*—

OVER-SEER: You woke up screaming.

SHARK-SEER: How we *will* be when we *will* be—

OVER-SEER: You woke up screaming.

US-SEER: And how we be, now that we iz.

ALL: You woke up screaming out—you woke me up.

OVER-SEER: Put on this. Around your head and over your eyes. It will help you sleep. See? Like me. Around your head and over your eyes. It will help you see.

KIN-SEER, US-SEER and SHARK-SEER: Gaw gaw gaw gaw—eeeee-uh. Gaw gaw gaw gaw eeeeeee-uh.

SOUL-SEER: Howzit gonna fit? Howzitgonnafit me?!

US-SEER: Bleached Bones Man has comed and tooked you. You fall down in-to-the-sea.

KIN-SEER: Should I jump? Should I jump?? Should I jump shouldi-jumporwhut?

SHARK-SEER: I dream up uh fish thats swallowin me—

SHARK-SEER and KIN-SEER: And I dream up uh me that is then be-camin that fish and I dream up that fish be-camin uh shark and I dream up that shark be-camin uhshore.

ALL: UUH!

SOUL-SEER: And where I be-camin from duhduhnt look like nowhere I been.

SHARK-SEER and KIN-SEER: And I whuduhnt me no more and I whuduhnt no fish. No new Self was uh 3rd Self made by thuh space in between.

ALL: UUH!

KIN-SEER: Rose up out uh thuh water and standin on them waves my Self was standin. And my Self that rose between us went back down in-to-the-sea.

US-SEER: EEEEEEEEE!

SHARK-SEER: Me wavin at me me wavin at I me wavin at my Self.

US-SEER: Bleached Bones Man has comed and tooked you. You fall down in-to-the-sea. . . .

KIN-SEER: Baby, what will I do for love?

OVER-SEER: Around your head and over your eyes. This piece of cloth will help you see.

SHARK-SEER: BLACK FOLKS WITH NO CLOTHES. . . .

US-SEER: This boat tooked us to-the-coast.

SOUL-SEER: THUH SKY WAS JUST AS BLUE!

KIN-SEER: Thuuuup!

HARK-SEER: Eat eat eat please eat.

SOUL-SEER: THUH SKY WAS JUST AS BLUE!

KIN-SEER: Thuuuup!

SHARK-SEER: Eat eat eat please eat. Eat eat eat please eat.

OVER-SEER: Around your head and over your eyes.

US-SEER: This boat tooked us to-the-coast.

SOUL-SEER: But we are not in uh boat!

US-SEER: But we iz. Iz uh-huhn-uh-huhn-iz.

OVER-SEER: There are 2 cliffs. 2 cliffs where the Word has cleaved. Half the Word has fallen away making 2 Words and a space between. Those 2 Words inscribe the third Kingdom.

KIN-SEER: Should I jump shouldijumporwhut.

US-SEER: Come home come home dont stay out too late.

KIN-SEER: Me hollerin uhcross thuh cliffs at my Self.

SOUL-SEER: Ssblak! Ssblak! Ssblakallblak!

OVER-SEER: That's your *soul* you're looking at. Wonder #9 of my glass-bottomed boat. Swallow it, you, or you'll be jettisoned

SOUL-SEER: UUH! UUH!

KIN-SEER: This boat tooked me from-my-coast.

US-SEER: Come home come home come home come home.

SOUL-SEER: The tale of who we were when we were, who we will be when we will be and who we be now that we iz:

US-SEER: Iz-uhhuhn-uhhuhn-iz.

KIN-SEER: You said I could wave as long as I see um. I still see um.

OVER-SEER: Wave then.

OVER-SEER, KIN-SEER, SOUL-SEER, SHARK-SEER and US-SEER: Gaw gaw gaw gaw ee-uh. Gaw gaw gaw gaw ee-uh.

SHARK-SEER: This is uh speech in uh language of codes. Secret signs and secret symbols.

KIN-SEER: Wave wave wave wave. Wave wave wave wave.

SHARK-SEER: Should I jump shouldijumporwhut? Should I jump shouldijumporwhut?

KIN-SEER:	SHARK-SEER:
Wave wave wave wave.	Should I jump shouldijumporwhut?
Wavin wavin	Should I jump should I jump
wavin wavin	shouldijumporwhut?

US-SEER: Baby, what will I do for love?

SOUL-SEER: Rock. Thuh boat. Rock. Thuh boat.

KIN-SEER:	SOUL-SEER:	SHARK-SEER:	US-SEER:
Wavin wavin	Rock. Thuh boat.	Shouldijump	Thuh sky
wavin	Rock.	shouldijump	was just
wavin	Thuh boat.	or whut?	as blue!
			THUP!

Wavin wavin	Rock. Thuh boat.	Shouldijump	Thuh sky
wavin wavin	Rock.	shouldijump	was just
wavin wavin	Thuh boat.	or whut?	as blue!

OVER-SEER: HO!

KIN-SEER:	SOUL-SEER:	SHARK-SEER:	US-SEER:
Wavin wavin	Rock. Thuh boat.	Shouldijump	Thuh sky
wavin	Rock.	shouldijump	was just
wavin	Thuh boat.	or whut?	as blue!
			THUP!

Wavin wavin	Rock. Thuh boat.	Shouldijump	Thuh sky
wavin wavin	Rock.	shouldijump	was just
wavin wavin	Thuh boat.	or whut?	as blue!

OVER-SEER: HO!

KIN-SEER, SOUL-SEER, SHARK-SEER, US-SEER and OVER-SEER: Gaw
    gaw gaw gaw gaw gaw gaw gaw.

OVER-SEER: I'm going to yell "Land Ho!" in a day or so and all of
    this will have to stop. I am going to yell "Land Ho!" in a day or
    so and that will be the end of this.

KIN-SEER, SOUL-SEER, SHARK-SEER and US-SEER: Gaw gaw gaw gaw-
    ee-uh. Gaw gaw gaw gaw-eeeee-uh.

OVER-SEER: What are you doing? What'reya doin. What'reya-
    doeeeeee! WHAT ARE YOU DO-EEE-NUH???!

KIN-SEER: —.—: Throw-ing. Kisses.

Part 4: Greeks (or the Slugs)

A.

MR. SERGEANT SMITH: I'll have four. Four shots. Four at thuh desk. Go ahead—put in thuh colored film. Mmsplurgin. Splurging. Uh huh. Wants em tuh see my shoes as black. Shirt as khaki. Stripes as green. No mop n broom bucket today! I'll sit first. No. Stand. I kin feel it. In here. Mmm gettin my Distinction today. Thuh events of my destiny ssgonna fall untuh place. What events? That I dont know. But they gonna fall intuh place all right. They been all along marchin in that direction. Soon they gonna fall. Ssonly natural. Ssonly fair. They gonna fall intuh place. I kin feel it. In here. This time tomorrow mm gonna have me my Distinction. Gonna be shakin hands with thuh Commander. Gonna be salutin friendly back n forth. Gonna be rewarded uh desk cause when uh mans distinguished he's got hisself uh desk. Standin at thuh desk. My desk. Sssgonna be mines, anyhow. Fnot this un then one just like it. Hands in pockets. No—out. Ready for work. Here is Sergeant Smith at his desk. Ready. Ready for work. Next, second shot: right hand on the desk. Like on the Bible. God and Country. Here is a man who loves his work. The name of this man is the name of Smith. You get the stripes in? They gonna be bars by evenin! Ha! Bars by evenin! Having a desk is distinguished. All of us have them. Because when there is danger from above, we stop. We look. We listen. Then we—dive underneath our desk (being careful that we do not catch our heads on the desk lip). Dive! Dive under our desks where it is safe. Like turtles. In our shells we wait for the danger to pass.—I don't wanna do uh shot uh that—don't want em tuh worry. Next, third shot: Here—oh. I will sit. Hands folded. Here I am—no. Arms folded. Next, shot number four. Ready? Hands on books and books open. A full desk and a smiling man. Sergeant Smith has got stacks of paper, but, not to worry, he is a good worker and will do well. Wait. Uh smile. Okay. Go head. Take it. Smiling at work. They like smiles.

(*Airplane sounds*)

B.

Mrs. Sergeant Smith and Buffy. A lovely home.

BUFFY: Mommie, what should the Biloxie Twins wear today?

MRS. SMITH: Sumthin nice.

BUFFY: The green one with pink stripes orange and yellow fuzzy sweater sets. Blue coat dresses. Double breasted. Which one's nicest?

MRS. SMITH: They all perm press? Put em in permanent press. You don't want em arrivin wrinkled. I vote for them two sharp little brown n white polka-dotted numbers. Put em both in thuh brown n white dotted swisses.

BUFFY: There iduhn't any brown and white swiss.

MRS. SMITH: Perm press is best. Put em in thuh swiss.

BUFFY: I'll press em with my hands. My hands get as hot as uh iron sometimes, Mommie. Here they go—ssss—tuh! Hot enough! Press press press.

MRS. SMITH: Don't press on thuh desk. Gotta keep your daddy's desk nice for im. Use starch? Starch!

BUFFY: Starch—starchstarch! Ooooh—starch made uh tab come off.

MRS. SMITH: Sssokay. It'll hold with three tabs.

BUFFY: What if thuh wind blows her dress? What if three tabs won't hold? She'll be naked. Thuh wind'll steal her clothes and then she'll be naked.

MRS. SMITH: Ssit pressed? Bring it here. Lemmie feel. Good, Buffeena—

BUFFY: But what is her dress whips off? What if she is naked? Can't be outside and naked people will see her she'll be shamed—

MRS. SMITH: Good tuh be pressed. Don't like crinkles—

BUFFY: What if thuh wind pulls like this and this and then she is naked and then—

MRS. SMITH: She kin hide behind her twin. They look just alike, don't they. They look just alike then Miss-Naked-Biloxie-with-thuh-three-tabs kin hide behind Miss-Fully-Clothed-Biloxie-with-thuh-four. Nobody'll notice nothin.

BUFFY: Where the Biloxie Twins off to, Mommie?

MRS. SMITH: Off out.

BUFFY: Off out where?

MRS. SMITH: Off out to thuh outside.

BUFFY: Off outside when they go who're they gonna meet?

MRS. SMITH: Their Maker. They're gonna meet their Maker. Huh! Sssimportant. Last furlough your daddy had, I tooked you tuh see him. Remember? Two thousand, oh hundred fifty-three stops. Three days on one bus. Was uh local. Missed thuh express. Changed in Castletin. Most folks waited in thuh depot. We waited outside. In thuh snow. Wanted tuh be thuh first tuh see thuh bus round thuh bend. That bus tooked us to thuh coast. Last tuh get on. Sat in thuh—rear. More even ride in thuh rear. Tooked us to thuh coast. Saw your daddy. Remember?

BUFFY: Uh huhn. The Biloxie twins are gonna—

MRS. SMITH: Huh! Good memory you got.—That was before you was born. I tooked you to see your Maker. Put on my green n white striped for thuh busride—it got so crinkled. Had tuh change intuh my brown with thuh white dots. Changed right there on thuh bus. In thuh restroom, of course. There's some womens that'll change anywheres. With anybody. Not this one. Not this Mrs. Smith. I gotta change my dress I goes to thuh restroom no matter how long thuh line. Goin in thuh mobile restroom's uh privilege, you know. They let me privy to thuh privilege cause I wanted tuh look nice for your daddy. Wanted tuh look like I hadn't traveled uh mile or sweated uh drop.

BUFFY: Biloxie Twinsss gonna wear their brown and whites—

MRS. SMITH: Got off that bus at thuh coast. Sky was shinin. Real blue. Didn't see it. All I seen was him. Mr. Smith. Your daddy. He tooked up my whole eye. "Mrs. Smith!" he yelled, loud enough for everyone tuh hear, "you ain't traveled a mile nor sweated a drop!"

BUFFY: You were just as proud.

MRS. SMITH: I was just as proud.

BUFFY: You were just as proud.

MRS. SMITH: I was just as proud. "Ain't traveled a mile nor sweated a drop!"

BUFFY: I'm gonna be just as proud.

MRS. SMITH: As what?

BUFFY: —As proud—.

MRS. SMITH: Uh huhnn. We're gonna have us uh big family. Your father's got uh furlough comin up. How'd you like uh—uh sister, Buffeena?

BUFFY: The Biloxie Twins don't need uh sister cause then they wouldn't be twins.

MRS. SMITH: We can put her in uh bed next tuh yours.

BUFFY: Where would the Biloxie Twins sleep?

MRS. SMITH: Men from thuh Effort come by?

BUFFY: 0-800.

MRS. SMITH: Whatja give em.

BUFFY: Thuh floor lamp.

MRS. SMITH: With thuh curlicues? Huh. Don't need it nowhow. Whatcha need is uh—uhnother girl. You and her—you'll have uh—uh sister. Get your twins off thuh desk, Buffy. Gotta keep it nice for your daddy. Two girls'll make things even. And thuh next time your daddy comes home we'll all do it up in brown and white.

(*Airplane sounds rise up*)

C.

MR. SERGEANT SMITH: Here I am on a rock. As you can see, the rock is near water! We of the 20-53rd are closer to water than you can guess. We are in the water! But we are not on a boat! But, we are not on a submarine! We of the 20-53rd are on an ISLAND!! A big rock in the middle of the ocean. Next time your mother takes you to visit the ocean, Buffeena, look very far out over the water and give me a wave. I will waaaave back! You may have to put on your glasses to see me, and I expect that to you I'll look like just a little speck. But if you look very far, you'll see me and if you wave very hard, I will waaaaaaave back! Next time your mother takes you to visit the ocean, Buffeena, throw me a kiss and I will throoooow one back! Now, Buffy, to reach me at the 20-53rd you are going to have to throw me a BIG kiss. Ask your Mother to help you. She will help you just as we here at the 20-53rd help each other, working together, to get the good job done. Here at the 20-53rd different men have different jobs. Some read maps. Some fly airplanes. Some watch guard over our island home. It is my job to keep watch over this rock. The rock I'm standing on right now. Our Commander, the man in charge, likes a clean rock. See my broom? See my mop? It is my job to keep this rock clean! My rock is very clean. My rock is the cleanest of all the rocks on our island home. I make the Commander very happy because I do a good job. I help him and in turn he will help me. My Commander, when the time is right, will reward me for a good job well done. My Commander will award me soon and put me in charge of bigger and more important—more important aspects of our island home. And your daddy will then have his Distinction. And your daddy will then come home. He will come home with bars instead of stripes and you and your Mommie will be just as proud! Well, it is time for work! Your daddy loves you, Buffy, and sends a big kiss and a big smile.

(*Airplane sounds rise up*)

D.

Mrs. Smith, Buffy and Muffy. A lovely home.

MUFFY: How come he didn't write tuh me?

BUFFY: Say "why is it that," Muffy, not "how come."

MUFFY: Why is that he didn't write tuh me? He didn't include me.

MRS. SMITH: You got thuh ledger, Buffeena? "Subject": uh letter. Check thuh "non bill" column. "From:"? Write—

MUFFY: How come he didn't say Muffy too?

BUFFY: Get out from under the desk, Muff. Mrs. Smith, write "Sergeant Smith"?

MRS. SMITH: Right.

MUFFY: Duhdun't he know my name? I'm Muffy. Duhdun't he know my name?

BUFFY: "Contents"?

MUFFY: Duddun't he know me?! I'm Muffy.

MRS. SMITH: Write—uh—"general news."

BUFFY: General news.

MRS. SMITH: Slash—"report of duties."

BUFFY: Good.

MUFFY: He duhdn't like me. Sergeant Smith dudhn't like me Buffy. He only likes Mrs. Smith he only likes Buffy Smith he only likes his desk. He duduhn't like Muffy. I'm Muffy. He duduhn't like me.

BUFFY: He likes you.

MRS. SMITH: "Signs of Distinction":—uh—uh—put "—." What'd we put last time?

MUFFY: He duhuhun't love me. HE DUDUHN'T LOVE HIS DESK!

BUFFY: Helovesyouheloveshisdesk.

MRS. SMITH: I hear you kickin Sergeant Smith's desk, Mufficent! I'm comin over there tuh feel for scuff marks and they're better not be uh one! Hhh. "Signs of Distinction"? What'd we put last time.

MUFFY: Why dudn't he love me? If he really loved Muffy he'd say Muffy. If he really loved me he would I'm Muffy why dudn't—

BUFFY: Last letter's Signs of Distinction were "on the horizon."

MRS. SMITH: Before that?

BUFFY: . . . "Soon." Before that he reported his Distinction to be arriving quote any day now unquote.

MUFFY: Mm wearin my brown and white. You said he likes his girls in their brown and whites.

MRS. SMITH: On thuh horizon any day now soon. Huh. You girls know what he told me last furlough? Last furlough I got off that bus and thuh sky was just as blue—wooo it was uh blue sky. I'd taken thuh bus to thuh coast. Rode in thuh front seat cause thuh ride was smoother up in thuh front. Kept my pocketbook on my lap. Was nervous. Asked thuh driver tuh name out names of towns we didn't stop at. Was uh express. Uh express bus. "Mawhaven!" That was one place—where we passed by. Not by but through. "Mawhaven!" Had me uh front seat.

Got to thuh coast. Wearin my brown and white. "You ain't traveled a mile nor sweated a drop!" That's exactly how he said it too. Voice tooked up thuh whole outside couldn't hear nothin else. We got tuh talkin. He told me that over there, where he's stationed, on his island home, over there they are uh whole day ahead of us. Their time ain't our time. Thuh sun does—tricks—does tricks n puts us all off schedules. When his time's his own he tries tuh think of what time it is here. For us. And what we're doin. He's in his quarters stowin away his checkers game and it's dark but you're whinin out thuh lumps in your Cream of Wheat, Buffy and Muffy, you're tearin at your plaits and it's Tuesday mornin and it's yesterday. And thuh breakfast goes cold today. I redo Miss Muff's head and fasten it with pins but it ain't today for him. Ssstomorrow. Always tomorrow. Iduln't that somethin?

BUFFY: I'll put "expected." Hows that.

MUFFY: I like his desk. I love his desk. I kiss it see? I hug it. Uuh! Hear me, Mommie, I'm kissing Sergeant Smith's desk. I am hugging it. Uuuhh! He likes his girls in their Swisses, right? Don't you, Sergeant Smith? I'm their Swisses! I'm their Swisses!!

MRS. SMITH: "Mention of Work": check "yes."

BUFFY: Check.

MUFFY: "Mention of Family": check NO.

MRS. SMITH: Check "yes," Buffeena.

BUFFY: Check.

MUFFY: Did not mention Muffy.

BUFFY: Censors, Muff.

MRS. SMITH: Scissors?

BUFFY: Censors. The Censors—they're uh family. Like us. They're uh family with Mr. Censor at thuh lead. Mr. Censor is a man who won't let Sergeant Smith say certain things because certain things said may put the Effort in danger. Certain things said and certain ways of saying certain things may clue-in the enemy. Certain things said may allow them to catch Sergeant Smith unawares. Sergeant Smith, Muff, deals in a language of codes—secret signs and signals. Certain ways with words that are plain to us could, for Sergeant Smith, spell the ways of betrayal, right, Mrs. Smith? Notice he only says "Commander." He isn't allowed to mention his Commander by name. We say

"Muffy" every day but for Sergeant Smith saying your name would be gravely dangerous.

MUFFY: Muffy's not gravely dangerous.

MRS. SMITH: Muffy—Muffy—Muffy sounds like minefield. What's uh mine, Mufficent?

MUFFY: A mine is a thing that dismembers. Too many mines lose the war.

MRS. SMITH: Good girl.

MUFFY: Remember the Effort.

MRS. SMITH: Good girl!

BUFFY: We all gotta make sacrifices, Muffy.

MRS. SMITH: Wouldn't uh named you "Muffy," but they hadn't invented mines when you came along.

MUFFY: They name mines after me?

MRS. SMITH: Go put on your Brown n White. We're goin tuh thuh beach.

BUFFY: She's got it on, Mrs. Smith.

MUFFY: Sergeant Smith's comin?!?

MRS. SMITH: You're not wrinkled are you Mufficent? Comeer. Lemmie feel. Hmmmm. Ssall right. Wouldn't want tuh be crinkly for Sergeant Smith. Huh. I remember when he first saw you. We traveled for miles and—when we walked off that bus! Brown-and-White polka dots uh swiss! Lookin like we hadn't traveled uh mile nor sweated uh drop!

MUFFY: Was he just as proud?

BUFFY: He was.

MRS. SMITH: Your Sergeant ssgonna be furloughin soon. How'd my two girls like uh—uh brother, huh? Seems like three is what this family needs. He always wanted uh—boy. Boy. Men from thuh Effort come by already, huh?

BUFFY: 0-800.

MRS. SMITH: Whatyuh give em?

BUFFY: Floor lamp.

MRS. SMITH: Thuh one with thuh green brass base?

BUFFY: And thuh phonograph.

MRS. SMITH: Records too? HHH. Don't need em no how. What we need is uh—

BUFFY: Uh brother.

MRS. SMITH: Uh brother! Your Sergeant Smith ssgonna be furloughin soon. Whatduhyuh say, Buffy? Muffy? Buffy? Muffy?

(*Airplane sounds rise up*)

E.

MR. SERGEANT SMITH: I expect it's today for you by now. Last night it comed to me: there's four hours every day that I kin say "today" and you'll know what today I mean. We got us whatcha calls "uh overlap." We got us uh overlap of four hours. Times when my day's yours—and yours is mines. Them four hours happens real quick and they look just like thuh other twenty-odd so you gotta watch for em real close. That little bit uh knowledge comed tuh me last night. Along with—my Distinction. Mrs. Smith, your Sergeant Smiths now—distinguished. They're etchin "Sergeant Smith" on thuh medals right this very moment as I speak I expect. Sssmy desk. Sssmy desk, this. Hhh. I saved uh life, ya know. Not every man kin say that, Mrs. Smith. I know you're gonna be proud. Make no mistake. Just as proud. Just as proud as—. Not every man saves uh life!

(*Airplane sounds rise up*)

F.

Mrs. Smith, Buffy, Muffy and Duffy. A lovely home.

MRS. SMITH: You ironed thuh Sergeant's desk today, Buffeena?

BUFFY: Yes, Mrs. Smith.

MRS. SMITH: Don't want it wrinkled.

BUFFY: No, Mrs. Smith. We'll get him another one tomorrow, K Muff? Duff too.

MRS. SMITH: Another what?

DUFFY: Are turtles mammals, Mommie?

MRS. SMITH: Mammals? Waas uh mammal?

MUFFY: Live births. Nurse their young.

MRS. SMITH: Waas today, Buffeena?

BUFFY: No, Duffy, they're not mammals. Today's Friday, Mrs. Smith.

MUFFY: Mind if I yo-yo, Buff?

BUFFY: Be careful, K?

MRS. SMITH: Be careful of thuh desk. Sergeant Smith's comin home n all we need's for it tuh be scored with your yo-yo welts, you!

DUFFY: Sergeant Smith uh mammal?

MRS. SMITH: Waas uh mammal?

MUFFY: Live births—round the world—whooosh!

BUFFY: Yes, Duffy.

MUFFY: Nurse their young. Whoosh! Whoosh!

MRS. SMITH: Today Friday?

BUFFY: Yes, Mrs. Smith.

DUFFY: He said he was uh turtle.

MRS. SMITH: Turtle?! Today's Friday. Waas uh turtle?

MUFFY: Masquerade as fish, Mrs. Smith. Round the world! Round the world!

MRS. SMITH: They catch on my line when I cast it out. Today's Friday. Fish on Friday. We'll have fish.

BUFFY: When Sergeant Smith said he was uh turtle that was uh figure of speech, Duffy. Sergeant Smith was figuring his speech.

MRS. SMITH: We'll go out. Out. Out. Have fish. You'll wear your swiss, Duffy. Same as us.

DUFFY: How do they breathe?

MRS. SMITH: Same as us.

DUFFY: Underwater?

MRS. SMITH: Same as us. Same as us. Sergeant Smith's comin. Soon. Today. Sergeant Smith's comin soon today soon.

MUFFY: Soon today today soon on the horizon today soon on the horizon today soon round the world round the world.

DUFFY: All winter through gills?

BUFFY: In summer they suck up lots of air. They store it. In the winter they use the stored air. Like camels use water.

DUFFY: Camels breathe water? Camels have gills?

MRS. SMITH: Course they got gills. You heard of thuh overlap, aintcha? Overlap's uh gap. Uh gap overlappin. Thuh missin link. Find thuh link. Put out thuh cat. Close thuh kitty cat flap mm feeling uh breeze. Seal up thuh flap mm feelin uh breeze.

BUFFY: Flap is sealed.

MRS. SMITH: Sscold. Mm feelin uh breeze. Mm feelin uh breeze.

MUFFY: She's feeling a breeze we're all gonna freeze round the world round the world.

BUFFY: Flap is sealed.

MUFFY: Round the world.

MRS. SMITH: Look for thuh overlap!

MUFFY: Round the world.

DUFFY: Overlap's uh gap!

BUFFY: Isn't!

DUFFY: Is!

MUFFY: Round the world round the world.

DUFFY: Overlap's uh gap!

BUFFY: Isn't!

DUFFY: Is!

MUFFY: Round the world round the—

MRS. SMITH: FREEZE!

MUFFY: —world.

MRS. SMITH: Sound off.

BUFFY: Buff-y!

MUFFY: Muff-y!

DUFFY: Duff-y!

MRS. SMITH: Mm feelin uh breeze. Stop that yo-in, Mufficent, or you'll have thuh Sarge tuh answer to. Still. Still thuh breeze. Anyone by at 0-800? Whatja give em? Don't need it no how. What we need is uh—. There was uh light in thuh sky last night. Don't suppose no one seen it. You all'd gone out. Through thuh gap. I was waitin up. There was uh light in thuh sky. I stopped. I looked. I heard. Uh man was fallin fallin aflame. Fallin at midnight. There wasn't uh sun. He was comin from another world. I stopped. I looked. I heard but couldn't do nothin. It all happened so far away. It all happened before you was born. Go put on your Brown and White, son. The Sergeant likes his family in their Brown and Whites. Muffy. Walk thuh dog.

MUFFY: Walking the dog walking the dog.

MRS. SMITH: Thuh sergeant'll want to see things in order. Nothin more orderly than uh walked dog.

MUFFY: Walk the dog. Walk the dog. Round the world. Walk the dog.

MRS. SMITH: Stand me in my walker. Go on—my walker, Private! Sarge is comin, gotta snap to attention.

DUFFY: Turtles lay eggs in thuh sand at night. Then they go away. How do they know which ones are theirs? Which eggs? Thuh eggs hatch and thuh baby turtles go crawlin out into thuh sea. How do thuh parents know em? How do thuh parents know em, Buff?

BUFFY: I don't think they much care.

MRS. SMITH: TEN-SHUN!

MR. SERGEANT SMITH: Hello, honey. I'm home.

BUFFY: Daddy is home!

MUFFY: Daddy is home!

DUFFY: Daddy is home!

BUFFY, MUFFY and DUFFY: Hello, Daddy!

MRS. SMITH: Hello, Mr. Smith. How was your day?

MR. SERGEANT SMITH: Just fine, Mrs. Smith. Give me uh kiss. Why, Mrs. Smith, you've lost your eyes. You've lost your eyes, Mrs. Smith. When did you lose your eyes?

BUFFY: What did you bring me, Daddy?

MRS. SMITH: For years, I had em lost for years.

MR. SERGEANT SMITH: When?

MRS. SMITH: YEARS. Years uhgo.

MUFFY: What did you bring me, Daddy?

MR. SERGEANT SMITH: Shoulda wroten.

DUFFY: What did you bring me, Daddy?

MR. SERGEANT SMITH: Shoulda called.

BUFFY: Daddy promised me uh china doll!

MR. SERGEANT SMITH: Shoulda given me some kinda notice, Mrs. Smith. Iduhn't no everyday uh wife loses her eyes. Where did you lose them and when did they go? Why haven't we ordered replacements? I woulda liked tuh hear uhbout that.

MRS. SMITH: Thought they'd come back afore you did. Shoulda informed me you was stoppin by.

MR. SERGEANT SMITH: I wrote. I called.

BUFFY: I'll get thuh ledger.

MRS. SMITH: What do you think of our brown and whites, Mr. Smith?

MR. SERGEANT SMITH: Who're you uhgain?

DUFFY: Duffy. You promised me an airplane.

MUFFY: I'm Muffy.

MRS. SMITH: You are Mr. Smith. You are our Mr. Smith? What do you think of our brown and whites, our Mr. Smith?

DUFFY: I'm your spittin image. Did you bring my airplane?

MR. SERGEANT SMITH: I was uh fine lookin man—like you—once. I got pictures. Uh whole wallet full. There. That's me.

DUFFY: Nope. That's me. We look uhlike.

BUFFY: They took thuh ledger. Thuh ledger was in thuh desk.

MRS. SMITH: Ssstoo bad. We needs documentation. Proof.

MR. SERGEANT SMITH: I wrote! I called!

MRS. SMITH: There's lots uh Smiths. Many Smiths. Smithsss common name.

DUFFY: You promised me uh air-o-plane!

MR. SERGEANT SMITH: I visited. We had us a family. That's proof.

MRS. SMITH: Lots uh visits. Lots uh families.

MR. SERGEANT SMITH: I got my Distinction. See? Here are my

medals here in my name. They let me be uh Mister. Mr. Smith's got his bars!

MRS. SMITH: Distinction? Waas uh Distinction?

BUFFY: You promised me uh Chinese doll.

MR. SERGEANT SMITH: Uh Distinction's when one's set upart. Uh Distinction's when they give ya bars. Got my bars! See?

MRS. SMITH: Lemmie feel.

MR. SERGEANT SMITH: I saved uh life! Caught uh man as he was fallin out thuh sky!

MRS. SMITH: You catched uh man? Out thuh sky? I seen uh light last night. In thuh sky. From uhnother world. I don't suppose you catched it, Don't suppose you're our Distinctioned Mr. Smith?

MR. SERGEANT SMITH: Was standin on my rock. I stopped. I heard. I seen him fallin—

MUFFY: You stepped on a mine. I read it in the paper. A mine is a thing that remembers. Too many mines lose the war. Remember the Effort. The mine blew his legs off.

MR. SERGEANT SMITH: You one uh mines?

BUFFY: He lost his legs.

MR. SERGEANT SMITH: You one uh mines?

DUFFY: He lost thuh war.

MR. SERGEANT SMITH: You one uh mines?

MRS. SMITH: Why, Mr. Smith, you've lost your legs, why, Mr. Smith, you've lost thuh war. When did you lose your legs, Mr. Smith, Mr. Smith, when did you lose thuh war? Men come by at 0-800. What do we give em? What we don't need nohow. BuffyMuffyDuffy? Your father's got hisself uh furlough comin up soon. That's just what we need. Uhnother boy. Always thought things should come in fours. Fours. Fours. All fours. I'll put it to him when he comes home. Whatduhyasay?

DUFFY: Are we turtles? Are we turtles, Mr. Smith?

BUFFY: Duffy—

MR. SERGEANT SMITH: No. No—uh—boy we iduhn't turtles. We'se slugs. We'se slugs.

(*Airplane noises rise up*)

G.

MR. SERGEANT SMITH: Always wanted to do me something noble. Not somethin better than what I deserved—just somethin noble. Uh little bit uh noble somethin. Like what they did in thuh olden days. Like in thuh olden days in olden wars. Time for noble seems past. Time for somethin noble was yesterday. There usta be uh overlap of four hours. Hours in four when I'd say "today" and today it'd be. Them four hours usta happen together, now, they scatters theirselves all throughout thuh day. Usta be uh flap tuh slip through. Flaps gone shut. I saw that boy fallin out thuh sky. On fire. Thought he was uh star. Uh star that died years uhgo but was givin us light through thuh flap. Made uh wish. Opened up my arms—was wishin for my whole family. He fell on me. They say he was flying too close to thuh sun. They say I caught him but he fell. On me. They gived me uh Distinction. They set me apart. They say I caught him but he fell. He fell on me. I broked his fall. I saved his life. I ain't seen him since. No, boy—Duffy—uh—Muffy, Buffy, no, we ain't even turtles. Huh. We's slugs. Slugs. Slugs.

(Airplane sounds rise up)

OUTSTANDING DRAMA

0452

☐ **THREE TALL WOMEN Winner of the 1994 Pulitzer Prize for Drama. by Edward Albee.** As an imperious, acerbic old woman lies dying, she is tended by two other women and visited by a young man. But it is who the women are that reveal Albee's genius. These "tall women" lay bare the truths of our lives—how we live, how we love, what we settle for, and how we die. "Stunning . . . A masterpiece."—*Time*
(274001—$9.95)

☐ **PRETTY FIRE Winner of the Los Angeles Drama Critic's Award and NAACP Theatre Awards. by Charlayne Woodard.** An enthralling celebration of life. Filled with earthy humor, it takes readers on a universal journey through a world in which the family bond is as strong as steel. "A remarkable feat of writing and performing . . . funny, flavorful and brushed with rich imagery and a tangy idiom . . . ripe with texture and language of a scruffy, vibrant world that appalls, enthralls and enriches us almost simultaneously."—*Los Angeles Times*
(273854—$8.95)

☐ **KINDERTRANSPORT by Diane Samuels.** In 1938, seven-year-old Eva Schlesinger is put aboard a train filled with other Jewish children and carried away from Nazi Germany in a little-known operation called "Kindertransport." A stunning dramatic creation, this play tells of a miracle amid unimaginable horror and probes the complexity of emotions in those who must lose everything they love . . . to live.
(274273—$8.95)

☐ **LOVE! VALOUR! COMPASSION! and A PERFECT GANESH Two Plays. by Terrence McNally.** *Love! Valour! Compassion!* gathers together eight gay men at the upstate New York summer house of a celebrated dancer-choreographer who fears he is losing his creativity . . . and possibly his lover. In *A Perfect Ganesh* the vacation of two suburban matrons to India begins as a hilarious serio-comic journey of very politically *incorrect* Americans abroad and becomes a dark passage of the soul. "The humor is uproarious and the pathos is abundant and genuine."—Howard Kissel, *New York Daily News*
(273099—$11.95)

Prices slightly higher in Canada.
